# NORTHERN SPRING

# NORTHERN SPRING

## THE FLOWERING
## OF CANADIAN
## LITERATURE

# GEORGE WOODCOCK

Douglas & McIntyre
Vancouver/Toronto

*To Pat Page, in admiring affection.*

Copyright © 1987 by George Woodcock
87 88 89 90 91  5 4 3 2 1

Douglas & McIntyre Ltd., 1615 Venables Street,
Vancouver, British Columbia   V5L 2H1

**Canadian Cataloguing in Publication Data**

Woodcock, George, 1912–
    Northern spring

        Includes index.
        ISBN 0-88894-536-1

    1. Canadian literature (English) – History and
criticism.*  2. Regionalism in literature.  I. Title.
    PS8101.R36W6 1987/     C810'.9     C86-091482-8
    PR9185.5.R36W6 1987

54,927

Cover and book design by Barbara Hodgson
Typeset by The Typeworks
Printed and bound in Canada by D. W. Friesen & Sons

# CONTENTS

# Part Two

# ACKNOWLEDGEMENTS

Most of the Introduction was published originally as "Northern Spring," a pamphlet commissioned by the Canadian Embassy to the United States, and "The Meeting of Time and Place" as the 1980 Lecture for the NeWest Institute of Western Canadian Studies, published by New West Press; the essays on Charles Heavysege and Patrick Lane were written for the series *Canadian Writers and Their Works,* published by ECW Press; the essays on Ethel Wilson and Timothy Findley appeared respectively in volumes III and IV of *The Canadian Novel,* edited by John Moss and published by NC Press; "The Journey of Discovery" appeared in *Colony and Confederation: Early Canadian Poets and Their Backgrounds,* edited by me and published by the University of British Columbia Press; the greater part of "Casting Down Their Golden Crowns" appeared in *The Human Elements: Second Series,* edited by David Helwig and published by Oberon Press, and "Metamorphosis and Survival" was included in *Margaret Atwood: Language, Text and System,* edited by Sherill E. Grace and Lorraine Weir and published by the University of British Columbia Press. Other pieces have appeared in *Canadian Literature, Journal of Canadian Studies, Canadian Ethnic Studies, Queen's Quarterly, Saturday Night, Room of One's Own, The Malahat Review* and the *Yearbook of English Studies.* In each case I extend my acknowledgements and my thanks to the editors and publishers.

# INTRODUCTION

This is the third of my books of essays on Canadian writers and writing. *Odysseus Ever Returning* appeared in 1970 and *The World of Canadian Writing* in 1980; both of them were concerned with modern Canadian writers, those who played their parts in the great literary upsurge that over the past half century has transformed Canadian writing from a colonial offshoot of the British tradition into a literature in its own right. But each book represented a stage in the transformational process that has seen a literary landscape once sparsely inhabited by writers of real individuality become visibly and thickly populated by scores of novelists and poets, dramatists and critics of high and idiosyncratic talent. Canadian literature, in other words, had reached maturity, and with maturity, as in all literatures, had come its necessary consequence, an escape from the garrison of enclosed attitudes. There was a time when Canadian writers often seemed obsessed with the process of liberation itself, and regarded nationalism as almost an obligatory theme; from Hugh MacLennan's *Barometer Rising* in 1941 to Margaret Atwood's *Survival* in 1972, thirty years later, the attitude held sway. It no longer does; with maturity has come—as in all literatures—variegation, the rejection of all orthodoxies of style and theme, and a growing assurance among writers in following their own unclassifiable paths.

It is with this movement of maturing and variegation, together with the related phenomenon of regionalism, that *Northern Spring* is largely concerned, and this is why it is not restricted to contemporary writers. It discusses some poets and novelists whose importance became evident after my earlier books were written, but it also takes into view the whole process by which Canadian literature came to maturity, and so it contains as well writers we can regard as significant ancestors.

There are two possible ways of approaching the theme of maturity and variegation which I have chosen: the literary historical, which subordinates individual writers to trends and movements, and the critical, which studies writers individually and allows general patterns to be inferred. The danger of the first method is that it may lead to critical superficiality; that of the second is that it may lose sight of general truths in an excessive concern for

9

the particular. To avoid these pitfalls, I have chosen a mixture of the two methods, mingling critical portraits of the writers I find significant in this context with more general essays—topographies as it were—that show varying vistas of the literary scene. The remainder of this introduction offers my own general vision of the way Canadian literature has developed, and so it serves as a sketch map of the whole terrain in which the individual essays that follow have their places.

*   *   *

One of the anecdotes often told by literary historians in Canada relates to the late nineteenth-century poet Archibald Lampman, who in 1880 read with delight a book called *Orion,* the first poems of another Canadian writer, Charles G. D. Roberts. It seemed to Lampman that Roberts showed an ability to write of the Canadian landscape as well as the English poets wrote of theirs, and he remarked: "It seemed to me a wonderful thing that such a work could be done by a Canadian, by a young man, one of ourselves."

At the same time Lampman also made a remark which has not so often been quoted: "A good deal is being said as to whether a Canadian literature exists. Of course it does not." And, at the time he was writing, just about a century ago, what he said was correct.

Ever since the British North American colonies came together in 1867 to form the Confederation of Canada, cultural nationalists like D'Arcy McGee had been talking of the need for a national literature. Indeed, the thought had been expressed even before Confederation when in 1864 an Upper Canadian clergyman named Edward Hartley Dewart published an anthology entitled *Selections from the Canadian Poets,* and in his introduction declared: "A national literature is an essential element in the formation of national character. It is not merely the record of a country's mental progress: it is the expression of its intellectual life, the bond of national unity and the guide of national energy." But a literature is not created by a collective act of will, and for many years Canadian writers were enslaved by the pioneer mentality, which seeks to recreate in a hostile wilderness the institutions and the cultural patterns of the lost homeland. Canadian poetry and fiction, until late in the nineteenth century, were derivative in their form and imagery, while other literary genres, like drama and criticism, hardly existed at all.

It was Lampman and his friends and contemporaries, Charles G. D. Roberts, Bliss Carman and Duncan Campbell Scott, who realized that their inspiration must be found at home. They wrote the first poetry that took the Canadian landscape and the life people lived in it as the source of their imagery; starting off with a style derived from the English Romantics, the best of them recognized in the end that their new content demanded a new

10

idiom. The first experimental Canadian poetry in a modernist sense was written by Roberts and Scott in their later years, while Roberts, because of his animal stories, and Carman, because of the popularity of his poetry among Americans, were the first Canadian writers to acquire an international readership.

These were the first true Canadian classics, but they hardly created a Canadian literature, for they had no immediate successors of equal stature, while Canadian fiction hardly developed at all until after the Great War. The good pre-1914 Canadian novels do not take even the fingers of a single hand to count: William Kirby's historical romance, *The Golden Dog* (1877); James de Mille's utopian fantasy, *Strange Manuscript Found in a Copper Cylinder* (1888); Sara Jeannette Duncan's ironic political novel, *The Imperialist* (1904), and Stephen Leacock's *Sunshine Sketches of a Little Town* (1912), less a novel than a series of linked humorous stories.

It was really in the 1920s and 1930s that Canadian literature began to acquire a distinctive identity. In the western plains a whole school of prairie realists emerged, led by novelists like Robert J. C. Stead (*Grain*), Martha Ostenso (*Wild Geese*) and—most important—Frederick Philip Grove. Grove, who had already written novels in German as Felix Paul Greve, began his Canadian career with a book of essays, *Over Prairie Trails,* which is still one of the best evocations of the mingling of beauty and dread in the prairie landscape, and followed them with a series of flawed, massive novels in which he applied European naturalism to the struggle of prairie farmers against both the land and their own passions. *Settlers in the Marsh* is the most darkly realist of these works, but Grove had too grandiose a mind to be a consistent naturalist, and his most ambitious book—and one of the true Canadian classics—was a symbolic epic on the onward march of mechanization, *The Master of the Mill*.

Grove's urban counterpart was Morley Callaghan, who accepted the lessons of an undecorated prose learned from his friend Ernest Hemingway, and in the 1930s published a series of novels that read like laconic moralist parables, notably *Such Is My Beloved* and *They Shall Inherit the Earth;* these novels admirably caught the ways of life and speech in the growing Canadian cities.

In poetry the centre of the ferment of the years between the wars was Montreal, which still had a vigorous anglophone culture. Modernism found its first Canadian expression when F. R. Scott and A. J. M. Smith worked together on the *McGill Fortnightly Review* and published in it a kind of verse that was cosmopolitan in form, since it took cognizance of experimental trends in both Britain and the United States, but sought to locate itself firmly in a Canadian setting and to find the rhythms of speech appropriate to the place. Because of the difficulties of publishing in the depression years, neither Scott nor Smith brought out a book during the

1930s, but with a few other poets they published in 1936 an anthology —*New Provinces*—that marked the beginnings of Canadian modernism and also of a separate Canadian literary tradition.

During the 1940s Montreal remained a notable centre for English-language poetry, and F. R. Scott was joined there by such younger poets as Irving Layton, Louis Dudek, P. K. Page and the English poet Patrick Anderson, while at the same time, in Toronto, Dorothy Livesay, Earle Birney and Raymond Souster were beginning to write and publish. The work of all these poets appeared in two historic Montreal journals, *Preview* and *First Statement,* which in 1945 united as *Northern Review,* and in the equally historic *Contemporary Verse,* which Alan Crawley published in Victoria and which became the centre of a poetry movement in western Canada.

The development of a national literature is dependent on a great many factors, emotional and even material. The modernist movement in poetry and the realist movement in fiction during the 1930s might have been ephemeral if World War II had not in many directions increased the Canadian sense of existing as a separate nation, finally detached from the old imperial links with Britain and anxious to defend itself from being absorbed into a continental culture in North America. And any national literature depends for its survival on the development of the type of infrastructure which we often call a "literary world," meaning the kind of ambiance in which writers are in touch with each other, in which responsible criticism develops, and in which there is a reasonable certainty of publication through a network of publishers, periodicals and media willing to use literary material. That a fair number of writers should earn enough to work without having to depend on academic appointments or journalistic chores is also one of the signs of a real literary world.

Such a world hardly existed in Canada before the mid-1960s, but the shifts in national consciousness that began during World War II were making it possible. In the 1940s the direction of Canadian fiction was changed by the appearance of two classic novels, Hugh MacLennan's *Barometer Rising* and Sinclair Ross's *As For Me and My House*. Ross's book was a single triumph, a sensitive study not only of the frustration of life in small prairie towns but also of the plight of the artist in a country only just emerging from a condition of pioneer philistinism. But *Barometer Rising* was the beginning of a distinguished career, for MacLennan dominated the late 1940s and the 1950s in Canadian writing with his didactic novels. They were popular because, like the quasi epics of E. J. Pratt and the early poems of Earle Birney, they mirrored the preoccupations of a people conscious that they were coming to terms with their own land and no longer depending on any of their various "Old Countries." MacLennan novels like *Two Solitudes* and *The Precipice* in various ways gave fictional expression to an emerging national and nationalist consciousness, and they

12

were widely accepted in spite of their conservative style and awkward characterization.

It is symptomatic of the change in Canadian writing that since the late 1950s no single figure has dominated any area in the way MacLennan then dominated fiction. This is due mainly to the rapid coming to maturity of Canadian literature during the past quarter of a century, and the notable variegation, in kinds of writing and in ways of writing, that has accompanied it. In 1976 Northrop Frye remarked on the "colossal verbal explosion that has taken place in Canada since 1960." And whether one looks at the number of books published, the number of magazines in circulation, the number of publishing houses and bookstores in operation or the number of Canadian books read by Canadians, there is no doubt that we have seen an enormous quantitative expansion in Canadian writing.

Let me give some examples. After *Northern Review* disappeared in 1953 with the death of its editor, John Sutherland, there was no literary magazine of any substance in Canada until *Tamarack Review* was founded in 1956. In 1982 *Tamarack* ceased publication after a distinguished career; it could do so because there are now several dozen Canadian literary periodicals in existence. When I started to edit *Canadian Literature* in 1959, it was the only critical journal in Canada, and criticism as a literary genre hardly existed. Now there are half a dozen critical magazines dealing with various aspects of writing in this country. In the same year of 1959 twelve books of verse were published in Canada. By the end of the 1970s the yearly average was about ten times that number. And these books were being published by a whole underground network of small publishing houses that had come into being to meet the need of the many new, and often good, poets who were emerging.

The magazines and the publishing houses became part of that essential infrastructure of a literary world. Linked in a symbiotic way to the expansion of the literary world was the emergence of the Canada Council, the organization for the administration of public patronage without political strings. The Canada Council came into being as the result of the Royal Commission set up in 1949, under the chairmanship of Vincent Massey, to investigate the situation of the arts, letters and sciences. The commission sensed the groundswell of interest in literature and the other arts that would produce Northrop Frye's "explosion" a decade or so later, and its recommendations led to the establishment of the council, which since its foundation in 1956 has been encouraging the arts in many ways that have improved both the working situations of writers and their chances of presenting their works to a responsive public. Grants of various kinds have given writers much-needed time to work without financial anxieties in a country where few writers have ever lived from their literary earnings. They have enabled magazines to survive and to publish both creative and critical writing. They have subsidized publishers willing to bring out books without guarantees of quick profits. They have sustained theatres, which in turn have employed writers, with the result that Canada, which in the past had a fine radio drama tradition, now has a young but vigorous tradition of writing for the stage.

Of course, the relationship between art patron and artist is a complex one. Patronage can always guarantee the quantity of writing or painting, as it has done in some totalitarian countries, but quality is a different matter. That cannot be produced by financing or organizing the artists. On the other hand, the good writer or artist can be encouraged where he exists by removing some of the difficulties he experiences in producing or distributing his work. In the case of Canada, the foundation of the Canada Council at just the time when Canadian writing was moving rapidly forward and outward was a happy conjunction. The rapid growth of public patronage after 1956 did not cause the ''verbal explosion,'' but it helped the best of the writers who appeared at this time—and some of the worst as well, since no patronage system is infallible in its decisions—to have time for their work and the means of reaching an audience.

Literary historians in the future are likely to spend a great deal of time speculating why in the 1960s and 1970s there was not only a spectacular increase in the number of Canadian writers but also a remarkable maintenance of quality. The literary landscape—once inhabited by a few isolated writers of real quality—has become populated by scores of novelists and poets, dramatists and critics, of high, idiosyncratic talent.

Perhaps the most impressive novelist of the 1960s and 1970s was Margaret Laurence; if I had to pick a notable Canadian prose epic I would certainly choose her prairie tetralogy (for the prairies are the heartland of her characters even when they wander), from *The Stone Angel* to *The Diviners*. It has a breadth of vision, a historical sense and a largeness of texture that are unique in Canadian fiction. Margaret Laurence is also important because she exemplifies how Canadian writers at this period were breaking out of the narrower patterns of the past. Some of her crucial years were spent in Somaliland and Ghana, and she perfected her craft by writing about Africa in her novel *This Side Jordan* and her travel book, *The Prophet's Camel Bell,* before she turned a very practiced hand to writing about Canada.

Margaret Laurence was not alone in this experience of leaving Canada and returning changed and culturally enlarged. It happened to older as well as younger writers, to Earle Birney and Dorothy Livesay, to P. K. Page and Irving Layton and Al Purdy, as well as to Dave Godfrey, Audrey Thomas and Marian Engel. In the case of elder poets like Birney, Livesay and Page, the remarkable second careers on which they embarked after they returned from their times abroad have been as productive as their earlier periods as young experimental poets, as can be seen from Livesay's *Ice Age,* Birney's *Collected Poems* and Page's *Evening Dance of the Grey Flies.* Al Purdy, Canada's great poet of place, had already written eloquently on his native Ontario and on Canada from Newfoundland to British Columbia and north to the Arctic when he set out on his world wanderings; the distillation of this mass of global experience is to be found in *Being Alive,* the most representative collection of his work.

In maturing literary cultures a related phenomenon to the travelling writer is the expatriate, who goes and stays away because only thus can he get a real perspective on his native world. The Englishman Malcolm Lowry and the Irishman Brian Moore were two expatriates from other countries who came to Canada and enriched its literature with books like Lowry's *October Ferry to Gabriola* and Moore's *The Luck of Ginger Coffey.* Among the Canadians who made themselves exiles, Mavis Gallant, whose stories have appeared often in the *New Yorker,* is a good example. She has lived in Paris since 1951 and has not yet returned home (although she came as writer-in-residence to the University of Toronto for six months in 1983). Many of her stories are about other expatriates, while one of her best books, *The Pegnitz Junction,* is a remarkable fictional study of postwar Germany. More recently she has reached the exile's logical goal by going back in memory to childhood and writing a superb series of stories on a past Montreal, *Home Truths.* Another Canadian writer who lived long abroad was Mordecai Richler, but his novels were often set in Canada and were always populated by Canadians. His period of residence abroad ended after the completion of *St. Urbain's Horseman* which, with *The Apprenticeship of Duddy Kravitz,* represented the high point of Richler's achievement in giving fictional expression to the vigorous multicultural society of Montreal.

The crossing of frontiers by Canadian writers has been more than a matter of foreign travel. It has also meant expansion into previously neglected fields of writing. Serious criticism, once mainly represented by Northrop Frye, developed into a significant literary genre in the 1960s, and many important younger critics emerged, including Margaret Atwood (*Survival*), D. G. Jones (*Butterfly on Rock*) and W. H. New (*Articulating West*). Significantly, some of the best of these critics are themselves fine poets, and this has meant that criticism in Canada has become a genuine dialogue within the world of writers. In the theatre there was in the 1960s a leap from radio drama to stage drama, led by writers like James Reaney (*Colours in the Dark*), George Ryga (*The Ecstasy of Rita Joe*), Sharon Pollock (*Walsh*) and David Freeman (*Creeps*). Canadian stage drama has tended to be radical in sentiment as well as presentation, and to be concerned largely with minorities, the poor, the despised. Another genre — the short story — which was long neglected in Canada and for years kept going by CBC radio, re-emerged with vigour in the 1960s in the hands of writers like Alice Munro, W. D. Valgardson and W. P. Kinsella.

The novel was a rather conservative form in Canada until the 1960s, with only a few experimental exceptions like Howard O'Hagan's *Tay John* and Sheila Watson's *The Double Hook*. But by the end of the decade experimentation of some kind had become almost *de rigueur* in prose fiction, and the result has been an enormous variation in the kinds of novels being published in Canada. Even comparatively realistic novelists like Mordecai Richler and Margaret Laurence have played with time and memory in adventurous ways. The period saw the emergence of Margaret Atwood, whose novels like *Surfacing* and *Bodily Harm* are tight and sinewy studies of neurotic frontiers; the quasi-mythical prairie novels of Robert Kroetsch (*The Studhorse Man*), and the later novels of the ironist Robertson Davies, which moved into a rich metaphysical vein (*Fifth Business* and *World of Wonders*). The pattern of variation has continued among younger novelists like Matt Cohen, with his excursions into rustic melodrama (*The Disinherited*) and futurism (*The Colours of War*); Jack Hodgins, with his elaborate manipulations of strange fiction and stranger fact (*The Invention of the World*), and Timothy Findley, with his elaborate pastiches of invented history (*Famous Last Words*).

In poetry the variation has been even greater, because more poets have emerged than fiction writers, and books of verse are more easily published than novels. It is hard to do more than indicate the contrasts in this crowded field. They have ranged from the ironic classicism of John Glassco (*A Point of Sky*) to the concrete idiom of bp Nichol (*The Martyrology*), and from the colloquial exuberance of Al Purdy to the lapidary restraint of Margaret Atwood, whose *Selected Poems* is her most substantial and representative selection. Other notable poets of recent decades have been Phyllis Webb, Leonard Cohen, John Newlove, Margaret Avison, Alden Nowlan, Gwendolyn MacEwen, Michael Ondaatje and George Bowering. An especially interesting trend (it is not organized enough to be called a movement) among the younger poets has been towards a return to the landscape, though in much less conventional ways than the Confederation poets a century ago. The writers representing this trend—among them some of the best of younger Canadian poets—include Patrick Lane, Dale Zieroth, Sid Marty, Tom Wayman and Susan Musgrave. They are mostly from the prairie provinces and British Columbia, and they show a westward inclination that in recent years has become very noticeable in Canadian writing.

The cultural forces of the country, like the political and economic ones, have been shifting radically in recent years, and the days when Montreal and Toronto were the literary centres of English-speaking Canada are already in the past. Not only the west but the Maritime provinces of the Atlantic coast are producing many interesting new writers and new movements in theatre and other areas close to literature. Northrop Frye once remarked that, whatever its political shape, Canada is culturally decentralist, and Canadian writers have recently been proving it by their variety of approach, which is as much regional as it is personal.

It is to illuminating this variety of approach, which signifies the maturing of the literary tradition in Canada, and to tracing some of its roots in the past, that the essays in this volume are devoted.

# PART ONE

# I

# THE MEETING OF
# TIME AND SPACE

## Regionalism in Canadian Literature

As the following essay suggests, the reality of Canadian experience is geography, variously shaped by history. That is why this vast country is inevitably regional in its cultural manifestations. The sense of locality, it is true, came before the sense of region, which is the product of living in time within a specific environment. The first of all Canadian writers, the explorers like Alexander Mackenzie and David Thompson, had a strong sense of locality, but almost none of region. Theirs was the literature of travel and movement, whereas the regional awareness involves finding what Al Purdy once called "a place to stand on." Here and there among the explorers a fitful sense of region appears, as in the narratives of Samuel Hearne, who wandered with an Indian band and absorbed their sense of territory as living space.

But for the most part the sense of regionality came with settlement, and that is why one is first aware of it among the Québecois and the Acadians, French peasants who had exchanged one terrain for another and had been forced to adapt a centuries-old Gallic rural way of life to existence on the verge of the wilderness. As the English-speaking immigrants came in their turn—Loyalists and others—and after them the continental Europeans and the Asians, the experience was repeated of adjustment between an Old World culture and a New World land. Out of these encounters came the strong regionalism that to this day marks off the areas of Canada by history—the shared memory of experience—and geography. It has been one of the most powerful forces in shaping not only the country's literature but also its visual arts.

Let me begin with four of my favourite quotations, which I think between them define the limits of what we call regionalism in literature. The first is a rather surprising remark by the English poet T. E. Hulme, who is generally regarded as the founder of the early twentieth-century movement in poetry known as imagism. Hulme had spent a period in North America, and in 1906 he remarked:

Speaking of personal matters, the first time I ever felt the necessity or inevitableness of verse, was in the desire to reproduce the peculiar quality of feeling which is induced by the flat spaces and wide horizons of the virgin prairie of western Canada.

Canadian poets did not become sufficiently aware of imagism to be influenced by it until the late 1920s, in the work of W. W. E. Ross and to a lesser extent of A. J. M. Smith, and only in the late 1960s would a notable group of western Canadian poets arise to give significant expression to the emotions aroused by "the flat spaces and wide horizons" of a prairie no longer "virgin." But Hulme's reference to "the peculiar quality of feeling" induced by a particular landscape nevertheless enters into the phenomenon I describe as regionalism. It is the sense of locality which is indispensable to a consciousness of regional identity, but which is not all of that consciousness.

The second of my quotations is from Margaret Laurence's *Heart of a Stranger*, that splendid collection of essays in which she reveals so much about her novels by relating herself in an autobiographical way to the places that have lived so vividly in her fiction. She implies that the sense of locality is itself not enough when she remarks, concerning her own part of Manitoba:

I doubt if I can ever live there again, but those poplar bluffs and the blackness of that soil and the way in which the sky is open from one side of the horizon to the other—these are things I will carry inside my skull for as long as I live, with the vividness of recall that only our first home can have for us.

Later, in the last pages of *Heart of a Stranger*, Margaret Laurence amplifies this first statement in a significant way:

This is where my world begins. A world which includes the ancestors—both my own and other people's ancestors who become mine. A world which formed me, and continues to do so, even while I fought it in some of its aspects, and continue to do so. A world which gave me my own lifework to do, because it was here that I learned the sight of my own particular eyes.

Here Laurence is adding to Hulme's geographical factor of locality the historical factor of human experience, direct and inherited, individual and social, the creating of a continuing pattern of interrelation between man and the landscape which is necessary before true regional feeling can come into existence—the sense of the region as a living polis as well as a mere area of land.

Margaret Laurence's reference to "other people's ancestors who become mine" is here most important because by no means every one of those whose artistic or literary expression becomes intensely regional in character can claim the region as his "first home," where he "learned the sight of my own particular eyes." The experience of being born again is not restricted to pentecostal religion; it can be the experience of any person who at a critical point in his or her life finds that a new setting, with its own geographical shape and historical resonances, offers a home to the emotions he needs to express. Strangers as well as natives can live in their minds the life of a region, so long as they accept "other people's ancestors." This is shown by the number of writers who have expressed in prose or verse the essential characters of regions where they were neither born nor had other than surrogate ancestors. Among these writers from outside who have given such splendid voice to the regions of Canada have been Frederick Philip Grove, Malcolm Lowry and Roderick Haig-Brown.

One of Haig-Brown's statements is the last of my quotations. He talks of provincialism, and provincialism of course is the word by which its critics so often derogate regionalism.

"I am not at all sure that provincialism is such an evil thing as that. No man becomes a great patriot without first learning the closer loyalties and learning them well: loyalty to the family, to the place he calls home, to his province or state or county."

The truth that Haig-Brown states in this sentence is the truth that Spaniards, the most intensely regionalist people of Europe, understood when they created the phrase *patria chica* (the little fatherland), a term that embraces all I have so far been describing—the geographical feeling of locality, the historical feeling of a living community, the personal sense of ties to a place where one has been born or which one has passionately adopted.

\* \* \*

In Canada at present there is a tendency to oppose regionalism to nationalism. I believe that to deny regionalism is to deny the Canadian nation as it historically and geographically exists and as it is likely to exist in any foreseeable future. For Canada is by definition a confederation, and a confederation is something quite different from the centralized and long outdated nation-state of the type that developed in eighteenth-century Europe. It is, as it was first created by the Swiss when the three forest cantons of Uri, Schwyz and Nidwalden met in 1291 to found their Everlasting League, a group of free and sovereign regions who come together to arrange certain matters for their mutual benefit and protection. The Swiss cantons have always been clearly defined physical and historical entities because of the sharp mountain barriers that divide their country.

In the case of Canada the diversity which in Switzerland existed in a concentrated but sharply divided geographical area is fostered by distance and grandiose natural barriers; these physical divisions have been intensified by historical factors, so that both ethnically and in terms of the actual history of settlement the Canadian regions are entities at least as distinct from each other as the cantons of Switzerland.

For Canada, like Switzerland, has never been a nation in the same way as classic centralized European states like England and France. The fact that the original provinces of Québec, Ontario, Nova Scotia and New Brunswick came together by mutual agreement to form the Confederation meant that they were autonomous entities entering into a compact; they did not surrender their freedom at any later stage, which means that when Canada became virtually independent under the Statute of Westminster in 1931, the provinces as constituent polities became independent and evolved into sovereign nations that had made an agreement to their mutual advantage. In the same way Prince Edward Island, Manitoba, British Columbia and later Newfoundland entered voluntarily into the compact of Confederation, and thus retained their sovereignties insofar as they did not assign them for mutual convenience. The cases of Alberta and Saskatchewan, which were created by the federal government out of the Northwest Territory, may be legally slightly different, but as they were admitted into Confederation as provinces equal to the others, one must assume that their rights are the same and that they are in fact sovereign polities, like the Swiss cantons, insofar as they have put certain rights into the trusteeship of the federal government, such trusteeship being voluntarily accepted and therefore revocable at any time.

This view of Confederation is different from the centralizing and Jacobinical interpretation of Canadian political structures once posed by Pierre Elliot Trudeau and his ruling Liberal Party, but I am convinced it is more in accord with historical truth, more fitting to geographical factors and closer to the cultural actualities of Canada, where literary and artistic traditions are not homogeneous, but have developed variously in various parts of our immense country and can only be seen in their full richness if we understand how they differ mutually and how they interweave into the general culture of the country.

Provincialism and regionalism are not exactly the same, since provinces can be created by the arbitrary fiat of superior governments, for they are merely political constructs, whereas regions come into being by more organic and less formalized processes. For this reason, while in political terms there are ten provinces and two territories in Canada, in cultural terms there have in fact been seven regions plus one intercultural community which in the circumstances of mediaeval Europe would undoubtedly have been a great and autonomous Free City. The potential Free City is of course Montreal, which has been as important in the artistic and literary life of anglophone Canada as in that of Québec considered as a francophone community, and which has always been the centre of Canada's fertile Jewish culture.

Newfoundland, first of the seven regions, is an island not merely physically. It had its own separate history from the late sixteenth century until 1949, for much of that period as a self-governing colony. During this time it developed linguistic patterns based on an ethnic mixture of Irish, West English and Acadian peoples that was unique in Canada, and an oral and written literature recording an austere way of life different even from that of the nearby Maritime provinces, though their existence also was based largely on fishing and seamanship.

The Maritime provinces of Prince Edward Island, Nova Scotia and New Brunswick share a great deal of history, in terms of French settlement, British conquest, Loyalist settlement, maritime prosperity and subsequent decline, which is markedly different from that of Newfoundland. Culturally they are distinguished by their special mingling of English-speaking Loyalist and French-speaking Acadian traditions, and by their early development of political autonomy and of a genuine local literary culture, both of which emerged before the middle of the nineteenth century.

The French language and a *canadien* culture dating from the sixteenth century have distinguished Québec from the beginning, but except for Montreal and the Eastern Townships it falls outside the scope of the present argument, devoted as it is to English-speaking regional cultures. However, there has never been any doubt of Québec's regional uniqueness within Canada. My object now is largely to show how, in ways other than linguistic distinctiveness, that uniqueness exists in each of the other regions.

Ontario, the heir to Upper Canada, with its Loyalist and Regency English traditions, its memories of the war of 1812 that shaped its special self-awareness, its old communities of German sectarians and its sharp geographical definition by lakefront and Shield, remains a distinct region even though its two greatest cities, Ottawa and Toronto, have become the foci of a political, economic and cultural centralism that goes entirely against the Canadian grain.

West of the Shield which insulates them so densely from central Canada, the three prairie provinces really form a single region, since, whatever the slight difference in their topographies and the somewhat larger differences in their political histories, they are united geographically in the great plains that sweep virtually without interruption from Lake of the Woods to the foothills of the Rockies. In cultural traditions they have great similarities, since, despite the original ambition of Ontario to annex the plains by populating them, they were in fact mainly settled by European strains, Germanic and Slavic, quite distinct from the so-called founding peoples, the French and the Anglo-Celts. The prairie provinces are also distinguished from the rest of Canada and drawn towards each other by the fact that for generation after generation they have bred the great protest movements in Canada, from the Métis rebellions of 1870 and 1885, down through the women's liberation movement early in the twentieth century, the Winnipeg General Strike, the emergence of the Progressive Party and the CCF, to the strength in the prairies even in our own day of essentially regional parties like the NDP and Social Credit. Politically, indeed, at least throughout the present century, the prairies have remained quite different from the rest of Canada, except British Columbia, in their largely rural radicalism. Out of this situation has emerged a unique literary culture shaped alike by the extremities of climate and of passion. Only the land is ever level between the Shield and the Rockies.

British Columbia, the "sea of mountains" parted by the Continental Divide from the rest of Canada, with its people living on small pieces of level land in the valleys that filter down to the steep fjord-bitten and forested coastline, with its mild winters and moist summers, has likewise its special historical pattern complementing a unique geographical conformation. The memory of the great native culture of the Coast Indians still broods over it and inspires much of its painting and poetry. White settlement began with sea traders and overland-travelling agents of the North West Company, and its towns started as fur trading posts before the coming of the gold miners, and afterward the CPR, turned them from tiny clusters of log buildings into mining or farming or communications centres or seaports. Even then much of the population came by sea from Europe or by coastal shipping or overland from California and the Oregon territory, bringing with it not only the San Francisco architecture which survives to this day in the wharfside streets of Victoria, but also the ruthless exploitative attitudes of lumber and mining barons and the labour radicalism of the IWW. An extraordinary combination of forest and dryland, of mountain and island and ocean, played its part in differentiating the literature of the Coast, while the mild climate and the relaxed and almost luxuriant way of living was attractive to writers and painters alike, so that British Columbia, and especially Vancouver and Victoria, has not only produced its own native writers in considerable number but has attracted many more from outside, from Ethel Wilson and Roderick Haig-Brown and Malcolm Lowry down to, in our generation, P. K. Page, David Watmough and Jane Rule. More than most other parts of Canada it is, for its writers, an adoptive *patria chica*.

Finally there is the North, the great sweep of territory mainly above the sixtieth parallel, which forms the southern boundary of the Yukon and Northwest territories, but also, because of the southeasterly pull of the dividing line between tundra and northern forest, embracing the northern parts of Manitoba and Ontario around Hudson's Bay, the Ungava peninsula of Québec, and the north of the Labrador coast which forms part of the province of Newfoundland.

The North has had its own great native culture, that of the Inuit, which flowered after contact with white culture into a splendid tradition of sculptural art, but which also developed an oral poetry that, like the superb hunting techniques of the northern people, was beautifully attuned to the nature of the region, as was shown in passages like this fragment which the explorer Knud Rasmussen took down from an anonymous hunter more than half a century ago:

And yet, there is only
One great thing,
The only thing:
To live to see, in hunts and on journeys
The great day that dawns
And the light that fills the world.

By ending in the North my definition of the seven true regions of Canada, I reach the appropriate point where one can begin to consider the processes by which regional literatures develop in vast and varied countries like Canada.

The first stage is that of the explorer, the traveller who never settles in the land, and there the recognition that ensues is not of region so much as of locality, since the explorer who writes his narrative usually lives a life outside the native culture that may exist in a region. Unless he is forced in some way, as James Jewitt was when he became the slave of Chief Maquinna on Nootka Sound, he never truly absorbs or understands that native culture, and thus does not truly enter the regional life, though he may change it by his presence.

Canadian literature really begins with the explorers, just as Greek literature began with that first great account of a Mediterranean voyage, the *Odyssey,* and Canada's *Odyssey* was Samuel Hearne's *Journey to the Northern Ocean,* published in 1795 but telling of Hearne's finally successful series of efforts to travel overland from Hudson Bay to the Arctic Sea between 1769 and 1772. No book written in or about the territory that later became Canada would for many years rival Hearne's splendid narrative. It owed its vividness largely to the aspect that made it so much more a truly regional piece of writing than the later narratives of North West Company explorers like Alexander Mackenzie and Simon Fraser and David Thompson. They were always fur traders travelling in their usual manner with armed crews of voyageurs, whereas Hearne found that the only way he could cross the tundra was to be actually adopted by an Indian band and to share their way of life with all its hardships and perils as they wandered northward over the Barren Lands, so that in the *Journey to the Northern Ocean* he gives a rounded picture not only of the locality but also of the patterns of human and animal living that made it in the full sense a region.

In a similar way, it was the accounts of explorers who actually lived like the native peoples and often with them, like V. Stefansson and John Rae, that later gave the truest sense of the North as a region. The explorers by sea, of whom so many came during the great searches for Franklin in the mid-nineteenth century, only projected a sense of locality, though sometimes they did this with a vividness that inspired great literature, as the *Strange and Dangerous Voyage* describing the adventures of Capt. Thomas James on his search for the Northwest Passage entered into the very texture of Coleridge's *The Ancient Mariner*.

The explorer journeyed and observed the land, and sometimes the sea and the ice, making the notations that would chart the hitherto unknown and, if he were a fur trader, setting down the features of the natural scene that might be exploited for financial gain. Our debt to such men for extending the area of the known world, the bounds of geographical perception, and for charting the lines of access along which settlement and communication would eventually move, is great indeed; but with rare exceptions like Hearne and Stefansson and—in his very different way—Jewitt, they wrote merely descriptively, and what they described were the geographical localities in which the history they brought on their snowshoes or their paddles had not yet exercised its transforming powers.

The settlers did transform the land, and with them locality and history came together. But they had time for nothing more than the task of transformation, and they failed to develop a true regional consciousness, partly because they created the actual human structures of regions, and few creators observe clearly what they make, but partly because their vision of the locality into which they came was paralysingly divided. As pioneers they regarded it as land to be conquered and tamed, and until this had been achieved, it was a wilderness that was often intractable and sometimes hostile. Yet as still incompletely detached inhabitants of the countries from which they had come, they looked back with nostalgia on what they had left; partly for the sake of the mental security gained by grasping at the familiar and partly because they knew nothing else except the terrifying new place they would have to inhabit, they tried to recreate in new settings the ways of life they had left behind them.

For this reason pioneers in Canada wrote in the forms with which they had been familiar in Britain or in Boston, and used the accepted literary language of the imperial centres. For a long time they also sought to perceive the new life in terms of the old, either to encourage themselves or to justify their disappointment.

The Canadian Oliver Goldsmith's early nineteenth-century poem, *The Rising Village*, which closely copies the form and manner of his celebrated relative's "The Deserted Village," is a case in point. Recollecting that the English Oliver had regarded emigration as an almost unbearable fate for good English villagers, the Canadian Oliver looks forward with confidence to a time when the trials of the pioneers will come to an end, and something very like the deserted villages of the homeland will be recreated. Recollecting his relative's lament in "The Deserted Village" over the destruction of English agrarian life during the period of the enclosures, he exhorts his readers:

> If then adown your cheek a tear should flow
> For Auburn's village, and its speechless woe;
> If, while you weep, you think the "lowly train"
> Their early joys can never more regain,
> Come, turn with me where happier prospects rise,
> Beneath the sternness of Acadian skies.

So far as his diction and his imagery are concerned, Goldsmith might have been in London arguing directly with the other Goldsmith, for he failed to develop a way of writing that would render convincingly the special character—the sheer difference—of the land to which he and the other settlers had come. There are, indeed, wild beasts and Indians who inhabit the background as threatening presences, but they are described in conventional English eighteenth-century ways. In other words, Goldsmith has negated the alarming strangeness of the New Brunswick forests, as the Loyalists encountered them, by presenting them—through the use of English pastoral conventions—with a curious but neutralizing familiarity.

There were other Loyalists, like Joseph Stanbury, who in their poems reacted with emotional violence against the locality they were forced to inhabit and hence against the historic and cultural region which their very presence was creating. Something of the horror they felt at exchanging their long-settled Pennsylvania or New England life for the perils and discomforts of the New Brunswick wilderness was reflected in the striking statement of an equally appalled English Methodist preacher and poet, Joshua Marsden: "There is a solitary loneliness in the woods . . . to which no language can do adequate justice. It seems a shutting out of the whole moral creation." But Marsden understood thoroughly the mental mechanisms by which the pioneer writer used his art to evade and not to understand the reality of his experience, and expressed it in eight lines of conventional English verse in a work called *The Backslider: A Descriptive Moral Poem.*

In this cold climate, where rough Boreas blows,
Pours his fierce hail, and spreads his dazzling snows,
Disrobes the green-wood, chills the solar beam,
And shakes his icy-spectre o'er the stream,
Let me beguile stern winter's frigid ire,
With books divine, a friend, and maple fire;
Or cheat the night-storm terrible and fierce!
With purest sweets of fancy-pleasing verse.

The writing of the pioneer generation in all parts of Canada shows a similar tendency to escape from experience in a new and untamed country by rendering it in familiar and artificial forms rather than developing the kind of perception which sees it as it is, and, finally, the language which fits that perception.

The case of the Stricklands in Ontario is a classic one. Members of a well-known English writing family, Samuel Strickland and his sisters, Susanna Moodie and Catharine Parr Traill, reached Canada at various times between 1825 and 1832 and remained there. All of them wrote memoirs of their experiences, and what is striking in every case is the extent to which they wrote from *outside* their experience, from outside the land in which they settled, lived and died. Samuel in his *Twenty-seven years in Canada West* is factually very informative about the settlement of Upper Canada, but one gets little real sense from his narrative of the kind of society which developed there and how it fitted into the locality, largely because there were whole sectors of that society whose way of living he neither shared nor understood.

Similarly, Susanna's first book, *Roughing It in the Bush,* is told from the viewpoint of a cultured English gentlewoman who sees the pioneer life from the outside even when she is forced to live it, and her much happier later book, *Life in the Clearings,* really expresses her relief in at last being able to move to Belleville where she found a small emigré society of writers, the contributors to 'the *Literary Garland* and the *Victoria Magazine,* whose styles were hardly distinguishable from their English early Victorian contemporaries and who usually sought their subject outside the uncomfortable realities of Canadian experience.

Of the three Stricklands, only Catharine Parr Traill emerges as a truly regional writer. There were two reasons for this. First of all, she was a devoted amateur naturalist, and became fascinated by the flora of the New World. This gave her observations of the environment a special touch of intimacy, which she extended to the details of immigrant life, so that while in works like *Rambles in the Canadian Forest* and *Studies of Plant Life in Canada* one gets the sense of a landscape not only observed but also accepted with deep feeling, in her books on the settler's life, like *The Back-*

*woods of Canada* and *The Female Emigrant's Guide,* one experiences a mature awareness of the new ways of existence, appropriate to the geographical and historic circumstance, that were emerging in the forest clearings of Upper Canada and forming a truly regional way of life.

Apart from *The Backwoods of Canada,* which appeared four years after she settled in Douro township, Catharine Parr Traill's most perceptive books were written during the 1850s. They were really part of the literature of a postpioneer period, and it is in fact during this later stage of settlement that the truly regional literatures begin to appear in all parts of Canada. The land has been farmed long enough and the forests have been sufficiently cleared and the fisheries sufficiently established for the early terror of the wilderness on land and the wild sea to have been greatly modified; toil has become less time and energy consuming; boundaries and communications have been established; political structures, from the community level upward, have been created or have naturally evolved; the geography of the land has been understood, and its history has begun to form even if it has not been written down; above all a large proportion of the population is native to the region, and the time is approaching when whole lives will be lived out there and the generations will succeed each other. Localities, in other words, have changed into geographic-historic regions, and in the process have begun to develop cultures out of which their own literatures emerge. And they are literatures which reflect in each region the special characteristics of the land—geography—and of its people—history.

*　　*　　*

The process by which the regions of this country have emerged into historical-cultural reality has of course been coterminous with the process of the making of Canada. In fact, region making and nation making are aspects of the same process, since the special character of Canada as a nation is that of a symbiotic union of regions, as organic as a coral reef, rather than a centralized state constructed according to abstract political concepts. The emergence of regional consciousness among English-Canadians, and its expression in literature, proceeds historically from east to west.

This, of course, is the same direction as the Laurentian impulse which forms the core of Donald Creighton's view of Canadian history. But the conclusions to be reached are not the same as Creighton's. Creighton confused two separate phenomena, that of trading with its necessary exploration, and that of settlement. The pattern of the trading epoch was one of constant movement into the farther wilderness as the stocks of fur-bearing animals were exhausted; in the process of establishing trails across the continent the traders created the communication links that unite Canada to this day. Settlement proceeded largely by way of these links, first into Upper Canada, then across the Shield into the great plains, and finally over the

31

Rockies by the land routes into British Columbia. But while trading moved constantly over these main routes, and the fur companies were necessarily continent-wide operations under centralized control, settlement developed autonomously in the regions, each creating its own centres to which the regional life related. Canada came into existence as a union of these regions, each of which had developed its own pattern of settlement and its own pattern of culture.

Creighton's model accords with presettlement Canadian history; a united organization of fur traders was needed to exploit the regional ways of life of the native peoples. And here the word *exploit* is the operative one, for the relation of centralized organizations like the HBC, the Ottawa government or the CPR to the regions has always been an exploitative one, causing resentment and conflict. This has been the case even in cultural matters, where openly centralized public corporations like the CBC and the National Film Board, and less overt centralized institutions like the Toronto publishing industry and the Ontario-based national magazines, have always worked against regional cultures, partly by centralizing the production of books and periodicals and partly by drawing into their orbit many of the best talents from Canada outside the St. Lawrence valley.

Despite such centripetal tendencies, and despite the constant political and economic efforts of central Canada to impose its hegemony on the rest of the country, Canadian literature, like Canadian painting, has always remained regional in its impulses and origins. In this respect, Canada resembles countries like Germany and Italy and Spain, which have a number of competing cultural centres, rather than Britain and France, where London and Paris have tended until very recent years to attract to themselves all but the most rebellious of artistic talents. All the really important innovative tendencies in English-Canadian literature have originated in the regions, especially if one regards anglophone Montreal as a region in its relation to the centralist axis of Toronto-Ottawa.

One can begin, in time as well as geographically, with the Atlantic provinces. The case of Newfoundland is special, since it remained for so long a separate polity, a separate society, a separate culture. But here as well the rule seemed to operate, that only after a genuine settlement had come into being did a true regional literature emerge. Through its pioneer era, the long-drawn-out period of conflict between fishermen and settlers, Newfoundland produced little literature of its own that was significant. Gentlemen colonizers, like Robert Hayman, the friend of Ben Jonson, wrote acceptable Jacobean verses which exaggerated like a public relation blurb the advantages of the real estate he was offering. And the common people from Ireland and the west of England who stubbornly survived around the edges of the great bleak island preserved the folk literature of their native regions in many cases longer than it survived in the homelands from which they had come.

But it was not really until the nineteenth century, when the attempt to preserve Newfoundland as a base for transient English fishermen was finally abandoned, that the characteristic famine-and-feast culture of the outports established itself, and the celebrated oral ballad literature of Newfoundland emerged. It was not in fact the kind of anonymous folk literature that has often been portrayed. The authors of many of the most famous ballads are known, and wrote within living memory, while the most remarkable characteristic of this kind of popular poetry was its topicality, its ability to keep pace with events, and particularly events that affected the people of St. John's and the outports, such as disasters at sea, and new and strange phenomena like mining on Bell Island. The ballads of Newfoundland, reflecting as they did the local social mores while they narrated the tragedies of a perilous way of life, have been true regional poetry in a country that until recent years did not offer a great deal to encourage the growth of a sophisticated written literature.

Yet one notable poet (who actually made himself a Canadian before Newfoundland entered Confederation) did emerge out of Newfoundland. He was E. J. Pratt, whose first volume of poems, *Newfoundland Verse,* showed how deeply as a boy and an itinerant preacher he had entered into the lives of the fishermen and the seal hunters and had learned the lore of seafarers and the precariousness of their existence. The forms he used tended to be conventional (in fact to the end he was inclined to use seventeenth-century verse metres for his mock epics), but the facts and the emotions were true to Newfoundland life, and they prepared the way for Pratt's earlier long poems, the best of which, like "The Cachalot," *The Roosevelt and the Antinoe* and *The Titanic,* were concerned with the sea and the courage of mariners as Pratt had learnt of them in his Newfoundland days. In a compelling way, though it did not directly involve his fellow islanders, *The Titanic* condensed into a single world-shocking episode all the centuries of endurance that had gone into shaping the Newfoundland character, and in the final chilling lines of the poem, after the great ship has sunk, there is an image of the vast indifference of nature which reflects the deep fatalism that was—and perhaps still is—the other side to the roistering view of outport existence which so many of the island ballads attempt to project.

> And out there in the twilight, with no trace
> Upon it of its deed but the last wave
> From the *Titanic* fretting at its base,
> Silent, composed, ringed by its icy broods,

The grey shape with the palaeolithic face
Was still the master of the latitudes.

Although the inhabitants of the three Maritime provinces shared to a great extent Newfoundland's dependence on the sea, the regional way of life that developed in Nova Scotia and in a somewhat different manner in New Brunswick and Prince Edward Island was in many aspects softer than that of Newfoundland and more hospitable to the development of an urbane regional culture. The Maritime provinces were not a mere fringe of bleak and spottily settled coastline around a virtually deserted interior. Settlement probed up the river valleys; agriculture and lumbering were from early days important elements in the regional economy; more clement and sheltered ports than St. John's fostered a thriving merchant marine and bustling shipyards; the garrison in Halifax, the Hanoverian settlers nearby in Lunenburg, the Loyalist settlers and their Acadian neighbours in New Brunswick, combined to form a society far more varied than the poor fishermen and the Grandgrindish St. John's merchants who formed the dispiriting polarity of Newfoundland life.

It is hard to find broader contributions to the Canadian literary tradition from Newfoundland than the work of individual writers (and perhaps in the last resort of one individual writer), but the regional culture of the Maritimes at least twice initiated trends which affected the general development of literature in Canada, though most of the best writers in these three provinces have always been intensely regional in their outlook and loyalties and still remain so.

If early Loyalist settlement in New Brunswick tended to produce mere imitations of Old Country writing, and the garrison society of Halifax produced almost nothing for several decades after its establishment in 1749, by the 1820s Nova Scotia was already at the beginning of a cultural renaissance that centred largely around Joseph Howe and the *Novascotian,* the newspaper he began to publish in 1828. Howe himself was an accomplished rather than an original essayist and poet, and his way of expression was that of Regency England, but he led the political movement which made Nova Scotia the first of the British North American colonies to gain responsible government, and he encouraged writers who were more innovative than he.

The special contribution of Nova Scotia to Canadian writing in this period was the development of the kind of satirical fiction that, down through Leacock and Richler, has become a recurrent form among our writers. It has been said, and experience seems to prove it, that the novel is a complex and sophisticated literary form that needs a fairly developed culture in which to thrive, and certainly the two notable Nova Scotian fictional satirists, Thomas McCulloch and Thomas Chandler Haliburton, confined themselves to the episodic form which Leacock later cultivated. McCulloch in *Letters of Mephibosheth Stepsure* and Haliburton in *The Sayings and Doings of Sam Slick* set out to reform the manners and politics of colonial Nova Scotia by mockery and a measure of constructive criticism. In the process they drew some memorable characters, largely out of local originals, revealed a great deal that has still documentary interest about Nova Scotian life, and wrote some very amusing prose. Their attention was closely fixed on local issues and circumstances, and since they saw their society as an established order—even if a sick one—what they wrote was in the best sense regional literature.

We move half a century forward to New Brunswick and Fredericton, where by the 1870s a small renaissance had emerged in the shadow of the recently founded University of New Brunswick and under the influence of George Parkin, who zealously taught the virtues of the major Romantic and Victorian poets and showed his students that they might be emulated even in North America. One young man who took such lessons to heart was Charles G. D. Roberts. In a long life of writing mainly for money, Roberts turned out a vast mass of work, most of it dull and ephemeral, but his best poems came as a revelation to other young writers, since he looked at the landscape of New Brunswick with a fresh and perceptive eye, and, though he used the forms and diction of Keats and Tennyson, he presented the most luminous images so far offered of the Canadian countryside, seen through eyes that were misted neither by pioneer hostility nor by the nostalgic desire to find in a new land the memories of a lost home. Roberts knew the region and belonged to it, and in poems like the famous "Tantramar Revisited" and such sonnets as "The Winter Fields" and "The Potato Harvest" he wrote about it with an accuracy of observation and expression that at times rival the achievement of another great regional poet, Thomas Hardy. There were times when Roberts's cousin, Bliss Carman, also wrote with true feeling on the landscapes of the Maritimes, but never with the power of emotion that in Roberts overcame the fact that he worked with conventional forms and a borrowed poetic language.

Ever since the days of Roberts and Carman, Fredericton has thought of itself as a centre of poetry, and there is no doubt that the exploration of the regional landscape and the regional way of life has been carried out in poetic terms by many fine writers, including, in our own day, Alden Nowlan and A. G. Bailey, Elizabeth Brewster, Fred Cogswell and Charles Bruce. When not a single literary magazine survived in the rest of Canada, during the dark days of the early 1950s, *The Fiddlehead* was being carried on by Maritime poets who sought to keep their art alive in the region and succeeded in doing so.

Perhaps the Maritimers have shown a greater stubbornness over a longer period in sustaining their own literary culture than the people of any other

Canadian region except francophone Quebec. Yet there has been nothing enclosed or parochial about such regionalism. It speaks to other Canadians today as eloquently in the poems of Alden Nowlan as in the past it did in the poems of Roberts, who was a major influence on his fellow Confederation poets (as Malcolm Ross described them), yet inspired them not to imitate his poetic renderings of the Maritime countryside but to perceive their own localities. The result of the process was the first poetry that expressed the real nature of Ontario as a region, Lampman's sensitive rural lyrics of the settled lands of the Ottawa valley, and Duncan Campbell Scott's poems of the northern woodlands, derived from his experiences as an Indian agent.

Scott has often been presented, like Roberts and Lampman, as one of the precursors of a national literature, and so he was. But he is also an example of the way in which even a national literature has its roots in the strength of local perceptions. Scott's best poems are those, like "The Forsaken," that show his awareness of the lot of the Indians as a stark conflict between man and nature in which the native way of life is doomed by historical rather than geographical necessity, and those other poems that emerge from a pure visual awareness of the landscape, expressed with a sharp, almost imagist clarity, and showing a dawning awareness that the traditional poetic forms still favoured by Lampman and Roberts must be broken up if a poetry that really fits the land is to be developed. One of the best of these is "En Route."

> The train has stopped for no apparent reason
> In the wilds;
> A frozen lake is level and fretted over
> With rippled wind lines;
> The sun is burning in the South; the season
> Is winter trembling at a touch of spring.
> A little hill with birches and a ring
> Of cedars—all so still, so pure with snow—
> It seems a tiny landscape in the moon.
> Long wisps of shadow from the naked birches
> Lie on the white in lines of cobweb-grey;
> From the cedar roots the snow has shrunk away.
> One almost hears it tinkle as it thaws,
> Traces there are of wild things in the snow—
> Partridge at play, tracks of the foxes' paws
> That broke a path to sun them in the trees.
> They're going fast where all impressions go
> On a frail substance—images like these
> Vagaries the unconscious mind receives

From nowhere and lets go to nothingness
With the lost flush of last year's autumn leaves.

Although Canadian poetry had emerged from pioneer escapism into the phase Roy Daniells has called High Colonialism, when poets responded directly to the land, it was not until the twentieth century was well advanced that poets began seriously to confront the problem of providing local perceptions with a local idiom. When that happened it was again a strongly regional development, though this time the region was less immediately recognizable as such, since it was an urban concentration rather than a rural expanse. Montreal from the 1920s to the end of the 1940s was a place of extraordinary energy; its phase as a predominantly English city in the demographic sense had come to an end, but it was still a society within which the tensions between the French and the English and the Jewish communities were strong and productive. In the late 1920s and the 1930s the group of poets centred around A. J. M. Smith, F. R. Scott, A. M. Klein and the *McGill Fortnightly Review* initiated the modernist movement that found expression in the anthology *New Provinces* (1936), and their lead was followed a decade later by the younger generation of poets, including Irving Layton, Louis Dudek, P. K. Page, Patrick Anderson and John Sutherland, who in the 1940s produced the magazines *First Statement* and *Preview*, which were consciously directed towards discovering a form and a diction that would be appropriate not merely to describing the landscape of Canada, which the rural poets had done, but also to rendering the very texture of Canadian life, in cities as well as in villages. This the Montreal poets admirably did, and so did their Toronto associate, Raymond Souster, whose poems to his own city have over the years been an unexpectedly poignant expression of local feeling in a place we are so often led to think of as the great enemy of Canadian regionalism.

In eastern and central Canada poetry—perhaps because it is so intensely personal a genre—reflected the regional nuances of Canadian living before the other literary forms, apart from satiric fiction. With one or two exceptions, of which Sara Jeannette Duncan's *The Imperialist* is perhaps the most striking, Canadian fiction before the First World War tended to be formulaic. Much of it was romantically historical; much consisted of what has been called "the regional idyll," the novel in which a pleasing and usually sentimental impression of rural life is created by the lavish use of authentic details to create local colour. *Anne of Green Gables* and *Jalna* were famous and popular examples of such pseudoregionalism.

But in the west the process was different, and Hulme's "desire to reproduce the peculiar quality of feeling which is induced by the flat spaces and wide horizons of the virgin prairie of western Canada" first found expression, not in the verse which he had thought an inevitable response, but in fiction. For it was in the prairies, and in the west in general, that the most important developments in the Canadian novel took place from the 1920s onward.

The society of the prairies differed from that of any part of Canada east of the Shield by the fact that there was no single past, no common Old Country, to which the pioneers could look back. The pasts of these people who came from so many countries were different, often dramatically so, but the present was the same, and for this reason the inhabitants of the great plains from the beginning were less inclined to seek consolation by reproducing old patterns; instead they confronted the present, the here and now. Thus prairie literature started not somewhere far away, but on the spot, in the realistic fiction which in books like Grove's *Settlers in the Marsh* and *Fruits of the Earth* and Robert Stead's *Grain* portrayed with a curiously appropriate clumsiness the harshness of pioneer life. The ancestral pasts were not forgotten, for the mingling of ethnic strains has always been an important element in the regional way of life in the prairies. Yet the emphasis was on the adaptation of traditional attitudes to the actual present experience of prairie life, exemplified in books like Martha Ostenso's story of Norwegian immigrants, *Wild Geese,* Laura Goodman Salverson's portrayal of the Icelanders of Manitoba in *The Viking Heart* and Adele Wiseman's powerful rendering of Winnipeg Jewish life in *The Sacrifice*.

Out of the trials of the pioneers emerged the small wheat-growing communities of the west, detached from the main centres of culture to a degree unimaginable in the days of radio and television, and now it was less physical hardness than the mental narrowness of prairie life that preoccupied a later generation of prairie novelists, such as Sinclair Ross, whose *As For Me and My House,* published in 1941, became a Canadian classic because it universalized the struggle of sensitive people against a stultifying environment by linking it to the wider struggle of the artist to find his identity in the philistine Canadian world of his time. It is more than accidental that in the same year as *As For Me and My House* there appeared a novel from the other end of Canada, Hugh MacLennan's *Barometer Rising,* in which a similarly close observation of a regional society at a point of crisis— Halifax in 1917 at the time of the great explosion—is used to illustrate a national theme, the emergence of a sense of Canadian self-sufficiency at the end of a long colonial slumber.

Grove and Stead and even Sinclair Ross were concerned with the prairie experience in the present, however much, in the end, *As For Me and My House* may suggest the inevitability of change and decay. But in Margaret Laurence's splendid quartet of novels, from *The Stone Angel* to *The Diviners,* whose action has its origin in the little fictional Manitoba town of Manawaka, the horizontal distances of the land are complemented by the vertical spaces of history. Few Canadian novelists are more rooted in a local culture than Laurence, and yet few expand their understanding more broadly in the world, journeying far without loosening their roots, as she travelled to the Africa that was the setting of her earlier books like *This Side Jordan* and *The Tomorrow-Tamers*. This ability to go away and return enriched is of course part of the regional experience, which in practice tends to liberate the mind from the narrowness of mere nationalism. An admirable example is Rudy Wiebe's broad timescape of the Mennonite experience, *The Blue Mountains of China*.

By their intermingling of history and geography, Margaret Laurence's novels take one beyond mere history into the realm of myth and to the edge of fantasy, where writers like Robert Kroetsch take over. And here there is a similarity with the development of fiction on the West Coast, where the fine realistic writing of Martin Allerdale Grainger in his classic logging novel, *Woodsmen of the West,* was followed by Ethel Wilson's urbane writing about Vancouver, the seacoast and the inland lake country in books like *Swamp Angel* and *The Innocent Traveller,* and then by the various fantasies of Malcolm Lowry, trying to live out a personal hell and heaven in the splendidly realized coastscapes of *October Ferry to Gabriola* and "The Forest Path to the Spring," and of Sheila Watson, who in *The Double Hook* gives a strange and universal portentousness to the living out of aboriginal myths in the interior drylands.

There is no doubt that regional developments in western Canadian fiction have initiated important trends in Canadian novel writing, from the realism of the 1920s down to the quasi-historical fantasy of more recent years; but equally important is the fact that in the end T. E. Hulme's insight was literally fulfilled, and the "necessity or inevitableness of verse" as applied to the great spaces of the prairies was recognized. With a few exceptions, like Roy Daniells's "Farewell to Winnipeg" and Anne Marriott's "Prairie Graveyard," no good poetry emerged until very recent years out of the great area between the Shield and the Rockies; the typical publication would be a nosegay of sentimental verse brought out by a smalltown printer at the author's expense. But in very recent years the great plains as visible facts and as spaces for living have begun to occupy the minds of poets in the same way as they occupied the minds of novelists in the preceding generation.

But a different prairie vision emerges from that of the early novelists who wrote realistically about pioneer experience, or the later writers who evoked the life of small communities when they were still filled with energy, however malign it might sometimes have been. The prairie poets came at a time when that way of life was decaying already, as mechanization changed the manner of farming and the trans-Canada highway virtually eliminated many of the small railwayside communities of the past. The new prairie poets tend to write of memory and loss, as John Newlove does in recollecting the Doukhobor-founded village of his childhood:

> all sights and temperatures
> and remembrances, as
> a lost gull screams now
> outside my window,
> a 9-year-old's year-long
> night and day in tiny
> magnificent prairie Verigin

Among the other poets of this lyrical renaissance in the prairies have been Gary Geddes, Andrew Suknaski and, perhaps the best of them all, Dale Zieroth. All of these poets tend to lament the history that in the form of settlement destroyed the elemental geography of the virgin prairie and that in its turn enters the cycle of decay where men begin to reject the land, and the young

> know that Winnipeg
> (200 miles south and not big enough
> for a place on the map of the world
> in the post office), that Winnipeg
> is where the world begins.

Zieroth himself is one of the young who departed, yet he knew that the regional impulse would remain when he said:

> still I will inhabit
> the bitter geography of my own making

and it was from far away across the mountains but as a native that he wrote so vividly and so exactly of rural Manitoba:

> Summer comes in from Saskatchewan on
> a hot and rolling wind. Faces
> burnt and forearms burnt, the men seed
> their separate earths and listen to the CBC
> for any new report of rain. Each day now
> the sun is bigger and from the kitchen
> window, it sets a mere hundred feet behind
> the barn, where a rainbow once came down.

The kind of regional poetry closely linked to the land and the physical experience of it in work and life which Dale Zieroth writes has its parallels in the mountain poems of Sid Marty and the poems of the coastal life which Pat Lane and Peter Trower have been writing over the last decade and more, and perhaps there is no better image of the way the mind makes regionalism out of locality than Marty's verse:

Each mountain
its own country
in the way a country
must be
a state of mind

Pat Lane's poems of British Columbia contain some of the best nature verse written by Canadians, as in his sharp-flavoured poem of the dry-lands, "Day after day the sun":

Day after day the sun hurts these hills into summer
as the green returns to yellow in filaments as hard
as stone.
Everywhere the old mortality sings.

Sagebrush breaks the bodies of the small.
Desiccated bits of fur huddle in the arroyos
as the land drifts away, melted by the wind.

And Peter Trower, as Al Purdy has said, is "a poet of mean streets, log-ging camps, pubs, and the immense blue and green sprawl of British Columbia." In his poems the wilderness and the comradeship of work, as well as the drudgery, that still linger in the British Columbian forests are vividly expressed, as in "The Last Spar-Tree."

Logging's larger than life. Keep your sailors and
cowboys!

I'm always stressing the sombre side
but there was much comradeship and laughter—
great yarns beside noon donkeys, hillhumour
between turns,
excellent shits behind stumps with the wind
fanning the stink away,
sweat smelling good and cigarette smoke celestial.

41

Dream on in peace old tree—
perhaps you're a truer monument to man
than any rocktop crucifix in Rio de Janeiro.

Poets like Pat Lane and Peter Trower remind one that British Columbia
has offered an active regional centre of poetry writing ever since the 1930s.
For a decade, from 1941 onward, when little magazines were rare, Alan
Crawley edited out of Victoria one of the best Canadian poetry magazines,
*Contemporary Verse,* and when I returned to Canada in 1949 Earle Birney,
Dorothy Livesay and Anne Marriott were all writing from British Columbia, and were soon joined by younger poets like Phyllis Webb, Daryl Hine
and Marya Fiamengo, with Pat Lane and his brother Red Lane following
afterward.

Some of these poets, like Dorothy Livesay and Earle Birney, have become in the best sense national poets, poets who speak to Canadians of all
regions; yet however they may travel and incorporate their experience into
poetry, the roots remain important. After the journeys that produced his
notable Asian and South American cycles, Birney could return to write
what is certainly his finest poem of British Columbia, and perhaps the best
of all his poems, marvellously universal and yet local at the same time,
"November Walk near False Creek Mouth," in which, as in some of his
other verse, he envisages the Canadian coast as the end of land, the extremity of wandering as he reflects on the human condition.

*in the last of warmth*
*and the fading of brightness*
*on the sliding edge of the beating sea*

The poetry of Earle Birney, like the fiction of Margaret Laurence, based
ultimately on the recognition of one's region—as Al Purdy put it, as the
only "place to stand on"—demonstrates what I feel to be the central and
important truth about regionalism, whether in literature or in politics: that
unlike nationalism, which is a matter of rigid and artificial political forms
and boundaries, regionalism is not limiting, any more than true confederal-
ism is. The full consciousness and experience of one's region in a non-
exclusive way enables one to understand better other lands and other
regions. Purdy himself is another poet whose work strongly illustrates this
truth. No Canadian poet has wandered farther, or brought back better
poetry from his wanderings, yet his loyalty to the countryside of Loyalist
Ontario has remained amazingly constant. It is the heart of his world, the
heart without which no mental vision can really live, as he makes clear in
one of the most moving of his poems, "My Grandfather's Country":

and if I must commit myself to love
of any one thing
it will be here in the red glow
where failed farms sink back into the earth
the clearings join and fences no longer divide
where the running animals gather their bodies
together
and pour themselves upward
into the tips of falling leaves
with mindless faith that presumes a future

In such poems, and in the novels that resemble them, the reality of Canadian experience, geography variously shaped by history, is truly expressed. But it is an experience that can only be lived, as Canada can only be understood, in regional terms. We are not a unitary nation. We are in cultural terms, as we should be in political terms, a confederation of regions.

# 2

# THE CHANGING MASKS
# OF EMPIRE

## Notes on Some Novels by Sara Jeannette Duncan

The development of a distinctive Canadian literature was hindered during the nineteenth century by two principal factors. One was the defensive conservatism of a pioneer society which clung to familiar ways of thought and expression brought from the Old Country as a means of emotional self-protection within what seemed a hostile environment. It was only when the land had been safely settled that people began to realize that a new kind of society had come into existence which called for a new way of giving expression to its unique pattern of life.

The other factor was the virtual absence in sparsely populated colonial societies of all the advantages on which a writer depends if he is to live by his work. A scanty readership, a rudimentary publishing industry, a scarcity of literary periodicals and an almost complete lack of literary critics: such inadequacies made it difficult before the very end of the century for any writer to gather a following or make a living. The recently published letters of Susanna Moodie, with their endless pleas for work and payment, and their revelations of periods of chronic poverty, show how hard the literary life was for those who remained in Canada, and make one understand why so many Canadian writers looked abroad for readers and publishers and why so much of our early literary talent drained away to foreign metropolises.

James de Mille, one of the most brilliant of our early novelists, wrote almost entirely for the American market. John Richardson, Charles G. D. Roberts, Bliss Carman, Ernest Thompson Seton and Gilbert Parker were examples of those who headed away to the literary markets of New York or London and either stayed for good or remained for long abroad.

Perhaps the most talented of these nineteenth-century errant Canadians was Sara Jeannette Duncan, who after a briefly brilliant journalistic career in Canada went off—not to New York or London—but to the India of the Raj; there, remote from her roots, she produced what is arguably the best Canadian fiction before the 1920s.

Sara Jeannette Duncan is a better and more interesting writer than the caprices of posthumous reputation have allowed. For almost forty years of her relatively short life (1862–1922) she was an industrious and capable journalist (writing for Canadian, American and eventually Indian papers) and she wrote twenty books which appeared in her lifetime or shortly afterward. Most of them were published in both London and New York, and some in Toronto as well. From the beginning of her career they were on the whole well received, and in the latter part of her career she generally gained the respect that is accorded a writer of acknowledged standing. Like other Canadian writers of her time she was probably more highly regarded abroad, where in any case she spent half her life, than in her native Canada.

The fate of posthumous oblivion after a life of success is not uncommon among writers, but rarely so complete as it has been in the case of Sara Duncan. She wrote six novels about India, where the last thirty years of her life were mostly spent, yet her name is not even mentioned in any of the recent studies of Anglo-Indian writing—such as Allen J. Greenberger's *The British Image of India* (1960) and Belinda Parry's *Delusions and Discoveries: Studies on India in the British Imagination* (1962)—though her novels of British life in India are better written than those of such contemporaries as Maud Diver and Flora Annie Steele, to whom considerable attention has recently been paid, and more interesting for the light they throw on the social life and the political motivations of the imperialists.

There is in fact only one book by Sara Jeannette Duncan, *The Imperialist,* that is now at all well known, and this owes its revived reputation to the attempt on the part of Canadian scholars and critics to create a past for the national literature which, as a recognizable tradition, is a comparatively recent one with few native roots. *The Imperialist* is a bright, perceptive and somewhat nostalgic novel about Canadian political life in a small Ontario town, which Duncan wrote more than a decade after she left Canada to become a *chota memsahib* in Calcutta. Reprinted in 1961 as a paperback in the New Canadian Library, it has been fairly widely read since then, and is now recognized as one of the few mature and sophisticated novels to be written by a Canadian before the Great War.

In a more general way, Sara Jeannette Duncan has undergone a rehabilitation among literary historians who recognize her importance as one of the first dedicated professional woman writers to begin their careers in Canada. But apart from *The Imperialist,* a volume of stories entitled *The Pool in the Desert* and a brief selection of her newspaper writings, *Sara Jeannette Duncan: Selected Journalism,* edited by Thomas E. Tausky, none of her work has been reprinted, and only during the 1970s have serious critical studies of her books (other than *The Imperialist*) begun to appear in Canadian journals, culminating in the publication of the sole book-length study of her writings, Tausky's sound and comprehensive *Sara Jeannette Duncan: Novelist of Empire* (1978). So far as I have been able to discover, this recent small surge of interest in Sara Jeannette Duncan has been limited to Canada; it has not spread to Britain or the United States, where her novels were most widely published and read during her lifetime, or to India, where she lived half her life and about which she wrote some of her best books.

The reasons for the neglect from which Sara Jeannette Duncan's reputation has only recently begun to emerge are closely connected with the character and even the virtues of her writing, and especially with the political vision with which her best-known works were associated. She was a remarkably good journalist in a style that became dated because its sometimes rather frenetic brilliance was a manifestation of the self-consciousness which their role in a world dominated by men imposed on young women writers seeking a career in the press (sometimes it also imposed on them masculine pretences, for there was a time when Sara Jeannette wrote under the nom de plume of Garth Grafton). She was also a novelist always tempted towards the didactic, which sometimes imposes a fatal topicality. She was particularly interested in the movement for imperial federation that rose and foundered about the turn of the century and which was especially associated with Joseph Chamberlain in England and with the remnants of the Canada First movement in Canada.

Although the influence of George Eliot is certainly visible in a book like *The Imperialist,* Sara Jeannette Duncan's literary inclinations were shown already in an early article she wrote on a visit to New Orleans in 1885, when she remarked that "literary taste is high in New Orleans. On the table in your boarding-house you will find Turgenev, Hawthorne, Arnold, James, where at home you would be greeted by such celebrities as Mary Jane Holmes, Mrs. Braddon, or the Duchess." She was to see herself always in the sophisticated company of the Turgenevs and the Jameses and outside the sentimental conventions of Victorian women's writing, though she was not lacking in her own kind of romanticism. And though her stress on realism made her sympathetic to Turgenev, it was to be largely in the United States that she found her literary models. In her generally clear-sighted way she recognized the reason for this inclination even before she took to writing books, when in 1888 she contributed a piece on "American Influence on Canadian Thought" to Goldwin Smith's magazine, *The Week:*

> The lack of moneyed leisure is not the only condition of life common to Americans and Canadians. If it were, American literature would be as impotent, at any price, to change the character of Canadian literature as it is to effect a literary revolution in England. But, like the Americans, we have a certain untram-

melled consciousness of new conditions and their opportunities, in art as well as in society, in commerce, in government. Like them, having a brief past as a people, we concentrate the larger share of thought, energy, and purpose upon our future. We have their volatile character, as we would have had without contact with them; volatility springs in a new country as naturally as weeds. We have greatly their likings and their dislikings, their ideas and their opinions. In short, we have not escaped, as it was impossible we should escape, the superior influence of a people overwhelming in numbers, prosperous in business, and aggressive in political and social faith, the natural conditions of whose life we share, and with whom we are brought every day into closer contact.

Appearing in the journal which Goldwin Smith, a former imperial federationist, was now using to put forward his pleas for commercial union with the United States, this passage reads more like an argument for the inevitability of American annexation than Sara Jeannette Duncan perhaps intended. For politically her loyalties always inclined towards the Empire, the British connection, and when she did leave Canada for good it was not to emigrate to the United States, along the road taken by so many Canadian writers from Maj. John Richardson onward, but to find her place in one of the poles of Empire, the city of Calcutta, which before the building of New Delhi was the capital of the Viceroys of India. Yet she felt always the distinction between Britain and parts of the Empire that had developed their own style of life, and an earlier piece in *The Week*, "Our Latent Loyalty," set out some of the reasons why, sharing so much with the Americans, Canadians had loyalties that lay elsewhere.

Sentiment is difficult of analysis, and the sentiment of the flag of the most difficult sort. We owe more to Britain than we are ever likely to pay; gratitude may be detected in it. We love our Queen: for the span of a long lifetime she has been to us the embodiment of all the tender virtues of a woman, all the noble graces of a queen. Thousands of her subjects in Canada were born in her kingdom; and nothing is more contagious than the loyalty they colonized with. Rideau Hall is an isolated fact in our social life. It has, and can have, no translatable meaning as a centre for the very irregular circumference it should dominate. Such old-world practices as obtain there we rather rejoice to see, feeling again in their dignity the bond of connection with the most dignified of commonwealths, and in their great incongruity, assurance that they can never become indigenous. We are glad to know that Her Majesty's representative is comfortable in Ottawa, and can be made so in his own way; and for esteeming his presence there or here an honour, with the history he bids us share, the traditions he commits to our keeping, and the flag he points our love and loyalty to, we cannot think of apologizing.

Such a passage helps to explain why, like the Canada Firsters who also embraced imperialism, Sara Jeannette Duncan rejected the idea of Canada as a colonial dependency, since she shared with them the vision of equal peoples accepting a realm of common interest based on past connections even if by now, as she also remarked, the ancient symbols of the loyalties involved might have become "alien to our social system."

Her sense of the complexities inherent not only in political loyalties but also in the relations between people from different cultures (even cultures using the same language) drew Sara Jeannette Duncan especially towards William Dean Howells and Henry James, the American writers for whom she expressed the greatest admiration. It is Howells with whom she shows the nearest affinity as a writer, for whenever she seems to be emulating James's complexities of manner her prose tends to lose the lucidity and springiness that are its most attractive qualities. Like Howells, she was always a novelist of manners, so that when we read books like *The Imperialist* and *His Honour, and a Lady,* we get the same sense of the living texture of everyday life, of the average as a setting for the exceptional, as Howells evoked, while, like Howells, Duncan used her experience of travel to illuminate the worlds she knew (Canadian, English, American, Anglo-Indian) by introducing into them sensitive and perceptive travellers from other cultures.

As a journalist, Sara Jeannette Duncan had already learnt that "she must have some unworn incident, some fiber of novelty or current interest to give value to her work" in the eyes of editors and the reading public, and her newspaper pieces contain many vignettes that still evoke vividly how ordinary Canadians lived a hundred years or so ago. When she went into fiction it was by way of travel journalism, for her first book, *A Social Departure* (1890), was a collection of travel dispatches written for the Montreal *Star* during a world journey, streamlined into a narrative and given a fictional form in which the interest is concentrated on the ways in which two young women of different backgrounds travelling together (the Canadian narrator and her archly named English companion, Orthodocia) experience their mildly exotic adventures in Japan and India and the Middle East. There is a triple movement in the book, embodied in the varying responses of the two travellers to strange settings, and the way in which they affect each other. On this level the claims of fiction are somewhat shallowly fulfilled, and a frame is provided for the bright but rarely more than superficial observations of unfamiliar societies and their strange life styles. From this pattern Sara Jeannette Duncan never entirely escaped. She always tended to be the victim of her own verbal cleverness, and to imagine that when she had brought people into amusing confrontation in settings that emphasized their peculiarities of character she had written a novel. Such charming fictions of manner and setting, which fail in her own requirement of "the development of human character," punctuate her career.

The first of her Indian books, *The Simple Adventures of a Memsahib* (1893), is an early example. A young man in trade in Culcutta, and therefore without expectation of ever becoming a *burra sahib*, sends for his fiancée from England, they are married, set up house in Calcutta, and young Mrs. Browne goes through all the exotic and often exasperating experiences of establishing a household and finding her level as a *chota memsahib* (little lady, as against *burra memsahib*, great lady) in the highly stratified Anglo-Indian society. An ironic touch is given to the narrative, since it is told by an older woman, Mrs. Perth McIntyre, who had gone through the same experiences as Mrs. Browne, and who watches the way in which the young woman's eager response to an unfamiliar way of life has been destroyed by the communal pressure to conformity; for the English in India, conformity was self-defence. The novel ends on a note of quiet pathos.

It was a very little splash that submerged Mrs. Browne in Anglo-India, and there is no longer a ripple to tell about it. I don't know that life has contracted much for her. I doubt if it was ever intended to hold more than young Browne and the baby—but it has changed. Affairs that are not young Browne's or the baby's touch her very little. Her world is the personal world of Anglo-India, and outside of it, except in affection for Canbury, I believe she does not think at all. She is growing dull in India, too, which is about as sad a thing as any. She sees no more the supple savagery of the Pathan in the market-place, the bowed reverence of the Mussulman praying in the sunset, the early morning mists lifting among the domes and palms of the city. She has acquired for the Aryan inhabitant a certain strong irritation, and she believes him to be nasty in all his ways. This will sum up her impressions of India as completely years hence as it does today. She is a memsahib like another. . . . I hope she may not stay twenty-two years. Anglo-Indian tissues, material and spiritual, are apt to turn in twenty-two years to a substance somewhat resembling chalk. And I hope she will not remember so many dead faces as I do when she goes away—dead faces and palm fronds grey with the powder of the wayside, and clamorous voices of the bazar crying, "Here iz! memsahib! Here iz!" . . . So let us go our several ways. This is a dusty world. We drop down the river with the tide to-night. We shall not see the red tulip blossoms of the silk cottons fall again.

*The Simple Adventures of a Memsahib* carries the process of fictionalization a step farther than *A Social Departure*. It is no longer through the eyes of two real people turned into characters, but through those of invented characters, that we are looking at and otherwise experiencing a strange world, but still the author is mainly engaged in writing graphically of the humanity about her, "its tricks of speech, its manner of breaking bread, its ideals, aims, superstitions." And we can reasonably take it that *The Simple Adventures* is Sara Jeannette Duncan's way of telling us something of how she adjusted to a strange life when in 1891 she went out to marry Everard Charles Cotes, the curator of the Indian Museum who shortly afterward went into journalism and became the editor of the *Indian Daily News*. Certainly neither of the Brownes emerges as a strongly delineated personality, and (except for a visiting and meddling British politician portrayed with acerbic dislike) the remaining characters are all shallow types of Anglo-India rather than people with interesting inner lives. Nor, indeed, do we have much access to the inner life even of Mrs. Browne, the central figure of the novel, and this is not entirely because her experiences are told from the outside, by the observant Mrs. Perth McIntyre. It is because she is so neutral as a person, so much the experiencing membrane, that she never takes on shape in our minds as a woman whose feelings are deep and real or whose relation to her world is much more than an excuse for the author to record her own impressions of India and its English expatriate community as she first saw them.

When Duncan did move into more substantial fiction, into novels where the characters were well developed and the action became tense with conflict, it was under the influence of the didactic impulse of politics. At her best, in *The Imperialist,* or in her more impressive works on India, like *His Honour, and a Lady* and especially *The Burnt Offering,* Sara Duncan became one of the few Canadians who have written genuine political fiction to which, as Thomas E. Tausky has pointed out, Irving Howe's classic definition clearly applies when he differentiates the political from the social novel, defining it as "the kind in which the idea of society, as distinct from the mere unquestioned workings of society, has penetrated the consciousnesses of the characters in all of its profoundly problematic aspects, so that there is to be observed in their behaviour, and they are themselves often aware of, some coherent political loyalty or ideological identification."

Early in her career as a journalist Sara Duncan wanted to become involved in political writing, and in March 1888 she gained her first opportunity when she was appointed parliamentary correspondent in Ottawa for the Montreal *Star*. It was a brief assignment, for in the late summer she was already in Brantford preparing for her departure in September on the world tour that led to her first book, *A Social Departure*. The columns she wrote suggest that she was more interested in the pageant and the personalities of Canadian government than in the issues at stake during the brief session she reported, for her dispatches are strong on description of parliamentary events and weak in analysis of policies, which may well explain why the *Star* was so happy to send her on the world tour where her descriptive powers would be more appropriately used.

However, her interest in politics remained and was put to journalistic use when she began in the middle 1890s to write editorials for the *Indian Daily News*. It surfaced in *The Simple Adventures of a Memsahib,* where she introduced, in the person of Jonas Batcham, M.P., her first sketch of the gullible travelling politician who visits India and acquires a superficial knowledge of the situation there which leads him to make misleading accusations regarding the administration of the local officials. On a very simple level, the attitude towards the Raj that Sara Duncan maintained in the thirty years of her connection with India was already established in this early book. She looked with a satiric eye on the social pretensions and the snobbish distinctions within the Calcutta Anglo-Indian community. She disliked the Bengali "baboos" who had received a partial education in the English manner and belonged to neither the new Western nor the traditional Indian culture. She looked on Indian princes as material for comedy, and when she did portray an Indian character in convincing depth he usually turned out to be something of a villain. An example is the Indian nationalist, Ganendra Thakore, in *The Burnt Offering,* who was based on an actual nationalist leader, Bal Gandhadur Tilak, a pious Hindu advocate of the use of extreme and violent means to rid India of British domination. Sara Duncan had clearly studied Tilak's record and his character very carefully, for Ganendra Thakore is a thoroughly believable Indian leader of the Tilak kind without being a literal portrait; he is also diabolically convincing in his pietistic evil.

Almost everything that Sara Duncan wrote of India spoke well of those Anglo-Indian idealists who saw themselves taking up the white man's burden and offering the Indians, despite their ungrateful opposition, the way to a more healthy and industrious life by which, in the long rather than the short run, they would be prepared to take their places within the Empire as equals. Sara Duncan's Indian politics were nearer to those of Lord Curzon than to those of the regular Indian establishment, and this means, of course, that they were more consciously imperialist in the ideal sense than most India hands allowed themselves to be in practice.

*His Honour, and a Lady* (1896), published three years after *The Simple Adventures of a Memsahib,* shows a considerable advance in Sara Duncan's understanding of the moral ambience of the Raj. Reading this and her other Indian novels, we have to remember the special position, almost ideal for ironic observation, which she held in Anglo-Indian society. As wife of the curator of the Indian Museum, she did not belong to the commercial strata of Anglo-Indian society, yet her husband was not one of the all-powerful members of the Indian Civil Service. Leaving the museum to become a newspaper editor, he (and Sara) remained somewhere between the commercials and the civilians, so that they never became *burra sahibs* yet had fairly free access to almost every Indian presence, whether in Calcutta or in the hot-weather capital of Simla. This mobility, combined with the special access to political issues conferred by her newspaper work, allowed Sara Duncan to write with irony on Anglo-Indian social relationships at the same time as she seriously considered the political issues that faced the rulers of India and the moral struggles out of which their decision and their subsequent actions arose.

*His Honour, and a Lady* shows admirably the dual aspects of Duncan's Indian novels. The title is more weightily ambiguous than most critics have realized. To begin, it refers to one of the leading figures, John Church, who as the novel opens is receiving the news that he has been picked out from his remote district commissionership to become acting lieutenant-governor of Bengal; he will be referred to as His Honour. By the time the book ends, Church has lost his post in a political storm and has died of cholera, and his secret enemy, Lewis Ancram, has been appointed lieutenant-governor and become His Honour. The Lady with whom both their Honours are involved is Church's wife, Judith, who married him, a man more than twice her age, because it meant an escape from spinsterhood in a grey English industrial town to the romantic possibilities of life in India. Judith does not love John, but she immensely respects his devotion and his idealism, and when she falls in love with Ancram, and he with her, she cannot sacrifice her marriage. Partly, we see, she is moved by fear of the unknown, of the consequences in the Victorian world of adultery or (even worse) of divorce, but she is also influenced by her deep loyalty to the man whose struggle to use his power for the good of Indians she entirely admires.

Church's great plan, on which he risks his position and his reputation, is to change education in Bengal, superseding Macaulay's system of English liberal-style education (which by the end of the nineteenth century had produced a host of unemployable and discontented graduates in arts and law), with a system more oriented towards technical training, which would benefit the sons of peasants rather than the sons of landowners and money-lenders educated under the existing system. Ancram, who is chief secretary to the Bengal government, pretends to admire Church and to support his proposal, but in fact despises him as a politician and intrigues with Bengali nationalists who seize on the educational issue to fan opposition to the regime; Ancram is the real author of the article in a Bengal paper which has most influence in Britain, forcing the secretary of state to demand Church's resignation. Fortuitously (perhaps too fortuitously) Church is already sick from the cholera of which he is to die when the news is communicated to him by the Viceroy.

What makes Ancram interesting as a character is the division between his love for Judith Church and his hatred for John Church. His lack of true passion is shown by the fact that he does not hate Church emotionally as a rival in Judith's love, but intellectually as an administrator whose reforms, whatever their merits, are not in accordance with what he regards as the experience of imperial rule. Nevertheless, when Church dies, Ancram hopes he will not only gain his position as lieutenant-governor but also win his wife. But Judith learns at the last minute how Ancram betrayed Church with his anonymous article, and she declines to marry him. And here the title takes on one of its secondary meanings. For this "Lady" there is only one "His Honour"; Ancram's title is shown to be specious as we realize that Sara Duncan is writing not merely about the honourific aspects of office but also about the honour involved in political morality. John Church is an honourable man because he carries out, to the point of risking and accepting death, the obligations of his office, and refuses to bow to political expediencies when he is devising a new system which he believes will be to the ultimate benefit of the people he rules as a surrogate monarch. Ancram is a man without honour, since he allows expediency to make him an ally of those who are seeking to frustrate, by their specious visions of independence, the positive efforts of the British rulers.

This battle of political ideals and personal honour takes place against the background of an expatriate society projected partly through the eyes of the narrator and partly through the shrewd observation of the second important woman in the novel, Rhoda Daye, an independent-minded young person with a witty tongue who is engaged to Ancram but jilts him because she recognizes his hollowness; there is a great deal in Rhoda, one feels, of her creator. In portraying the meretricious Anglo-Indian social life, Sara Duncan's talents as a novelist of manners are well deployed, and the "composite dinner party" given by Mrs. Daye, Rhoda's mother and the wife of a commisariat colonel, shows admirably how she could balance sharp dialogue and analytical narrative.

Mrs. Daye always gave composite dinner parties, and this was one of them. "If you ask nobody but military people to meet each other," she was in the habit of saying, "you hear nothing but the price of chargers and the prospects of the Staff Corps. If you make your list up of civilians, the conversation consists of abuse of their official superiors and the infamous conduct of the Secretary of State about the rupee." On this occasion Mrs. Daye had reason to anticipate that the price of chargers would be varied by the grievances of the Civil Service, and that a touring Member of Parliament would participate in the discussion who knew nothing about either; and she felt that her blend would be successful. She could give herself up to the somewhat fearful enjoyment she experienced in Mr. Ancram's society. Mrs. Daye was convinced that nobody appreciated Mr. Ancram more subtly than she did. She saw a great deal of jealousy of him in Calcutta society, whereas she was wont to declare that, for her part, she found nothing extraordinary in the way he had got in—a man of his brains, you know! And if Calcutta resented this imputation upon its brains in ever so slight a degree, Mrs. Daye saw therein more jealousy of the fact that her family circle was about to receive him. When it had once opened for that purpose and closed again, Mrs. Daye hoped vaguely that she would be sustained in the new and exacting duty of living up to Mr. Ancram.

"*Please* look at Rhoda," she begged, in a conversational buzz that her blend had induced.

Mr. Ancram looked, deliberately, but with appreciation. "She seems to be sufficiently entertained," he said.

"Oh, she is! She's got a globe-trotter. Haven't you found out that Rhoda simply loves globe-trotters? She declares that she renews her youth in them."

"Her first impressions, I suppose she means?"

"Oh, as to what she *means*—"

Mrs. Daye broke off irresolutely, and thoughtfully conveyed a minute piece of roll to her lips. The minute piece of roll was Mr. Ancram's opportunity to complete Mrs. Daye's suggestion of a certain interesting ambiguity in her daughter, but he did not take it. He continued to look attentively at Miss Daye, who appeared, as he said, to be sufficiently entertained, under circumstances that seemed to him inadequate. Her traveller was talking emphatically, with gestures of elderly dogmatism, and she was deferentially listening, an amusement behind her eyes with which the Chief Secretary to the Government of Bengal was not altogether unfamiliar. He had seen it there before, on occasions when there was apparently nothing to explain it.

"It would be satisfactory to see her eating her dinner," he remarked, with what Mrs. Daye felt to be too slight a degree of solicitude. She was obliged to remind herself that at thirty-seven a man was apt to take these things more as matters of fact, especially—and there was a double comfort in this reflection—a man already well up in the Secretariat and known to be ambitious. "Is it possible," Mr. Ancram went on, somewhat absently, "that these are Calcutta roses? You must have a very clever gardener."

"No"—and Mrs. Daye pitched her voice with a gentle definiteness that made what she was saying interesting all round the table—"they came from the Viceroy's place at Barrackpore. Lady Emily sent them to me: so sweet of her, I thought! I always think it particularly kind when people in that position trouble themselves about one; they must have so *many* demands upon their time."

The effect could not have been better. Everybody looked at the roses with an interest that might have been described as respectful; and Mrs. Delaine, whose husband was Captain Delaine of the Durham Rifles, said that she would have known them for Their Excellencies' roses anywhere—they always did the table with that kind for the Thursday dinners at Government House—she had never known them to use any other.

Mrs. St. George, whose husband was the Presidency Magistrate, found this interesting. "Do they really?" she exclaimed. "I've often wondered what those big Thursday affairs were like. Fancy—we've been in Calcutta through three cold weathers now, and have never been asked to anything but little private dinners at Government House—not more than eight or ten, you know!"

"Don't you prefer that?" asked Mrs. Delaine, taking her quenching with noble equanimity.

Sara Jeannette Duncan did not become so preoccupied with Anglo-Indian society or with the politics of the Raj that she easily forgot her Canadian links, and in an article ("Imperial Sentiment in Canada") published in the *Indian Daily News* in the same year as *His Honour, and a Lady* appeared, she sketched a theme that eight years later would be fictionally fleshed out in her only completely Canadian novel, *The Imperialist*. In this piece she made clear that her own sympathies were with Joseph Chamberlain and his idea of a "practical Federation of the British Empire based on a mutual system of preferential tariffs," an idea that would be kept alive into the 1930s by a Canadian expatriate politician operating from Britain, Lord Beaverbrook. Sara Duncan castigated Sir John A. Macdonald for paying lip service to Canada's British links, while his National Policy "was conceived and carried out in plain opposition to British interest as a whole, and many of its tariff provisions were directly aimed at British manufactures." And she was encouraged by a statement of the newly elected Liberal prime minister, Laurier, that "he and his Liberals looked with favour upon designs for Imperial Federation based on a preferential tariff for the goods of British Columbia and her colonies." She was gratified that Joseph Chamberlain "should find the first sincere welcome to his scheme for Imperial Federation offered by the Liberals of Canada, with whose economic principles it accords, and who are proud to claim a part in the greatness it prefigures." Sara Duncan was expecting too much from Laurier, for Canada at no time committed herself to the cause of Imperial Federation. Eight years later, in *The Imperialist,* she used this Liberal betrayal, as it seemed to her, for her basic situation.

*The Imperialist* is not, any more than the other novels by Sara Duncan that I am discussing, entirely a political novel. The aborting of Lorne Murchison's parliamentary career through the conflict between ideals and practical politics in the Ontario town of Elgin is only one of the novel's leading strains, and though the fiasco of young Murchison's election campaign provides the most visibly dramatic action, his sister Advena's finally successful efforts to achieve a marriage of true minds with the preacher, Hugh Finlay, is almost as important in balancing the structure and heightening the emotional tension of the novel. The contrast between the intellectual Advena's steadfastness in love and the fickleness of the shallow-minded

Dora Milburn, who jilts Lorne for a visiting English snob, parallels the contrast between Lorne's steadfastness to his imperial ideal once he had adopted it and the calculating expediency of the Liberal party hacks who veer immediately they see the vote endangered by idealist politics and who eventually desert Lorne when a re-election is ordered and they feel they need a more cynical candidate.

*The Imperialist* is as much a social as a political novel, and much of its lasting appeal in Canada lies in the nostalgic vividness with which Sara Duncan recreates, in the small town of Elgin, the Brantford in which she spent her childhood and her youth. A great deal of the local colour that she shared with Howells enters the passages of urban description in which she sets the scene for her political drama. It is there with a special felicity in the opening passage of the book where the bizarre figure of the half-mad gingerbread seller, "old Mother Beggarlegs," introduces the celebration in loyal Elgin of the Queen's Birthday, and it appears in a more solid way, giving a sense of the devotion of Elgin people to the immediate advantages of life, in the passage describing the market square where Lorne's legal office is situated.

During four days in the week the market square was empty. Odds and ends of straw and paper blew about it; an occasional pedestrian crossed it diagonally for the short cut to the post-office; the town hall rose in the middle, and defied you take your mind off the ugliness of municipal institutions. On the other days it was a scene of activity. Farmers' wagons, with the shafts turned in, were ranged round three sides of it; on a big day they would form into parallel lines and cut the square into sections as well. The produce of all Fox County filled the wagons, varying agreeably as the year went round. Bags of potatoes leaned against the sidewalk, apples brimmed in bushel measures, ducks dropped their twisted necks over the cart wheels; the town hall, in this play of colour, stood redeemed. The produce was mostly left to the women to sell. On the fourth side of the square loads of hay and cordwood demanded the master mind, but small matter of fruit, vegetables, and poultry submitted to feminine judgment. The men "unhitched," and went away on their own business; it was the wives you accosted as they sat in the middle, with their knees drawn up and their skirts tucked close, vigilant in rusty bonnets, if you wished to buy. Among them circulated the housewives of Elgin, pricing and comparing, and acquiring; you could see it all from Dr. Simmons's window, sitting in his chair that screwed up and down. There was a little difficulty always about getting things home; only very ordinary people carried their own marketing. Trifling articles, like eggs or radishes, might be smuggled into a brown wicker basket with covers, but it did not consort with elegance to "trapse" home with anything that looked inconvenient or had legs sticking out of it. So that arrangements of mutual obligation had to be made: the good woman from whom Mrs. Jones had bought her tomatoes would take charge of the spring chickens Mrs. Jones had bought from another good woman just as soon as not, and deliver them to Mrs. Jones's residence, as under any circumstances she was "going round that way."

This is not mere stage scenery, for the mixture of formality and calculation shown in the market behaviour of Elgin housewives is extended into the whole of the little town's society as it is laid out before us, dominated by the materialism of its factory interests yet led also by more tenuous considerations of class and convention that derive from a history different from that of the Americans. It is of course the tendency for material self-interest to compete with wider and more nebulous loyalties that Lorne Murchison has to fight in his effort to win election on the basis of a policy that, by dismantling Sir John Macdonald's tariff barriers to let British manufactures in, might harm the profits of Elgin factory-owners and the wages of Elgin workers. The full bitterness of Lorne's situation emerges when we realize that it is material self-interest on the lowest level, the eagerness of a few men to earn bribes which the political "boys" offer them, that puts Lorne's marginal electoral victory in jeopardy. And this leads to the situation in which the rival political machines agree to a "saw-off" that will halt investigations of corruption on both sides provided the judges order a new election. It is when the party bosses send for him that Lorne finally understands how ideals are used in practical politics, being adopted and discarded as expediency dictates.

They had delegated what Horace Williams called "the job" to Mr. Farquharson, and he was actually struggling with the preliminaries of it, when Bingham, uncomfortable under the curious quietude of the young fellow's attention, burst out with the whole thing.

"The fact is, Murchison, you can't poll the vote. There's no man in the Riding we'd be better pleased to send to the House; but we've got to win this election, and we can't win it with you."

"You think you can't?" said Lorne.

"You see, old man," Horace Williams put in, "you didn't get rid of that save-the-Empire-or-die scheme of yours soon enough. People got to think you meant something by it."

"I shall never get rid of it," Lorne returned simply, and the others looked at one another.

"The popular idea seems to be," said Mr. Farquharson judicially, "that you would not hesitate to put Canada to some material loss, or at least to postpone her development in various important directions, for the sake of the imperial connection."

"Wasn't that," Lorne asked him, "what, six months ago, you were all prepared to do?''

"Oh, no," said Bingham, with the air of repudiating for everybody concerned. "Not for a cent. We were willing at one time to work it for what it was worth, but it never was worth all that, and if you'd had a little more experience, Murchison, you'd have realized it."

"That's right, Lorne," contributed Horace Williams. "Experience—that's all you want. You've got everything else, and a darned sight more. We'll get you there, all in good time. But this time—"

"You want me to step down and out," said Lorne.

And after a little more conversation he agrees and leaves the other men, "and they stood together in a moment's silence, three practical politicians who had delivered themselves from a dangerous network involving higher things."

One ends *The Imperialist* with more than a suspicion that Sara Duncan is skeptical of the ability of democratic politics ever to rise above the level of expediency and self-interest, and this attitude is developed further in the second political novel about India which I am here discussing, *The Burnt Offering*. If *His Honour, and a Lady* is about how practical politics destroys honour, and *The Imperialist* is about how it erodes ideals, *The Burnt Offering* is really about how ideals applied without sufficient knowledge of a situation can be as destructive as the most cynical of manipulative policies; in fact mistaken ideals and political manipulation, in Sara Duncan's view, seem to work together and feed each other.

*The Burnt Offering* draws its life from the political ferment that arose when India was released in 1905 from the glacial bureaucratic peace of Lord Curzon's viceroyalty. In 1906 a Liberal government came to power in Westminster, intent on introducing reforms that would hasten India on the road towards constitutional government. The Anglo-Indian community, led by the Viceroy, Lord Minto, was skeptical of the practicality of John Morley's reforms, which in the Indian Councils Act of 1909 introduced the elective principle into the selection of legislative councils; justification seemed to be given to this caution by the fact that between 1907 and 1910 the Bengali and Mahratta terrorists became powerful in the Indian independence movement and, under Bal Gandhadur Tilak, challenged the moderates led by Gopal Krishna Gokhale, Gandhi's predecessor. Tilak was imprisoned for sedition in 1908, and a rash of terrorist attempts followed, including one on Minto's life. The British replied by restricting freedom of speech, press and meeting and by other stringent emergency measures.

Sara Duncan was in India throughout this turbulent period and recognized the opportunities it offered for a powerful political novel. *The Burnt Offering*, which appeared in 1909, while the terrorist campaign was in progress and the British were buttressing their regime by strong police action, was therefore extremely topical, and its very topicality in 1909 is one of the reasons why it is historically so interesting in the 1980s. It gives a vivid sense of the ambience in which both the English and the educated Indians lived in Calcutta, which was still the capital of India as well as of Bengal, and if Sara Duncan has taken the liberties with the actual pattern of events that fiction demands, she still evokes, both vividly and authentically, the political forces then at work in India.

Indian characters are more numerous in *The Burnt Offering* than in any of Sara Duncan's earlier novels, and their variety suggests how closely she had observed the types with which an enquiring Anglo-Indian was likely to come into contact. The common people other than servants (coolies, policemen, peasants, cabbies) are seen from the outside, portrayed as a genre painter might do, with a quick stroke that sets them in the mind's eye: "Lower down a steamer had been coaling, and along the footpath on the riverside trooped some scores of blackened coolies, each in his rag of loin-cloth, chattering and gesticulating as they pressed on to the shelter and the meal that stood for their share of life." The coolies are seen not without compassion, but with no sense of how, given the nature of Indian life, their lot can be changed.

The changes in Indians who have been in contact with Europeans are evident. Ganendra Thakore longs to return to the old ways of Brahminical India, but to that end willingly condones forms of violence that require weapons and explosives imported from Britain and in one instance disguised as Brand's Essence, which as an extract of beef is of course repugnant to all good Hindus. In the case of Bepin Behari Dey, the young son of a family belonging to the reformed sect of Brahmo Samaj, his education in Oxford, London and Paris had turned him into a nationalist extremist willing to sacrifice himself in an act of terrorism. Sir Kristodas Mukerji, the pious Brahmin judge, is torn between his lawyer's sense of the fairness of British administration and his traditionalist's longing that, fair or not, the rule of the aliens shall come to an end.

It is Sir Kristodas who sentences Thakore for sedition (he gives him ten years while Tilak got only six) and then resigns his judgeship and his Order of the Indian Empire to become a pilgrim wandering through the sacred places of India with his daughter, the Rani Janaki, who has eaten of Western culture and found it a dusty Dead Sea Fruit, and the Swami Yadava, who combines the role of a *sanyasin* with that of a spy for the British police. Yadava is the least authentic of all the characters who populate the book, whether Indian or British, and this is perhaps because he is too obviously derived from the Tibetan lama who played a similar double role in Kipling's *Kim,* while the other Indian characters are clearly related to, though not directly modelled on, the real Indians whom Sara Duncan encountered either socially or as a journalist.

The catalytic figures in the novel are the two English people who come from outside the Anglo-Indian world: Vulcan Mills and his daughter Joan. Vulcan Mills is the most developed example of one of Sara Duncan's recurrent types, the globe-trotting British M.P. who is sketched out in the unpleasant Jonas Batcham, M.P., of *The Simple Adventures of a Memsahib* and appears fleetingly as a boring dinner guest in *His Honour, and a Lady.* For Vulcan Mills, Sara Duncan took as her model the Scottish labour leader, Keir Hardie, who made a trip to India in 1907, travelled around with open eye, and in his book, *India: Impressions and Suggestions,* was predictably critical of British methods, which he regarded as authoritarian but unstatesmanlike. A little sympathy and conciliation, he felt, would achieve more than a great deal of oppression, and he believed that the extension of the Indian participation in governmental affairs should be carried on with a view to eventual Dominion status. His book was moderate, sensible and perceptive, and it was obvious that Hardie was nobody's fool.

Vulcan Mills, on the other hand, is represented as pompous, vain and easily misled, and his daughter Joan as an ecstatic enthusiast of the most gullible kind. Such figures Sara Duncan evidently felt necessary to stress the central message of her book: that India's problems must be solved by those who know the country and have brought it forward into the nineteenth century, and that benevolent intruders from outside who do not realize the complexity of the situation are likely to play into the hands of forces which, under the cloak of patriotism, will turn India back towards its dark ages. Ganendra Thakore feeds Vulcan's sense of the total injustice of the Raj and flatters him with suggestions of how his influence in Britain may change the situation. But Vulcan in his turn challenges Thakore to greater extremities and eggs him on to make the speech that will lead to his imprisonment. The imprisonment in turn provokes Thakore to give the secret sign that will trigger Dey's self-destructive attempt on the Viceroy's life, so that Mills, who sees himself as a man of peace, unknowingly precipitates a sequence of deadly violence.

In *The Burnt Offering* the moderate Congress adherents of G. K. Gokhale never appear. Doubtless this was because Calcutta, where Sara Duncan lived, was the centre of terrorist action at the time she was writing the novel. At the same time the stress on Thakore and his fellow conspirators makes for a more dramatic book than the intrusion of moderate nationalism would have allowed, and if Sara Duncan disturbs political actuality by this choice she also enhances the fictional intensity, as Conrad did in his departure from the true history of anarchism in *The Secret Agent,* which Sara Duncan may well have read, since it appeared in 1907 and she had already expressed her admiration for Conrad's work in a review of *An Outcast of the Islands* which she wrote in 1896.

Thus the internal dynamics of the novel led Sara Duncan to make Vulcan

Mills very different from Keir Hardie in real life, just as they led her to violate the sentimental conventions of her time by showing how love as well as idealism are mangled by political realities, so that there is no neat pattern of happy amorous conclusions. The lovers, each in his or her own way, are destroyed by the situation in which they are trapped. John Game, a high official, falls in love with Joan Mills, which means the disappointment and eventual withdrawal from the world of the Rani Janaki, who loves him. Joan, however, falls for the blandishments of Dey, and agrees to marry him (which Thakore thinks will be a great gain for the nationalist cause), but before their wedding can take place he has shot himself after his failed assassination attempt. The only victim of the attempt, apart from a pariah dog, is John Game, who is thrown from the Viceroy's carriage and dies, not from the explosion, but agonizingly from tetanus; Calcutta mud has got into his blood through his grazed skin. And Joan, who thinks to serve Dey's memory by remaining in India and working for the cause, is forced to leave by his female relatives, whom events have scared back into conservatism, and who no longer want the daughter of Vulcan Mills among them.

*The Burnt Offering* shows a far deeper understanding of the undercurrents of Indian life than Sara Duncan's first book on the country, *The Simple Adventures of a Memsahib,* and it is more sophisticated and more critical in its portrayal of Anglo-Indian society than *His Honour, and a Lady.* Duncan's awareness of the divisions between political ideals and political realities is as certain as it was in *The Imperialist,* which in my view rivals *The Burnt Offering* as her best novel. And if, in the end, I consider *The Burnt Offering* the better, if not the more plausible book, it is because Sara Duncan has not been afraid to shake off verisimilitude when she found it necessary to give dramatic or grotesque form to the shape of political violence, whether in the mind or in the streets. She showed her understanding of Stendhal's maxim: "Politics in a work of literature is like a pistol-shot in the middle of a concert, something loud and vulgar, and yet a thing to which it is not possible to refuse one's attention."

# 3

# INNOCENCE AND SOLITUDE

## The Fictions of Ethel Wilson

The fact that at this point two essays about women writers follow each other is in accordance with the general spirit of *Northern Spring* and also with the general pattern of Canadian literary history. Of fourteen essays devoted to individual writers in this volume, seven are exclusively about women writers, and one makes a comparison between the work of a man— Rudy Wiebe—and that of a woman—Margaret Laurence. This proportion reflects the extraordinarily important role that women played in the great resurgence of Canadian literature between the 1950s and the 1980s, and which they continue to play today.

But the importance of women writers in Canada is nothing new. The first novel written about Canada was by a woman: Frances Brooke's *The History of Emily Montague* in 1780. The first novel written by a native-born Canadian was a woman's: Julia Catherine Beckwith Hart's *St. Ursula's Convent; or, The Nun of Canada,* which appeared in Kingston in 1824. Throughout the nineteenth century, even if the women writers were less numerous than the men, some of them were among the most interesting literary figures of their time, such as the Strickland sisters (Susanna Moodie and Catharine Parr Traill), Anna Jameson, Rosanna Leprohon, Agnes Maul Machar, Isabella Valancy Crawford and, of course, the subject of the last essay, Sara Jeannette Duncan.

Thus Ethel Wilson is part of a powerful continuing tradition in Canadian writing. But she also plays an important role among modern Canadian women writers—and indeed among modern Canadian novelists in general —as a transitional figure, old enough in years to have been an Edwardian and to have retained a premodern sensibility, yet stylistically sophisticated and in tune with the period of the 1950s and 1960s in which, a literary late-starter, she actually wrote.

Ethel Wilson always stood somewhat outside the general currents of Canadian writing in her time or any time. She was a great deal older than most contemporary novelists and belonged by experience as well as birth to an earlier generation. She did not publish her first short story until she was forty-nine in 1937, when "I Just Love Dogs" appeared in the *New States-man,* and her first novel, *Hetty Dorval,* appeared in 1947, when she was fifty-nine. Her career, after that, was remarkably short, for the last of her six books, *Mrs. Golightly and Other Stories,* appeared in 1961, and the last of her contributions to literary periodicals in 1964. Although Ethel Wilson lived long afterward, until 1980, she withdrew in her later years into the silence of bereavement and sickness. The two items that repre-sented the end of her career as a published writer, both appearing in the autumn of 1964, were a short story in *Tamarack Review* ("A Visit to the Frontier") and a slight autobiographical essay ("Reflections in a Pool") in *Canadian Literature.*

Thus Ethel Wilson's career as a writer lasted only twenty-seven of her ninety-two years, and her books all appeared within an even briefer period of fourteen years. In terms of publication she was the junior contemporary of much younger writers like Hugh MacLennan and Sinclair Ross, both of whom published first novels six years before *Hetty Dorval,* but in terms of age and experience she was the contemporary of writers we regard as be-longing to much older generations. She was three years younger than D. H. Lawrence and six years younger than Virginia Woolf and James Joyce; she was six years older than Aldous Huxley and J. B. Priestley, and as a child she had known Arnold Bennett. When she reached Vancouver, she and the city were both in their early teens, youthful and growing, and when King Edward VII died she was a young woman in her early twenties.

I suggest that in this temporal disjunction between experience and crea-tion lie many of the clues to the special character of Ethel Wilson's writing. For, as I remarked in my essay "On Ethel Wilson" in *The World of Cana-dian Writing,* "she had retained, I realized, an Edwardian sensibility, but she had developed a contemporary ironic intelligence, and it was the inter-play of the two that gave her books their special quality."

When she began to write, Ethel Wilson carried with her—in terms of personal memories and family traditions—the rich past to which she gave fictional form in *The Innocent Traveller,* that intriguing chronicle in which the history of the young city of Vancouver is interwoven with the group biography of a transplanted Victorian family. At the same time, coming of a literary lineage (Matthew Arnold as well as Arnold Bennett haunted its past), she had remained aware of what was happening in the literary world of her time, and in her correspondence she showed a sensitive appreciation of the special qualities of novelists as varied in time and kind as Defoe and Proust.

The breadth of Ethel Wilson's literary sympathies extended to her Cana-dian contemporaries, and she followed with enthusiastic interest the up-surge of writing in this country during the 1950s and the early 1960s. She expressed her admiration for the achievements of Gabrielle Roy, Morley

Callaghan and Robertson Davies and recognized the originality and the lyrical power of a novel so unlike her own work as Sheila Watson's *The Double Hook*. Her very use of the adjective *dissimilar* when she talked of these writers implied that she did not need to identify herself with them. Indeed, one of the aspects of the literary calling she always emphasized was the fact that it was solitary and hence individual. In a late essay, "A Cat Among the Falcons" (*Canadian Literature* 2, 1959), she talked of her misgivings about Creative Writing courses, and went on, discussing the writers she admired:

> I am impelled to think that most of them—equipped with their natural and varied gifts and their early acquired processes of language—travelled their own legendary way. I cannot avoid the conviction that a writer who can already handle his tools and write, is thereafter self-taught by writing (how the view opens out), and thus a literature is made. . . . It is possible that a preference for early and thorough familiarity with the language, for privacy of intention, and the individual road in the matter of "creative writing" (I borrow the term, it is not mine), is a personal idiosyncrasy only; but as I look over the wide reaches of writing and at the highly personal art and act of writing, I don't think so.

Clearly Ethel Wilson saw her own writing in this way—as an activity that in its creative phases was private, individual, unruled by any collective imperative. In the same essay she talked of how, in her experience, the act of creation went beyond the conscious direction even of the writer herself:

> There is a moment, I think, within a novelist of any originality, whatever his country or his scope, when some sort of synthesis takes place over which he has only partial control. There is an incandescence, and from it meaning emerges, words appear, they take shape in their order, a fusion occurs.

It was this passionate sense of the personal and unconsciously motivated development of original literary works—a far cry from the doctrines of art breeding from art that Northrop Frye developed out of Oscar Wilde's *Intentions*—that made Ethel Wilson distrustful of fashions in fiction and intent on going her own way and, as she put it, "simply writing." This made her appreciate writers unfashionable among the literary intelligentsia who handled their medium lovingly and carefully. Writing to Desmond Pacey, she defended Arnold Bennett against what she regarded as Virginia Woolf's blindness to "his view of poor persons, poor houses, poor places, mean streets, and their relative beauty to those concerned—both dwellers and observers." And in the *Canadian Literature* essay already cited she took up the defence of another writer often despised by academic critics and cultural snobs:

Somerset Maugham does not pretend to sit upon Olympus, but I wonder if there is any novelist anywhere in the English-speaking world today who can write a straightforward story like *Cakes and Ale,* full of humanity and dextrous exposure.

In Ethel Wilson's approach to literature there was a great deal of what she called "innocence" when she applied it to her characters—the power to look at the world with clear eyes and live with what one sees. Once she talked of the "artlessness" that is "very artful indeed," and it is this quality that is evident not only in her writing but also in her perceptions of the qualities in other people's writing that she admires. Writing about some of the writers she most admired—again to Desmond Pacey—she remarked that "my taste runs to economy in writing—with some glorious exceptions," and went on to say of the novelists she liked:

> I would say that the limpid style of most of them, the lack of pretentiousness, the fact that these people have something to say, with skill, with good heart, often with deep feeling yet with some cynicism, their detachment as well as their involvement, give one inexpressible pleasure. They have *style,* each his own, and without style . . . how dull.

Ethel Wilson did not pretend to be a critic, though at times she wrote with great insight about her craft, and for the purposes of this essay it is not important whether what she says about her favourite writers is objectively correct, though generally speaking I believe it is. The point is that in delineating the qualities of others she seems to speak of her own aims in writing, and certainly that all her works strive at—without invariably attaining—the limpid and unpretentious style, involvement distanced by detachment, irony without the loss of feeling.

Ethel Wilson was not one of those novelists who regarded critics as vermin on the body of literature. She saw the value of the critic as mediator, but she was as unhappy about fads in criticism as she was about fads in fiction, and though she herself handled symbolism sparingly but skillfully, she was especially perturbed by any broadly symbolic interpretation of her work. The critic who discusses Ethel Wilson's work should be guided by this preference on her part, for her great virtue lies in her power to record experience, not literally, but faithfully, and it is out of this recording and out of her extraordinarily clear observation of people and places that her symbolism and the formal structure of her novels emerge by natural extension; one never has the feeling that any symbol appearing in her books is deliberately invented, either for its own sake or to evade the difficulties of clear and direct expression.

I talked a moment ago about the clear observation of "people and places," and in that phrase, it seems to me, is contained the dual pattern that gives so much of its interest to Ethel Wilson's work. For she presents the unusual combination—especially in Canada—of the novelist of manners and the novelist concerned in a lyrical way with the natural world and man's place in it. She is greatly interested in the details of daily life and the modes of human behaviour and intercourse, and in representing them she has something of the wit and playfulness of a Congreve or a Peacock as well as the wry understanding of a Jane Austen. Yet she is so intensely open to the appeal of the natural setting, of the places she and her characters inhabit, that she writes of them with a shimmering intensity that reminds one—though it in no evident way imitates him—of the young D. H. Lawrence, the Lawrence of *Sons and Lovers* and *The White Peacock,* celebrating the English countryside.

It is significant that what Ethel Wilson found intriguing in Proust was not so much his more obvious and celebrated preoccupation with Time, but his concern with Place, from which, as she once said, "he took his text." For her, Proust writing on Paris and Combray and Balbec seemed to be reaching the universal through a regional awareness, which she was careful to point out was something quite different from provincialism. She was willing to admit that there were some writers—and good writers—who were not affected by Place. But for her it was so essential that, with all her awareness of the universal implications of literature and of the intense privacy of the act of creation, her writing must be centred where her life had mainly been experienced.

In stressing that Ethel Wilson is so intent an observer of human behaviour, and so sensitive to the setting where her novels or stories are mostly placed, I do not suggest she is ever a mere recorder, for the inventive imagination works strongly as she melds together the detail out of which her fictions are constructed. However authentic their lives may be, her characters seem rarely to be taken largely from life, and sometimes it is clear that they have sprouted and grown from a very small germ of actuality. In a late essay, "The Bridge on the Stokehold " (*Canadian Literature* 5, 1960), Ethel Wilson tells us:

A novel of mine or its main character, grew directly from a few words dropped almost at random in a previous book. The words were, ". . . formed other connections." What connections? I had never seen and did not know the girl in question. She did not exist in my knowledge any more than a fly in the next room, but I considered certain aspects and likelihoods, and wrote a book called *Lilly's Story.* On the way, characters multiplied, their outlines at first dim, later clear. I cannot imagine willingly employing even a marginal character without knowing his outside appearance so well that he could be identified in the street by myself and for my own purposes.

This imaginative construction of her characters to the point of actually visualizing them is related to the economy Ethel Wilson has been able to achieve in the text as well as in the structure of her concise yet complex novels. If she is not excessively concerned with the process of symbolization, she has always been skillful in tense, evocative writing that stimulates the mind's eye; this allows her to dispense with lengthy passages of explication and at moments to achieve the visualized shorthand of a kind of prose imagism, as in the brilliant and counterbalancing sentences that open and close *Swamp Angel:*

Ten twenty fifty brown birds flew past the window and then a few stragglers. . . .

When all was still the fish, who had fled, returned, flickering, weaving curiously over the Swamp Angel. Then flickering, weaving, they resumed their way.

By such simple means the whole novel is looped into its environment.

\*    \*    \*

In the first part of this essay I have been relating what I see as the essential qualities of Ethel Wilson's fiction to her personal attitudes towards the art of fiction, which are those of an acute, honest and somewhat ironic self-observer. The appearance of simplicity which her work offers demands, I suggest, this approach. We must have some idea of her general strategy to understand how the imagination uses this limpid style, this illusion of glittering verisimilitude, this deceptively didactic manner of narration which implies more than it ever states. Now I shall suggest how this strategy is translated into the tactical patterns of her various novels.

*Hetty Dorval,* the first of these novels, is perhaps the most striking example of the combination of a Victorian sensibility and a modern ironic consciousness that I have noticed as especially characteristic of Ethel Wilson. Indeed, it is the failure of these two aspects of her literary persona to coalesce at this point that makes it a less than perfect, though an extraordinarily pleasing book. Ethel Wilson herself described it as an "innocent novella," and indeed it is based on the encounter of two kinds of innocence — that which grows into experience in the sense of embracing and seeking to understand the collective life of humanity, and that which does not.

The plot is a simple one, with strong elements of the conventional Edwardian romance. A beautiful but mysterious young woman, Hetty Dorval, arrives to occupy a bungalow on the outskirts of Lytton, a small town in the British Columbian interior at the confluence of the Fraser and the Thompson rivers. Frankie Burnaby, the narrator, is attracted by her charm, and for a few years Hetty weaves in a pattern of coincidences in and out of Frankie's life, a temptress with a shadowy past of which we learn only by vague conversational allusions. In the end, when Hetty attracts a cousin to whom Frankie—now a young woman—is deeply attached, there is a confrontation between them, and Hetty leaves the field and goes off with an Austrian lover to Vienna.

Six weeks later the German Army occupied Vienna. There arose a wall of silence around the city, through which only faint confused sounds were sometimes heard.

*Hetty Dorval* is a tightly knit little book, simple in plot and written with a kind of casual candour that fits and illuminates Frankie's character as we watch it developing. In its combination of conciseness and completeness, *Hetty Dorval* is much nearer to a French récit—by Gide or Camus, for example—than it is to the Edwardian romances usually populated by characters like Hetty. Considered in herself, Hetty Dorval seems an improbable *femme fatale,* with her strange and literally two-faced beauty.

We remained standing there and gazing at the empty sky. Then Mrs. Dorval turned her face on me and I realized all of a sudden that she had another face. This full face was different from the profile I had been studying, and was for the moment animated. Her brows, darker than her fair hair, pointed slightly upwards in the middle in moments of stress and became in appearance tragic, and her eyes which were fringed with thick, short, dark lashes opened wide and looked brilliant instead of serene. The emotion might be caused by pain, by the beauty of flighting geese, by death, or even by some very mild physical discomfort, but the impact on the beholder was the same, and arresting. Ordinarily, Mrs. Dorval's full face was calm and somewhat indolent. The purity was not there, but there was what I later came to regard as a rather pleasing yet disturbing sensual look, caused I think by the over-fullness of the curved mouth and by those same rounded high cheek-bones which in profile looked so tender. Whatever it was, it is a fact that the side face and the full face gave not the same impression, but that both had a rapt striking beauty when her eyebrows showed distress.

Hetty's life is that of an adventuress who becomes involved with men not because she can love them but because they are rich and powerful; at times she turns her charm upon other people, like Frankie and her cousin Rick, and one is never certain whether she is practising her power or acts out of an indolent unloving good nature. There are times when Hetty's life moves into melodrama, and on no occasion more strikingly than in the scene in which Mrs. Broom, her long-suffering housekeeper, shatters

Hetty's illusions of being an orphan without ties of any kind by revealing that she is actually her mother. It could have been the episode that spoilt the book, but Ethel Wilson handles it with exemplary skill and locks our attention with a final memorable visual image.

> And Hetty did exactly what Hetty would do. She did not speak to her mother. Without a word or a look she rose and slowly went out of the room, closing the door behind her, and left her mother standing there, looking after her with a ravaged face.
>
> Mrs. Broom had forgotten me. She now looked down at her hands, and so did I. Her hands, with the pressure upon the table, were red and looked swollen and congested. She held up her hands and regarded them strangely, turning their roughness this way and that to the light. What she thought as she regarded her worn hands so strangely I could only guess.

If one makes the leap of credulity and accepts Hetty as something near to an allegorical figure, then the novel takes on two aspects. It is first, as I have suggested, a study in two kinds of innocence, and secondly a fascinating study of the process of growing up, in which flesh-and-blood Frankie becomes the central figure and Hetty becomes a foil to Frankie's changing attitudes to existence.

Hetty's innocence is the negative kind that manifests itself in a failure to feel for or with other people, and, more than that, a dominant desire to remain untouched by them. Hetty is not wholly insensitive; she responds with deep feeling to the wild geese in whom she sees made manifest her own desire to fly forever free. But she is incapable of developing loves or loyalties. "People only existed when they came within her vision. Beyond that she had neither care nor interest." She has no malice, as Frankie observes, but she resents attachments that limit her freedom or interfere with her "self-indulgence and idleness." "It is preposterous, the way other people clutter up and complicate one's life," she says. "It is my own phobia. . . ."

Thus Hetty's innocence takes the form of an inability to proceed beyond the self-bound world of the infant, an inability to acknowledge herself "a piece of the Continent, a part of the maine." Frankie, on the other hand, has been taught by her mother the truth of John Donne's statement (which is the epigraph to the novel) that "No man is an Island, intire of it selfe," and so she shows the natural growth from innocence into experience.

John Donne was to Ethel Wilson much more than a convenient source of epigraphs. "My own discovery of John Donne, almost before he had again entered the Re-Establishment, dazzled me," she remarked in "A Cat Among the Falcons," and there is no doubt that Donne's central statement about the unity of all mankind continued to be an inspiration throughout

69

her writing life, so that her characters can be divided between those who through love move into the world of experience and realize that they are irrevocably "involved in Mankinde," and those who cannot love.

It was less the spiritual content of Donne that Ethel Wilson absorbed than his abounding sense of the reality of existence and the unity of all beings. She pays tribute to the pious, like the mystical and saintly Annie Hastings in *The Innocent Traveller,* but it is the people who belong to the visible rather than the invisible world that she portrays with the greatest understanding and involvement. Life as she projects it in *Hetty Dorval* no less than in her other novels is the whole world in which we live, including the human communities to which we belong, as Frankie belongs to Lytton and the country around it with its mixed population of whites and Indians and Chinese, but also the whole environment, for everything that happens in the human heart finds its echoes and correspondences in the natural world.

This is why Ethel Wilson's precise and lyrical description of the country of sagebrush hills and great rivers in which so much of *Hetty Dorval* takes place is so important. We read it not merely for its evocative representation of the natural setting but also because we are aware of being offered a kind of mirror in which the human condition is illuminated, just as Frankie's room in Vancouver contains a mirror in which she sees the mountains framed into forms whose power she had never realized before. Frankie herself recognizes the importance of the "genius of place," and remarks:

> My genius of place is a god of water. I have lived where two rivers run together, and beside the brattling noise of China Creek which tumbles past our ranch house and turns our water wheel, and on the shore of the Pacific Ocean too—my home is there, and I shall go back.

And water does indeed play a constant and varying role in Frankie's existence. A sea voyage to England marks the beginning of her growth into maturity; she leaves Canada a girl and quickly in Europe becomes a sophisticated and responsible young woman. And perhaps the most potent image in *Hetty Dorval*—an image generating a vast symbolic power—is that of the confluence of the two rivers, the Fraser and the Thompson, and the bridge from which one sees them; it is an image to be repeated in Ethel Wilson's best novel, *Swamp Angel,* which shares so greatly the terrain of *Hetty Dorval*. She describes it thus in her first novel:

> Ever since I could remember, it was my joy and the joy of all of us to stand on this strong iron bridge and look down at the line where the expanse of emerald and sapphire dancing water joins and is quite lost in the sullen Fraser. It is a marriage, where, as often in marriage, one overcomes the other, and one is lost in the other. . . . Ernestine and I used to say, "Let's go down to the

Bridge,'' and there we would stand and lean on the railing and look down . . . at the bright water being lost in the brown, and as we walked and laid our own little plans of vast importance for that day and the next, the sight of the cleaving joining waters and the sound of their never-ending roar and the feel of the frequent Lytton wind that blew down the channels of both the rivers were part and parcel of us, and conditioned, as they say, our feeling.

The image—like all potent images—can be read in several ways. It can stand in potent isolation, like the image in a haiku, suggesting everything, stating nothing. It can be read as a rendering of direct experience, and, given the plot of the book, as a portent of what follows, for soon Ernestine will be destroyed by the "sullen Fraser" when she plunges in to try and save a dog (thus providing the extreme contrast to Hetty's persistent noninvolvement with other beings). It can be read symbolically. Rivers run together and all rivers run into the sea, which means much the same as Donne's imagery of islands and continents. Lives run together, as rivers do, so, irrevocably, something from Hetty's life (the brown of the Fraser or the blue of the Thompson?) has flowed into Frankie's life. Or, finally, we can return to our concepts of innocence and experience and learn that no life continues forever in the innocent blueness of origin; experience muddies and hides it, just as Hetty's sparkling and careless beauty in fact flows into a river of murky consequences.

*The Innocent Traveller* is a more complex and also a more ponderous book than *Hetty Dorval,* mainly because it attempts to be two things, the life story of an eccentric personality and the history of a family. In both respects it is highly readable and conducted with wit and wisdom, but the fusion is incomplete.

The novel begins in Staffordshire, Ethel Wilson's ancestral county, and there is no doubt that family traditions and her own memories have contributed to its content, just as one of the younger members of the fictional family, Rose, shares much of Ethel Wilson's youthful experience and perhaps also her point of view.

The innocent traveller is Topaz, at the beginning of the novel a small child, "innocent as a poached egg," telling Matthew Arnold with embarrassing enthusiasm about the newly installed water closet in the Edgeworth house that goes "Whoosh! Whoosh!" She ends far away in space and time from her Staffordshire home, for she has passed a hundred when, in Vancouver, she finally dies, as self-centred, as avid, as innocent, as she had always been.

"Let me go immediately . . . immediately . . ." she murmurs in her imperious way. "A hundred years . . . I shall be late . . . me, the youngest." Then the small face lightens. "Quick, get me some fresh lace for my head,

71

someone! I'm going to die, I do declare!'' Evidently she is pleased and confi-
dent. What an adventure, to be sure!

Away she went. Now she is a memory, a gossamer.

Topaz becomes ''a memory, a gossamer'' because she had no love or
true attachment. Yet, thanks to circumstances and especially to the love of
others, she has been able to live out her life with happiness and zest and to
retain to the end the special kind of innocence that enables her to survive in
emotional insularity until death gathers her in to the continent of the one
experience that, after birth, all mankind must share.

In this way, of course, though it reads as a very different kind of book,
much busier and more crowded, *The Innocent Traveller* is an extension of
*Hetty Dorval,* presenting the comic rather than the tragic face of innocence. If Topaz is incapable of love, she has an extraordinary zest for
living, yet in her own strange way she remains immune from the effects of
experience, which leaves her unchanged while it moulds and modifies the
other major characters in the novel. The very innocence that keeps her
from forming deep personal attachments also enables her to confront each
encounter in life with an open kind of enthusiasm. It also makes her
tolerant, so that she suffers neither from snobbery nor from any other
prejudice and is willing to accept people as she sees they are. Conventions
and conventional distinctions mean nothing to her, and she is as devoid of
prejudice as she is—like Hetty—lacking in malice.

One of the crucial scenes in the book concerns the black man, Joe
Fortes, an actual figure in Vancouver's history who used to teach the children to swim at English Bay and who rescued many from drowning. A
woman taught by Joe is presented for membership of the Minerva Club,
and a ''pudding-faced lady'' asserts she has been ''seen more than once in
a public place, bathing in the arms of a black man.'' Topaz valiantly
defends both Joe Fortes and the maligned woman, who is elected to the
club with acclamation, and when she gets home tells her saintly sister Annie and her niece Rachel. And Rachel, who has often been annoyed with
Topaz, listens to the tale, and then remarks: ''I have never heard you say
an unkind thing about anyone. I have never heard you cast an aspersion on
anyone. I really believe that you are one of the few people who think no
evil.''

What Rachel says takes on its full meaning only if we think of it in relation not only to Topaz but also to Hetty, that other innocent incapable of
self-denying love. For Topaz is able to retain and nurture the honesty and
fairness that represent the positive side of her innocence only because she
has been brought up and protected to the end of her days in the warm nest
of the family. Hetty seems less kind and more devious because she has
never lived in the emotional shelter a family like the Edgeworths provides.

The only relative she knew—and she did not know until the end that this was a real relative—had been Mrs. Broom, the mother masquerading as a servant, and all her years since girlhood had been a long campaign to gain the life of ease she desired without sacrificing the freedom that made the wild geese almost her totem birds. In one poignant scene on an Atlantic liner, Hetty approaches Frankie and her mother and begs them not to reveal what they know about her, because she hopes to achieve a marriage that will bring her the security she had never known. Topaz's innocence has always flourished in security, and so it has manifested itself in genial eccentricities and a fearless acceptance of life.

Topaz could never have survived as she did, mentally and physically, without the support of that family, some of whose members understood better than she the reality of love. But the family could have survived without Topaz, and in the reader's eye it takes on a life of its own, as a kind of collective character that provides the other stream of interest in the novel.

We encounter the Edgeworths in the first chapter as a solid Staffordshire pottery family which has made money on teapots admired by Queen Victoria at the Great Exhibition and on chamber pots which an African tribe ordered in large numbers, reportedly for use as headgear. The Edgeworths are cultured enough to be the guests and associates of local politicians, though they have remained chapel folk, true to the Methodism that was the militant cult during the industrial revolution.

The Victorian patriarchs die, the children spread over the Empire, to die in India, to prosper in Australia and South Africa and Canada, and finally the remaining nucleus of the family—the saintly Annie, her daughter Rachel and the feckless Topaz—emigrate to Canada. Once again a sea voyage brings a change of perspectives, and the Edgeworth women find in the new land a place where their natures can expand into a new fulfilment.

> Topaz had at last reached open country. British Columbia stretched before her, exciting her with its mountains, its forests, the Pacific Ocean, the new little frontier town, and all the new people. Here was no time limit, no fortnight's holiday. Here she had come to live; and, drawing long breaths of the opulent air, she began to run about, and dance for joy, exclaiming, all through the open country.

Vancouver, when the family arrives, is still little more than the rough settlement that sprang so quickly into existence when the CPR reached over the mountains.

> Modest one- or two-storied buildings rose, to everyone's admiration, where the nobler forest had lately been. The forest still was, and winding trails through

73

the woods ended at small hidden shacks, almost within the town itself. Vancouver was only a little town, but prophetically it called itself a city.

Vancouver's growth into a real city is one of the themes of *The Innocent Traveller,* but it is so woven into the experience of the novel's main characters that one perceives it rather as one perceives Balzac's projections of Louis Phillippe's France—as a living fictional entity, with Joe Fortes who was a historical individual and Yow the Chinese cook who was a historical type at home within the half-imaginary, half-documentary but wholly self-consistent world of Topaz and her relatives and their middle-class friends of British origin.

It is not the relative authenticity of the imaginative vision that troubles one in *The Innocent Traveller*. It is rather the awkwardness of the structure. The novel is highly episodic in form. Three chapters, "Down at English Bay" (about Joe Fortes), "The Innumerable Laughter" (about Topaz scaring herself by sleeping out one night in the Gulf Islands) and "I have a Father in the Promised Land" (an ironic and amusing account of a revivalist meeting) were all published separately in periodicals, where they stood happily on their own, as self-contained as short stories. This autonomy of the chapters gives the book as a whole a somewhat jerky motion. It is no great improvement that the cracks which result are often papered over by passages of authorial comment, sometimes too ponderous and sometimes too arch. Occasionally such comment actually serves as a flashforward, telling the reader with clumsy confidentiality the future consequences of acts committed in the present.

Ethel Wilson never again attempted a novel as large or as complicated in structure as *The Innocent Traveller*. She returned to shorter fiction with relatively simple structure and a single dominant line of development. Her next two novels, *Tuesday and Wednesday* and *Lilly's Story,* were in fact so short that they were published in a single volume, *The Equations of Love,* which altogether—with its ninety to a hundred thousand words—is no longer than an average novel.

At first sight, except that each of them is concerned with the varieties of emotion and relationship we bring together under the name of love, these two novels—or novellas—seem very different. *Tuesday and Wednesday* is entirely urban, set in a later Vancouver than the little town where Topaz and her sister first arrived. Its action, leading through comedy into tragedy, is completed in the two days of the title. Its characters have no time to change and grow; they merely reveal their true natures through the harrowing of stress and calamity. *Lilly's Story* encompasses the greater part of its heroine's life. It begins in the city and takes refuge in the country. And its very core is the changing and maturing of a personality. Lilly Waller, the pale girl with taffy-coloured hair who works in Lam Sing's restaurant and arouses the passions of Yow (the Edgeworths' cook) is in the beginning an innocent very much like Hetty Dorval, but she is born into life on a lower level, so that her struggle to survive is necessarily more ruthless and predatory. Experience changes her when she devotes her life to providing the best possible future for the child, Eleanor, whom she has by a passing liaison.

It is curious that no previous critic has linked these two novellas with Ethel Wilson's admiration for Arnold Bennett. For in fact they present just what she thought to be good in Bennett—a "view of poor persons, poor houses, poor places, mean streets, and their relative beauty to those concerned." They are, apart from a few stories, the only writings in which Ethel Wilson left the middle class to which she belonged and imaginatively entered the minds and lives of people who lived outside the sophisticated world that was her own.

There is no suggestion in these novels that Ethel Wilson had been led to write about the poor by any political imperative. In her inclinations she was indeed liberal, and she had read widely in political polemics ever since she was introduced to the *New Statesman* in the 1920s, but, though politicians appear as characters in at least two of her novels, and she would have agreed that the novelist cannot ignore the political any more than other dimensions of life, the idea of writing to make propaganda for any partisan viewpoint was remote from her view of the role of literature. But to show through the glass of the imagination the true lives of poor people—to show them with compassion and understanding—was to her, as much as it had been to Dostoevsky, a part of the novelist's function, provided it were done in a work of literary art, true to and within itself.

*Tuesday and Wednesday* carries an epigraph from *Bleak House*—Mr. Chadband asking, "Now, my young friends, what is this Terewth . . . firstly (in a spirit of love) what is the common sort of Terewth . . ." And, somewhat like jesting Pilate, the novella proceeds to consider how we can judge of human actions, and how the same actions, seen by different people, can seem heroic or despicable, without either viewpoint being objectively correct. Mortimer and Myrtle Johnson (Mort and Myrt) are a feckless working-class couple living in an untidy room off Powell Street near the docks in Vancouver. Mort is good-natured, lazy, a born fantasist who turns every gardener's job he loses from idleness into a big landscaping contract. Myrt, who goes out cleaning, is less given to dreaming of this kind, for her small, acrid personality is self-contained and self-fuelling. Losing one job during the days of the novel, Mort almost gets another, and is walking home in a self-congratulatory glow when he encounters his dearest friend, the high-rigger Eddie Hansen, who is—according to his wont—roaring drunk on Powell Street. Eddie forces Mort to accompany him down to the docks on a futile search for a lost suitcase. Eddie staggers over the end of the wharf, and Mort either falls or dives after him—it is never quite clear which—and is dragged to his death by the panic-stricken logger, who cannot swim.

Later, in the Johnsons' flat, various versions of the truth are brought in confrontation with each other. Myrt believes the policemen who tell her of Mort's death. According to them, the two men were seen staggering together down the street, and therefore they were presumably both drunk. Myrt thinks only of herself and bitterly laments what Mort has done to her by getting drunk again with the detested Eddie. But shortly afterward her timid cousin, Victoria May Tritt, makes an appearance. On her way to church Vicky has seen Mort walking soberly along the street and being accosted by drunken Eddie. On her way back from church, she has heard Mort's name mentioned by a group of men talking in the street about the tragedy. On the spur of the moment, it occurs to her to vindicate Mort's memory by invention, and, reproaching Myrtle with uncharacteristic vigour, she declares that Mort acted heroically, deliberately diving in to rescue his drunken friend. Neither version is the whole truth, but Victoria speaks with the passion of conviction, and Myrtle in astonishment accepts her story.

> Something grew warm within Myrtle and she saw the simple picture of Morty putting his hands together and diving in to rescue Eddie Hansen and she became, as Victoria May had said, the widow of a hero, and she became proud of Morty, but prouder of herself for being the widow of a hero. Vicky, seeing what she had achieved, expelled a long breath, and relaxed. How simple it had been!

It is a world of simple, ill-educated people with primitive reactions among whom Ethel Wilson moves, a dripping Vancouver world where minds are inclined to be as foggy as the skies, and one wonders, when the equation of Mort's and Myrt's love is worked out, just how the sum comes out. For underneath the comic, almost Dickensian masks worn by Myrt and Mort and Vicky and the self-indulgent Mrs. Emblem, Myrtle's aunt, one senses emotions of compassion and loyalty and love that are unarticulated or at best articulated in the debased language of the cinema and the radio. (Television had yet to come.)

*Lilly's Story* begins in the same depressed area of Vancouver as *Tuesday and Wednesday,* for the gambling houses where Yow spends his nights and the café where he meets and becomes obsessively enamoured of Lilly, a runaway girl working as a waitress, are not far from the Powell Street area where the Johnsons lived.

Yow had already appeared in *The Innocent Traveller,* as lacking in innocence as Aunt Topaz was full of it, yet capable of love. He boasted, and probably truthfully, of having killed two men in China, one quickly and one slowly, but he was devoted to the saintly Annie, Topaz's sister, and he loved Lilly with a ferocity that led to his ruin, for he stole on a large scale from the Edgeworths to win her heart. When Yow was arrested, Lilly—who had never loved in her life—thought only of saving herself from the police, and became a "pale slut who is running through the dark lanes, stopping, crouching in the shadows, listening, hardly daring to look behind her."

If Aunt Topaz stands on one side of Hetty Dorval as the innocent who was sheltered and so saved from having to live in the appalling amorality of endangered innocence, Lilly stands on the other side—the child who never knew even the strange love with which Mrs. Broom had protected Hetty, her unproclaimed daughter. When she flees from the police and disappears to surface again on Vancouver Island, Lilly knows the meaning of love even less than Hetty or Topaz.

> No one had loved her, and she did not even know that she had missed love. She was not bitter, nor cruel, nor was she very bad. She was like the little yellow cat, no worse and no better. She expected nothing. She took things as they came, living where she could, on whom she could, and with whom she could, working only when she had to, protecting herself by lies or by truth, and always keeping on the weather side of the police.

In Nanaimo Lilly goes to live with a Welsh miner, but there is no love. Lilly is still as innocent and uncaring as an animal, as Ethel Wilson suggests in the strangely harsh way in which she describes the relationship:

> Ranny was only a kennel into which a homeless worthless bitch crawls away from the rain, and out of which she will crawl, and from which she will go away leaving the kennel empty and forgotten.

The rest of the novel tells of Lilly's transformation from "a homeless worthless bitch" into a loving and responsible human being, her difficult passage from innocence into experience. With one of those haunting resonances that in Ethel Wilson's work pass on from novel to novel, there is a second echo here of *Hetty Dorval*. The young Lilly, the taffy-haired girl for whom Yow lusted, may have been a debased counterpart of Hetty, but her later life uncannily resembles that of Hetty's mother, Mrs. Broom. Pregnant by Ranny the miner, she leaves him to have her child, and then assumes another self. She is no longer Lilly Waller, the slut who has an illegitimate child. She gives herself a new name, and with the new name a different history, so that she is now Mrs. Walter Hughes, the widow of a prairie farmer, better bred than herself, who was killed by a horse before their daughter was born. In this guise she sets about finding the circumstances in which she can best bring up her daughter and give her the kind of life she has missed.

To begin she becomes housekeeper to a British ex-officer and his wife at Comox, and there are some idyllic years until Lilly realizes that in the village Eleanor is known as "the maid's daughter." She departs and becomes housekeeper at a hospital in the Fraser valley; here she ages as her daughter grows up, and lets her looks fade, and resists the approaches of men, for all she can feel is the possessive love that binds her to her daughter.

The final opening out of that love comes when Eleanor has gone to Vancouver for training as a nurse, has married and herself had children. Lilly, in her hospital, seems to be withering into a loveless existence, when fate and coincidence thrust her back into the stream of life. One day, looking out of the window of her cottage at the hospital, she sees a figure of dread walking in from her past. It is Yow, come to work at the hospital as cook.

Reappearing with such melodramatic suddenness, Yow paradoxically liberates Lilly from the life of fear and concealment into which her care for Eleanor has involved her. She flees once again, this time to Toronto, where she works as chambermaid in a hotel. There she meets widowed Mr. Sprockett, and Mr. Sprockett falls in discreet love with her, and Lilly, for the first time since Ranny, accepts a relationship with a man. But this time it is different. Ranny was the unloved provider in whom she found refuge as a fugitive. But Sprockett talks of love, and asks her for love, and Lilly begins to see love as a mutual caring:

> If loving Mr. Sprockett meant looking after him and thinking for him and caring for him and guarding him from harm and keeping things nice like she'd always done for Eleanor and for Matron, then she could love him, and she was his, and he was hers.

She senses, in this relationship where she would give as much as she would be given, "She would be without fear; nothing, surely, could touch her now." And so, after the long years of love as sacrifice, Lilly comes to the realization of love as mutual caring, love as union.

Just as in some ways *Lilly's Story,* that modest and moving novella, develops elements that had their origin in *Hetty Dorval,* in other ways it anticipates *Swamp Angel;* perhaps most notably in the way it develops the correspondence between human life and the natural world. Its most dramatic scene is one of conflict between wild creatures, when Lilly and Eleanor, still a child, are on a little promontory at Comox, with the child's kitten. They see a robin attacking a tiny snake; the kitten stalks the robin until the shadow of an eagle falls upon it, but before the eagle can swoop down he in turn is attacked and driven away by a crow and a seagull. The scene makes Lilly uneasy; she relates it to her own life, and to her it "seems like everything's cruel, hunting something." It is beyond Lilly to see—though her daughter Eleanor may—what Ethel Wilson describes on the next page in one of her authorial asides as

> the incorporeal presence in air, and light, and dark, and earth, and sea, and sky, and in herself, of something unexpressed and inexpressible, that transcends and heightens ordinary life, and is its complement.

Nowhere in Ethel Wilson's work is this sense of a spiritual force imminent in the natural world more powerfully expressed than in *Swamp Angel,* the best of her novels. Maggie Vardoe, the leading character, runs away from her present, as Lilly Waller had done. She too changes her name to indicate her change of living, though in her case she takes back an old name, Maggie Lloyd, which means that she is rejecting the interlude in which she sought to live according to bourgeois conventions with the pathetic materialist Edward Vardoe.

Maggie Lloyd is a much more complex figure than the earlier characters with whom one naturally compares her, Hetty and Lilly. She has always known and understood the reality of love, in her relations with her father and later with her first husband, killed during the war. Her love for that dead husband does not vanish, but she marries Edward Vardoe for compassion, and only when she realizes that this vain, coarse man is unchangeable does she decide to leave him. Having made her decision, she plans her departure carefully, earning money secretly, arranging her flight with care, and leaving no clues that will enable Vardoe to track her down. In this respect she resembles Lilly saving and planning before she leaves Ranny the miner to have her child.

But Maggie is not really choosing a new way of life. She had been brought up at a fishing lodge beside a lake in New Brunswick, where she helped her father and learnt from him the skill of fly-tying which she uses to finance her flight. It was in that past that she developed the self-reliance, manifesting itself in both resourcefulness and secretiveness, to which she now turns.

> Maggie, brought up from childhood by a man, with men, had never learned the peculiarly but not wholly feminine joys of communication, the déshabille of conversation, of the midnight confidence, the revelation. And now, serenely and alone, she had acted with her own resources . . .

There is something uncanny, even slightly repellent about the serenity with which Maggie makes her plans and acts and deals with people. For cruelty is never far from compassion, not only in her view of nature, but also in her own actions. Perhaps compassion has failed with Edward Vardoe, but the way Maggie leaves him, slipping out in the middle of dinner, seems calculated to create the greatest bewilderment and pain, and the same duality exists in her attitude to nature. She loves the wild and the creatures of the wild, yet fishing and all that goes with it are at the heart of her life, and—not being callous—she is aware of the cruelty. After she leaves Vardoe on her flight into the hinterland, Maggie stops for a couple of days beside the Similkameen River and fishes there.

In the pleasure of casting over this lively stream she forgot—as always when she was fishing—her own existence. Suddenly came a strike, and the line ran out, there was a quick radiance and splashing above the water downstream. At the moment of the strike, Maggie became a co-ordinating creature of wrists and fingers and reel and rod and line and tension and the small trout, leaping, darting, leaping. She landed the fish, took out the hook, slipped in her thumb, broke back the small neck, and the leaping rainbow thing was dead. A thought as thin and cruel as a pipe fish cut through her mind. The pipe fish slid through and away. It would return.

At the moment of landing the fish, Maggie is as totally and naturally absorbed in her task and unconscious of its implication as the osprey she will later watch with such admiration, until the thought like a pipe fish slips through her mind and separates her from the world of nature.

Maggie goes on, through Lytton, where the meeting of the waters is again splendidly described, and on to Kamloops, where, up in the hills, she gets a job as cook at the lodge run by the Gunnarsons at Three Loon Lake. From now on this is her world and her life, and she cannot even envisage returning to the city. The lake, like her, is both cruel and kind. It gives Maggie physical and mental vigour, but two people are almost killed by it, and brought back to life by Maggie's care. A strength emerges in her. She is no longer the discontented powerless wife of Edward Vardoe. She moves to create a life in which her self-reliance can flourish, a life without attachments, though not without the desire to help others as she helps the Gunnarsons. But as she helps she shapes, dealing as capably with Vera Gunnarson's jealousy as she deals with the practical problems of running and expanding the lodge. She uses her very decency to impose her will on others, manipulating them even if it is for their own good, so that in the end one has a sympathy for poor weak Vera's obsessive feeling that Maggie is running the Gunnarsons' lives. There are times when her very helpfulness robs other people of their personal sense of dignity.

In this way the main plot and the subplot of *Swamp Angel* come together and the title is explained. Leaving Vancouver, Maggie has left not only Edward but also her real friends, Hilda Severance and her old mother, Nell.

Hilda's unlikely marriage comes about and flourishes as Maggie's own marriage with Vardoe ends, and in the background the eccentric Nell Severance plays with her souvenir of a lost life, the pistol known as the Swamp Angel. For Nell has been a professional juggler in her day and remained romantically attached to the circus world of illusion, yet curiously practical as she now juggles with other people's lives, turning Vardoe aside from his murderous anger towards Maggie and pushing Hilda into making up her mind to marry Albert Cousins. It is appropriate that when Nell feels the Swamp Angel is a dangerous toy to keep, she sends it to the other juggler, Maggie, and when Nell dies it is Maggie who takes the pistol and throws it into the lake as if it were Excalibur.

> She stood in the boat and with her strong arm she threw the Angel up into the air, higher than ever Nell Bigley of the Juggling Bigleys had ever tossed it. It made a shining parabola in the air, turning downwards—turning, turning, catching the sunlight, hitting the surface of the lake, sparkling down into the clear water, vanishing amidst breaking bubbles in the water, sinking down among the affrighted fish, settling in the ooze. When all was still the fish, who had fled, returned, flickering, weaving curiously over the Swamp Angel. Then flickering, weaving, they resumed their way.

The Swamp Angel, which "in its eighty years or so has caused death and astonishment and jealousy and affection," nevertheless belongs to the temporal world of human artifice, and when it is gone, it will soon be "not even a memory, for there will be no one to remember it." The lake into which it falls represents the timeless world of nature where the fishes flicker and weave a dance that never ends. And so another duality of the novel is projected; we live in time but belong to the timeless, just as the land in which we live is rocks and trees and water but also in other ways a map of the human heart.

*Swamp Angel* offers Ethel Wilson's most successful structure as a novel, every part tuning with the other, just as Maggie Lloyd is her most developed and most convincing character. Perhaps there is a shade too much of the melodramatic in Nell Severance; perhaps Edward Vardoe is too absurdly contemptible, but otherwise the characters and their relationships exist entirely convincingly in their autonomous world.

Ethel Wilson's last novel, *Love and Salt Water,* was also her least successful. It is a neatly written and well enough constructed book about the growing up of a middle-class girl and her difficulties—which finally end—in achieving the kind of marriage that satisfies her. But the urgency of feeling that burns through the other books is no longer present. The essential plot is perhaps no more unpretentious than that of *Hetty Dorval,* but Ellen Cuppy does not develop through the same sensitively evoked opening of the perceptions as Frankie Burnaby, and there is no enigma in the book as interesting as Hetty. Even the minor characters are less tellingly portrayed than those that crowd *The Innocent Traveller,* and the wit has somehow faded from the narrator's tongue as the irony has from her eye. There is only one point in the whole book at which the reader becomes urgently involved. That is when Ellen takes her little nephew Johnny out in a dinghy in Active Pass to look for seals, and they are nearly drowned when the riptide overturns the boat. The feeling of the British Columbia coast and its waters is at times pleasantly recalled, but rarely does it become the commanding environment of *Hetty Dorval* and *Swamp Angel*.

It is perhaps significant that this was the time when Ethel Wilson began to think consciously about her art as a writer and to write about it almost as a critical outsider. For what is lacking in *Love and Salt Water* is precisely the sense that here is a writer led on half-consciously and only half-willingly by her own creation, which was so strongly present in her earlier books. *Love and Salt Water* is a well-made novel of manners, but the clear flame of feeling and insight one remembers from her earlier books does not shine through the translucency of its prose.

Thus Ethel Wilson's significant novels embrace an even shorter period than the full list of her books suggests. They were published in a mere seven years, from *Hetty Dorval* in 1947 to *Swamp Angel* in 1954, and the period over which they were written was doubtless no longer. But these few short books have an unchallengeable place in the record of Canadian fiction, not only for their own qualities and their influence on younger writers, but also because they were the first successful attempt to bring the physical setting of western Canada convincingly into fiction, so that their comedies of manners and their dramas of feeling were played out against superbly described backdrops of landscape, for Ethel Wilson was unrivalled in her time as a novelist of Place.

# 4

# SURROGATE FATHERS AND ORPHAN SONS

## The Novels of Hugh MacLennan

There is always an inclination in emergent nations for writers to be didactic. There are messages to be given, lessons to be taught, and who better equipped for these tasks than the men of words? Even the imaginative giants in the literatures of such times tend to write books with messages; Shakespeare's *Henry V,* with its glorification of the nationalism which the Tudor kings were trying to inculcate in sixteenth-century England, and Tolstoy's *War and Peace,* with its populist attack on the "great man" theory of history, are notable examples. Nor has the didacticism of writers in such times been restricted to political ends; times of national readjustment are often also times of spiritual crisis, when men seek in the City of God a compensation for the deficiencies of the City of Man, and so both *The Divine Comedy* and *Paradise Lost,* for all their imaginative splendour, are as didactic as any evangelist's tract.

Given the conditions of Canada's emergence into nationhood, it was inevitable that there should be a strong element of didacticism among its writers. Hugh MacLennan is perhaps the most striking example, though there are many others; Margaret Atwood, for example, is—in her fiction at least—rarely without a lesson to offer, and sometimes a bitter one, as in *Bodily Harm* and *The Handmaid's Tale.* But the successful didactic novel, though its closeness to actuality tends to rob it of inventiveness, needs a strong imaginative element to carry its message, which emerges in its symbolic structure as much as in its language. In Hugh MacLennan especially we see a writer who uses archetypal myths, notably those of Oedipus and Odysseus, to make his message appealing to the emotions as well as to the intelligence.

On first reading, Hugh MacLennan appears a simple writer. His fictional techniques are traditional; not only has he never written anything that could in any way be termed experimental but he has publicly expressed his distaste for avant garde writers like Samuel Beckett and even Marcel Proust. For himself he has even disclaimed any pretence of being an intellectual:

I have never been particularly intelligent, and abstract ideas are usually incomprehensible to me. My brain is far slower than my intuitions, and in every novel I have written my brain has hung me up because it keeps refusing to accept what my intuitions shout at it. That is why I have taken so long to write my novels.

MacLennan's views of the proper nature of fiction have wavered from verisimilitude to autonomous invention and back again. In 1951, refuting all those who had tried to find actual people in his novels, he remarked that "the surest way to write fiction that rings false is to make it accurate in its representation of the people you know." But in 1955, writing of Dickens with qualified approval, he remarked that "his characters, no matter how preposterous, have never seemed incredible to me. At times they are caricatures, but I am sure all of them except his heroines were drawn from life. If his pages squirm with grotesques, so did the world he lived in." The fact, it seems to me, is that while MacLennan has paid lip service to the belief that novelists must be "creative," in the sense of being wholly inventive, in practice—like Defoe and Dickens—he has recorded life as he knew it to be, and exercised his imagination, which is a different faculty from invention, mainly in ordering the known.

Invention finds its logical end in fantasy, and nothing that MacLennan has written can be described as fantastic. But imaginative recording almost always touches on the didactic, as it did in the dawn of the novel with Defoe, and as it has done ever since when emergent literatures coincide with the growth of national consciousnesses, as happened in Canada at the very period when MacLennan began to write.

After producing a group of never-published novels set outside Canada, MacLennan turned to his own country as the setting for *Barometer Rising*. At that time, in the early 1940s, Canada—he remarks—was "virtually an uncharacterized country," and it is quite evident that he believed the attempt to portray it in "pure" literature, detached from the facts and problems of Canadian society, would be self-defeating.

It seemed to me that for some years to come the Canadian novelist would have to pay a great deal of attention to the background in which he set his stories. He must describe, and if necessary define, the social values which dominate the Canadian scene, and do so in such a way as to make them appear interesting and important to foreigners; whether he liked it or not, he must for a time be something of a geographer, a historian and a sociologist, to weave a certain amount of geography, history and sociology into his novels.

Not merely did it seem to MacLennan essential that the Canadian writer, at least in his generation, should project Canadian "social values"; he also regarded it as essential that he should be "engaged," should take his side and play his part (and here he cited Aeschylus standing in the ranks at Marathon) in the political crises and moral issues of his time.

> A true child of my epoch, I believed that a writer should also be a citizen. I am disturbed by the kind of detachment that enables some writers to rub their hands over the crimes, follies and misfortunes of mankind because they furnish such exciting materials for literature.

Given such views of the role of the writer in a society discovering itself, like that of Canada, there is small wonder that MacLennan at times speculated on the limitations imposed by the fiction writer's aim of creating a new, autonomous world of the imagination, and that he should see the initiative moving towards writers who could separate the shaping function of the imagination from mere invention, as the great historians have always done, from Herodotus down to Toynbee. In 1967, the year of his novel *Return of the Sphinx,* MacLennan declared that we were witnessing a great revolution in prose literature: "In a sentence, non-fiction writers have learned how to write better stories than the novelists are now capable of writing."

This was said before the broadening of the vistas of Canadian fiction that produced the novels of new writers like Margaret Atwood, Matt Cohen and Rudy Wiebe, and the later and more complex works of Robertson Davies and Margaret Laurence, while some of the nonfiction "stories" that MacLennan praised so highly twelve years ago (like Barbara Tuchmann's *The Proud Tower* and *The Guns of August*) have not worn well, as then seemed probable. But whether or not MacLennan would now stand by his statement of 1967, the fact remains that at a crucial time in his career, when he published a novel strongly projecting his views on the present state of Canada, he expressed the opinion that nonfiction might be a more effective instrument for his ends than the fiction he composed so slowly and painfully, as he has often told us.

One cannot fail to relate such a conclusion to the fact that more than most Canadian writers MacLennan had approximated to the European type of the *homme de lettres* who writes—as Gide and Camus and Malraux and Heinrich Mann and many others did—in a variety of genres without creating a hierarchy of values that places a poem or a novel on a necessarily higher plane than an essay or a work of history. MacLennan, who started off as a historian with a very interesting doctoral thesis on a Nilotic town in the Roman era (entitled *Oxyrynchus,* it was eventually published in Amsterdam in 1968), has always written essays while he was writing novels and in the intervals between them, and there have been many critics who would say, as Arnold Edinborough did in reviewing *Return of the Sphinx,*

"MacLennan is not a novelist, but an essayist, and a very good essayist too."

Yet it is a mistake to divide MacLennan's nonfiction from his fiction, to see him as primarily either novelist or essayist. The two forms in his work relate closely to each other. Often, in essays like "An Orange from Portugal" or "Orgy at Oriel," MacLennan is creating situations and characters as imaginatively through the manipulation of memory as ever Proust did. And equally often in his novels he raises arguments and makes points which even friendly critics often feel are blemishes on fiction and would be much better stated in essays. The ultimate fact is that, like so many *hommes de lettres,* MacLennan has always been unashamedly didactic in his writing. He has had little use for Wildean doctrines proclaiming the autonomy of art, though, unlike George Orwell, he has never gone so far as to assume that the didactic and the political were identical.

But while it is easy to identify Hugh MacLennan as a novelist in the realist tradition with didactic inclinations, it is not so simple as it appears to relate the various facets of his writing, which include not only his didacticism but also his deep sense of place and history, his powerful gift for describing human action on a dramatic scale, his curiously uneven characterization (good with men and poor with women) and his equal unevenness in portraying human relationships (profoundly evoked in the case of generational relationships and shallowly in the case of sexual ones). Not least of the difficulties the critic faces in such a quest is that, far more than appears at first sight, MacLennan's novels do present a kind of cumulative unity that makes it difficult to deal with all, except perhaps the first of them, singly.

I embarked on this essay with the impression that if I were to take MacLennan's perhaps most didactic novel, *Return of the Sphinx,* I could relate it to the essays and establish the connections between the two main contents of MacLennan's writing, the imaginary world of his fiction, and the arguments about existence that belong in his essays but also surface at many places in his novels. But I realized immediately that *Return of the Sphinx* lost a great deal of its significance if one read it in isolation, which may be one of the reasons why it was so coolly received by the critics.

Genetically it is related to *Each Man's Son,* for its central character, Alan Ainslie, is the "son" of the earlier novel, and much that happens to him in *Return of the Sphinx* is related to the boyhood in which he lost a real father and found a surrogate one.

Thematically, and even structurally, *Return of the Sphinx* is also related to *Two Solitudes.* Not only does it deal with the question of the two Canadas, French and English; its central family, like the Tallards of *Two Solitudes,* comes from a marriage of the two main Canadian peoples, so that the sons in both families, Paul Tallard and Daniel Ainslie, are part

French and part Celtic (Irish in Tallard's case and Scotch in Ainslie's). And the father in the family is in each case a good man fallen among politicians, who finds his idealism constantly frustrated by the pragmatic realities of political life and who in the end is destroyed by his enemies' manipulation of public opinion.

Finally, with its concern over the future of Canada, which *Return of the Sphinx* presents as almost fatally imperilled, this novel is linked by inversion with MacLennan's earlier novels, not only *Two Solitudes* but also *Barometer Rising,* where the emergence of the nation into consciousness is a dominant and hopeful theme. MacLennan recognized this shift in his own basic viewpoint. His early novels, as he remarked, "had been essentially optimistic."

> I had believed the barometer was really rising; I had believed (and in this I may have been partially right) that the two solitudes were bound to come together in Canada. But my last two novels had been tragic. My original title for *The Watch* was a dead give-away; it was *Requiem*. Requiem for one I had loved who had died, but also for more; requiem for the idealists of the thirties who had meant so well, tried so hard, and gone so wrong. Requiem also for their courage and a lament for their failure on a world-wide scale.

And if *The Watch That Ends the Night* was a requiem for a generation of idealists, *Return of the Sphinx* became a litany in extremis for the vision of a nation which Neil Macrae developed with such confidence in *Barometer Rising*.

Thus, in considering the didactic element in MacLennan's fiction, one has to view all his books and not one of them. The blemishes which didacticism created mar every one of his novels with the exception of *Each Man's Son* and, to a lesser extent, *The Watch That Ends the Night*. Many critics have noted the way in which MacLennan's plots tend to take on a mechanical impetus, and his characters veer towards allegorical types in order that the right lesson may emerge out of the interaction of human beings that is the proper concern of fiction. There are times also at which a bald statement of a novel's theme tears jaggedly into the unity of mood and style, as when, in *Barometer Rising,* Neil and Penelope, at last united, are leaving devastated Halifax, and one expects the warmly personal thoughts of people united after many trials and dangers. Instead, Neil lapses into notions that might fit well into an essay but which jarringly spoil the final pages of a novel.

> He looked down the car and saw the lines of quiet bodies sway gently with the train's motion. Why was he glad to be back? . . . For better or worse he was entering the future, he was identifying himself with the still-hidden forces

which were doomed to shape humanity as certainly as the tiny states of Europe had shaped the past. Canada was still hesitant, was still hamstrung by men with the mentality of Geoffrey Wain. But if there were enough Canadians like himself, half-American and half-English, then the day was inevitable when the halves would join and his country would become the central arch which united the new order.

The ending of *Two Solitudes* is even more boldly didactic, for here MacLennan takes his conclusion entirely into the area of authorial reflection and makes his final chapter an essay on Canada as it moves into the second of the great wars, and on its awakening sense of nationhood (which he now shifts from the 1918 of *Barometer Rising* to 1939). He ends:

> Then, even as the two race-legends woke again remembering ancient enmities, there woke with them also the felt knowledge that together they had fought and survived one great war they had never made and that now they had entered another; that for nearly a hundred years the nation had been spread on the top half of the continent over the powerhouse of the United States and still was there; that even if the legends were like oil and alcohol in the same bottle, the bottle had not broken yet. And almost grudgingly, out of the instinct to do what was necessary, the country took the first irrevocable steps toward becoming herself, knowing against her will that she was not unique but like all the others, alone with history.

Such open and almost naive didacticism would not have been accepted, at the time MacLennan was writing, in either of the mother literatures of Canada, English or French, and no novelist of any consequence now at work in Canada would write in this way. We read such a novel already in a historical way, bearing in mind the decade to which it belongs.

Yet the fact remains that Tolstoy perpetrated similar didactic solecisms in writing *War and Peace,* yet it became a classic on publication and has remained so without effective challenge ever since. And MacLennan dominated the Canadian literary scene of the 1950s and the early 1960s, and is still widely read, because in his novels there was a quality that overbalanced, even in the minds of critical readers, their obvious flaws. Somehow the didacticism was always eventually subsumed in the imaginative fabric; whether we accepted or rejected the messages encapsuled in his novels was irrelevant to our acceptance of their literary power and validity.

So the appropriate question becomes: how did MacLennan, obsessed as he was with the fate of his country and the role of his generation in determining it, bring his didacticism under control? How did he avoid becoming consumed by it, as the socialist realists were by their political doctrines?

Partly, I suggest, it is because MacLennan's has always been a personal and not a partisan vision: especially, not a political one. But even more important than the personal and unpolitical vision as a control of MacLennan's recurrent didacticism is the fact that there have always been structural elements that control the course of action, the interrelationships and inner developments of the characters, and that originate at levels deeper than the didactic.

One of these elements is the common mythical structure that unites MacLennan's major novels. A decade ago I devoted much of a small book on MacLennan (*Hugh MacLennan,* 1969) to the argument that the "great unifying myth of his novels is the *Odyssey* translated into terms of modern life." The Odyssean pattern of the wanderer returning to the waiting woman begins in *Barometer Rising,* where the heroine is actually called Penelope, and continues in *Two Solitudes,* in *Each Man's Son,* in *The Watch That Ends the Night,* even obliquely in *The Precipice,* with results that vary from happiness and fulfilment in *Barometer Rising* to tragic disaster in *Each Man's Son,* whose particular Penelope—Mollie MacNeil—puts aside her tapestry too soon and is slaughtered with her lover by her returning husband, the prize fighter Archie MacNeil.

In *Return of the Sphinx* there is a shift in the mythical structure. Alan Ainslie is indeed a wanderer, and his life has been a kind of Odyssean quest filled with testing experience. Yet it leads to no journey's end in Ithaca, and there is no waiting Penelope, for Ainslie's wife, Constance, has been killed before the action of the novel begins. The myth that now assumes dominance is suggested by the very title: *Return of the Sphinx.* It concerns a world from which what seemed to be certainties have vanished; an unsure world once again in the power of the enigma. And in that world the conflict of fathers and sons is the central human encounter.

Hugh MacLennan once told me that, despite his lifelong enthusiasm for the *Odyssey,* he had not deliberately based his books on the Odyssean quest, though he recognized its presence once they had been written. And it is possible that the *Odyssey* reflects archetypal patterns so deeply lodged in the unconscious that a novelist or a poet might call up the myth without being at the time aware of it. Yet the fact remains that a knowledge of the *Odyssey* is a most useful aid to the interpretation of *Barometer Rising* and *The Watch That Ends the Night,* and a knowledge of the Oedipus myth is as useful in interpreting not only *Return of the Sphinx* but also a whole series of relationships that play key roles in the earlier books and assist MacLennan in reconciling the didactic and the imaginative, in teaching us—as I remarked in *Hugh MacLennan*—"social truths through the credible encounters of human beings."

When we go back to the real Oedipus myth we see that it has complexities which are not recognized in the Freudian concept of the Oedipus complex as it is commonly understood. The hostility towards the father and the rivalry in love for the mother which Freud postulates do not in fact occur in the myth, since Oedipus does not know that Laius is his father when he kills him in a chance encounter and does not know that Jocasta is his mother when he marries her. These are fatalities outside his desires.

Hostility between father and son does indeed exist in MacLennan's novels, but so do a number of features of the original Oedipus myth of which the Freudian concept takes no real account. One is the surrogate father: cast out to die by his real parent, Laius, Oedipus is brought up by Polybus whom he believes to be his father. Then there is the orphan theme: Oedipus appears to be an orphan when Polybus's shepherd discovers him, and makes himself an orphan in the end by killing his real father and causing his mother's suicide. The violent death of the mother is an essential part of the myth which again the Freudian concept does not take into account. Finally, there is the fact that the ''orphan'' son has unusual perception; he alone in the myth solves the riddle of the sphinx.

All these elements of the Oedipus myth recur through MacLennan's novels, parallel to the Odyssean returning theme. When Archie MacNeil murders Mollie in *Each Man's Son* and himself dies of a stroke, the guilt-stricken doctor, Daniel Ainslie, becomes Alan's surrogate father and shapes him into the questing, tragic intellectual we encounter in *Return of the Sphinx*. The great conflict in *Barometer Rising* is not between Neil Macrae and his real father, dead a decade ago, but between him and Geoffrey Wain, the uncle who took on a father's role when Neil's mother died in bearing him. Captain Yardley in *Two Solitudes* assumes many of the functions of a father towards Paul Tallard after his real father, Athanase, dies. Jerome Martell, born of his mother's casual encounter with some unknown man, never knows his father or even his real name; after his mother is murdered, he is taken into the home of a pastor named Martell who brings him up as his own son. Martell, in turn, assumes a surrogate father role towards the narrator George Stewart in *The Watch That Ends the Night,* whose real father is wholly ineffective as a parent: ''He had not been my actual father but for a time in the Thirties, when I was spiritually and emotionally fatherless, I had virtually allowed him to become so.''

In showing the abundance of surrogate fathers in MacLennan's works I have necessarily emphasized the prevalence of orphans. In fact, they are even more numerous in key roles than I have suggested. As well as Alan Ainslie, at least two of the more important characters in *Return of the Sphinx* are orphans: Latendresse, the revolutionary separatist who is the evil genius of Alan's son Daniel, and Bulstrode, the demagogue who wields a malign influence over Alan's political fate.

Mothers die violently or at least with shocking abruptness in at least four of MacLennan's novels: Mollie MacNeil murdered in *Each Man's Son* and

Jerome's mother in *The Watch That Ends the Night;* Jamsie Macrae dying of childbirth in *Barometer Rising* and Constance Ainslie crushed to death by a runaway truck in *Return of the Sphinx.* They are startling deaths when one remembers the self-conscious and chivalric tenderness with which MacLennan treats women in other circumstances, but they emphasize the bleak isolation of the orphan son, which is concealed but not eliminated when he finds a surrogate father. Complementary to that isolation is the autonomy and acuteness of the orphan's insight as he passes, like Neil Macrae in the trenches of France and the Halifax explosion, and Jerome in the horrors of concentration camps, through a living death into wisdom.

The discord between father and son in MacLennan's novels (as in Turgenev's eponymous masterpiece) is hardly a matter of Oedipal conflict in the Freudian sense, since there are no evident rivalries over the mother's love. It is more a matter of the alternation of generations, a process MacLennan has discussed widely outside his novels, particularly in essays like "Reflections on Two Decades." Perhaps the most significant characteristic of these relationships is their ambivalence. In *Two Solitudes* Marius Tallard, the elder and entirely French son of Athanase, repudiates his father's attempts to promote political unity between the two Canadas, and becomes a fervent Quebec nationalist of the 1914 vintage. Yet we are told that "his hatred of his father collapsed in a longing for his father's approval, never attained because stubbornness of pride made him refuse consistently to do a single thing his father wished." And Daniel Ainslie, reenacting the role of Marius in the context of 1960s separatism, can empathize privately with his father at the same time as he opposes him publicly. They meet:

> To Daniel his father looked much older than he remembered him, his face more noticeably divided between the injured side and the other one. To Alan his son also looked older and he recognized from a new expression on his face that he had crossed a frontier of some sort in his life. In their mutual recognitions was a deeper recognition that made them both afraid and self-conscious.

In fact, it is only in MacLennan's earliest novel, *Barometer Rising,* that unrelieved hostility exists between the generations, in this case the surrogate father Geoffrey Wain and the orphan Neil Macrae.

All these elements shared by his novels and the pre-Freudian Oedipus myth, MacLennan uses on two levels, and here we may find a clue to his relative success in handling didactic impulses. On one level he is using archetypal situations to give power to his presentation of human encounters. What happens in a MacLennan novel may sometimes seem contrived, but it is contrived in the same way as a classic tragedy to stir feelings that are universally experienced and recognized; as he himself has said: "But we

91

can't escape ourselves for ever, and more of ourselves than we choose to admit is the accumulated weight of our ancestors.'' Turns of events may at times seem mechanical, but human relationships in general are credible and convincing. As readers we can enter into them, more deeply in the case of generational relationships or male friendships, and less so in the case of sexual relationships, where MacLennan never quite sheds the Cape Breton puritanism that, in *Each Man's Son*, so relentlessly pursued Daniel Ainslie. It is this power to use archetypal patterns to create dramatic and acceptable human situations that allows MacLennan to use the same patterns, on another level, for his didactic purposes. There is in his novels a constant process of transference from the intimate to the general, from the personal to the political.

In a very curious passage in his essay ''Reflections on Two Decades,'' MacLennan, in defending himself against accusations of excessive didacticism, in fact seems to invert what actually takes place in his works; he says:

> My last novel, *Return of the Sphinx*, took four years from my initial notes in 1962 to its completion in the fall of 1966. My mental hangups ceased only when I realized that the separatist movement, its external theme, had no more to do with the real theme than a revolver with the mind of a man who uses it to shoot somebody. The real story was the destruction of a well-meaning father by an unhappy, ambitious, confused, guilt-ridden, idealistic son.

First of all, one could argue with a good deal of plausibility that, as MacLennan projects the situation in *Return of the Sphinx*, Alan Ainslie is destroyed as much by his own mental confusion, his own blindness to the meaning of events, as he is by his son's actions. And, of course, one cannot equate a physical object like a revolver—as MacLennan tries to do—with a movement of opinion like separatism that affects minds and emotions in a way no firearm in itself can do. Separatist or otherwise, the ''movements'' in MacLennan's novels, if we see them as wide collective shifts of thought, are as important as the individual relationships, which sometimes reflect them.

Despite what he says in ''Reflections on Two Decades,'' MacLennan uses the interplay of the personal and the social to further his didactic ends in *Return of the Sphinx*. For example, in one of the key scenes between the Ainslies, father and son, the state of being an orphan is clearly equated with the condition of French Canada.

> A wild exasperation entered Daniel's eyes and he cried out at his father, ''Why do you have to be like the rest of them? We scream it from the housetops

and not even you can understand. Even *you* ask me what we want and what we mean. Don't you understand words?''

"Words can be disguises, Daniel. I learned that in the 1930s."

"The 1930s!"

"You still haven't told me why you've joined the movement."

Daniel looked away. "What's the use? How can anyone like you understand what it feels like to be an orphan?"

Tears filled Ainslie's eyes; he reached out and put his hand over Daniel's wrist.

"I certainly know what it feels like to be a widower," he said quietly.

Daniel wrenched his wrist from his father's grip and made an impatient sweep. "I wasn't talking about *that*! I was talking about the whole French Canadian race. You grew up a part of the British Empire with the United States beside you and talking your language, with the whole huge, insensitive, crass, clumsy, conceited, interfering, hypocritical Anglo-Saxon System behind you. But we're orphans and at last we've found the courage to admit it. We don't want to spend the rest of our lives in an orphanage—and that's all the Province of Quebec will ever be unless it becomes an independent state and regains the pride that was milked and crushed out of it." He stared at his father. "Oh, what's the use? You'll never understand. Not in a thousand years would you be able to understand a thing like this. . . ."

Ainslie turned and said, "I've decided to tell you something I perhaps should have told you long ago. It's strange, your comparison of French Canadians to orphans. I happen to have grown up an orphan myself. I dare say it's had a bigger effect on me than I've been willing to admit."

In the last resort, if we extend the concern over Québec in this passage to MacLennan's own wider concern for Canada as a whole, what more potent image can a writer find who is dealing with the fate of a country barely emerging from British colonialism before it is threatened by a greater and closer imperialism—an image that at the same time disguises and justifies his didacticism—than the relationship of orphan son and surrogate father that recurs so often in the novels I have been discussing?

# 5

# PRAIRIE WRITERS
# AND THE MÉTIS

## *Rudy Wiebe and Margaret Laurence*

In a society as divided as Canada's by barriers of race and language, it has been inevitable that the divisions between various groups should often be polarized into patterns of Them and Us, with Them appearing as the hostile Other. This has been especially the case where the factor of conquest has come into play, whether between English and French, or between whites and native peoples, or, in a different way, between other Canadians and minorities they have tried to force into their own patterns, like the Doukhobors. In such cases the loser resents the victor and longs to turn the tables on him, and the victor sees the loser as a threat to his own sense of superiority.

The result of this situation is very often mutual isolation and the creation of stereotypes based on mutual ignorance. Writers have often tried to bridge the gap between what, in a famous novel, Hugh MacLennan (borrowing a line from Rilke) called the "two solitudes" of the French and English. Even in the nineteenth century English Canadian writers like William Kirby, Gilbert Parker and Duncan Campbell Scott sought to extend understanding of the French of Québec by writing romantic novels and stories about them. In more recent years the tragedies of the Métis uprisings, bred of a sense of vast injustice, have struck the imaginations of Canadians; Louis Riel has become a national martyr and Gabriel Dumont something of a national hero.

But such official tributes often seem to have the facility and falseness of belated amends to the past that can be made at no cost to the present. It is the writers who have dealt most imaginatively with the issues, realizing, as Margaret Laurence has said, that we must reach the point "when it is no longer necessary to say Them and Us . . . or perish."

For the majority of Canadians, even those of French ancestry, the story of the Métis has been almost as distant as a rumour. It has passed from a history of small rebellions into the myth of a dying nation defending itself against impossible odds, and in the process Louis Riel has been transformed from a criminal agitator into a national hero, celebrated in stage shows performed in the country's capital, commemorated with street names and postage stamps. But the condition of the Métis people has not changed materially as a result of this shift in the national mythology. They have remained socially and economically an underprivileged group, kept on those margins of our world and our consciousness to which they retreated after the defeat of the 1885 rebellion. And they continue to live mainly in the prairies where they were once the dominant people, and in the Northwest Territories, to which many of them withdrew in an attempt to sustain the traditional nomadic hunting pattern of their lives. It is only in this region that they retain any cohesion as a people and show a degree of militancy in attempting to defend and extend their rights. A Métis who moves to Québec or British Columbia is usually seeking absorption into the larger society, and very often he does not choose to proclaim his origins.

This means that most Canadians outside the prairies and the northern territories have no direct knowledge of the Métis as a social group or even as individuals, and for them Riel and his followers are historical figures as remote and as isolated in the great sweep of the past as, say, Tecumseh and his warriors. This lack of real contact is doubtless the reason why the Métis have played so slight a role in Canadian literature up to the present. In recent years a number of Métis, Maria Campbell notable among them, have begun to write evocatively of their people's way of life, and the memoirs— usually dictated—of a few Métis hunters and guides who lived during the classic period before 1885 have been published and have added considerably to our background knowledge of them.

But mainly, as far as the general reader is concerned, the Métis appears as a character in the novels of prairie writers of other backgrounds and communities, and his presence usually—at least in contemporary fiction— acts as a moral touchstone so far as the writer, the reader and the other characters are concerned. This applies even to the one novel I shall be discussing in which Métis are the principal characters, Rudy Wiebe's *The Scorched-Wood People*. The other novelist I am discussing is Margaret Laurence.

It seems important, to begin with, that in the novels by both Wiebe and Laurence in which Métis are involved, the representatives of this people who do appear are not introduced merely to heighten the local colour of the prairie setting, as they were introduced earlier into the novels of Ralph Connor. Even when they are not major characters, Wiebe's and Laurence's Métis play important roles in affecting the attitudes, the actions and even the fates of the people involved with them, while in each case their presence, in terms of what they represent collectively as well as how they act as individuals, is necessary to the development of the basic themes.

Rudy Wiebe's fiction has always been linked to his Mennonite background and to his personal struggle as an intensely religious man to shape a viable Christian life. His first novel, *Peace Shall Destroy Many*, concerns conflicts of power and conscience in a Mennonite prairie community, and his best novel up to the present, *The Blue Mountains of China*, is an epic narrative based on the wanderings of Mennonite communities from Germany to Russia, and then to Canada and Paraguay, in search of some haven where they can live what seems to them the just and holy life without interference or temptation.

As soon as one considers Wiebe's preoccupations as developed in these two books, one reason for his interest in the Métis becomes evident. Not only have Mennonites settled on land which the Métis once treated as a domain exclusive to them and their Indian cousins and rivals; they are, like the Métis, a minority people, resented and misunderstood by the ordinary Canadians around them, and often self-condemned to wander, as the Métis wandered from the Red River to the Saskatchewan and then, after their final defeat at Batoche, scattered over the prairies and into the trackless northland.

In *Peace Shall Destroy Many* the differences in attitude from their Métis neighbours on the part of the strict Mennonites in the northern wilds of Saskatchewan are related to the divergences within the community itself—divergences accentuated by the impact on the group of the modern world and especially of World War II, which challenged their traditional pacifism and strained their image of themselves as a German community.

The relationship between the Mennonites and the Métis emerges on various levels in the novel, some of them dramatic in their physical effect on the lives of individuals, others involving shifts and conflicts of attitude, but all of them in some way or other challenging the strict Mennonite view that it is possible to be and remain a Christian by isolating oneself, and even by isolating the word of God through insisting that it be uttered only in their own Low German dialect and by refusing to preach it to non-Mennonites.

Deacon Block is not only the practical leader of the Mennonite community, who guides them towards prosperity by acting on their behalf in business; he is also the self-appointed censor of morals and guardian of the purity of Mennonite doctrines. While he is willing to hire the Métis Louis Moosomin because of the wartime shortage of labour, he is nevertheless intent on keeping a strict division between his own people and the "breeds," as he always calls them. Most of the Mennonites, realizing in a vague way the difference between themselves and their improvident neighbours, choose to enquire no farther.

But Joseph, the Mennonite teacher of the village school to which the Métis children also go, finds himself forced to discover why they are slower than the children from his own community, and he begins to learn something of their shiftless existence, which results from their parents' dependence on the nomadic hunting life when their unplanned farming leaves

96

them unprovided for. Joseph and his young friend Thom Wiens believe they must help the Métis children, and one of the ways they do it is by starting Bible classes in English, which the Métis can understand.

To Deacon Block, this attempt to reach out to the Métis is anathema. He sees it as a threat to the defensive unity of the Mennonite congregation, and the use of English is one aspect of that threat. When Joseph leaves the village to join the army medical corps, Block forces Thom to give up teaching the Métis children. He justifies himself by declaring that

> the great matters of moral and spiritual discipline have been laid down once and for all in the Bible and our fathers have told us how we should act according to them. They cannot change. . . .
>
> That's why we have to remain apart from the world. And that includes the breeds, who are culturally and morally backward. They—their world—has been trained by its fathers to despise the things we hold precious: cleanliness, frugality, hard work, moral decency, peacefulness. . . . We are not of this world, the Bible says. We have to live separated to prepare ourselves for the world that is coming. Our knowledge and attitude therefore creates a certain distance between us and—the breeds, for example. It is right that it do so.

But Deacon Block cannot keep his people separate forever, and the outside world he fears penetrates even his own tightly controlled family. He has refused to allow his daughter Elizabeth to marry Herman Paetkau, who was the son of a Mennonite girl seduced by a Russian labourer in the Ukraine; the purity of his family might be destroyed by such a union. When Herman moves out of the community to a bush farm near the Métis and decides to marry a Métis girl, she is refused permission to join the congregation lest other Mennonites should be tempted to follow Herman's example. But when Elizabeth Block is suddenly taken ill and dies giving birth to a premature child, it turns out that the father is Louis Moosomin, the young Métis whom Block had employed, and—worse—that Elizabeth, fearing to die an old maid without sexual experience, had taken the initiative and begged Louis to lie with her. Block cannot see his own responsibility for what seems to him this appalling corruption within his family; the threat still seems to him to originate in the temptations of the outer world, and he reacts by buying out all the local Métis farmers so that temptation will be removed. But his iron pride is finally destroyed when his beloved son Peter fights in public with other young Mennonites over a non-Mennonite girl who has come to take Joseph's place as teacher in the local school.

Rudy Wiebe is a frankly didactic writer, and his books have clear messages. The message of *Peace Shall Destroy Many* is that in Christianity there is no chosen people. Its teachings cannot be restricted to one group, or taught in any one language; nor can they survive by denying the natural needs of men or by attempting to evade the world and its temptations. The relationship between the Mennonites and the Métis, two fugitive, despised and persecuted peoples, who are yet so different in their attitudes to existence and to God, is used admirably to develop these themes. None of the leading characters is a Métis; all the great struggles take place in Mennonite hearts. However, lightly sketched as they often are, the Métis serve well not only to present another view of existence from that of the Mennonites but also to display the kind of human need which a self-protective and exclusive religion is tempted to ignore, yet ignores at its peril.

There is no reason to suppose that Wiebe is rejecting the essentials of Mennonite beliefs, or the idea of a Mennonite community, or that he is proposing the present-day Métis way of existence as a desirable alternative. But his thinking about both Mennonite and Métis is bound up with his sense of the need for a community of will and values. Talking to Alan Twigg about *The Scorched-Wood People,* he said:

> It's the story of a people, a people who have almost disappeared because they no longer live to express a communal will. The Métis are scattered now. For a long time they have shown very little communality of purpose . . . The world has broken down their whole sense of community. History has broken them down. Riel saw this coming. In his prayers he prayed that his people would not lose sight of what they were and what they could be together. Not just as individuals.

I shall return to consider *The Scorched-Wood People* more closely, but before that it is helpful to glance at its predecessor, *The Temptations of Big Bear*. In a historical sense *Big Bear* is related to *The Scorched-Wood People,* since the Frog Lake incident was part of the rebellion of 1885, yet it was entirely isolated, in terms of action, from what the Métis were doing on the South Saskatchewan. Although Gabriel Dumont is mentioned in the first pages of *Big Bear,* he does not play the active role in the novel one expects, and the Métis in general appear only indirectly in references to past encounters between the Indian leaders and Riel. The novel concentrates on Big Bear in his role as a Cree chief who understands—as Wiebe told Twigg —even better than Riel that "you can't fight the white man with his own weapons." And Big Bear, who understands those other powers, appears in the novel, if not in history, as a "man of spirit," a prophet to his own people, even if they do not accept his exhortations, and to others even if they do not know of his existence. But a prophet who is also a martyr, as Big Bear eventually became because of his early death from the rigours of imprisonment, tends to assume a mythic stature, and in enlarging Big Bear as he does, Wiebe is really taking him out of his Indian context, giving him a universality he did not and could not claim for himself. Frank Davey, in *From Here to There,* comments acutely on this aspect of *The Temptations of Big Bear.*

> In Wiebe's view, there is no escape for the Crees from the vise-grip of circumstances; only Big Bear's continuing refusal to follow the tempting ways of total surrender or total resistance can temper the inevitable Indian collapse with dignity and nobility. In this refusal to accept the conventional human responses to persecution, Big Bear takes on the role of the Christian martyr; like Christ himself he stubbornly clings to a non-violent but fixed moral stance that with equanimity accepts the risk of death. Thus the least Christian of Wiebe's novels in its overt content is the most powerful in its Christian implications.

Just as in *Big Bear* Wiebe is not writing historical fiction, in spite of his elaborate and effective use of documentary material, as much as religious myth, so in *The Scorched-Wood People* he is trying to show in Riel a spiritual vision that leaps beyond the fate of his people, condemned by history, to the thought of a more universal human community. As Wiebe shows it, Gabriel Dumont remained throughout no more than a leader of the Métis, and because of this it was appropriate that he should escape and return to live out with his people their transformation from a self-conscious nation into a scattering of disoriented groups. But Riel saw the Métis as something more than they were, a community that might have a mission in the world if it could survive and keep together, just as he saw himself having a God-given mission; the defeat and scattering of the Métis left Riel only the martyrdom he chose consciously when he elected not to be defended on the grounds of insanity, and the opportunity to proclaim his faith for a last time from the dock.

Wiebe asserts of *The Scorched-Wood People* that "it's the voice of the Métis people that writes this book," but anyone who has read the surviving Métis accounts of the 1885 rebellion, notably the transcripts of Gabriel Dumont's oral accounts, will be bound to disagree. To an extent, indeed, the voice of Louis Riel does "write" the book, since much that he actually said or wrote is included, but, like any other novel, *The Scorched-Wood People* is an invention of its author, and the Métis are there, as they were in *Peace Shall Destroy Many,* to pose a recurrent Wiebe theme, which is the relationship between spirit and community.

If one sees *The Scorched-Wood People* as an imaginative presentation of Louis Riel, the religious visionary whom fate cast in the doomed role of a minority rebel leader, then it must be respected as the study of a man tortured by the conflicting demands of the world of action and the world of spirit. But in many ways Riel was not a true personification of the Métis community, however he may seem in the myth that has grown up in hindsight; his education and his experience in exile had by 1885 given him an entirely different kind of outlook from that of the Saskatchewan hunters, who found in Gabriel Dumont their truer spokesman and, when Riel had failed them, their exemplar—the man beside whom they finally fought and beside whom many of them died. And this is why Wiebe is mistaken in believing that "the voice of the Métis people," or even the voice of history, wrote *The Scorched-Wood People*.

For Rudy Wiebe in *The Scorched-Wood People* has failed to separate the legitimate purpose of historical fiction, which is to give us a plausible image and a true feeling of the past, from that of the historical moralist, which is to apportion blame, signal merit and formulate lessons. In all his books the moralist has been predominant over the historian, which means that the facts of the past, and even its essential character, are subordinate to dogmatic purposes that lie outside history and perhaps outside art.

One sees this in the enlargement of Louis Riel, the man of spirit, at the expense of Gabriel Dumont, the man of action, which is achieved by the distortion of history. By distortion I mean something different from the use of facts about the past by a good historical novelist like, say, Mary Renault, who accepts what is known as a kind of skeletal structure and invents in the areas of obscurity, so that probability and imagination do not conflict. In *The Scorched-Wood People* Wiebe deliberately rejects the structure of probability and introduces, along with invented incidents that could have occurred because we know nothing to the contrary, other events which our knowledge of the facts of the Red River Rising tell us could not have taken place.

The improbabilities that verge on impossibility begin with Wiebe's choice of a narrator; he is a Métis oral poet, and we are led to identify him with Pierre Falcon, the most famous of the Métis bards who was present at the skirmish at Seven Oaks in 1816, when he composed his famous song that became something of an anthem for the Métis "nation." But Falcon died in 1876, nine years before the events that mark the end of *The Scorched-Wood People*, and we are forced to assume that he has dictated his memoirs from the spirit world, which seems an unnecessary implausibility.

After this implausibility, it is not surprising that Wiebe should so distort history as to have Gabriel Dumont present at the Red River through the whole period of Riel's ascendancy there; though in fact Dumont was certainly at Red River for a period in 1870, he equally certainly arrived well after the rising began and left well before the appearance of Garnet Wolseley, Riel having refused his offer to bring a corps of Métis from the western prairie and ambush the Canadian expeditionary force. In *The Scorched-Wood People* Dumont is even shown as being present at such events as the turning back of McDougall at the border, which was the first act of insurrection, and the trial and execution of Thomas Scott. But, since Dumont's name appears in no account of these incidents, Wiebe cannot give him important roles, and he thus appears in the same inconsequential and demeaning manner as Shakespeare's attendant lords.

In such treatment the diminution of Dumont begins; it continues through the crucial events of 1884 and 1885. Indeed, it affects his whole role as a leader of the Saskatchewan Métis, for Wiebe shows him as the petty chieftain of a few hunters. His role in creating the quasi republic of St. Laurent in the early 1870s is minimized, and the clash between him and the Hudson's Bay people in 1875, which led to his first encounter with the North-West Mounted Police and became an imperial issue with repercussions in Whitehall, is treated as a very minor affair rather than the real beginning of the chain of events that led to the North West Rebellion. Finally, so as to make the "earthy" Dumont a suitable foil for the "spiritual" Riel, he is represented as a crude and violent figure (a "savage" as he calls himself in *The Scorched-Wood People* but never did in history). He is made to speak like a badly educated Canadian, an insensitive backwoods hick, whereas in fact Dumont (who spoke six languages even if he wrote none) was a man of considerable subtlety of expression and in his own way a highly sophisticated as well as a great and courageous man. Only the courage remains in *The Scorched-Wood People;* the intelligence and the grandeur are somehow lost. Dumont emerges as a muscular oaf, and that is neither fictional nor historical justice.

Just as Dumont is dwarfed to make a giant out of Riel, so the Métis in general are diminished. For even if, as Wiebe suggests, Riel "prayed that his people would not lose sight of what they were and what they could be together," he more than any other individual assured by his indecision— his failure to choose either the way of Gandhi or the way of Dumont—that the Métis defeat should be sharp and so shattering that they never recovered. Wiebe evades dealing with this failure; perhaps, because he was writing a religious and not a political novel, he cannot be expected to do otherwise. But the fact remains that in placing Riel's spiritual conflict at the heart of the book, he belies his own claim that it speaks with the "voice of the Métis"; nowhere in *The Scorched-Wood People* is justice done to the freedom and the natural nobility that characterized Métis life at its best, before history drifted that life into obsolescence. As in *Peace Shall Destroy Many* the Métis are used, even in this novel where they occupy the centre of the stage, not for their own sakes as individuals or as a people, but to illustrate a religious theme. Once, replying obliquely to my criticism, Wiebe remarked that "Woodcock . . . doesn't like to believe in the power of the *Christian* spirit." My criticism has nothing to do with the power or otherwise of the Christian spirit. It was and is that a religious novel about the Christian spirit and a historical novel about the fate of a people are two different things, and that Wiebe, in *The Scorched-Wood People,* has fallen between the two, and in the process does justice neither to his own abilities nor to the Métis.

Margaret Laurence has never written a novel about the Métis, though her stories about Africans in *The Tomorrow-Tamer* lead one to believe that she might be able to make the leap of mental identification that has been beyond Rudy Wiebe's powers. There is little evidence that she thought greatly about the Métis during her African period, for the comparison she makes in *Heart of a Stranger* between the North West Rebellion of 1885 and the anti-colonial campaigns of Mahammed Abdille Hasan, the famous "Mad Mullah" of Somaliland, dates from 1964, when she had already written *The Stone Angel,* her first Canadian novel. But from *The Stone Angel* itself, the Métis appear in all but one of Margaret Laurence's novels, and the role they play increases in complexity and importance.

Before observing how Margaret Laurence has treated the Métis in fictional terms, it is valuable to note how she has considered them in nonfictional terms and especially in the essay on Gabriel Dumont, "Man of Our People," which appears in *Heart of a Stranger* and is her most direct statement on the role of the Métis not only in Canadian history but also in the changes that are necessary in our attitude to the Canadian land if we are to avoid environmental suicide. The final paragraphs of her Dumont essay not only argue the importance of the Métis past as an example in shaping a viable future for our society, but also help us to understand why the survivors of this people who once ruled the prairies gain a steadily growing importance in Margaret Laurence's novels.

Has the voice of Gabriel Dumont anything to tell us here and now, in a world totally different from his? I believe it has. The spirits of Dumont and Riel, of Big Bear and Poundmaker, after the long silence, are speaking once again through their people, their descendants. Will we ever reach a point when it is no longer necessary to say Them and Us? I believe we must reach that point, or perish. Canadians who, like myself, are descendants of various settlers, many of whom came to this country as oppressed or dispossessed peoples, must hear native peoples' voices and ultimately become part of them, for they speak not only of the soul-searing injustices done to them but also of their rediscovered sense of self-worth and their ability to tell and teach the things needed to be known. . . . Those other societies which existed before imperialism, industrialism, mass exploitation and commercial greed were certainly far from ideal, nor can we return to them, but they knew about living in relationship to the land, and they may ultimately be the societies from whose values we must try to learn.

There are many ways in which those of us who are not Indian or Métis have not yet earned the right to call Gabriel Dumont ancestor. But I do, all the same.

His life, his legend, and his times are a part of our past which we desperately need to understand and pay heed to.

Métis characters appear in all of Margaret Laurence's Canadian works of fiction but one, *A Jest of God,* and there they are perhaps left out because the Ukrainian, Nick Kazlik, representative of another minority people, performs a very similar role of challenging stranger to that which the Métis assume in *The Stone Angel, The Fire-Dwellers, A Bird in the House* and *The Diviners.* All of her Métis belong to the same family, the Tonnerres, brought up in a cluster of cabins outside Manawaka and offering a perpetual reproach to respectable prairie smalltown society and in various ways perturbing the lives of the leading characters. In the earlier novels the relationship between the Canadians and the Métis is still clearly one of Them and Us. Slightly in *A Bird in the House,* and notably in *The Diviners,* the relationship changes, and the images of reconciliation appear.

In *The Stone Angel* the Métis appear as challengers and, ultimately, as destroyers. They are there generation after generation. Hagar's brother, Matt, wishes to go with Jules Tonnerre to set traplines on Galloping Mountain. His father, old Jason Currie, refuses permission because "he wasn't having any son of his gallivanting over the country with a half-breed." Later on Matt, who has obsessively saved his dimes and nickels to fulfil some boyhood goal, spends his nest egg on a fighting cock; pitted against Jules Tonnerre's cock, it is destroyed.

Hagar's own most loved son, John Shipley, later becomes involved with the sons of Jules Tonnerre:

> Once when I was out picking saskatoons near the trestle bridge, I saw him with the Tonnerre boys. They were French half-breeds, the sons of Jules, who'd once been Matt's friend, and I wouldn't have trusted any of them as far as I could spit. They lived all in a swarm in a shack somewhere—John always said their house was passably clean, but I gravely doubted it. They were tall boys with strange accents and hard laughter. The trestle bridge was where the railway crossed the Wachakwa river a mile or so from town. The boys were daring each other to walk across it. There were great gaps between the beams, so they teetered along on the thin steel tracks as though they were walking a tightrope.

Hagar yells at John, and not only almost scares him into falling, but humiliates him in front of the Métis boys. But the fatal link between John and Jules Tonnerre's son Lazarus continues, for one day John tells Hagar:

> After you told me not to walk the trestle bridge, we dreamed up another game there, I and the Tonnerre boys. The trick was to walk to the middle and see who

could stay longest. Then, when the train was almost there, we'd drop over the side and climb down the girders to the creek. We always meant to stay there while the train went over. We figured there'd be just enough room, at the very edge, if we lay down. But no one ever had the nerve.

John is doomed by his relationship with the Tonnerres, for he dies when he makes a bet with Lazarus to run his truck over the trestle bridge and collides with a special relief freight which nobody in Manawaka knew was coming through. So the bridge, which seems at first a symbol of reconciliation, becomes a place of death.

In *The Stone Angel* our links with the Métis are indirect, for we always see them through Hagar's eyes when she is considering the fate of her menfolk. We never know at first hand why Matt and John are drawn towards them, although the element of male challenge is always there, and the result is, in Matt's case, defeat for the white man, and, in John's case, his actual destruction. In this novel it is hard to regard the Métis as else than Them, the Other, carrying out some unconscious and undeclared campaign of revenge.

Métis generations are short, and in the scope of the Manawaka novels we are involved with at least four of them: Jules Tonnerre and his sons, especially Lazarus, in *The Stone Angel;* Lazarus and his children in the three other novels I have mentioned, with his daughter Val most important in *The Fire-Dwellers,* his other daughter Piquette in *A Bird in the House* and his son Jules in *The Diviners.* Finally, in *The Diviners,* a fourth generation emerges, with the daughter Pique whom Jules has by the novelist Morag Gunn, and the children of his brother and his sisters.

Val appears in *The Fire-Dwellers* as a challenger of values rather than as an aggressor. Stacey Cameron, daughter of the undertaker in Manawaka, has become a frustrated Vancouver housewife, obsessed with her children and unwillingly entangled in her husband's career as the typical salesman for the typical North American miracle drug. Everything about her life, except her feelings for the few people to whom she is possessively attached, is phony. She tries to escape through furtive and half-hearted affairs, but her adventures always end in a return to the protective shelter of her bourgeois life. One day Stacey is downtown in Vancouver, near Skid Road.

Stacey hears, strangely, her name being spoken by a woman's voice, a voice raucous as the gulls'.

Stacey    hey Stacey

She blinks. Coming towards her is a woman whose black hair has been upfrizzed until it resembles the nest of some large wild bird. Her dark eyes and her features are prairie Indian but not entirely. Her skin, or what can be seen of it under the thick crust of make-up, is a pale brown. Her mouth has been lipsticked into a wide bizarre cupid's bow. She is wearing a smeared hem-drooping mauve silkish dress which reveals her body's blunt thickness, the once-high breasts that are dugs now.

It *is* Stacey, ain't it? Stacey Cameron? I dunno your married name.

Yes    that's right    I    I

Valentine Tonnerre, Val. Doncha remember me?

Well, for heaven's sake. Well, sure I do. Of course.

Val tells Stacey that their sister Piquette has burned to death, drunk in her blazing cabin, with her children. Val, it emerges as she talks on, is resigned to dying soon, and when Stacey goes on to tell of her own anxieties and her fears, they seem petty in comparison with Piquette's tragedy and the combination of bitterness and fatalism she perceives in Val. Val does not appear again in *The Fire-Dwellers,* nor do the other Tonnerres, but the point has been made, and as the novel from this point draws quickly to its end, we look on Stacey's misfortunes—as they seem to her—with an ironic view. For though the alienation of modern urban man is real, he himself has created and cherished it, and so—however real his agonies—they are different from those whose alienation has been thrust upon them through the destruction of their way of life by historical change and of their community by alien forces, as happened to the Métis.

The death of Piquette Tonnerre casts its shadow over all of Margaret Laurence's last three works of fiction. Although the collection of interrelated stories entitled *A Bird in the House* was published a year after *The Fire-Dwellers,* the reference to Piquette's death in the latter novel sounds like a summarization of the final pages of "The Loons," which appeared in the later book, and it is likely that this story was in fact written before *The Fire-Dwellers.* "The Loons" is really a transition story, anticipating the change in the role of the Métis, and in the potential relationships between whites and Métis, that differentiates *The Diviners* from *The Stone Angel* or even from *The Fire-Dwellers.* It takes us towards the point where the Métis are no longer the Other, where the relationship is not necessarily between Them and Us.

Vanessa MacLeod, who tells of her childhood in the stories of *A Bird in the House,* is the daughter of the local doctor in Manawaka. Jules Tonnerre, the young man of *The Stone Angel,* has become a drunken old man living in his memories of the 1885 rebellion, Lazarus is the father of a large family, and his daughter Piquette is in Vanessa's class at school.

She was older than I, but she had failed several grades, perhaps because her attendance had always been sporadic and her interest in schoolwork negligible. Part of the reason she had missed a lot of school was that she had had tuberculosis of the bone, and had once spent many months in hospital. I knew this

105

because my father was the doctor who had looked after her. Her sickness was almost the only thing I knew about her, however. Otherwise, she existed for me only as a vaguely embarrassing presence, with her hoarse voice and her clumsy limping walk and her grimy cotton dresses that were always miles too long. I was neither friendly nor unfriendly towards her. She dwelt and moved somewhere within my scope of vision, but I did not actually notice her until that peculiar summer when I was eleven.

That summer, when the MacLeods are going off to their vacation cottage, Dr. MacLeod proposes that they take Piquette with them, to make sure of a recovery which he thinks will be spoilt if she stays at home with Lazarus. Vanessa's mother objects, but withdraws her objection when she realizes that if Piquette goes to the lake her mother-in-law will not. Vanessa looks forward to Piquette's presence for the wrong reasons; she has romantic ideas about Indians and hopes Piquette will live up to them. In fact she finds herself with a resentful, surly companion who is not even interested in the loons inhabiting the lake, who fascinate Vanessa and her father: "I could not reach Piquette at all, and I soon lost interest in trying. But all that summer she remained as both a reproach and a mystery to me."

Dr. MacLeod dies and Piquette ceases to attend the school. Then, four years later, Vanessa runs into her in a Manawaka café. She has changed, become loudly gay, and greets Vanessa like an old friend, telling her that her father—the doctor—was "the only person in Manawaka that ever did anything good to me." Yet Vanessa still finds the gulf between her and Piquette impossible to leap.

> I knew a little more than I had that summer at Diamond Lake, but I could not reach her now any more than I had then. I was ashamed, ashamed of my own timidity, the frightened tendency to look the other way. Yet I felt no real warmth towards her—I only felt that I ought to, because of that distant summer and because my father had hoped she would be company for me, or perhaps that I would be for her, but it had not happened that way. At this moment, meeting her again, I had to admit that she repelled and embarrassed me, and I could not help despising the self-pity in her voice. I wished she would go away. I did not want to see her. I did not know what to say to her. It seemed that we had nothing to say to one another.

Piquette tells her she is going to marry an Englishman in Winnipeg, and for a moment Vanessa sees the true person behind the defensive guise Piquette has created.

> For the merest instant, then, I saw her. I really did see her, for the first and only time in all the years we had both lived in the same town. Her defiant face,

momentarily, became unguarded and unmasked, and in her eyes there was a terrifying hope.

Vanessa does not see Piquette again, and eventually she goes away from Manawaka to college. She returns for the summer, and then it is that she learns of Piquette's death and the terrible way she died, her marriage having failed and failure having turned her into a drunkard. Once again, in Vanessa's reactions, one senses the strange cross-purposed distance that exists when people from the world of success and the world of failure meet.

> I did not say anything. As so often with Piquette, there did not seem to be anything to say. There was a kind of silence around the image in my mind of the fire and the snow, and I wished I could put from my memory the look that I had seen once in Piquette's eyes.

Morag Gunn, the novelist narrator and central character of *The Diviners*, was a fellow student of Vanessa, Stacey and Piquette in the school at Manawaka, but she lived there in a middle ground between the children of respectable homes and the Métis. An orphan, she was brought up in the poor part of the town by the municipal scavenger, Christie Logan, and is accordingly despised by most of her fellow students and their parents. It is between her and Skinner Tonnerre, the young Jules who is the son of Lazarus and brother of Val and Piquette, that a bridge of understanding is built that is not, like the trestle bridge of *The Stone Angel*, a way to destruction.

Morag, in the beginning, is half-frightened by Jules and half-fascinated by him; he represents a kind of freedom which complements the defiance of convention personified by Christie Logan, the man so embittered with the world after World War I that he deliberately chooses the occupation of scavenger and the contempt that goes with it.

The fact that Morag and Jules are both outsiders draws them together. Once, ineffectually, they try to make love, and then Jules goes away to fight in the war and narrowly escapes death at Dieppe. Morag, obsessed with writing, becomes the only reporter for the *Manawaka Sentinel,* and this leads her back towards Jules and his family, for she is sent out to report on the burning of the shack in which Piquette and her children have died, and the scene eats itself into her mind, as the memory of Jules has done, for when she meets him in Toronto as her marriage to the English professor Brooke is lurching to an end, they immediately become lovers, and their relationship is cemented by the memory of tragedy in a terrible scene in which Jules more or less forces her to tell what her senses recorded at the scene of Piquette's death.

Jules raised his head.

"When they came out—did you see—"

She is shaking and cannot stop. It is not her right, but she cannot help it.

"No, they—Niall and your dad—they took a stretcher in, and it was covered when they came out—a blanket or something, covering the—"

"Okay," Jules says steadily. "What else?"

"It was the coldest part of the winter," Morag says, and now her own voice sounds oddly cold and meticulous, as though the memory of that chill had numbed her. "The air smelled of—of burnt wood. I remember thinking—crazy—but I thought Bois-Brûlés."

"Shut up!" Jules cries out in some kind of pain which cannot be touched by her.

Silence.

"Go on," he says finally.

Why does he have to inflict this upon himself? Why can't he let it go? Perhaps he has to know before he can let it go at all.

"I guess I vomited, as they brought the stretcher out. I realized then that the air didn't smell of smoke and burnt wood. It smelled of—well, like roasted meat, and for a minute I wondered what it was, and then—"

Jules lies across the table once more. Then slowly he raises his head and looks at her.

"By Jesus, I hate you," he says in a low voice like distant thunder. "I hate all of you. Every goddamn one."

Morag gets up and puts on her coat. There is nothing more can be said. He watches her walk towards the door. Then speaks, the cry wrenched out of him.

"No. Wait awhile, eh?"

They hold on to each other again, and make love or whatever it is, throughout the dark and terrifying night.

Morag and Jules do not remain together. Each lives in their own half-world. Both have come out of the isolations of their childhood, Morag as a well-known novelist and Jules as a folk singer, yet neither is accepted entirely into the respectable white world, for the artist is, in a different way, as much an outsider as the Métis. Each belongs to a peculiar tribe. And, while their differences as well as Jules's nomadic habits make any established relationship impossible, and their intermittent contacts are broken by vast gaps of time, Morag and Jules are bound to each other by deep emotional ties, and their daughter Pique becomes the image and the concrete fact of their relationship, which in its turn is an image of reconciliation.

But it is an image that should not be pushed too far. There is no doubt that in her Manawaka novels Margaret Laurence has ideas about the relationships between peoples of different origins which she wishes to work out in her fiction, and this she does successfully. But she never loses sight of her characters as human beings; she is always observing them from within, in their own rights, for their own sakes, so that one never has the feeling one gets from Rudy Wiebe's novels, that the Métis are being used as vehicles to work out some aspect of the Christian life. Margaret Laurence is not a religious novelist; she is not even a historical novelist, though she writes with a great sense of history. And that is why she sees the problems of a people like the Métis not in terms of the action within a community of a faith larger than either the community or its members, but rather in terms of human relationships, of the erosion of prejudice through experience and understanding and ultimately empathy. Piquette is not a Christ figure; she is suffering humanity calling for our compassion, at the same time as she is an individual caught up in the collective fate of her people. And this approach, which sees everything in concrete and personal terms is, I suggest, more true to the art of fiction and also to the nature of human existence.

# 6

# CASTING DOWN THEIR GOLDEN CROWNS

## The Novels of Marian Engel

Marian Engel's death in 1985 was a great loss to Canadian writing. She was only in her early fifties, but already she had written and published seven novels that had placed her high among the writers of her time. She combined inventiveness, imaginative depth and a prose style—excellent in its simplicity and perfect pitch—that some critics considered the best among living Canadian writers.

Her novels are remarkable in their variety. She could write light "entertainments," as Graham Greene would call them, and these—*Joanne* and *Lunatic Villas* are examples—could parody popular styles and the sentiments of soap opera without failing in the sureness of their satirical touch. Her more serious novels (though none is devoid of humour) span the range of human potentialities, so that in her inimitable fable, *Bear,* she reminds us of the animal within us, our links with the natural world, while in her brilliant psychological novel, *The Glassy Sea,* she reaches over to the other side of the dual nature of humanity, and in the story of the nun who finds enlightenment in being persistently Martha rather than Mary, she tells us we are angelic also, spiritual beings no matter how earthy our concerns.

The choice of a heroine who was Martha rather than Mary was appropriate for Marian Engel, since in her own way she was a person dedicated to serving others. The stance of the writer aloof from life was alien to her. She was extremely active in the movement to give writers a collective voice to protect their interests, and she became the first chairperson of the Writers' Union that resulted from this initiative. She would, I think, have regarded her best monument the fact that in 1986, the year after her death, the Canadian government finally instituted a scheme—for which she had fought many years—to pay writers compensation for the use of their books in libraries.

In Marian Engel's *The Glassy Sea,* her leading character, the on-and-off nun, Sister Mary Pelagia, alias Rita Heber, says that her "life has always been a quest for simplifications, patterns, stylizations . . ." and one can gain a great deal of insight into Engel's array of novels by applying this remark to them. For I suspect the reason why critics are reluctant to discuss them is that they are so clearly written, so simply formed, so deftly patterned and rendered in window-pane prose, that they appear to be more transparent than in fact they are, and we shy away from discussing them for fear of seeming to say what may have appeared obvious to any perceptive reader.

In fact, Engel's novels are neither simple nor obvious, but the fact that they should appear so is a good point from which to start discussing them. They are all, to begin with, small books, as unupholstered as Shaker furniture. *The Honeyman Festival,* set in a single night of incident and recollection, is a mere 131 pages. *Joanne,* the diary of a woman whose marriage is going adrift, is a shade longer at 134 pages. *Bear* has 141 pages. None of the others attains 200 pages, except for *Monodromos,* which runs to 250 pages; its heavier use of background detail makes this the least typical and perhaps the least effective of Engel's novels.

But even in the other, briefer books, there is a complexity of structure and content that makes them more than mere novellas that develop a single extended thread of interest, and perhaps there is no accepted genre in English fiction that quite contains them. The French category of récit, which Camus and Gide applied to most of their medium-length fictions, seems to me to fit them best. The récit is a lucidly told but not necessarily simply constructed or simply understood narrative that does not attempt the grand sweep and structure and the somewhat realistic use of detail that one associates with the novel proper.

The récit also, at least as it was practised by Gide and Camus, tended to be a moralist kind of fiction, seeking to find in some individual predicament the basis for a statement that might be applied more widely to the human condition, and here also I suspect that every one of Marian Engel's first six novels would fit into the tradition. They are simple, patterned, stylized, moralist, as the masterpieces of minor French fiction have been in our time—and as Sister Mary Pelagia saw her life. And Sister Mary Pelagia's life, so closely Canadian in its setting, swings me back to the fact that, however interesting we may find the formal parallels between Engel's work and that of certain French writers, she is always writing very solidly within the Canadian social ambience (even if sometimes the Canadians encounter each other abroad); the moralism that haunts her work is Anglo-Celtic, not Gallic, and the very sureness of her use of language places her work firmly in the English tradition, even if the channel she follows through the broad delta that Anglo-Saxon literatures have formed in the late twentieth century happens to be a Canadian one.

If she does have literary ancestors, as distinct from analogues, they are in the English past, before the novel sprawled into Dickensian amplitude: Jane Austen, but even more Defoe with his earthy plausibility and his prag-

111

matic closeness to the real problems of ordinary people, and perhaps as much, if one can take a hint dropped more than once in *Bear,* Mrs. Aphra Behn, whose *Oroonoko* was greatly admired by the ursophilous Colonel Cary, and who had an economical and lucid style and a wry view of life which she expressed with befitting acerbity. In *Oroonoko* Mrs. Behn could, as Engel does in *Monodromos,* indulge herself in a rococo lushness of description as she establishes the background scene of Surinam, but it is in her less well known little novels, like *The Wandering Beauty, The Unfortunate Happy Lady* and *The Court of the King of Bantam* (with its inimitable opening sentence, "This money certainly is a most devilish thing!") that one finds a combination of wit and feeling, and a concern for the fate of women in an abruptly changing world (in which the Restoration so largely resembled our own age) that seems to be echoed in Marian Engel's best novels.

To draw this comparison out of literary history is of course only justified if it illuminates our understanding of the subject of this essay, which is Marian Engel and her work. I think the advantage of evoking it is that Aphra Behn offers us an exemplum of a writer who insisted on asserting her rights as a woman to recognition in her chosen world (she was the first of all successful professional women writers and became so in an aggressively male-dominated situation), who was willing to struggle with men and with the accepted mores to achieve her end, and underwent a great deal of vilification in the process, and yet who remained, after all the struggle, unchanged in her femininity. Whether much of this would apply, given the difference of age and situation, to Marian Engel, only her biographer will be able to say, though I suspect a great deal of it does. I know it applies in various ways to the women to whom she has devoted her writing.

For all of Engel's novels are about women, their problems and predicaments, their avenues of escape. Every time the central character is a woman, and in four of the novels the story is actually told first-person by the woman, in diary, letter, interior monologue, while even in the two third-person novels, *The Honeyman Festival* and *Bear,* the point of view is consistently that of the heroine.

I have used the word *heroine* quite deliberately, for though these central women characters may have the antiheroic qualities that emerge in any realistic presentation of people acting in the contemporary world, each of them has a quest of her own, grows in self-recognition and self-realization as her quest continues, and emerges with a clearer understanding of existence and a sense of personal purification and integration. All passion may perhaps by the end be spent, but the eponymous heroine of *Joanne* ends by finding herself "halfway to seeing life steadily and whole," for Sister Mary Pelagia "the chapel still smells of roses," and Lou, at the end of *Bear,* "remembered the claw that healed guilt. She felt strong and pure."

They have endured their own special *rites de passage;* they have earned the title of "heroic." There are no unhappy endings in Engel's novels, and if none of the endings is in the conventional way happy, we can certainly call them triumphant, in the sense that each of her women finds the truth that is proper to her and her environment.

What Marian Engel writes about is women who become conscious of the need to find their way through emotional predicaments that derive from their particular roles as women in the modern world. The predicaments are not new ones; what is new about the way they are treated is the sense that there are means of escape from them without denying or violating one's nature as a woman. Here—as in the books of other Canadian women novelists—there are sharp differences from the literature of the New Woman written at the turn of the century, mostly by men, like Ibsen and Shaw, like Wells and James. By such writers, the New Woman was observed as a phenomenon of the age; her struggle to establish a place in the world and shake off the dependence of the Victorian wife-and-mother was to be watched with interest and to be portrayed with sympathy. For after all, it was an age of liberation, and male writers hailed the emergence of women into freedom just as middle-class writers hailed the emergence of the workers into social and political consciousness.

Some fine feats of insight came out of that movement; Hedda Gabler and Major Barbara and Ann Veronica and the American lady who became the Princess Casamassima are remarkably true likenesses of types of women emerging out of the breakdown of the Victorian social order. But they remain characters seen from outside, no matter how penetrative the vision; in a sense there is always a double point of view at work in the plays and novels they dominate—the inward point of view of the woman who is at the centre of the work, and the shaping and external point of view of the man who creates her. It is not accidental that one of Bernard Shaw's most brilliantly written plays should have been a retelling in modern terms of the Pygmalion myth.

I do not think a writer like Marian Engel is really seeking a New Woman at all; that characteristically male vision was swept away in the storm of the first great war. She knows—unlike some of the more naive women's liberationists—that there is a feminine nature that is biologically and psychologically different from masculine nature, and she recognizes that this feminine nature has not changed in any meaningful way since the Greek poets created Helen and Penelope and Electra. What have changed are the social contexts that women inhabit, and the different perceptions that women and men have of the woman's role in those contexts.

But it is the way of perception that is different. For the sympathetic insight of the men writers who observed the New Woman, Marian Engel, like many other contemporary women writers, substitutes the empathetic insight, and one of the results is that while the situations of her women characters may in many respects be typical, the women themselves exist as characters lived through at all levels of their existence—physical, emotional, intellectual—by the novelist's understanding. They are individuals, and their ways of liberation, of self-recognition and self-integration, are individual.

In terms of the typology of situations, one can see Marian Engel's first six novels as a gallery of feminine roles in late twentieth-century Western society. *No Clouds of Glory* presents the woman as academic, challenging men in the career world; *The Honeyman Festival* the woman as the quintessential earth mother; *Monodromos* the woman as divorced wife moving back through surrogate sisterhood towards renewed individuality; *Joanne* the woman as wife and mother finding her way through the ruins of a failed marriage; *Bear* (whose fabulist aspect demands separate consideration) the woman as humanity recognizing and uniting with its animal nature; *The Glassy Sea* the woman as nun—humanity uniting reluctantly with its angelic nature. In establishing such a pattern, I am reminded of the building that is the central monument in *Bear*. Colonel Cary's splendid faceted house is octagonal in shape, and Marian Engel's present achievement is only a hexagon, but perhaps the real point of the house is not how many facets it contains, but that the light that falls from all of them is united in the great crowning lantern into a single luminosity. There is this kind of unity, built up light on light, to the corpus of Marian Engel's fiction.

*     *     *

At the opening of *No Clouds of Glory,* Sarah Porlock stands at an end which is a beginning.

> Of a sudden seven ducks . . . everything goes up in smoke. Job, family, *erotiko* and *agapo,* beginning of a reputation. Here I stand naked, if anyone had eyes to see, waiting for the evaluator; feeling, for that, almost nothing. Self-pity, perhaps, as if the doctor had commanded a salt-free diet. Simple, empty, in spite of myself nourished in hope: waiting for the new era to begin. Finally satisfied to be alone? Finally free?

The life on which Sarah looks back, after her father's death, after the two men she has loved have rejected her, after she has expelled herself from the academic life, seems in the end like a pattern of illusions, as she views it reminiscently with the present editing the past.

> Sarah is not the girl she was; truth has aged and been cobbled as well. Not even to myself do I tell it true, now. It has become One of My Funny European Stories.

Well, kid Sarah, that era has ended. You are about to remove yourself from a position whence you tell Funny European Stories. Say on, and purge.

It all begins, as she senses, in the feeling of unacceptance that makes her refer to herself as "Sarah Porlock, Bastard and Fool." From childhood she had been jealous of her beautiful, imperturbable nearest sister Leah, the prototype of a series of blonde bitches with whom the heroines of most of Engel's books have to contend.

Blonde Leah effortlessly moves herself from the narrow rustic Ontario background into which the sisters are born and bred, to marry a chance-met wealthy Venetian and to move with bored ease through the fashionable places of Europe. Sarah takes the route of effort in the hope that her academic achievement can prove, to her at least, that the ugly duckling is as good as her swan of a sister.

The homegrown, homespun world of small Canadian academies is splendidly satirized when Sarah moves up among her dullard colleagues, as a specialist in Canadian and Australian literatures: she discovers among the writers she studies "a host of Sarahs looking for themselves."

Sarah's quest for herself takes her off in the customary Canadian postwar pilgrimage to the cultural motherlands of Europe, where she prolongs a dull academic kind of affair with a fellow student, Joe. "Joe didn't belong to me. We were borrowers of each other, in need of a laugh or a poke, or a proofreading. . . ." Unexpectedly, invited with Joe to a *thé dansant* in a crumbling French château, she encounters and is outshone by Leah, masquerading as a rich American. To Sarah's surprise, Leah's husband finds her robust figure attractive as a change from his wife's gilded meagreness; he strikes the chord that has already made her feel: "before I am inevitably sealed and packed away in the academic I want once to deceive myself in this direction: become beautiful, vulgarly gorgeous, gross, wanted." For a while Sandro gives her these illusions as their smoky affair begins and continues, after Sarah's return to Canada as a full-fledged "lady Ph.D.," whenever Sandro's business takes him from Venice to North America.

But really, far from reassuring Sarah, far from building up her feminine confidence, the affair with Sandro has merely resurrected her sense of inferiority to Leah, who is clearly impervious to all challenges. Envious of the handsome children Leah has borne with superb indifference to Sandro, Sarah longs for her own child by him, whom she calls—in her reveries—Antonio. But the conditions of their relationship mean that, after being conceived, Antonio ends as the debris of an abortion, and this experience, followed as it is by Sandro's discreet withdrawal from their relationship and Joe's attachment to a crazed flower child—leads Sarah to the moment of truth when she recognizes that her academic career has been mere competitive pretentiousness. She is—she realizes with sickening insight —neither a literary genius nor an original scholar, not even an authentic *belle laide,* and she aggressively abandons all her dreams, even her dreams of succeeding by shock (she has been inhabiting a Toronto slum while teaching in her respectable little college), and sets off for Montreal. "Jump, or you'll die, Sarah," she tells herself. "And there'll never be green landscape or a sweet face again."

There is a crude apprentice directness about *No Clouds of Glory,* which Engel seemed to shed as soon as that book was finished, for nothing quite like its irascible manner, projected in veritable dum-dum bullets of sentences, ever appeared again in her novels. Once was often enough to declare that "in the country of the zombie the rebel lives," though the understanding of zombiedom and the permutations of rebellion do in various less explicit ways occupy her later novels. And always the need to risk a change ("Jump, or you'll die") is present. At an early stage in Engel's career—as W. H. New has remarked—"the search for an authentic identity formed the substance" of both *No Clouds of Glory* and of *The Honeyman Festival;* one can accept the phrase as appropriate to all of Engel's first six novels. And one can add that at no point does Engel suggest that any human being is exempt from that search or from the self-examination it necessitates; at the same time she is honest enough to recognize she must embark on the quest admitting the particular limitations of viewpoint that being a woman imposes on her.

*The Honeyman Festival,* Engel's briefest novel, draws in from the temporal disjointedness and structural eccentricity of *No Clouds of Glory* to observe the Aristotelian unities even more strictly than Joyce did in *Ulysses,* for while he allowed himself a day and night of twenty-four hours and the whole scope of Dublin, Engel restricts herself to about twelve hours of evening and night and the space of a single rambling house. But the evening is a Proustian one, and the house, which Minn Burge has allowed to be used for a party celebrating the Honeyman Festival, becomes an echo chamber in which the past reverberates, not only in Minn's memories but also in the people whom the party sweeps in from her past and deposits like flotsam before her.

Minn's present is dominated by pregnancy with her fourth child; she is married to a journalist who is at present away in Nepal, so that she has to handle the problems of the party herself. Her pregnancy is a riskier one than the others, and it draws her back mentally towards her earliest past, her childhood in the small western Ontario town, dominated by a stern mother and a puritan ethic of work; it "had once been the only place in the world, and all hers, and then she had found that that was hollow; and now she thought it was a fine place to have started her life."

Minn broke away, via a provincial university, into the European

Bohemia to which so many Canadians graduated in the 1950s and 1960s, the accepted place of escape and self-discovery. She departed in the company of a crazy scientist named Ziggy (who in one of Engel's later stories appears as an expert on taming gorillas) and falls in with the film producer Honeyman who, on the evening of the novel, is being celebrated in a festival at an arty local cinema that will spill over into the party at her house. To have consented in her condition to act as hostess is itself a Quixotic gesture to the past, and also a challenge to her present as a mother and housewife, to the present when her house is partly occupied by the flower children of a less motivated generation of rebels than her own. As the evening passes, she remembers Honeyman, seeing that youth in which she knew him shed of its romance, yet in its own way authentic:

> What a good rich life it was then, when you were young and had a Honeyman, and could walk into Paris offices and come out employed, dubbing, translating, rewriting a script, holding a pile of props at the edge of a set. It was no small thing to be equipped to survive.

Yet at the same time she sees how romance is being created out of what was never intended to be romantic, and the festival in which she has half-willingly become involved is an example; Honeyman, she recognizes, would have viewed such a celebration of him with contempt.

> But clearing glasses from the mantelpiece she found Reiner's folder and looked at the photograph of Honeyman and read the pseudo-scholarly text. God, they were making cult-figures as fast as they could find them; had Christianity gone out for film-worship? The man was a craftsman, knew what to do with a frame, how to build a sequence, but he wasn't Leonardo. The airs and graces they gave him he would have laughed at. What he wanted was money for a villa behind Cannes. What he loved were the blossoming dry Midi hills, like California, but with castles and good cheeses in them, best of both worlds. He made pot-boilers at Cinecittà and Westerns in Hollywood. It was a job, a thing he did, man. He crafted it, but he didn't open it up at the end, he wasn't an artist, he was only interested in the finite. He said he knew his limitations. He said the ones who thought they were artists always got into trouble. All he wanted was to do a good job and eat well, he said.

As the evening continues, actual inhabitants of Minn's past begin to appear: a college boyfriend, frayed by time; a Junior-League volunteer appointed to help with the problems of her pregnancy, who turns out to be "Jane-Regina Magill, the only girl she had absolutely hated in her life, the bitch-goddess of her year at boarding-school" (another detestable beautiful blonde); Honeyman's unbalanced son for whom she had at times played surrogate mother. And as the night ends it is not the past but the present she defends, as she thrusts her pregnant bulk into the doorway to prevent a policeman without a warrant molesting her hippy tenants. What Minn comes to, at the end of a night torn between the ideal of a free life she has carried over from her wild youth and the realities of her present with its multiple ties and obligations, is a recognition of the actuality one must accept without illusion.

> Whatever happens, the universe will roll on somehow. It's big enough to do without us, there's a comfort. The tides will ebb and flow, the moon rise even if she isn't cheese or snow. *Das ewig Weibliche* will whip us from her dog-cart. *Das ewig Maennliche* will slog across the moor.
>
> There will be war and murder and long winters and hot summers. You will have to have strong legs.
>
> We will sit in a circle longing for the lights of Moscow. We will bite each other's fingers out of boredom, to see the blood. We will continue to clean our houses. We will make artifacts.
>
> And the morning will come, and so will the night again. Won't it?

For self-recognition goes with recognition of the objective realities of existence, and both are conditions of survival.

There is already in *The Honeyman Festival* a characteristic and almost obsessive preoccupation with physical objects as the correlatives of mental states; it recurs in Engel's later books and gives some of its special solidity to her narrative manner. Minn is portrayed in a kind of panic, tidying up her room against the arrival of Jane-Regina with her prying and censorious eyes.

> Minn went down the long steep staircase, caressing the sticky bannister, to the back kitchen to crush the ice for Jane-Regina's daiquiri. She put the ice in the freezer (once again moving the snowball she had put away in a plastic bag for Louisa) and went to tidy the living-room, which belonged to their early, over-decorated period, when she had been clever with curtains and remnants and fringe, had had time to go to the sales and reconstruct the Victorian room; furniture collected annually from home, odd chairs and tables from the Salvation Army, half a dozen wicker plantstands containing dying aspidistras and ferns in the bay window; on the walls, articles associated with the lovers' game "our past": a case of surgical instruments which had originally (gleaming in a midnight store window on the Boulevard St. Germain) prompted them to go to bed, a row of covetable, childish wooden spoons, a bad map of Paris and a good one of Alexandria, a Majolica plate, a Portobello photograph: nonsense, all, but pleasing. The upholstery would have been more impressive in velvet rather than corduroy, and the staples were showing badly.

One notices in this list its selective particularity, the way it helps to set the tone of a place and a time and a personal history. One of Engel's special qualities as a novelist is the way in each of her books she gives a new situation in human relationships its own new physical world. And her passages of richly detailed description are what set the individual tone of these new worlds. Spectacular among them is the now famous list of the items for sale in the bazaar of the Cypriot city that is the setting of her third novel, *Monodromos:*

Lemons, fat-rinded oranges, bay on the branch (Daphnis), tomato paste on paper squares, Jerusalem artichokes, purple French artichokes, onions, potatoes, carrots, tin toys, frozen octopus from Greece, dead hanging sheep on hooks, rice puddings, Indian custard like rosewater junket, Armenian pancakes spread with meat and sumach—like the socca we had in the bar in Nice, behind the lawcourts, with wine mixed with lemonade—cheese pies, pumpkin pies, and curled sheets of dried apricot paste that look like sheets of fly poison put out in summer in a pie plate; water jars with vestigial penises and breasts; pin-headed penny banks like the Venus of Willendorf with the slot in the wrong place, Lapithos jugs with splashed copper in the glaze, bowls, plates, casseroles, Yoghourt pots, all undecorated, spindles, hand-made whiskbrooms, whorls. Poets don't know the domesticity of Byzantium, they're all too busy looking for mosaics, gyres and mechanical birds.

When Audrey Thomas reviewed *Monodromos* in *Canadian Literature* she noted with disturbance that "Cyprus lives and breathes and takes on depth through the heroine's observations," but that "the place is much more interesting than the people Ms. Engel chooses to write about." And this, I think, is just. *Monodromos* is a larger and more complex book than Engel's others, and this is mostly because she has been led into the temptation (and has not resisted) of presenting an exotic setting and a strange way of life in all their complexity and richness, and has produced, as some reviewers at the time remarked, a travel book in fiction rather than a real novel.

The real core of the book, the emotional situation with its moral implications, is in fact less substantial than those of Engel's briefer and sparser novels. Audrey, the heroine, is working in London and living with the poet Max when she receives a message that her divorced husband Lafcadio (generally known as Laddie) is in distress and needs her presence. She and Laddie parted years ago after she found him strangely engaged with a male friend in the loo; in Cyprus, while earning his living as a music teacher, he had let his homosexual inclinations flourish. Arriving, Audrey finds that Laddie's plight has been exaggerated by a well-meaning woman friend; though poor and distressed at being deserted by his lover, Lord Edward, he strongly resents Audrey's presence even if he may have perversely engineered it. However, since she has no money to go back to England, she settles down in one of the cells of the converted Armenian priory in which he lives, posing for the skeptical local people as his sister.

There is really not enough blood left in the relationship between Audrey and Laddie to sustain a novel as long as *Monodromos,* and Audrey's liaison with Max becomes little more than a narrative device which enables her to report in letter form at least some of her experiences and impressions, and so vary the pattern of reminiscent narrative and diary notes. When Max dies the appropriate tears are shed and lushes drink libations, but one feels it is a matter of not striving "officiously to keep alive." The real substance of the book lies in Audrey's explorations of the island, her contacts with the inhabitants, her relationships with the other expatriates. There are some beautifully sharp character sketches, but the best of them are of minor figures, such as feckless Greek traders and English gents gone to seed, who are never deeply involved in Audrey's life. The one amorous relationship of her stay on Cyprus, with the cultured Xanthos, is blandly uninteresting in comparison with the highly comic account—packed with topographical description and local colour—of her visit to an island monastery, famous for its icon of a dog-headed saint, where the bishop, excited by the rank stench of her unwashed body after several days travelling on a donkey through the mountains, tries valiantly to rape her.

All of this results in a very readable book, vivid and racily written, but the point it makes about human relationships is curiously muted in comparison with the conclusions of Engel's other novels. It is that when they last long, the very continuity creates a bond, and that bond cannot be rejected however sordidly habitual it may seem, and however much it may be twisted by resentment. So we have Audrey parting from Laddie; Lord Edward has returned, bringing two pretty Arab boys, and Audrey has been warned that the Cypriot police are unlikely to look favourably on foreign pederasts who are not content with local catamites.

> I have not had time [says Audrey in the letter to the dead Max that ends the book] to talk to him about the boys because the day after I returned from the mountains, I moved in with Aphroulla, and I know, now, if I speak about the boys, how he will react. But I suppose I ought to say something to him. I have known him longer than I have known anyone else in my life except my mother and my brother. Old friends are a kind of serial story, which is why you keep up with them even after they've turned into enemies.

She talks about the boys and Laddie reacts scoffingly, as she has expected, and she departs. And even though a Cypriot says to Audrey after she has left, "Do not mourn for that island, it is not a person, only a place," it is the place that resonates in the mind and memory after one has read *Monodromos,* not any single person. But that is in the tradition of novels that English-speakers write about the Mediterranean. *Monodromos* is in the succession from *South Wind, The Rock Pool* and *The Alexandria Quartet,* which makes good company if one is willing to accept fiction that is somewhat less than fully human in its scope of comprehension.

Marian Engel's fourth novel, *Joanne,* brings one sharply back into the heart of a disintegrating human relationship and keeps one there until the end. And, to anyone involved in the actual processes of writing, the story of its conception and genesis is interesting. For *Joanne* is one of those rare pieces in modern times, a novel produced to order as a serial by a fastidiously craftsmanly writer. Dickens did it and so did other major novelists at least as late as Thomas Hardy, but it has not happened often in our age. When the CBC invited Marian Engel to write a fictional diary of a woman whose marriage was on the rocks, and to do it in four- or five-minute episodes to be broadcast five days a week, she was intrigued, perhaps alarmed, certainly challenged, and accepted the assignment after only a moment's thought. She found that for the time being she had to abandon her accustomed ways of writing: "The ordinary literary process is a very slow one. It allows for all the rewriting, rethinking and reconsideration in the world. It turns even the most mercurial people into tortoises. *Joanne* was another kettle of soup: on-the-spot fabrication."

Marian Engel discovered—as anyone does who writes to a great extent for radio—that "*Joanne* increased my facility," led her to rely less on "fine writing" and to discover how, when a continuous narrative is not possible, "you can build with vignettes and epiphanies." She also found, like Dickens, that the serial rendering of a novel created a continuing two-way relationship between writer and audience, and as she went along she sometimes changed direction in response to the flow of criticism.

When it was all broadcast, Engel recognized that *Joanne,* written in the choppy form of short daily scenes, had to be extended to give it the shape and continuity needed for publication as a book and that the prose had to be changed in places "because print is more formal than speech." But the episodic form of diary entries, roughly equal in length, remained, and gave the book a special rapidity and urgency that differentiate it from Engel's other novels.

The basic situation is simple. Joanne's marriage is breaking up. Her husband is becoming inexplicably hostile. It is obvious that he is tired of their relationship, and what seemed at first a rational—if resentful—arrangement for their parting is worked out. As Joanne realizes: "Marriage, like anything else worth having, is hard work. Unifying two independent spirits requires an enormous effort. We tried to do it through our lifestyle—with things, objects, possessions. It didn't work." At this point the whole situation changes, because Joanne's mother-in-law kidnaps her two children. After a few days of hectic plotting and amateur detective work, Joanne manages to steal them back, and then herself vanishes with them to an old-fashioned western Ontario town she had known in the past. At this point Joanne is really slipping back towards the childhood whose difficulties she starts to remember as her marriage begins to die.

Her father, a violent embittered man, regularly beat his wife with a blackthorn stick. "When I was five my mother pulled herself together and marched the three youngest of us down that clay road and away." And this is what Joanne essentially does now, starting out again with an ill-paid secretarial job in an old-fashioned school, and going to live in a so-called garden flat that is "hallmarked with the characteristics of the lower class in this country: linoleum, cheap paint, cracked ceilings, gold threaded upholstery, tippy tables." In one way it is shocking to her, since she has been accustomed for years to the showy, wasteful life of an executive's wife, and her children have known nothing but spoiled suburban prosperity. But in another way it is reassuring. She is dropping back into the safe womb of the past, when she lived in "a little house where a heap of children huddled on straw mattresses in a stuffy attic," while her children enjoy the novelty of a situation in which so much has to be improvised. There is a touch of smugness to this latter part of the book, a too easy identification with the smalltown way of life, and the ending does read as if, when Marian Engel was mastering the craft of writing for radio, her prose became slightly infected by the soap opera tradition.

> I look out of the window now; the sun is slanting low across the river, gilding the bridge and the Federal Building, whitening the stone foundry walls, glazing the ogival dome of the Globe Insurance Building. I think, we've started a new life here. It's not as easy and privileged as the old one was, but it has its own flavour. We have a few friends, we'll find more, we can go to the Y and the library, and out in the country to Rosie's and Merrill's. We've a landlord, a doctor, Mrs. Brodhurst and a list of babysitters. Why, we exist. That's a miracle.
>
> It's halfway to seeing life steadily and whole and probably as far as ordinary mortals like Jen and Andrew and me will ever get.

*Joanne*, I suggest, can best be regarded as an interesting sport among Marian Engel's novels. It brings one back quite sharply, after the bemusement with exotic scenes and historic echoes that characterized *Monodromos*, to the ordinariness of Canadian life, to the actuality of human relationships muddied by commercial values, to the realization that "faith, passion and innocence are too long out of style." And if it is marred by the simplistic approach imposed by its origins, and by a facility of feeling that too often slips into sentiment and *faux-naiveté*, it also represents an advance in fluency of prose and in clarity of construction whose effect is shown in two other Marian Engel novels, *Bear* and *The Glassy Sea*. The difference of quality between these books and the earlier Engel novels is remarkable, and *Joanne* must be regarded as the humble bridge that links the two periods and styles.

Both of them are written with a brilliance of craftsmanship so sustained and so spare that they emerge as marvellously luminous and self-sufficient artifacts. *Bear* is on one level a kind of animal story—a genre that has had an honourable past in Canada and—always—an essential ambiguity. On one side lay the temptation to anthropomorphize the animal in the British manner, to make him a human being in fur or feathers, hero or victim. On the opposite side (in the American manner) the animal was irrevocably the Other, emanation of the hostile wilderness and at the same time of the irrational forces within himself that nineteenth-century man feared as much as he feared those of the natural world. *Animal Farm* is a good example of the British variety; Faulkner's "The Bear" of the American. Canadian animal stories have been different from either.

Canadian writers ever since Charles G. D. Roberts have been turning back, in theme and symbol, towards primitive man's sense of man as part of the natural world and not as that Other whose separateness animals instinctively feel when they flee from human scent. Such writers recognize man's place in the natural world, his kinship with the animal world reflected in the power of his unconscious, which is both animal and spiritual in its nature. Recent novels like Margaret Atwood's *Surfacing* have testified to this awakening to the enigmatic relationships between man and his fellow creatures with their delicately balanced world of relationships. But none so far has made quite the same leap back towards early man's sense of closeness to the natural world as Marian Engel in the bizarre daring of *Bear*.

In choosing her central situation she has of course picked on one of the most persistent cults of human prehistory—that of the bear, whose skulls were found arranged in ceremonial circles in Neanderthal caves, who were killed and eaten with ceremony by Ainu and Haida alike, and about whose kidnapping of women and cohabiting with them there are a number of interesting Coast Indian legends.

*Bear*'s audacity is to bring such cults and legends into the modern Canadian world, and this essentially is what makes it a fable rather than a novel in the ordinary sense. It is a tale, told with impeccable plausibility, of an improbable encounter between human and animal and, like all true fables, it has not only its theme but also its moral.

*Bear* concerns a woman archivist whose emotional life has narrowed to a weekly copulation among the maps on her desk with the director of her institute, and who is given a chance to catalogue the contents of the house of a certain Colonel Cary. An acquaintance of Byron, Cary received as his grant of land in Upper Canada an island where he built a jewel of an octagonal house, lived an alienated British life that he transmitted to his descendants (the last of them a virile lady christened "Colonel" to meet the conditions of the original Cary will), and made his terms with the new land by becoming fascinated with bears to the extent of making their lore the subject of desultory lifetime research and of acquiring the first of a succession of pet bears.

The last of the pet bears is there when the archivist Lou arrives and the plot of *Bear* is Lou's growing erotic obsession with this aging and strong-smelling plantigrade. She swims with the bear, eats with him, caresses him, teaches him to thrust his tongue into her most private parts. In one intoxicating moment she witnesses his magnificent erection, but, on turning herself like Pasiphae in animal-fashion towards him, she is merely slashed reproachfully across the back with his needle-sharp claws. It is Homer, the neighbouring resort owner, who enters her with his long and serviceable prick; it is Bear she loves.

An absurd tale, on the face of it, but Marian Engel has the skill that makes the absurd credible in a way, it seems to me, writers like Mordecai Richler and Robertson Davies have never done in their more fantastic novels. She writes a plain kind of Defoesque prose, which makes everything, as Margaret Atwood remarked curiously in her comment on the book, "plausible as kitchens." The descriptive urge that ran wild in *Monodromos* is tamed into an obedient servant of the plot, and visual and tactile details are used skillfully to enhance the authenticity of the action. The bear is never made to act like a man; he remains convincingly animal throughout in his actions and reactions, even though there are times when his behaviour seems more canine than ursine. And poor Lou, used by a succession of men, rises through clouds of pathos into the self-integration of those who have pushed themselves to the margins of human possibility and survived. At the end, when the bear has been taken away by his Indian friends and Lou departs:

> She went up the river slowly. She felt tender, serene. She remembered evenings of sitting by the fire with the bear's head in her lap. She remembered the night the stars fell on her body and burned and burned. She remembered guilt, and a dream she had where her mother made her write letters of apology to the Indians for having to do with a bear, and she remembered the claw that had healed guilt. She felt strong and pure.

But pure, one feels inclined to emphasize, because of the rejecting claw that maintained the proper distances in an ordered ecology. A prosaic person, Marian Engel is, in the best sense of knowing just what prose can do, so that in *Bear* the earthy and the fantastic dance in proper harmony.

Two other bits of writing came compellingly into my mind when I was reading and thinking about *Bear*. The more obvious was, of course, *Surfacing*. After all, it is also on an island in the Canadian Shield that Atwood's narrator has her confrontation with the wilderness, and the narrator becomes aware of the wildness within her and is reconciled. But there, perhaps, is the operative element of difference. The wilderness is *within* Atwood's narrator; it is a matter of coming to terms with oneself and hence with the natural world. The difference is crucial and represented formally in the fact that *Surfacing* is told in the first person and hence is avowedly subjective, and *Bear* is told in the third person and has the curiously transparent objectivity of a fable. But this does not prevent the two novels from complementing each other and forming a composite paradigm for humanity as an endangered species.

The other work that occurred to me was Earle Birney's "The Bear on the Delhi Road." And here I could not help sensing an advance—by both Atwood and Engel—out of the simplism of another generation. For with Birney it is really a matter of alternatives. Either the bear is left in his own world, away from man and his culture, to follow:

>     the tranced
>   wish forever to stay
>   only an ambling bear
>   four-footed in berries

or he is subjected to human demands, as his teachers

>     rear this fellow up
>   to lurch     lurch with them
>   in the tranced dancing of men

For an Ainu or a Haida there would be no such division; no bear would be "only an ambling bear," and the alternative to exploiting him would not be merely to ignore him, but to recognize kinship, as Marian Engel has done.

Although in appearance *The Glassy Sea*'s story of an Anglican nun's withdrawal into secular life and marriage and her eventual return to conventional religion may seem very different from *Bear*, it does in fact complement the earlier novel in the sense of going back to the dual basic nature of man, so that where *Bear* was based on a recognition of the animal within us, *The Glassy Sea* pleads the acceptance that we are angelic also. *Bear* is a fable of reconciliation with the natural world to which by origin we belong; *The Glassy Sea* is a psychological novel about the search for the spiritual perfection to which we aspire.

*The Glassy Sea* is such a sufficient novel that, reading it and contemplating this essay, I felt for the moment tongue-tied. What more was to be said than the book contained—and contained with such marvellous clarity that the mediation of the critic did not seem necessary? One emerges of course from such dumbfoundings, as one does from stagefright, but enough of the feeling they generate remains to leave me convinced, in this case, that *The Glassy Sea* is a book exceptional in its intensity and its almost perfect crafting, and even an exceptional one in terms of Marian Engel's other books.

It is not that *The Glassy Sea* falls outside the basic patterning of Engel's fiction, which is always "about" women caught in crises, and usually the crisis of failed marriage. It is rather that she has used this customary predicament to produce a remarkable meditation on faith, hope and charity and on the impossibility of being Mary if you are indeed Martha. The novel really combines an elaborate parable, in which the theological points are expertly made, and a deeply human drama of the interplay of existential facts and spiritual verities within a single life.

*The Glassy Sea* has a certain topicality, since it was written during the late 1970s, at a time when the tide of nuns escaping from their convents was beginning to turn, as more and more women scarred by marriage began to feel the need for some kind of religiously oriented refuge from the world. Its leading character—Rita Heber, later Sister Mary Pelagia, then Rita Bowen and finally Sister Mary Pelagia again—goes through all these stages, being attracted into a small Anglican order, the Eglantine Sisters, going back into the world to marry and bear a hydrocephalic child, seeing her marriage collapse, and, after a period living alone beside a deserted Maritime shoreline, returning at the request of her bishop to become the mother superior of her former convent, with the mission of turning it into a useful institution in the late twentieth-century world.

It is largely a memory novel. It begins in the present, with Mary Pelagia back in the great Victorian house that became the convent. The nuns with whom she once lived are dead or dying. She is waiting in the empty building for the novices of the renewed order to appear. She has gone through her consecration and the clergy who officiated have departed. One of them was the bishop, Philip Huron, and she now sits in the kitchen, brewing tea and reading the immense letter which she had written to him the previous summer from her seaside solitude, explaining why she could not fit in with his plans to re-establish the Eglantines and make her—the last real survivor of the older order—its mother superior.

The letter actually forms four-fifths of the novel. Although it is protestation, it is also confession, and in some ways very Augustinian in its probing of motives and descriptions of spiritual ambushes, if one can imagine an Augustine capable of irony who had also read Kierkegaard and Heidegger. But at the same time, it is an extraordinary study of the way society shapes the expression of religious impulses and often turns them awry. Religious experience is highly personal, as lonely a process as artistic creation, but it is also universal, and the voices of the mystics echo each other from religion to religion and from century to century with a surprising uniformity. But as soon as the manifestation of religion becomes collective, then social forms inevitably affect it, as institutions and their rituals seek to channel its impulses into accepted ways. It is the attempt of the individual seeker to find his or her own route through these patterned labyrinths that provides much of the drama of the religious life, with which Marian Engel is essentially concerned.

Rita Heber's religious life begins at a United Church in backward rural Ontario and is embodied first in the sound of rejoicing hymnary.

> We sang, though, in that church. Oh, we sang. It was the hymns that made the theology, not the preaching, which was so often done by temporary ministers, or students with many charges, men in black gowns with tabs for ties, so that they looked like professors, but not quite. It wasn't they who made the church, even when we had a whole half-share in one of our own with East China, it was the hymns. We flung them out like a banner, and . . . when we sang, we sang as one foundation.

She begins to awaken to other dimensions of the religious life when, one summer, a few encounters onward, she goes to a retired Anglican clergyman for tutoring. He leads her through the English poets to the religious ones: "Donne, Herbert, Vaughan, Crashaw." They bring that special tone of Anglican devotion one so associates with seventeenth-century verse, and when Rita does enter Mr. Laidlaw's church—a rather High one—it is for the words rather than the sound that she goes.

> I went to Mr. Laidlaw's church for the language, as many students of English literature do. It seemed sane and dignified and, above all, stately; the hymns had no salvationist gore in them; it sanctified the saints. It was the place I belonged in, as a student of English literature.

It is through Mr. Laidlaw, who is their confessor, that she first visits the Eglantine Sisters and eventually becomes one of them. Her vocation is always uncertain, for her feelings seem to hover between the spiritual and the aesthetic, which is the besetting temptation of High Anglicanism, and when spiritual understanding appears to come to her, it is always fragmentary, evanescent.

> Perhaps that is what attracted me to Eglantine House; I sensed in my first visit there that there was something beyond my grasp, something that flitted in and out of my consciousness like a moonbeam, a firefly, or a broken rainbow on a hall carpet that might be there possessed; and it was indeed in Mary Rose's office that I sometimes, fragmentarily, understood that firefly—love, grace, understanding itself; and then I was happy.

As Sister Mary Pelagia, Rita endures the benevolent duplicity of Mary Rose, the mother superior, who, seeing she is not fitted for the completely cloistered life of prayer and meditation, invents the benign fiction that the convent is poor and needs someone who will work outside and earn money for subsistence, and sends her to teach in various schools beyond the convent gardens. As the years go on, and the older nuns become more feeble, Mary Pelagia has to share more and more in the administration of the house. The difficulties of both teaching and in her other hours virtually running the convent when Mary Rose is sick seem to destroy the very aim with which she had joined the Eglantines. "My spiritual life had died—if it ever existed—in the practical details of the house."

She had come as Mary—part of her conventual name—and she had turned into Martha, and in Martha's role at this time in her life she could see no religious value. In accordance with the other half of her conventual name, she has the Pelagian hungering after perfection, and her religious life has brought her nowhere near it.

Nor does her life outside, when wifehood and motherhood seem equal challenges to her longing to be perfect, and she fails in both roles, and becomes the victim of a sanctimonious predator, whose condition for maintaining her at subsistence level after their divorce is that she should live in virtual retreat on the Maritime shoreline where the birds become her most constant companions. And there, in inaction, she gets as near perfection as she ever will. At the end of her great letter to Philip Huron, when she has recounted all the vagaries of her life up to the present, she tells him:

> Now I'm the crazy lady by the shore. That is what I want to be. No mystic, gnostic, hermetic, self-flagellating solitary anchoress; but a woman living by the shore. She reads a lot. Gets a little mail. Walks (but not naked; what would the locals think?) a little when the tide is out. Plays solitaire, thinks, not about her loss, but about her gain; this world, this finally painless life.

But the flaws of all teachings of inaction, except perhaps for the Taoist overflowing with nature, is that they are ultimately life-denying. In the end Mary Pelagia finally re-emerges, as Rita Bowen finally agrees to the urgings of Philip Huron and his emissary, Brother Anthony, and in the conversation she has with Anthony after her consecration the theme arises.

"Oh, Anthony, there always will be a reservation in me, if that's what you're worried about. Why do you think she called me Pelagia?"

"Mary Rose? Why?"

"Not for Aphrodite, I can tell you that. Oh, it's my ghastly Puritan background, the perfectionism. I can't work it out of myself. You can't either."

"I'm no Pelagian."

"Don't take umbrage. It was drummed into us both at school and at Sunday school: 'Be ye perfect as I am perfect.' "

"One can't."

"But one tries. And perfection is death."

"You said it was perfect by the sea."

"It was. But it was a kind of death."

The return to life means the return to life's material obligations. If the Eglantine Sisters are to be refounded in the late twentieth-century world, they can no longer provide merely a retreat for gentlewomanly contemplatives. As Mary Pelagia thinks, after she has reread the great letter she wrote to Philip Huron: "The religious life is a luxury in times of war," and she considers that she finally accepted the call to service because "there is a war on now" and she was "brought up to believe that sensible people rolled up their sleeves and pitched into the war effort."

It is to Florence Nightingale rather than to the women contemplatives she once aspired to imitate that Mary Pelagia is driven back when she now seeks a model.

What interested me most was, of course, her relationship with her mother; what caught me up was the way she later despised ladies, particularly the religious ladies—both Catholic and Protestant nuns—she took with her to the Crimea (though some of the Sellonites were excused, if I remember). The need, she said, was not for soul-saving, but for life-saving. When men are dying in corridors running with filth, you get down on your knees and scrub, not pray; when governments have to be convinced, you collect statistics, not tears; when men are dying you apply bandages of sterile cotton, not of prayer.

The war that Mary Pelagia sees raging around her is "the battle of the sexes," the men "running scared" because of the rise of feminism and acting out "a ghastly woman-hate" that is in the air, and the women "responding with either aggression or fear." Mary Pelagia refuses to react with the sex hatred that her experience with her former husband Asher Bowen might lead her to feel. "I don't believe we're essentially better or essentially worse than men."

And so Mary Pelagia has come by her own route to the Pauline equation in which charity turns out to be greater than either faith or hope. Her lack of spiritual experience, her irreversible involvement in the world, have led her to the point of challenging Christian doctrines when she refuses to accept "that stuff about women bringing sin into the world and therefore having constantly to be beaten for it." As for hope, in the conventional Christian sense, when Brother Anthony challenges her to declare her belief in an afterlife, she shelves the question, and later she declares, "I'm living in the here and now," and clearly means this in an existential way, in the way that led Camus to warn us against the delusiveness of hope, which prevents one living one's life and one's death to the full. But charity remains, the need to support and help others, to fight the battle of life without hatred. "It is easier to choose to be a Martha in a war."

But in becoming Martha, she remains Mary, and Pelagia also. If it had not been for the spiritual search, the search for perfection that seemed to fail, she would never have seen the strand of meaning in the chaos of brutal existence that led her to choose in the end a life of service. As Marian Engel rightly understands and rightly shows, the spiritual house has many mansions, and Martha—as the sister of Mary—has found her place in all religious systems. Even Hinduism has its role for the Karma Yogin, the person who finds his way through action, so long as he does not covet action's fruits.

What is especially striking about *The Glassy Sea* is the feeling one has of its universal application. Sister Mary Pelagia's experience, like the experiences of all Marian Engel's leading characters, is a feminine one; it is, in its specificity, the kind of life in which only a woman could be involved, and it is seen through feminine perceptions in an introspective first-person novel. Yet there is no exclusiveness about the vision. Any sensitive reader, whatever his or her sex or age, can empathetically enter into and understand Mary Pelagia's life and her acceptance of the final calling.

But *The Glassy Sea* is much more than an eloquent statement of the relationship between spirituality and works in the religious life. It succeeds as a novel for quite other reasons, and not least because Mary Pelagia is so convincing a human being in all her weakness and strength that we believe in the didactic structure of the novel because we believe in her and in the intensely credible world she inhabits. *The Glassy Sea* is Marian Engel's best novel. It is beautiful, concise and positively exemplary in the way every word tells and adds; the compassion, the lyricism, and the resonance of prose that throughout characterize Engel's novels find here their most flawless expression.

Thus, like all of Marian Engel's books, *The Glassy Sea* is to be valued for a great deal more than its content. Others have written about the difficulties of faith, the experience of losing one's life to find it, and have failed to be more than didactic because they have lacked the right kind of imagination. In this connection our appreciation of Marian Engel reflects the change that has taken place recently in our expectations of Canadian fiction; we are far less concerned with what is said than we were in the days of Hugh MacLennan's great fictional sermons on our national problems, and far more concerned with the way of telling, with the quality of the work as artifact as well as with its relevance as statement. Marian Engel's prose style, with its excellent simplicity and perfect pitch, may well—even more than her imaginative characterization—have been her prime virtue as a writer.

# 7

# THE PLOTS OF LIFE

## *The Realism of Alice Munro*

The short story has long been a favoured genre among Canadian writers. From Duncan Campbell Scott and Stephen Leacock, the succession has been continuous, including writers like Morley Callaghan in the 1920s and Sinclair Ross in the 1930s, and continuing to contemporary storytellers like Mavis Gallant and Audrey Thomas, W. D. Valgardson and John Metcalf.

The devotion of Canadian writers to the story is all the more striking since it has never been a very profitable medium and for a long period during the 1940s and 1950s it was hardly publishable, for the popular magazines had ceased to print short fictions and the publishers to accept collections of them. But the writers kept on producing them, and for a long time the only considerable outlet for them was the CBC, where Robert Weaver would accept them for broadcast on radio and then publish the best of them in anthologies issued by the Oxford University Press.

It was during this discouraging period that Alice Munro began to write and to submit her stories to Weaver, who immediately recognized the unique combination of a documentary approach and a clear luminous style that gave them their special feeling of magic realism. Later, Alice Munro's work was more widely recognized and found publishers. She turned to novel writing as well, but remained essentially a tale teller, and her novels became discontinuous series of episodes differing from books of stories mainly because they centred on a single heroine and were arranged roughly in the chronological sequence of a life. Any episode in any of her novels can be taken on its own and read as a self-contained story, and the fact that they were turned into novels resulted from the demands of publishers rather than from the writer's inclination. But they were never harmed by this kind of arrangement. In whatever she has written, Alice Munro has remained *par excellence* the storyteller.

> *But the development of events on that Saturday night; that fascinated me; I felt that I had had a glimpse of the shameless, marvellous, shattering absurdity with which the plots of life, though not of fiction, are improvised.*
>
> Alice Munro, *Dance of the Happy Shades*

There is a challenging ambivalence in Alice Munro's stories and her open-ended episodic novels, a glimmering fluctuation between actuality and fictional reality, or, if one prefers it, a tension between autobiography and invention which she manipulates so superbly that both elements are used to the full, and in the process enrich each other.

The paperback edition of Munro's second novel, *Who Do You Think You Are?*, bears on its cover the reproduction of a neorealist painting by Ken Danby, called "The Sunbather." It has no illustrative function; none of the episodes that make up the novel concerns or even mentions sunbathing. Yet it is hard to think of a painting that could have been better chosen to convey the special tone and flavour of Munro's writing.

A girl sits naked on a partly shaded patch of grass, her knees drawn up, her arms resting on them, her cheek resting on a wrist. Everything is rendered with the meticulous exactitude that only tempera, as a medium, makes possible—the tones of the gently tanning skin perfectly caught, the grass blades spiky yet pliable in the darkening green of high summer; the girl's face shows neither joy nor discontent, but a kind of indrawn pensiveness. Yet the realism, precise and particular as it may be, is much more than mimetic. The artist is not merely representing life, not merely recording how a particular girl with rather greasy hair and a largish bottom looked when she sat on the grass on a certain day in July. He is creating an image, outside time and place, that stands in our minds not merely as a painted surface but as an epitome, a focussing of several generalities that come together in its eternal moment—generalities like youth and girlishness and the benison of sunlight and the suggestion of fertility that we sense in the girl's broad hips and at the same time in the springing green of the grass and weed leaves among which she sits.

And this, except that she is using words rather than paint to impress her images on the mind, is very near to what Alice Munro tries to do. Just as magic realist painters create a kind of superreality by the impeccable presentation of details in a preternaturally clear light, and in this way isolate their images from mere actuality, so Alice Munro has combined documentary methods with a style as clear as the tempera medium in painting. In this essay I propose to discuss the methods in the hope of illuminating the ends.

Alice Munro has always been rightly reluctant to offer theoretical explanations of her methods, for she is quite obviously an antidogmatic, the kind of writer who works with feeling ahead of theory. But even on the theoretical level she is shrewd in defining the perimeters of her approach, perhaps negatively rather than positively. She once, for example, in an essay written for John Metcalf's *The Narrative Voice*—entitled "The Colonel's Hash Resettled"—cautioned against attempts to read symbolism excessively into her stories. And she was right, for essentially her stories are what they say, offering their meaning with often stark directness and gaining their effect from their intense visuality, so that they are always vivid in the mind's eye, which is another way of saying that she has learnt the power of the image and how to turn it to the purposes of prose.

Her visuality is not merely a matter of rendering the surface, the realm of mere perception, for she has understood that one of the great advantages of any effective imagist technique is that the image not merely presents itself. It reverberates with the power of its associations, and even with the intensity of its own isolated and illuminated presence. Munro herself conveyed something of this when John Metcalf, remarking on the fact that she seemed to "*glory* in the surfaces and the textures," asked whether she did not in fact feel " 'surfaces' not to be surfaces," and she answered that there was "a kind of magic . . . about everything . . . a feeling about the intensity of what is *there*."

When Alice Munro first began to write, her work was undervalued, except by a few exceptionally percipient readers like Robert Weaver, because her tales of Ontario smalltown life were taken to be those of a rather conventional realist with a certain flair for local colour. And realism at that time, following its decline in the visual arts, was going into a somewhat lesser eclipse in literature. Canada was becoming aware of modernism, and this meant that for a time at least writers were concerned with thematic and symbolic fiction rather than with anything that savoured of the mimetic.

Alice Munro has always been one of those fortunate and self-sufficient writers who never really become involved in movements or in literary fashions. From her start she had her own view of life, largely as she had lived it herself, and her aim was to express it in a fiction distinguished by craftsmanship and clear vision rather than by self-conscious artifice. It was a curiously paradoxical method of self-cultivation and self-effacement that she followed, for she has always written best when her stories or the episodes in her novels are close to her own experience in a world she knew, yet at the same time she cultivated a prose from which authorly mannerisms were so absent that it seemed as though the stories had their own voices. In the process Alice Munro became, next to Marian Engel, perhaps Canada's best prose stylist.

But linked to the pellucid clarity of that voice—or voices—there was always the intense vision—and in this context I mean vision as a power of visualizing. The comparison with magic realist painters that I made early in this essay is not merely an analogical one, for Munro is always deeply concerned with describing, with establishing scenes and people clearly in the mind's eye, and as in real life, so in her stories, we establish our conception of the character of people first by recognizing what they look like and how they speak, and then, such familiarity established, proceeding inward to minds and feelings. The photographic element in her presentation of scenes and characters as visualizable images is an essential factor in her writing.

The camera, of course, does not always lie, but through the photographer's conscious selectiveness and even more through the tendency of the lens to isolate the image from the chaos of actuality, it does offer us a different reality from that we normally perceive. In an interesting essay entitled "Alice Munro and the American South," J. R. (Tim) Struthers discussed the influence on Munro of writers like Eudora Welty and James Agee, and in doing so he talked of the way in which both these writers were fascinated by the possibilities of photography as a medium and its relationship to the kind of realistic writing they carried on. They saw the special literalness of photography not as a usurpation of the role of imaginative perception but as a means of enhancing it. In this sense Struthers talks of Munro as having a "visual or photographic imagination," and as an example he cites the ending of a harrowing little story of the scalding death of a baby—"The Time of Death"—in her first volume of short stories, *Dance of the Happy Shades*. The story drifts away into its intended anticlimax as the little shabby neighbourhood absorbs the minor tragedy, and then, at the very end, the narrator steps backward out of the stunted lives of the characters and stands like a photographer taking a middle-distance shot of the setting.

> There was this house, and the other wooden houses that had never been painted, with their steep patched roofs and their narrow, slanting porches, the wood-smoke coming out of their chimneys and dim children's faces pressed against their windows. Behind them there was the strip of earth, plowed in some places, run to grass in others, full of stones, and behind this the pine trees, not very tall. In front were the yards, the dead gardens, the grey highway running out from town. The snow came, falling slowly, evenly, between the highway and the houses and the pine trees, falling in big flakes at first and then in smaller and smaller flakes that did not melt in the hard furrows, the rock of the earth.

This paragraph, which terminates the story, is not only a good example of Munro's ability to create sharply visual images, still shots, that stir our feelings, in this case pitying despair; it also, by an echo many readers must have recognized, establishes her links with an earlier strain of realism, that of the James Joyce of *Dubliners*. The Joyce story I mean, of course, is "The Dead"; though the title of the story is reminiscent of Munro's, the main action of the story is quite different from hers, but in the end there is the final paragraph in which, as in "The Time of Death," the idea of death and the image of snow are brought together.

> Yes, the newspapers were right: snow was general all over Ireland. It was fall-ing on every part of the dark central plain, on the treeless hills, falling softly upon the Bog of Allen and, farther westward, softly falling into the dark mutinous Shannon waves. It was falling, too, upon every part of the lonely churchyard on the hill where Michael Furey lay buried. It lay thickly drifted on the crooked crosses and headstones, on the spears of the little gate, on the bar-ren thorns. His soul swooned slowly as he heard the snow falling faintly through the universe and faintly falling, like the descent of their last end, upon all the living and the dead.

The resemblance is tenuous and haunting, but the echo is quite clear. I am not suggesting that there is a conscious borrowing here, for, as all writers know, recollections of their reading can lodge in recesses of the mind until they are called up to fit into the *bricolage* that the imagination makes out of its resources of memory, conscious and unconscious alike. More important, perhaps, is the general resemblance between the kind of realism that Alice Munro developed during the 1950s and that of the early days of modernism, the kind of realism one finds not only in the early Joyce and—more lyrically expressed—in the early Lawrence, but also in their continental European contemporaries like Thomas Mann and Italo Svevo. There is the same tendency towards the *Bildungsroman,* whether manifest in a novel or disguised in a cluster of related stories; the sense of a society observed with oppressive closeness from within by someone who wants to escape; the concern for the appalling insecurities created by what was then called social climbing and now is called upward mobility; the agonized awareness of the perils of moving through the transitions of life, from childhood to adolescence, from adulthood to age.

While Alice Munro's approach has a great deal in common with this European realism of the early part of the century that trembled on the edge of modernism, without herself going forward—as some of the modernists like Joyce and Wyndham Lewis did—from realism to the extremes of for-malism, it has little in common with the kind of prairie writing that repre-sented realism for Canadians during the decades between the two great wars. Writers such as Robert Stead, Martha Ostenso and Frederick Philip Grove were concerned with the pioneer farmers and their struggle with the frontier lands of the great plains. Alice Munro was dealing with a society that had long passed out of the pioneer stage and represented a decaying es-tablished culture rather than a frontier one. The problem of those who in-habited it was not—as it had been with Grove's characters—to conquer the wilderness without being destroyed in the process, but to escape before one had been dragged down into the mental stagnation and physical decay of the marginal farmlands of Ontario.

Alice Munro herself grew up in this background, and much of the content of her stories and novels, if it is not strictly autobiographical, does echo the experiences of her youth. Like Del Jordan in *Lives of Girls and Women,* she was brought up on a farm where her father bred silver foxes without ever prospering greatly; her mother, like Del's, was a bright, frustrated woman with an iconoclastic cast of mind, who died of Parkinson's disease. Again, like more than one of her heroines, Munro married and moved west to British Columbia, which gave her another terrain for her stories; also like them, she stepped out of a disintegrating marriage and returned to Ontario. In other words, she wrote of what she knew best, and while each of her stories lives within its own complete world and is not a mere mirroring of the writer's life, it is inevitable that the fictions she drew out of the intensely remembered country of her childhood should be more convincing than those she conceived in British Columbia, where she was never completely at home.

Turning to the books themselves, there are three collections of short stories, *Dance of the Happy Shades, Something I've Been Meaning to Tell You* and *The Moons of Jupiter,* and two novels, *Lives of Girls and Women* and *Who Do You Think You Are?* They have appeared at fairly symmetrical intervals, between three and four years from one book to the other, and up to now they have alternated in form, a novel of related episodes following a collection of miscellaneous stories.

*Dance of the Happy Shades* appeared in 1968. It was a late date in terms of Munro's writing life, for she had been publishing stories sporadically since the early 1950s, and I remember when I met her round about 1955 I did so with pleased recognition, since I had already read and admired some of them. I am sure I became aware of them through Robert Weaver, who— more than anyone else—"discovered" her, broadcasting her stories on various CBC programs he ran.

It was only in the later 1960s, largely because of the success with which Weaver had introduced stories to radio audiences, that publishers once again began accepting collections of stories and finding that willing readerships existed. Once Munro's *Dance of the Happy Shades* appeared, her acceptance by Canadian readers was assured, and her later volumes were successful not only in Canada but also in the United States, where the marginal agrarian communities she portrayed were recognized as familiar, and where reviewers, ignorant of other Canadian writers, almost automatically compared her with American analogues like John Cheever and Joyce Carol Oates. In fact, like Al Purdy with his poetic rendering of the "degenerate Loyalist" heritage of Ameliasburgh and thereabouts, Munro offers the portrait of a distinctively Canadian society and does it in a distinctively Canadian way. Her sense of the interplay of setting and tradition is impeccable, so that there are really two ways of reading Munro—the exoteric one of the reader who knows a good story when he comes upon it and reads it with enjoyment and not too much concern for authenticity, and the esoteric one of the Canadian who is likely to read it with a special sense of its truth to the life he knows.

Perhaps because, unlike the later collections of stories, it is gathered from the writings of a relatively long period—at least fifteen years as against three or four—*The Dance of the Happy Shades* is more varied and tentatively venturesome than the later volumes. It shows the author trying out different modes and approaches. There are stories, like "The Office," that rather self-consciously explore the problems of women setting out as writers in an unsympathetic environment. There are others, like "The Shining Houses," a study of the callousness young property owners can show in defending their "values" (such as the selling prices of their homes), that are as ambivalently suburban as anything by John Updike. "Sunday Afternoon" is a little social study, highly class-conscious for a Canadian writer, of the relations between a country girl hired to serve in a rich middle-class home and her brittle-brainless employers. And in "Thanks for the Ride" Munro makes a rare foray across the sex line and tells in the voice of an adolescent boy the story of his first lay; in fact, the point of view is deceptive, since the real interest of the story lies in the portrait of his partner, Lois, a fragile yet tough working girl, much used by men and yet—in her coarse independence—strangely inviolate.

Most of the remaining stories fall into a group of which the main theme is childhood and growing up in the Ontario countryside, with action centred sometimes on the farm operated by the father of the central character and sometimes in the nearby small town where the mother at times lives separately and where the girl attends school. The father-dominated farm represents the world of nature and feeling, a world devoid of ambition. The mother-dominated house in town represents the world of social and intellectual ambition, just as the school is the setting where the heroine establishes her relationships with her peers among the smalltown children but also develops her desire to escape into a broader world. In some of the stories the mother—living or remembered—is shown advancing into the illness—Parkinson's disease—that will accentuate the oddity which most of her neighbours have already mocked in her.

The three stories of childhood—"Walker Brothers Cowboy," "Images" and "Boys and Girls"—are perhaps the most important of this group, both for their vivid evocation of the decaying rural life a century after the pioneers of Upper Canada and for their delineation of the relationships between parents and children in hard times.

"Walker Brothers Cowboy," the opening story of the book, takes us to a time when the silver fox farm has failed and Ben Jordan has taken up peddling the patent medicines, spices and food flavourings distributed by Walker Brothers. The story—told by his daughter, who does not name herself—begins by relating this time of stress and scarcity to the slightly better past on the farm. The girl's mother, also unnamed, tries desperately to maintain self-respect in a situation she sees as a demeaning loss of social face, even though in fact she lives physically better in the town than on the farm.

> Fate has flung us onto a street of poor people (it does not matter that we were poor before, that was a different sort of poverty), and the only way to take this, as she sees it, is with dignity, with bitterness, with no reconciliation. No bathroom with a claw-footed tub and a flush toilet is going to comfort her, nor water on tap and sidewalks past the house and milk in bottles, not even the two movie theatres and the Venus Restaurant and Woolworths so marvellous it has live birds singing in its fan-cooled corners and fish as tiny as fingernails, as bright as moons, swimming in its green tanks. My mother does not care.

The father, more self-contained, more ironic, finds ways to live with depression conditions and salvage his pride. As the story opens we see him walking with his daughter beside Lake Huron and telling her how the Great Lakes were gouged out of the earth by the ice coming down from the north. Clearly the girl prefers her father's company to her mother's:

> She walks serenely like a lady shopping, like a *lady* shopping, past the housewives in loose beltless dresses torn under the arms. With me her creation, wretched curls and flaunting hair bow, scrubbed knees and white socks—all I do not want to be. I loathe even my name when she says it in public, in a voice so high, proud and ringing, deliberately different from the voice of any other mother on the street.

Travelling his route of the desperate dusty farmlands, Ben Jordan makes fun of his situation by improvising as he rides a kind of endless ballad of his adventures on the road, and this becomes a *leitmotiv* one day when he sets out with the girl and her brother and, leaving his Walker Brothers territory, takes them to a farmhouse where a woman who was once his sweetheart is living. The clean bare farmhouse with Catholic emblems on the wall and an old woman dozing in a corner becomes a kind of stage on which it is revealed to the girl that people we know may have dimensions to their lives of which to this point we have been unaware. The sense of something theatrical and unreal and different from ordinary life is given by the fact that Ben Jordan and his old sweetheart—Nora Cronin—name each other, but nobody else in the story is named. The strangeness of the hitherto unknown past is framed within the nameless ordinariness of the present.

In "Images" a different kind of framing takes place. The story begins with the girl, again unnamed and again mainly a spectator, remembering the coarse cousin, Mary McQuade, who comes in to act as a kind of nurse in family crises, and who is now filling the house with her overbearing presence because the mother is ill. The father, once again Ben Jordan but now an unspecified farmer, runs a trapline down by the river, and one day he and the girl go down to harvest the muskrats. On their way they encounter a crazy recluse, Joe Phippen, who patrols the river bank with an axe in search of imagined enemies. They go to the cellar where Joe has been living since his house burnt down; for the girl it seems like an underground play house, except for its sinister smells and a mad cat whom the hermit feeds whisky. As they leave the cellar Ben Jordan cautions the girl when she gets back to tell nobody in the house about the axe. At table with Mary McQuade he relates the story of Joe and his drunken cat, and Mary is filled with indignation.

"A man that'd do a thing like that ought to be locked up."

"Maybe so," my father said. "Just the same I hope they don't get him for a while. Old Joe."

"Eat your supper," Mary said, bending over me. I did not for some time realize that I was no longer afraid of her. "Look at her," she said. "Her eyes dropping out of her head, all she's been and seen. Was he feeding the whisky to her too?"

"Not a drop," said my father, and looked steadily down the table at me. Like the children in fairy stories who have seen their parents make pacts with terrifying strangers, who have discovered that our fears are based on nothing but the truth, but who come back from marvellous escapes and take up their knives and forks, with humility and good manners, prepared to live happily ever after—like them, dazed and powerful with secrets, I never said a word.

In this story the filial link is complete. The father puts his trust in his daughter, and she keeps it in a kind of complicity to protect the strange and eccentric and unpopular in human behaviour—a complicity that will re-emerge in Munro's fictions.

But in "Boys and Girls" the trust between father and daughter is broken, and that is one of the complex aspects of growing up, involving as it does the girl's gradual realization of the difference between the sexes that in the end, and no matter what Freud may have said, makes fathers see sons as their successors and makes men stand together.

The action of this story takes place entirely on the fox farm. In a passage of admirably clear and restrained description Munro creates the feeling of the place and details the daily tasks the girl performs as she helps her father, keeping the pens supplied with water and spreading grass over them to prevent the foxes' pelts from being darkened by sunlight. Her little brother also helps, but she jealously guards the main tasks for herself and resents her mother's attempts to trap her into household tasks. The curiously detached centre of all this activity is formed by the foxes, which despite generations of captivity have not ceased to be wild animals, hostile and intractable.

> Naming them did not make pets out of them, or anything like it. Nobody but my father ever went into the pens, and he had twice had blood-poisoning from bites. When I was bringing them their water they prowled up and down on the paths they had made inside their pens, barking seldom—they saved that for nighttime, when they might get up a chorus of community frenzy—but always watching me, their eyes burning, clear gold, in their pointed, malevolent faces. They were beautiful for their delicate legs and heavy, aristocratic tails and the bright fur sprinkled on dark down their backs—which gave them their name— but especially for their faces, drawn exquisitely sharp in pure hostility, and their golden eyes.

One has the sense that although loyalty to her father would never allow her to admit the thought, these wild captive creatures have earned the girl's sympathy, and what happens shortly afterward seems to confirm this. She begins all at once to realize that her cherished position in the little world of the farm has become insecure.

> This winter also I began to hear a great deal more on the theme my mother had sounded when she had been talking in front of the barn. I no longer felt safe. It seemed that in the minds of the people around me there was a steady undercurrent of thought, not to be deflected, on this one subject. The word *girl* had formerly seemed to me innocent and unburdened, like the word *child;* now it appeared that it was no such thing. A girl was not, as I had supposed, simply what I was; it was what I had to become. It was a definition, always touched with emphasis, with reproach and disappointment. Also it was a joke on me.

The critical point comes shortly afterward, when her loyalties are all at once tested, and her response is as astonishing to her as it is to anyone else. Her father buys superannuated horses to slaughter for fox food; occasionally there will be a perfectly healthy animal among them for which in those days of increasing mechanization a farmer no longer has any use. A horse of this kind, whom they call Flora, is bought and kept over winter. She is a nervous animal, in some ways almost as proud and intractable as the foxes, and on the day she is being taken out to be shot she breaks away into a meadow where a gate has been left open. The girl and her brother are sent to close it.

> The gate was heavy. I lifted it out of the gravel and carried it across the roadway. I had it half-way across when she came in sight, galloping straight towards me. There was just time to get the chain on. Laird came scrambling through the ditch to help me.
>
> Instead of shutting the gate, I opened it as wide as I could. I did not make any decision to do this, it was just what I did. Flora never slowed down; she galloped straight past me, and Laird jumped up and down, yelling, "Shut it, shut it!" even when it was too late.

The horse, of course, is eventually caught and killed. And then, at midday dinner, her brother Laird tells on the girl:

> My father made a curt sound of disgust. "What did you do that for?"
>
> I did not answer. I put down my fork and waited to be sent from the table, still not looking up.
>
> But this did not happen. For some time nobody said anything, then Laird said matter-of-factly, "She's crying."
>
> "Never mind," my father said. He spoke with resignation, even good humour, the words which absolved and dismissed me for good. "She's only a girl," he said.
>
> I didn't protest that, even in my heart. Maybe it was true.

Two themes that will recur in Munro's later writing have been introduced: the burden of femininity, and the need to break free. They take on increased importance in her first novel, *Lives of Girls and Women*. This appears to have begun as another collection of stories that had enough of a common strain for the publisher to suggest she might turn them into a novel; its origin survives in the episodic and rather discontinuous structure of the book.

*Lives of Girls and Women* really completes the three stories I have just been discussing. The inconsistencies that existed between them are ironed out. Ben Jordan is still the father, and he runs a fox farm. The other characters are now all named—the girl becoming Della, the mother Ida, the brother changing to Owen—and with this naming everything becomes more precise in intent. Even the locality is named, for the farm is on Flats Road in the disreputable outskirts of the town of Jubilee, and the action alternates between the farm and the town where Ida takes a house where she and Del live except in the summer months.

The eight parts (significantly they are named but not numbered, so that they seem as much stories as chapters) really serve two functions. Each is an exemplary episode, self-contained and written, even though its characters spill over into other episodes, so that it can stand on its own. Yet, in the classic manner of the *Bildungsroman,* each episode builds on the last, revealing another side of Del's education in life, and as the progression is generally chronological, the continuity becomes that of a rather conventional novel, which begins in the heroine's childhood and ends when, as a young woman who has just allowed a love affair to divert her from winning a scholarship, she turns to the world of art and begins her first book.

The general inclination of *Lives of Girls and Woman* is indeed that of a portrait of the artist, and the first-person voice in which it is told is appropriate. The sense of art as a miracle, and the sense also of some special kind of intelligence that recognizes it, recurs in Munro's books, and it is linked with the idea that there are levels of access to truth which have nothing to do with what in the world passes for wisdom or intelligence.

This is shown quite clearly in the first chapter—or story—"The Flats Road," where the central character is an eccentric, Uncle Benny, who lives in a house full of junk on the edge of the bush and works as a hired man on Ben Jordan's fox farm.

> Probably the reason he kept on working for my father, though he had never worked steadily at any other job, was that my father raised silver foxes, and there was in such a business something precarious and unusual, some glamorous and ghostly, never realized, hope of fortune.

It is through Uncle Benny that Del and her brother begin to learn the perilous wonders of the natural world, represented by the great bog with its ravenous quicksands that stretches beyond his home; it is through him that they begin to recognize the inexpressible strangeness of human relations, represented by his disastrous adventure with a mail order wife.

> So lying alongside our world was Uncle Benny's world like a troubling distorted reflection, the same but never at all the same. In that world people could go down in quicksand, be vanquished by ghosts or terrible ordinary cities; luck and wickedness were gigantic and unpredictable; nothing was deserved, anything might happen; defeats were met with crazy satisfaction. It was his triumph, that he couldn't know about, to make us see.

Through the remaining chapters of *Lives of Girls and Women* runs the recurrent theme of people who, whether they intend or know it, "make us see." In "Heirs of the Living Body" it is the old great-aunts preserving a model of the idealized Victorian Ontario farm life as they provide for their brother, Uncle Craig, who spends his time writing a vast prosaic chronicle of the history of his district. When he dies, his sisters give Del his manuscript, remarking: "He had the gift. He could get everything in and still make it read smooth." This is what her narrative seeks to do—to get everything in that is of importance, and to "make it read smooth"—the realist's ambition.

In other chapters her mother's intellectual restlessness, her own search for a faith that seems to meet her poetic expectations of religion, and the frenetic dedication to a parody of art which inspires the hysterically flamboyant teacher Miss Farris who produces the school operetta every year (and having lived to the limit of her own style commits suicide), are all stages on the path to self-realization and to realization of the true nature of the world along which Del is proceeding. So in the strangely poised title chapter, "Lives of Girls and Women," Del's sexual fantasies about middle-aged Mr. Chamberlain come to a climax in more ways than one when he takes her out to the country and masturbates in her presence. It could have been a shocking and traumatic experience, but Del takes it in her ironic stride, already at heart the observer-writer to whom everything is grist to the mill. This comes out at the end of the chapter when her mother makes the statement that gives chapter and book their common title.

> There is a change coming I think in the lives of girls and women. Yes. But it is up to us to make it come. All women have had up till now has been their connection with men. All we have had. No more lives of our own, really, than domestic animals.

It sounds like a good feminist statement until, talking of self-respect, Ida Jordan makes it clear—at least in Del's mind—that she is talking about the caution and calculation which "being female" must impose on women: "Whereas men were supposed to be able to go out and take on all kinds of experiences and shuck off what they didn't want and come back proud, without even thinking about it. I had decided to do the same."

And this is precisely what Del attempts, becoming involved in a love affair with a fervent young Baptist, being so submerged emotionally as to lose the scholarship her brilliance at school has led her to expect, but retaining enough of a will to reject finally his desire to overpower her mentally as well as sexually; resisting his attempt to baptize her forcibly, she brings their relationship to an end.

Her love burnt out, her scholarly ambitions abandoned, Del turns to the writing she has dabbled with over the years, and starts on a highly Gothic novel about a Jubilee family all of whose children have ended tragically, in suicide or madness. And then, by chance, she meets one of the sons, recently released from his mental home, and finds how false her perceptions have been, like the distortions of a bad photographer. Writing, she decides, must be true to the spirit of what it portrays, to its often unsensational reality. And it is in this realization, we are free to assume, though Munro never says it directly, that Del has written the book we have just read.

If one reads it in connection with the earlier stories to which it is so closely linked, *Lives of Girls and Women* is a remarkable achievement both in human understanding and in technical prowess, presenting a psychologically and emotionally convincing episodic narrative of a questing child's development into a young woman on the edge of artistic achievement, and using a quasi-documentary form so effectively that we are always aware of the imagination shaping and illuminating the gifts of an obviously vivid memory.

The second novel, *Who Do You Think You Are?*, is a much less convincing book than *Lives of Girls and Women*, in both emotional and aesthetic terms. It too is a *Bildungsroman*, extending well beyond childhood into the darker times of middle age with its failed marriages, humiliating love affairs and mundane careers. The story of Rose, her upbringing in the rural slum of West Hanratty and her subsequent and doomed marriage to a rich fellow student, develops the theme of social climbing and its perils that is already present in *Lives of Girls and Women*. The novel—again a series of loosely connected episodes—is written in the third person, and this shift in point of view accompanies—perhaps even creates—a notable change in tone from the earlier book. In *Lives of Girls and Women* the sense of familiar authenticity was sustained by the fact that the aspirant writer as central character was assumed to be both participant and observer. In *Who Do You Think You Are?* the participant is observed, and there is a kind of hard objectivity to the book with its relentless social documentation of low life in West Hanratty at the end of the 1930s. Although Munro does make a largely successful attempt to project the inner life of her principal character, the other leading figures in the novel, like Rose's crochetty stepmother, Flo, her violent father and her snobbish husband, are shallow projections, almost caricatures, portrayed with none of the feeling and understanding that characterized the presentation of the father and mother, Ben and Ida Jordan, in the earlier novel.

Yet, though the general tone of *Who Do You Think You Are?* is at once harsher and more brittle than that of *Lives of Girls and Women*, there is a variation of quality within the book, and the first four chapters, which deal with childhood in Ontario, are the most effective. When the action moves into other places, notably the alien realm of British Columbia, the documentary background becomes more uncertain, and as Munro deals with the problems of adults living out their erotic fantasies, she seems too near her subject for the special kind of luminous objectivity that characterizes the stories of childhood and adolescence to develop.

A similar criticism applies to the later stories contained in *Something*

*I've Been Meaning to Tell You* and *The Moons of Jupiter*. Reading them, one becomes aware how little Munro has changed as a writer since the early period of the 1950s and the 1960s when she first attracted the attention of readers. She is still at her best as the magic realist. She has not moved, like so many of her contemporaries, into fantasy, or into an experimental use of memory like that of Margaret Laurence, while the episodic and open-ended form of her so-called novels arises not from any deconstructionist intent, but, I suggest, from the kind of perception that sees life discontinuously, episode by episode.

In making these remarks I do not mean to suggest that the later stories are unimpressive. They are always skillful in their presentation of human situations, and the prose never falters. There is not a sloppily written piece among them. As studies of generational distancing, some of the stories seen from the viewpoint of old people, like "Walking on Water" and "Marrakesh," are thoroughly convincing, while here and there there are still marvellously lucid evocations of childhood and adolescence, like "The Found Boat" and "The Turkey Season." Much less satisfying are the stories of middle-aged women with elusive lovers, and here the very impeccability of the writing seems to emphasize the psychological hollowness. At times, in recent years, one feels that Munro has fallen into the trap of virtuosity. She is so good at the kind of story she has always written that she seems never to have felt the need to try anything different. The result has been a certain leaching of character from her writing; some of her later stories are so well made that they seem anonymous, like those *New Yorker* stories which might have been written by any one of a number of North American virtuosi; indeed, the Munro stories of which this seems especially true, like "Dulse" and "Labour Day Dinner" in *The Moons of Jupiter,* in fact appeared in the *New Yorker*.

I am conscious, remembering what I expected of Munro when I read her early stories and *Lives of Girls and Women,* of a disappointment with her career seen as a whole. Most of her early stories and some of the later ones are among the best ever written in Canada. But those we think of as major writers, while they do not necessarily evolve in the sense of becoming always better, do tend to metamorphose and so indefinitely to enlarge their scope, as poets like Earle Birney and Dorothy Livesay and novelists like Robertson Davies and Timothy Findley have done. In this respect Alice Munro has remained fundamentally unchanged, applying the same realist techniques with the same impeccable skill and merely varying the human situations. Her potentialities have always been major; her achievements have never quite matched them because she has never mastered those transformations of form with which major writers handle the great climactic shifts of life. She has written of all the ages as she wrote of childhood, and that is why her lives of girls are so much more convincing then her lives of women.

# 8

## CRITICAL COMPLICITY

### *John Metcalf and the Ambiguities of* General Ludd

Critics have long viewed fiction in a double way, with an eye first to the overt text, and then a look at what the narration hides. Take, as an example, a novel that has been subjected to much critical attention, Sinclair Ross's *As For Me and My House*. It is told by the pastor's wife, Mrs. Bentley, who is herself one of the active characters. How reliable is Mrs. Bentley, as the chronicler of a series of incidents in which she is always an interested party, an aggrieved wife? How true is her pose of reasonable understanding? What distortions of the truth are concealed by that wry, ironic tone? Is she an honest woman wronged or a glib hypocrite? Much in our final view of the novel depends on our judgement of her character and motives.

But novelists themselves have also led their readers to examine their narratives, to doubt their protagonists, to recognize that fiction is indeed a work of artifice rather than of mimesis, and finally to enter with the author into an examination of his strategies. This, of course, is not a new development in literature. It is at least as old as *Don Quixote* with its elaborate mirror games between author, character and reader and its frank acceptance of the origins of the Don and his adventures in the literary imagination rather than in the imitation of life.

Recent novelists, passing beyond modernism into postmodernism, tend to pursue such metafictional courses, and in this way multiply the number of levels of understanding of their works. The surface may often seem realistic—for neorealism is part of the same movement—but the reader is encouraged to probe beneath, to mistrust everything that is told him, and in one way or another to deconstruct the fictional edifice so that in art as in life the certainties are dissolved and the imagination breaks free. By its very nature, postmodernism is not in any real sense a movement or an orthodoxy, and there are many ways in which metafiction works. John Metcalf's novel *General Ludd* exemplifies one of them.

Towards the end of *General Ludd,* when the poet-protagonist Jim Wells is about to make his abortive foray into the Communications Arts Complex

(CAC for short) at St. Xavier University, his lover, Kathy Neilson, is trying to dissuade him.

"And if you did something like this," she said, "you'd go to prison."
"Or the bin," I said.
"And that doesn't bother you, of course."
I looked up at her.
"I don't really think it does," I said.
The realization surprised even me.
The words lay flat on the air.
I seemed to hear them echoing in my head.

The incident is anticipated at other points in the novel, when Jim Wells shows his inclination to identify with poets like Christopher Smart and John Clare, who at times were judged insane, or with the painter Sir Edwin Landseer, who was "deranged . . . for the last four years of his life." And the novel ends with Jim being wheeled away from a psychiatrist's office, presumably to face a long stay in a mental institution. We can therefore fairly assume that, as a last twist in the black comedy that propels the whole book, the narrator is telling his tale from the "loony bin" with which he has been threatened. And thus, unless we agree with the psychiatrists who have adjudged Jim Wells a dangerous lunatic, the ultimate message of *General Ludd* would seem to be that we live in a world so mad that those who do not accept its values will inevitably be made to appear insane.

The novel, of course, is far less simple than that, for its very form—a tale told in the first person by an immoderate, self-involved and undoubtedly paranoid narrator—gives it multiple layers of ambiguity. We see the world even through Jim Wells's eyes with a strange double vision; he perceives the world of things and shapes around him with a dispassionate clarity, but he views the world of men with an angry and distorting moral passion.

At the same time, as readers, we are aware of the narrator as well as his narrative, and of how his varying perceptions both filter and pollute reality. Most of the other characters are clearly too much absorbed in their own follies or fantasies for their opinions of Jim to be relevant or even evident, but we do gain a fairly consistent view of him through the eyes of Kathy Neilson, whom in his own way he appears to love, and even if she finds him ultimately incomprehensible and is led to betray him, that represents a point of view which shows how far he has gone beyond the normal patterns of thinking and feeling in the world where he finds himself living.

But ultimately we judge Jim Wells by listening to his voice, and as much through the covert codes of his ways of speaking and perceiving as through what he says—the content of his recollections. Yet what he says has its importance, for the final level of ambiguity appears at this stage. *General Ludd* is not merely black comedy. It is also satire, and here the character of Jim Wells, the Luddite poet, becomes a persona for John Metcalf, the mask through which he can utter his contempt for the contemporary world and its ersatz values, a contempt he has not been reluctant to utter in more direct forms than fiction. On this level the novel is unashamedly didactic.

Essentially, *General Ludd* is about two worlds, or perhaps rather two eras, in conflict. The original Luddites were English handloom weavers during the industrial revolution who revolted and smashed the new machines that were depriving them of employment; it was in defence of them that Lord Byron made his only speech of any importance as a member of the House of Lords. There is no doubt that the motives of the Luddites, as Jim Wells at one time realizes, were mainly economic; they smashed the machines not from any sense of the greater dignity of manual labour as opposed to serving machines, but because machines were replacing men and forcing those who could get employment to accept starvation wages. Yet historically the Luddite movement did seem the last resistant impulse of the old pre-industrial England, and as a poet Jim finds its rhetoric irresistible: the phrases of one Luddite letter ring through the novel to its end. Written by an emissary coming by "General Ludd's Express Commands," it warns its recipient:

Remember the time is fast approaching when men of your stamp Will be brought to Repentance, you may be called upon soon. Remember you are a marked man.

yours for Gen Ludd
a true man.

The novel tells the series of incidents and revelations, the growing and complex anger and despair, that lead Jim Wells from fantasizing about a destructive role to actually becoming "a true man" for General Ludd, involved in a real if frustrated attempt at a symbolic act of destruction directed against a new technological tyranny.

His first encounter with St. Xavier's University shows Wells to be already out of sympathy with the milieu he is about to enter for a year as writer-in-residence. "They are, I thought sadly, what they eat": these are the opening words, and as the welcoming party for the visiting poet goes on, with bad cheese eaten on paper plates, and Canadian "Warm Duck" served as wine, and the Reverend Father President orating about the leaven of creativity causing the academic dough to rise, and the head of the department revealing that a desk has not yet been found for the new member of the staff, we are introduced to a burlesque sampling of the kinds of frauds and incompetents who have long found refuge in the English Departments of universities in Canada.

Jim Wells is a poet with a true devotion to his *craft,* to the "singing chastity" of the line, but, in accordance with the general ambiguity of *General Ludd,* he has a false and romantic notion of the poet's *role.* He is a precariously reformed rake whose urges towards women become, at St. Xavier's, subsumed in his relationship with crisp Kathy Neilson, a fine scholar (on George Herbert) with a nature wounded by tragedy. He is also a falling-down-drunk poet in the Dylan Thomas tradition with an obsessive attachment to the older poet and suicide, John Caverly, from whom he acquired the notion of the poet as trickster and guerrilla, pitted against the modern world with its synthetic products and plastic values. The discovery of Caverly's *Collected Poems* remaindered in a chain bookstore at 99 cents a copy is one of the incidents that leads up to Jim's final desperate act, the attack on the Communications Arts Complex, which in his brief residence at St. Xavier's has become for him the grand manifestation of all that is negative and evil in the modern world.

St. Xavier's is a small liberal arts college that has been "secularized and grown big," so that its "once gracious grounds" are defaced by the "concrete bunkers of the new disciplines." The new disciplines, and the pseudodemocratic attitude they have insinuated into the process of education, have even permeated the elder disciplines, so that the rule in the English Department at St. Xavier's (as it actually was in an American university where I briefly taught in 1954) is that everyone, no matter how stupid, must pass. As writer-in-residence, Wells is faced by a series of would-be poets who have no ear for language. At their best they equate poetry with sincerity, and at their worst they are represented by the pathetic and wholly amoral Itzic Zemermann, an atrocious versifier who exploits his past as a victim both of the concentration camp and of polio to achieve an entirely undeserved acceptance as a poet from people who fear to reject him: "Whatever my criticism and however put, he always managed to make me feel like a latter-day member of an Einsatzgruppe. He aroused in me exasperation and rampant guilt."

Perhaps the most blackly comic passage in the novel comes when Jim Wells, looking out from the window of his office over a gaggle of jogging professors, is admonishing Zemermann on the importance of safeguarding the integrity and purity of language, and, with tears in his eyes, quoting to him those pretentious and meretricious verses which Auden wrote at the time of Yeats's death and himself later rejected as spurious.

> Time that is intolerant
> Of the brave and innocent

And indifferent in a week
To a beautiful physique

Worships language and forgives
Everyone by whom it lives;
Pardons cowardice, conceit,
Lays its honours at their feet.

In this darkly ironic scene one realizes how near Jim, who elevates the words over the meaning, in fact is to Zemermann, who inverts the same process by not caring how words are used so long as the meaning emerges. Both, one realizes, have false perceptions of the nature and role of literature.

But the scene is made even grimmer by the fact that, as Jim rants, behind his back Zemermann is dying in his wheelchair of a real heart attack, having repeatedly feigned such seizures in the past to gain the sympathy of his teachers. This precipitates in Jim a breakdown that, in accordance with the pervading ambiguity of the novel, can only partly be attributed to guilt over Zemermann's death.

Even before that event he is distressed by the consciousness of growing old and of losing his poetic powers. Having carried out a minor guerilla feat in John Caverly's memory—stealing a Department of English IBM typewriter and flogging it to a pawnbroker—he sits in a bar and feels sad instead of triumphant.

As a dolmen might loom out of a fog sudden and massive confronting the traveller lost in the wild expanses of a moor, the sadness assumed a shape, a shape which expressed itself in the realization: I was getting old.

It no longer lay ahead.

And a little later, after another pathetically inadequate "guerrilla" exploit—ludicrously letting down the Canadian side before some visiting Russian writers—he stands, drunk again, in the faculty club toilet where he has just been trying to frighten one of the Russians with threats of exposure to the KGB.

I leaned my hands on the sides of the washbasin and stared into the mirror. I felt that I could weep. Kathy said my greying hair was attractive. Kathy was going to be angry again. It wasn't that kind of old I cared about. It was being tired. Used up. Too old and tired for the words to move again. I felt frightened. I stood in the roaring white-tiled washroom waiting for Borkh to emerge.

151

But is it merely an anxiety that the words may not move again that is troubling Jim? Is it not also an anxiety over the words that *have* moved, a crisis of doubt about his own creativity? For during the whole present of the novel he writes no poems, though he had earlier been inspired by photographs in an old *National Geographic* of cargo cultists in New Guinea ludicrously seeking to unite the primitive world and the Atomic Age. "This impossible juncture of worlds, this attempt by the Stone Age to control the power had started the movement of words in my mind." But though he had let the "words and pictures ferment . . . all I'd produced since coming to Montreal I'd scrapped as sloppy, tired, out of focus."

"And the reason was Kathy Neilson," he tells us. But does not his infatuation with Kathy Neilson, a woman who neither understands his ideas nor shares his way of living, indicate a doubt regarding his whole past, including his past as a poet? It is surely significant that, though Zemermann's bad poetry is quoted freely, and John Caverly's last poem features more than once in the novel, not a single poem by the poet hero is ever offered. He quotes Auden to Zemermann, he recites anonymous bawdy limericks to the visiting Russian literati, but when he gives a poetry reading we are not offered a single line of his poetry; we are only told the trickster pleasures of performance.

> I wear my watch on the inside of my wrist so that I can glance at it unnoticed while I'm working—it's a trick I picked up from watching musicians in bars and night clubs. Watching the time in the middle of intricate solo fingerings when the emotion generated is at a peak—I enjoy that paradox. A good performance is always calibrated seductively. One evokes emotions one does not feel—actors, singers, dancers, politicians, poets—every single one a feigning whore. I enjoy that too.
>
> I gave them the works.
>
> Lovely the voice, lovely the flow of words, the sudden denial of the ear's expectation, the rise, the climb, the house of words like a card castle building, bound to tremble, tumble, saved sudden, turned, inverted, the melody resolved, restated, rest.

Whoredom is on Jim's mind, and a little later on the same evening, when he is sitting with Kathy Neilson in a sleazy bar she detests, it takes on a different negative aspect. Now he's no longer the whore as trickster; he's the whore, selling himself as poet-in-residence to academic fakers, when he bursts out: "Perhaps we might say I'd rather be here getting drunk with a lot of whores who confess themselves as whores rather than be with the whores by whom I'm employed. And for whom I whore."

In this light the last poem which John Caverly left to Jim as a kind of legacy before he committed suicide takes on a sharper relevance. It is called "What to Dream About," and in a way it is about the strange combination of vision and deliberation that goes into the very conception of a poem, even before the craftsmanship begins.

> How long does it take you to decide
> what to dream about? Do you think
> carefully beforehand of women
> you never enjoyed and who
> would never agree to enjoy you?

> Do you desire to dream of the deaths
> of those you love so your sorrow
> will be splendid among your friends?

> Do you carefully build in your mind
> your own car crash the police will announce
> in tones that know your loss so well?

> Do you rehearse your best tragedies
> distilling them into your dreams
> night after night before you sleep,
> your hair growing grey in your bed
> your pleasant tears huge in your head?

> Or do you dream of a real loss,
> the bent caverns of the dark sea,
> the glass trees rough, shining at night,
> no other animal at sight.

Towards the end of the novel it is the penultimate verse of Caverly's poem, "Do you rehearse your best tragedies . . .," that stands in Jim's mind as an accusation, leading him to murmur, "You horrible old man, John," and burn the treasured poem before he sets off on his mission to destroy the Communications Arts Complex.

At this point the whole series of events in the novel takes on an even more complex ambiguity. There is no doubt that the synthetic world of modern urban society, which he contrasts with his personal dream of a revised pastoral order represented by the decrepit farmhouse he owns in the country and is always planning to bring back to life, genuinely disgusts Jim. When he visits the Communications Arts Complex, at the invitation of the director, Cosimo O'Gorman, SJ, it is as if he were going on a mythical journey into an underworld like Orpheus, into a labyrinth of darkness like Theseus. "In the raw concrete bowels of the building behind the mir-

153

rors, the corridors and rooms off rooms seemed like a maze. I could get no sense of where we were."

O'Gorman is the monster at the heart of the maze, a grotesque caricature of Marshall McLuhan, carrying that guru's meretricious ideas to their ultimate absurdity as he gloats over the appliances that will bring an end to anything we now think of as art or poetry. "The over-riding virtue of video," he declares, "is that it has no aesthetic value whatsoever," and he builds this negative insight into the rationale of a doctrine which is a parody of McLuhan's concept of the Global Village: "In order once again to become whole, in order to draw mankind together with a common culture, a common polity, outmoded and irrelevant concepts of art and communication must be eradicated, the delusion of quality discredited utterly."

O'Gorman is obviously mad, but he is also powerful, and he represents in Jim's mind not only the end of the civilization he values but also the beginning of something worse. In Jim the Luddite urge grows, a rage building up beneath the calm and quietude his relationship with Kathy at first appears to confer on him, and in the aftermath of his guilt over the death of Zemermann, he finally decides to carry out the plan he has long toyed with in fancy, the destruction of the costly apparatus in the Communications Arts Complex. Like the original Luddites, he does not pause to consider that one machine—or one computer—destroyed is unlikely to change the general trend of events around him. The act of destruction has become an emotional necessity for him, not so much a symbolic act of protest as a deed compensating for his own failure of creativity.

His action is aborted, for as he is jemmying open the mirrored doors of the CAC, Kathy betrays him, bashing him on the head with a lump of quartz that had belonged to her dead geologist husband. It is one of the few objects introduced into the novel with multiple metaphoric intent. Jim had already found it, lying on the table in Kathy's sitting room, and glittering with its flecks of iron pyrites, a menacing if fascinating object.

> The crystal sat there, roadblock, monolith, cairn and guardian of *terra incognita*.
> Here be dragons.

"Fool's gold," says Kathy when she sees him weighing the rock in his hand, and he is plunged in speculation whether her remark is meant to be merely denotative or whether—given her preoccupation with George Herbert, the poet of *Sacred Poems and Private Ejaculations*—it is metaphorical, "that life itself, men, relationships, children, were 'fool's gold,' that only a fool would put trust in them. Fairy gold that turned to withered leaves. That in the assay, even real gold was base metal. Was the remark pointed at me, at us. Fools rush in.''

When the lump of quartz finally plays its decisive role in the novel, it is as material object, not as metaphor, clouting Wells behind the head when he is on the point of realizing his Luddite purpose. But Jim, lying in his hospital bed after being several days unconscious, and realizing what has happened to him, immediately turns the material back into metaphor: "So," I said, "all I'm suffering from is a head full of fool's gold. . . ." Which indeed may be what is wrong with his view of life and, by implication, with his poetry.

This question of the material and the metaphorical, and of the clear division which at this point Metcalf seeks to put between them, takes us through the content of the novel back to its structure, back to the way that Metcalf writes and—in so writing—reveals a whole philosophy of art and life.

Metcalf has always opened himself to international influences, to influences beyond his British origins and his Canadian adopted setting, to—as he has said—"the influences . . . from whoever is good and whoever is being innovative anywhere.'' He has always been the enemy of the abstract in writing, the friend of the concrete and particular, and perhaps the most important single influence on him has been not a movement of prose writers, but a movement of poets: imagism, which fascinated him in his youth and has continued to shape his attitudes ever since. By adapting to prose the old imagist doctrine, "no ideas but in things," he has come near at times to the *choseistes* of the French *nouvelle roman,* though he has never carried this inclination as far as it has been taken by writers like Alain Robbe-Grillet, for whom things become so important that persons are reduced to their reflections. The most resonant passages of *General Ludd* are often those in which clusters of pure visual images are associated to create a mood, to echo an emotion. For example, at one critical point in the novel, when he awakes in Kathy's apartment after they have begun to know each other on an epic pub crawl, everything is visual, and it is the imagery that controls his emotions, and that in thinking of it he relates to eventual poetry.

I awoke in a white room to the mutter of distant typing. I was lying in a double bed. Facing me was a window. Hanging inside the recess of the window's white woodwork was a fern in a brass bowl. The sunlight burnished the bowl, glowed in the fern fronds. The green of the fern was strong but delicate. I stared at the white panes and angles of the casement corner, the curve of the glowing bowl, the emerald fern. The sunlight held them timeless like an intense detail of a *trompe l'oeil* painting. It was imperative that I concentrate on them, incorporate them, before the sudden beauty vanished, before clouds broke the spell.

No need for a notebook. Things seen in such a way burn in my memory. These things seen would, I knew, appear at some time in a poem. As seen now, transmitted perhaps, translated. I didn't know how I knew, but I'd learned not to think about it.

In fact, the poem in which "these things seen" might appear translated or transmuted, or in their natural innocence, is never written. Jim Wells is caught up in the nonpoetic pursuit of ideas, not the poetic pursuit of the images of things. He is led by the ideological enemies of art into turning art itself into a salutary ideology, and so, as the novel proceeds and his obsession grows, the moments of clear, sharp perception become fewer and briefer, until in the final hectic chapters, when Wells drives around the city with Kathy in taxis, trying to shed the guilt for Zemermann's death and at the same time becoming ever more deeply obsessed with the synthetic and inhuman character of the culture around him, these moments become condensed into ever briefer vignettes, caught between squalls of anger. In a moment of calm, after days of near breakdown, the two go off on a shopping expedition, and for a moment Jim's poetic eye collects its images: "As the cab carried us along residential streets, I watched mailmen, dogs on their busy errands, toddlers in bright snowsuits being hauled over snowbanks. A woman on a porch between cedars sprinkling salt from a yellow paper sack." But then the traffic clots and the two of them enter the great impersonal warren of a shopping plaza in which he finds Caverly's poems remaindered, and reality drifts into obsession, leading to the climax of action aborted by betrayal.

In *General Ludd*, John Metcalf projects an aesthetic and a moral vision, both of which are offended by the world in which we live and most of all—because it is nearest—by the world in which Canadians consent to live. The two visions are shown at once in concord and in conflict. The moral and the aesthetic vision come together when they find a common literary ground, and in parody the novelist destroys the pretences of the professors and the presumptions of the O'Gormans and, by implication, of their real-life models, the McLuhans and all the other enemies of art and intelligence. Satire may not succeed in its aims, but it does not fail so catastrophically as a wrecking bar in a poet's hand.

The two visions come into conflict when the novelist arranges his hero's crusade and downfall and eventual enlightenment in the form of a mock epic. Epic and mock epic are both essentially episodic in structure, encounters and epiphanies marking the stages in the great circular journey that leads back home. This pattern of a necklace of highlighted episodes perfectly fits John Metcalf's fictional style, which in *General Ludd*, and even more in his earlier novel, *Going Down Slow*, is shaped by the fact that he began as a short story writer and still likes to construct his novels as interconnected set pieces.

The mock epic, of course, is a palimpsest form, both erasing and retaining, so that it projects—reduced to pretentiousness—some of the grandiosity of the true epic, at the same time as in its contemporary variants it perpetuates the basic incongruities of the earlier mock epics, like *Don Quixote*, in which the idealistic hero tries to fight the forces of darkness with their own weapons of violence and outrage, and inevitably fails. Don Quixote is often mentioned in *General Ludd*, and Kathy, who does not understand Jim's Luddite rhetoric, is always accusing him of seeking to destroy windmills.

In its very self-consciousness the mock epic becomes a metafictional genre, involving the reader's complicity through his recognition that one of the basic literary forms—the epic—is being manipulated for a satirical purpose. So the reader becomes involved with the writer as well as with the protagonist, and there are always two levels of intent: that of the protagonist who is following his own obsession to its end, and that of the novelist who is observing him ironically and inviting the reader to share in his observation. This does not necessarily mean that the writer is detached in every way from his protagonist. And perhaps the major ambiguity of *General Ludd* lies in the fact that, while Metcalf presents Jim Wells as an absurd and risible character because of the ways in which he puts his ideas into action and detaches them from his poetic function, he is not out of sympathy with those ideas. Indeed, in one possible reading, *General Ludd* is just what the protagonist means his narrative to be: a great denunciation of the pseudocivilization in which history has condemned us to live.

But *General Ludd* is also, as both epics and mock epics tend to be, a journey of initiation and self-discovery, which is a prolonged and bitter agony whether it happens to Odysseus or Don Quixote or Jim Wells. In his journey Jim Wells progressively shakes himself free of illusions. He finally rejects his dependency on the model of the vatic poet which John Caverly had projected. He rejects the promise of true contented love that Kathy had seemed to offer him. He rejects the Luddite dream. And when at the end he stands in the psychiatric ward, seemingly in the grip of his enemies, there is a sudden highly ambiguous point of recognition in which writer, reader and protagonist seem to come together in ultimate understanding. Wells has talked to Dr. Chawn (as clearly maniacal a psychiatrist as one could fear to meet) about Marshal Blücher, "a respected and competent commander'' who nevertheless apparently "lived his whole life in fear of giving birth to an elephant." At the end of the interview Dr. Chawn looks up from his notes and says:

"Interesting."
"What is?"
"Marshal Blücher."
"What are you talking about?"
"He's one of your central fears, isn't he?"
"He is?"
"You fear that had he been cured of his delusions, he wouldn't have been a successful soldier."
I stared down at him.
Then smiled.
And smiled.

And at this point we sense the writer smiling and we smile too. For the Luddite cause, which fails with action, can hold its own by evasion, by the artist's trickery.

# HISTORY TO THE DEFEATED

## *Some Fictions of Timothy Findley*

History is an odd discipline. Some of its modern practitioners choose to treat it as a science, but the ancients had no doubt at all that it was an art and assigned it a muse, Clio. And history does share with the arts the fact that of necessity it gives a pattern to the chaos of life. The great historians create an overriding concept or myth, as Gibbon did in *The Decline and Fall of the Roman Empire* and Donald Creighton in *The Empire of the St. Lawrence;* what they show is not the past as it actually was, which would be meaningless to us, but the past rearranged so that we can take an image of it into our minds and by an act of thought understand it.

The frontiers of literature and history have always marched close together. After all, a whole group of Shakespeare's plays have always been called Histories, and the historical novel has a long pedigree. Historical fiction has over history proper the advantage that it can flesh out the bare bones of known facts with invention, and the conjunction of these two elements, what history gives and what the writer's imagination adds, make it an easy territory for romancers to annex, so that historical novels have stretched from the unlikely fantasies of a best-selling purveyor of escape literature like Rafael Sabatini to the marvellously plausible reconstructions of the ancient past by writers like Robert Graves and Mary Renault.

Like that of most new nations, Canadian literature has been somewhat dominated by history. A poet like Al Purdy is almost defined by the nature of his historical vision; the novels of Hugh MacLennan and Margaret Laurence weave into the pattern of our past in such an intimate way that it is not surprising such writers have admired our historians, like Donald Creighton and A. L. Morton.

But there are more ways than one of being historical, and recent writers have been bold in reshaping the raw material of history to suit their imaginative visions rather than allowing the accepted shape of history to control their invention. And so we reach what one can best describe as the remarkable parahistorical novels of Timothy Findley.

*The stars are dead; the animals will not look:*
*We are left alone with our day and the time is*
   *short, and*
*History to the defeated*
*May say Alas but cannot help or pardon.*
                              W. H. Auden, "Spain 1937"

History, as *The Wars* and *Famous Last Words* have shown, is Timothy Findley's favourite though not necessarily most tractable material. In these books we look back into a past that in the minds of most of us is completed and closed off: the Great War in *The Wars;* World War II with the apprehensive years leading up to it in *Famous Last Words*. He is not trying to revive these lost ages as they were. He is taking history into the world of the imagination and in the process is creating his own myths which are also his own history.

But to suggest that Findley is a mythographer is not to subscribe to the Frygian clichés by means of which some of his critics have interpreted *The Wars* as a re-enactment of archetypal myths that are to be regarded as lying somehow outside history. My use of the concept of myth in this context presupposes a relation between myth and history quite different from that proposed by Frye. I cannot accept that myth is autonomous and apart from history and our apprehension of the phenomenal world, nor do I believe primitive man saw or sees it in this way.

To give an example, even today anyone who discusses with the Nishka Indians of British Columbia the matter of their land rights comes up against an attitude that depends on the historicity of myths, for most of the advocates of Indian rights accept as *historical fact,* not as symbolic fantasy, the legends that make their ancestors the autochthonous inhabitants of the land, and reject, on these grounds of myths interpreted as literal history, the anthropologists' arguments that they too were immigrants, coming over the Bering Strait. In treating myth in this way, they are typical of primitive man, for whom it was intimately related to the phenomenal world and was indeed its true history. Myth, in other words, is a product of the emergent historic imagination, of the attempt to give the world we experience an origin and a meaning. Each culture develops its own myths to the same effect.

It is a similar emergence of the historic imagination, giving our collective life an origin and a meaning, that has tended to shape Canadian writing during recent decades and to induce its formative myths. The upsurge of actual historical and biographical writing is one aspect of it. But more important than the quantity of historical works published in Canada has been the imaginative quality of the best of them. Historians like Donald Creighton have not been content to provide us with a well-documented account of what they believe actually happened. They remember that, for the ancients, history, like poetry, had its muse, and writers like Creighton recognized the extent to which they were servants of Clio, not merely by cultivating the art of writing so that the best of their books could rank as literary masterworks, but also by shaping their accounts to draw a grand pattern, a myth, out of the mass of heterogeneous facts. Such historians are important not only for the information they have provided but also for what they have led us to believe; in a way perhaps more literal than any of their heroes, they have *made* history.

This creative element in the writing of history drew historians and other kinds of writers together. The myths Creighton created had their political importance in the extent to which they helped inspire the more intellectual types of Canadian nationalism during the 1960s and the 1970s. But they went beyond politics just as they went beyond history considered as a mere academic discipline in offering the themes and images, even the historic personae, that would inspire novelists and poets. The tributes that Margaret Laurence has paid to A. L. Morton, perhaps the greatest historian of the Canadian west, and other writers to Donald Creighton, are not, however, merely statements of indebtedness. They are rather acknowledgements of affinity, indications that the poets and novelists themselves had developed a historic consciousness, almost a historic sensibility; that for them history had become not merely a rich source of imagery and subject matter but also, even, a shaping influence. An imaginative vision of the form of the past has given shape to Margaret Laurence's novels as certainly as it did to Stendhal's or Tolstoy's. An imaginative grasp of local traditions has dictated the very speech rhythm and therefore the prosodic form of Al Purdy's poetry. The dense vitality that our brief history takes on in the works of so many of our writers of fiction and poetry is one of the distinguishing characteristics of modern Canadian writing.

In applying this generalization to Timothy Findley, I would go a step farther and say not merely that he shares a historic consciousness widespread among Canadian writers of his generation but also that he is, in a more specific sense, a historical novelist. I am aware that the historical novel, highly respected as a genre in the nineteenth century, has become in our age a somewhat derided form of fiction, largely practised by popular novelists who write according to formulae for readers who see the past as a place of escape and history as romance. But the best of historical novels were and always are works of elaborate and often very self-conscious literary art, and they tend to fall into two main categories.

The novelist can take what information he has of the past and out of it creates an imaginary world that is certainly not identical with the past, but is complete and self-consistent within itself. Flaubert writing *Salammbo* out of the relatively few facts known in his time about Carthage is an example of this kind of historical fiction, which is not really very far removed from the product of an artist historian, like Gibbon in *The Decline and Fall of the Roman Empire*, who creates a vision of the past that, even when it has been superseded by later evidence and later interpretations, nevertheless remains as a literary artifact. The other type of serious historical novelist is the writer who gives history a fictional form in order to draw some moral or political implication. The grand example is, of course, *War and Peace*, in which Tolstoy made his major statements on the nature of war and on the illusory nature of political power. Here again there are analogues among historians, like Spengler using a cyclical interpretation of history to project a pessimistic philosophy.

Reshaping events to make moral or political points is only a step away from reshaping events for aesthetic purposes, as novelists like Robert Graves did in his Claudius series and Ford Madox Ford in *Parade's End*, both of them creating portraits of civilizations at critical turning points but at the same time writing with a high consciousness of form and of style, so that their novels stand as literary artifacts outside any question of their historical authenticity or of the thoughts about human societies that, almost incidentally, they induce. Timothy Findley's *The Wars* and *Famous Last Words* both fall—I suggest—into this last category. Indeed, I am somewhat surprised that none of the critics has yet studied the resemblances between *The Wars* and *Parade's End*—not only between their respective visions of the horror and waste of trench warfare in the Great War but also between Ford's Tietjens (that noble, outraged man) and Findley's Ross as characters, and between the visions of sexual relations as brutally rapacious that both novelists offer. However, such a comparison is not the aim of this essay, and I make it mainly to suggest how clearly *The Wars* rests within the tradition of historical fiction.

In both the novels I am discussing Findley uses formal frameworks based on historical methods even when, as in *Famous Last Words*, he combines them with a boldly fictional device, making the author of the memoirs about real persons, which Lieutenant Quinn so laboriously transcribes, that invention of Ezra Pound's early poetic fancy, Hugh Selwyn Mauberley. "You begin at the archives with photographs," says Findley two pages into *The Wars*. Whether the shaping intelligence of the book is actually addressing the researcher, or the researcher addressing the reader, or whether *you* is meant in the more neutral sense of *one*, is not at all clear, and doubtless the ambiguity is intentional. The fact is that the novel is presented as a kind of secondary record, derived from rummagings among archival relics—"Boxes and boxes of snapshots and portraits; maps and letters; cablegrams and clippings from the papers"—and from taped interviews given by a couple of survivors from the events that fill the book. The illusion of authenticity is quite deliberately created, and that illusion is part of the fiction. Somehow or other, we are expected to assume, all the scenes that are described directly in the third person have been created out of the debris of fragmentary records and surviving memories. There have even been hints, in accounts of conversations with Findley, that some at least of the incidents in *The Wars* are based on the Great War experiences of members of Findley's own family. Be that as it may, we are faced with fiction as historical pastiche, and with a consequent problem in the relationship between style and moralism in fiction.

On the surface, indeed, *The Wars,* with its neonaturalist determinism that makes its characters appear the victims of both heredity and circumstance, and even more *Famous Last Words,* with its cavalier blending of historical and fictional personages and its concentration on people who are devoid of the pride of principle, seem divorced entirely from fictional moralism. In a brilliant essay on Timothy Findley as novelist ("Look! Listen, Mark my Words!", *Canadian Literature* 91), John F. Hulcoop has related Findley's practice to Oscar Wilde's theories on the importance of style, in literature and in life alike. And a pair of Wildean phrases—part of the series of epigrams that prefaced the first edition of *The Picture of Dorian Gray*—can very appropriately be applied *on one level* to the type of fiction Findley has developed. "All art is at once surface and symbol. Those who go beneath the surface do so at their peril."

All this is true, of Wilde's work as well as of Findley's. For in Wilde's case those who have risked going below the surface, who have dared to read the symbols, have discovered the ultimate Wildean contradiction: that, as I showed long ago in *The Paradox of Oscar Wilde* (1949) and Joyce Carol Oates more recently in *Contraries* (1981), the dandy's emphasis on surface and style is often the thin ice concealing a moralism of almost Dostoevskian intensity.

The case is rather similar with Findley. Discussing any of his novels, one inevitably says much about style and surface, and by doing so acknowledges not merely his special literary dexterity, but also the growing sophistication of a Canadian fictional tradition that has come to the point where forms and artifices, parodies and pastiches, are the serious concerns of serious writers. Yet they are not their only concerns, and one would lose a great deal of Findley's two most recent novels if one's understanding of them ended with the aesthetic, or if one assumed, given they have such a strong vein of determinism, that they are ultimately pessimistic.

One can indeed apply Auden's lines which I use as the epigraph for this essay to both Robert Ross of *The Wars* and Mauberley of *Famous Last Words,* each in his own way irrevocably on the wrong side, Mauberley for his involvement in a quasi-fascist cabal, Ross for his defiance of the British army in a Quixotic attempt to rescue horses from the insane carnage that was eating up men by the thousands on the Flanders front. Mauberley is in the end horribly murdered, and Ross lives the last years of his truncated life a prisoner in mutilated inactivity. Both, by any normal standards, are utterly defeated. And history, indeed, can neither help nor pardon, for there is no possible reversing of their destinies.

But there is a difference here between literature and history, considered merely as the sequence of events. For the imagination may not be able to help or pardon, but it can offer understanding and compassion. When Clive, the soldier poet in *The Wars,* is asked, "Do you think we will ever be forgiven for what we've done?" ("we" meaning his generation), he answers: "I doubt we'll ever be forgiven. All I hope is—they'll remember we were human beings."

It is the retention of his humanity, the power, after all he has endured from the inhuman forces of war, to make a gesture in favour of life, that is Robert's final triumph at the moment of his apparent defeat. Having shot his senior officer and deserted, he rescues a hundred and thirty horses from almost certain death, only to be trapped and surrounded by pursuing soldiers. The barn in which he and fifty of the horses are sheltering is set on fire.

> But just as the walls began to fall in on top of the fifty horses—all of them standing in their places while they burned—Robert turned the mare and she leapt through the flames—already falling—with Robert on her back on fire.

The burning hero; it is a kind of apotheosis as well as a destruction. And Robert's triumph comes in his strange tenacity, in his clinging to life, through pain and hopeless mutilation, so that when the nurse Marian Turner in her pity offers him an overdose of morphine, his answer is "Not yet."

> Do you see? He might have said "No". He might've said "never". He might've said "Yes". But he said "not yet". There, in those two words, in a nutshell—you have the essence of Robert Ross. And perhaps the essence of what it is to be alive. *Not yet* has been my motto ever since—and here I am.

A few moments before she tells this incident Marian Turner—that ancient lady who still says "Not yet"—had described the bombing of the field hospital at Bois de Madeleine and had evoked an image that was not only related to Robert's holding on to life but also potently expressed one of the dominant structural as well as symbolic relationships of the book, that between men and animals.

> We nurses lived in tents, you understand, and these were all destroyed as well as the damage done to the hospital which was in someone's house. I remember the strangest sight when the raid was over. I'd been hiding under a bed and

when I crawled out and stood up I looked down the rows of platforms where the tents had been and there, at the edge of the step, sat a pure white cat we'd had as mascot. It was cleaning its paws! Serenely cleaning its paws. Well . . . life goes on—and a cat will clean its paws no matter what.

The cat is clearly, at this point, being introduced as a fabulist exemplar, offering man a model of conduct. There are other similar exemplary uses of animals in the novel; the toad who survives a gas attack because he is able to go underwater and control his breathing; the coyote behind whom Robert runs on the prairie and who leads him to a secret water hole, showing the combination of intelligence and instinct by which the animal takes advantage of its environment but does not, like man, attempt to dominate it and—by dominating—to destroy.

But animals are not used merely in a fabulist manner. They become extensions of the human characters, or perhaps rather their reflections in a different realm of consciousness, where culpability is replaced by innocence. Robert, running with the coyote, running later with the horses in an English paddock, is declaring a kinship, just as his friend Harris does when he lies dying in an English hospital and remembers how he would swim with shoals of mackerel, as if theirs were his element, and hear the music of the whales. One of the most appealing and elusive characters in *The Wars* is Robert's fellow officer, Rodwell, who keeps in his dugout a small menagerie of animals he had rescued when they were injured by artillery bombardments. Only the toad survives, and when Rodwell is sent to a part of the front that has been subjected to a terrible attack by flame-throwers, he confides the animal to Robert, who eventually liberates it in its native mud. Rodwell—who shortly afterward commits suicide because he cannot prevent shellshocked soldiers from torturing rats and cats to death—also leaves with Robert the books of sketches on which, as an artist, he has spent his spare time in the trenches. Later, in a train on the way to "Blighty", Robert dips into the sketchbooks:

There was the toad. Quite, as Rodwell had promised, realistic—lacking entirely any sentimental nuance. Just a plain, bad-tempered grumpy toad. Robert smiled. He leafed through the pages. There were birds and mice. The rabbit and the hedgehog. More toads. A frog and some insects. Then, towards the back of the book, he found himself. "*Robert*". He was lying asleep by the candlelight in the dugout. His mouth was slightly open. One hand reposed on his breast. He was wearing Harris's bitten gloves. The other hand hung down towards the earth. The likeness was good. Unnerving. But the shading was not quite human. There was another quality—speckled and fading into brightness where his clothes touched his neck and cheek. Robert could not decipher what that quality was—until he'd finished leafing through the book and glanced through the others (there were five, all told). In all of them—on every page, the drawings were of animals. Of maybe a hundred sketches, Robert's was the only human form. Modified and mutated—he was one with the others.

What had Rodwell meant by this? Or was it just the way he drew?

Whether or not Rodwell meant anything at all, his insight prefigured Robert's subsequent actions—his first unsuccessful attempt to liberate horses he sees as doomed by artillery bombardment, and later, after he becomes a deserter, his more successful liberation, this time of the trainload of a hundred and thirty horses he finds shunted into a siding. When he finally becomes cornered, he identifies himself completely with the horses; his pursuer, Major Mickle, calls on him to surrender, and he answers—though there is no other human being with him—"We shall not be taken." "It was the 'we' that doomed him. To Mickle, it signified that Robert had an accomplice."

The motives that underly Robert's acts are left deliberately unclear; we have, like the researcher who comes sixty years after the event, to piece them together from the given fragments. But it is clear that his anger at the death of the first batch of horses and his killing of Captain Leathers are merely the climax of a long process in which he has come to the point when he must make some manifestation for life against the mindless carnage and destruction that he has so far passed through undestroyed, and there seems no better way of doing so than to attempt the rescue of those innocent beings, the animals, and especially of the horses, which are regarded as the utterly dispensable material of war. In their subjection to the destructive elements that war imposes on them, men and animals are together, though it is only man that is culpable, and in half-conscious ways both Rodwell and Robert offer themselves as sacrifices to redeem man's culpability, which gives a final point to the poet Clive Stourbridge's hope that the humanity still existing in his generation may be remembered.

Like the relationship between man and animals, which provides one of the great balancing features in the structure of *The Wars,* the elements also play a significant symbolic and formal role in the novel, and here again the implications are dualistic. "Earth and Air and Fire and Water" are the words that Juliet d'Orsey had written on Robert's tombstone, and their presence is more than the revival of ancient science. Throughout the novel they are present destructively—in the water of the great shellholes where Robert almost drowns, in the earth that almost smothers him when his dugout collapses, in the air that is made blue and deadly by the presence of poison gas, and above all in the fire that rages during the artillery bombardments, and especially in the ersatz apocalypse of the terrible flamethrower attacks which the Germans release as Operation *Gericht.*

Fire storms raged along the front. Men were exploded where they stood—blown apart by the combustion. Winds with the velocity of cyclones tore the guns from their emplacements and flung them about like toys. Horses fell with their bones on fire. Men went blind in the heat. Blood ran out of noses, ears and mouths. Wells and springs of water were plugged and stopped by the bodies of men and mules and dogs who had gone there for safety. The storms might last for hours—until the clay was baked and the earth was seared and sealed with fire.

And it is fire that in the end destroys Robert. One is reminded too of the part that destructive fire plays in so many of Findley's works—for instance, the fires of *The Butterfly Plague* ("Real fires, symbolic fires. All burning—all eating—most of them conjuring death"), and the fire that turns Wallis Simpson's great fête in *Famous Last Words* into a black comic disaster.

There is a doubtless intended irony in recording the German name for their flamethrowing operation, since the result is in its way a *Gericht,* a judgement, on those who let loose such destructiveness on the earth. And all the elements have also, in the novel, their regenerative side. Water is another home for Harris. The earth on which he runs with coyotes and horses gives strength to Robert. The novel ends with breath, which is air—a photograph of Robert with his dead sister, Rowena. "On the back is written: 'Look! you can see our breath!' And you can." Even fire mirrors the rage and the spirit within Robert, so that the image of him at the end "on fire" is tragic but also triumphant. This dual aspect of the elements reinforces one's impression of *The Wars* as, in some inexplicit way, the product of a quasi-Zoroastrian vision; it is there in the determinism one uneasily feels to be such a dominant factor, and in the sense of a perpetual conflict of opposing forces for which fire is the uniting image, Ormuzd and Ahriman its double faces. It is this double vision that gives the book not merely its meaning but also its form.

*Famous Last Words* is in appearance a very different novel from *The Wars,* more cynical, more blackly comic, more stylized. Yet in the way Findley goes to work there is much in common between the two books, for in the later one also he is mingling the literary genres and turning the actual world—the world of history—into the raw material, to be manipulated at will, of an art that acknowledges no myths but its own, no models but preceding artifacts. Findley's concern with literature as the offspring of literature leads him in *Famous Last Words* to seek characters of two kinds: those who actually come out of literature and those who come out of life and may even be famous but whose roles are so artificial and so lacking in consequence that through them history can be manipulated easily into a writer's artifact.

As his narrator, Findley takes a character entirely out of literature: Hugh Selwyn Mauberley, the aesthete whom Ezra Pound conceived and then thought out of existence in 1920. A verse from *Hugh Selwyn Mauberley* seems to set the tone for the world of *Famous Last Words:*

> There died a myriad,
> And of the best, among them,
> For an old bitch gone in the teeth,
> For a botched civilization.

It is the botched civilization that we encounter at the novel's first point in time, 1924, when Mauberley meets Wallis Simpson in Shanghai and remarks: "It was a dreadful time; there was so much dissolution of the past and fear of the future. Nothing to stand on, nothing to reach for."

Findley's Mauberley defies the fate Pound laid out for him, for he does not pass "from man's memory in *l'an trentiesme / De son eage* . . ." but lives on to become, like his creator in real life, an apologist for fascism, and to die at the hands of Nazi agents during the chaotic aftermath of World War II. In the intervening period he had become deeply involved in a reactionary cabal, of which Ciano, von Ribbentrop, Lindbergh and Mrs. Simpson are members, plotting to supersede the reigns of Hitler and Mussolini by a new European order of which the figurehead will become that pathetic shell of a princeling, the briefly reigning King Edward VIII. As world events show, the plot fails; it may not have existed at all in actuality. It exists for the purposes of the novel, which is sufficient, since it provides Mauberley with the material for the memoir that is his posthumously discovered masterpiece.

There are two verses in *Hugh Selwyn Mauberley* that seem to have given Findley the clues on which to base the circumstances of Mauberley's composing the masterpiece Pound had denied him. The first:

> The "age demanded" chiefly a mould in plaster,
> Made with no loss of time,
> A prose kinema, not, not assuredly, alabaster
> Or the "sculpture" of rhyme.

And the second:

> "His true Penelope
> Was Flaubert,"
> And his tool
> The engraver's.

Fleeing from Italy, Mauberley finds refuge, not only from the Allies but also from Himmler's agents, in a deserted luxury hotel high in the Alps. There, awaiting his pursuers, he takes a silver pencil, which becomes his engraver's tool, and scores on the walls and ceilings of four of the rooms the contents of the notebooks he had brought with him—the record of the barren conspiracy in which peripherally he was involved. His enemies eventually track him down, murder him and burn his compromising notebooks, but before they arrive he has completed his work and added on the ceiling the sign of his own hand outlined by candle soot. Mauberley's record is read and recorded by the young American lieutenant, Quinn, who is part of a bizarre reconnaissance unit which provides a kind of low comic chorus to the mock heroic drama that is, as the "age demanded," written "in plaster," with "no loss of time," and is in its own way a "prose kinema, not, not assuredly, . . . / the 'sculpture' of rhyme."

In Mauberley, as the script unfolds, we become aware of a dual persona. He is in one aspect the weak and neutral man, scared by the physical contacts that may entrap him, so that he lives all his affairs in the mind, but led by his very lack of will into the associations that eventually must destroy him. In the other aspect, he is the artist who feels a complete power over what he creates, and who writes on the wall, for Lieutenant Quinn to read with troubled delight: "All I have written here is true, except the lies." Quinn is justifiably puzzled when he tries to understand "how Mauberley, whose greatest gift had been an emphatic belief in the value of imagination, could have been so misguided as to join with people whose whole ambition was to render the race incapable of thinking."

And when we read what Lieutenant Quinn—with the help of many candles and cigarettes—gleans from the scored walls, we realize that Mauberley has in fact claimed his privilege as an artist to chronicle but also to imagine and invent. And so the story he tells is not merely what he has seen, for there are whole incidents narrated in which he does not appear; it is also what he invents when his imagination plays over the actions of people he has known.

On the way Findley, rather like Tolstoy, presents us with views (perhaps not his own) on the nature and effects of war and the real character of history. "A war," Mauberley tells us, "is just a place where we have been in exile from our better dreams." And, describing an occasion when he sat with Wallis and von Ribbentrop, he remarks:

So this is history as she is never writ, I thought. Some day far in the future, some dread academic, much too careful of his research, looking back through the biased glosses of a dozen other "historians", will set this moment down on paper. And will get it wrong. Because he will not acknowledge that history is made in the electric moment, and its flowering is all in chance. At the heart of everything that shakes the world, there need be nothing more than a casual remark that has been overheard and acted on. There is more in history of impulse than we dare to know.

Yet, in the ironic event, it is history as process rather than accident that sweeps Mauberley to his destiny.

For all its inconsistencies, Mauberley's account goes far beyond what Pound attributed to his original: "Nothing, in brief, but maudlin confession." It is, uncompromisingly, literature as style, with Wallis Simpson as its ultimate example in life.

> The face she saw in her private mirror was a face no other human being had seen. It was her midnight face, and mostly in her mind. The true face—lifted and lacquered—was the one she showed to others and the world.

Which is nothing more than Wilde's doctrine of the truth of masks.

But just as in Wilde, that kindest of men, a moral being underlay the dandy, so in *Famous Last Words* we are never free from the moralism that goes with the territory of fiction. It is there, at the beginning, in raging Ezra, whose morality may be upended, but whose rage is nevertheless against a world lost in corruption. And certainly it is there in the two eventual commentators: Quinn, who believes in the understanding that forgives, and his superior officer, Captain Freyberg, who believes that to understand the enemy is to betray one's cause, which is Quinn's truth inverted. And finally, as a manifestation of the urge to live on that lies at the heart of even the most extreme aestheticism, there is Mauberley's own remark, as he remembers the caves of Altamira and reproduces their smoke-ringed handprint above his own engraved messages: "Some there are who never disappear. And I know I was sitting at the heart of the human race—which is its will to say *I am*." In such a statement—which echoes that of Clive Stourbridge in *The Wars*—style becomes its own morality and understanding becomes more important than help or pardon.

*     *     *

Findley's most recent novel, *Not Wanted on the Voyage,* may appear to fall outside the pattern of the new historical fiction that accommodates *The Wars* and *Famous Last Words*. Presenting a version of the story of Noah's flood, it may seem less a revision of history than the remythologization of a myth. But we are really back with the argument regarding history and myth that I used at the beginning of this essay. For primitive people history and myth are indistinguishable, myth on one level at least being regarded as a record of what actually happened. In the same way, *Not Wanted on the*

*Voyage* presents a critical rewriting of a tale that to most Jews and Christians and Moslems has been for many centuries credible history: a literal account of what happened in the days of our not too distant forefathers.

So, by virtue of the place it has held in the minds of so many people, the story of Noah can be taken as a kind of history, embedded so deeply in our traditions that a fictional retelling of it is as much an act of reconstructing history into art as either *The Wars* or *Famous Last Words*. Also, *Not Wanted on the Voyage* has a further historical aspect, since it presents us with an interpretation of the story of Noah, the flood and the ark that recollects the ancient controversies at the beginning of the Christian era regarding the nature of the Creator and his relationship to the true God.

The account of the ark and the flood in Genesis seems, when one returns to it, surprisingly sparse and concerned more with God's offended vanity than with the results of his appalling edict or the nature of the world it destroyed. That some survived and the deluge was never repeated are the facts that sanctify the story in our imagination, and Findley has caught the spirit of that reaction in his epigraph: Against Despair. For the wonder that emerges out of this book, as it does out of any realistic examination of human history, is that we have survived.

Like Timothy Findley's other books, *Not Wanted on the Voyage* is a fiction on several levels. In the conventional sense of a more or less realistic study of human relationships, it is hardly a novel at all, since, except for Mrs. Noyes (Noah's long-suffering wife), the characters are types rather than personalities and their relationships are allegorical rather than actual. It can probably best be described as a combination of fable and prose mock epic, which performs the same kind of bold and illuminating outrages on revealed religion as *Famous Last Words* performed on history.

We are presented with the world before the flood, hauntingly enough like our own to give us a poignant sense of déjà vu, yet also different so that although we are in a realm of whimsical anachronisms where Mrs. Noyes drinks her crocks of gin and plays Edwardian popular songs on the piano, it is still a premechanical world and also a world like that of the legends of primitive peoples and the fables of many literatures, in which the animals can also speak to each other and even to human beings. The law of Yahweh establishes the rule of man over the realm of nature, and to Noah it is given, as it was given to Adam, to wield that rule. The result is a record of cruelties and sacrificial slaughters which remind one of Schopenhauer's remark that in the world of animals men are the devils; it culminates in Yahweh's own super-holocaust of the flood in which mankind, except for Noah and his family (including the fallen archangel Lucifer, who has decided to join the human race and in the guise of the woman Lucy marries Ham), shares the destruction wreaked on the animal kingdom and on all the strange magical beings, like dragons and demons and fairies

171

and gryphons, who evolved between the Fall and the flood and have deco-
rated our myths and our dreams ever since.

The moment of truth for the old world comes when Yahweh, old and
fragile, arrives with his entourage of angels to visit his old friend and single
remaining loyal supporter, Noah. The Creator has been wandering through
his world and finding it in full revolt against his authority; orgiastic cults
are in the ascendant, and men insult and assault him at every turn. It is
when he arrives at the peaceful welcoming haven of Noah's estate, a fusty,
failing, senile parody of deity, that Yahweh decides on his great revenge
on mankind and on the whole of his creation. He will submerge it under
water, but he will allow his old friend, Noah, who in the half-blind eyes of
the cat Mottyl is a veritable demon of cruelty, to survive and to shape the
world that will emerge as the flood recedes and the earth dries out and the
animals preserved in the ark repopulate it. The privilege that Yahweh
grants to the survivors of mankind is to be the curse of animalkind, as recorded in those cruel, unacceptable words of Genesis: "And the fear of
you and the dread of you shall be upon every beast of the earth, and upon
every fowl of the air, upon all that moveth . . .; into your hand are they
delivered."

Having made this decision, Yahweh departs, and Mottyl the cat—alone
among mortal witnesses—hears the sound of flies in his coach and knows
its meaning, a meaning already discussed by Lucy and his / her brother,
the archangel Michael, when they meet in loving hatred.

> Lucy looked up the Hill towards the Blue Pavilion—shining, translucent, in the
> dark. Her mood swung wide of the banter she and Michael had been trading.
> "Tell me how He is," she said. "He looked so old . . . so ill . . ."
> "He's dying," said Michael.
> Lucy stared at him and then, very slowly, back at the Pavilion.
> "He can't die," she said, almost whispering.
> "Why not?"
> "He isn't able to die . . ."
> "I though that, too. But He *is* God. And if God wants to die . . ."
> "Then God is able."
> "Yes."

Yahweh, the evidence of his silence suggests, does indeed die, and so a
modish preoccupation of recent theologians is added to the complex
strands of Findley's parodic vision. But although Noah's exhortations to
his old friend arouse no response, this makes little difference to the real situation. Yahweh has drowned the earth as his last act of divine malice, and
the ark floats on as he intended. The primeval communication between
men and animals is shown to have broken down when the choirs of sheep

so well trained by Mrs. Noyes no longer respond with hymns but merely answer "Baaa!" And the war between man and the animal world that will characterize the postdiluvian dispensation is foreshadowed when the dolphins surge around the ark seeking to make friends with its human crew; Noah declares them to be pirates and enemies, and Japeth slaughters them as they jump smiling on to the deck. There is no need to remark how the concerns of the contemporary ecological movement—of all our struggles to end the massacre of the intelligent mammals of the sea—are reflected in such passages of a book that is sensitive and thought-provoking on so many levels.

As we have seen, *Not Wanted on the Voyage* is in some ways a recreation of the myths of primitive peoples like Pacific Coast Indians and Australian aborigines that envisage a past when all creatures could communicate with each other. Also, by virtue of its moral content, it belongs to the European fabulist tradition whose last great example was *Animal Farm,* while at times there is an element of touching and melancholy whimsicality, when Mottyl and her friends Whistler the groundhog and Bip the lemur converse, that reminds one of classic children's animal stories like *The Wind in the Willows.* Findley is calling in these various ways on a great reservoir of past associations at the same time as the death-of-God theme and the enmity-to-dolphins theme remind us that this is a book to be read with the preoccupations of our own world in mind. Using as its basic structure the great universal myth of the deluge, dramatically recorded by Greeks and Babylonians as well as by Jews, and relating the existence of antediluvian man to our own by an ingenious pattern of anachronisms, *Not Wanted on the Voyage* becomes a tract not for any single time but for all human time, giving fictional expression to a view of the natural order and the nature of God that may not be as old as the flood but is certainly as old as the high days of Alexandrian philosophizing and which had its remoter roots in Achaemenian Persia.

I am referring to Gnosticism, whose real origins can be found in the teachings of the early Iranian sage Zoroaster (c. sixth century BC) regarding two great conflicting powers at work in the universe, Ormuzd, the Lord of Light, and Ahriman, the Lord of Darkness. This dualism passed into Mithraism and Manichaeism, but with the emergence of the Gnostics in Alexandria at the beginning of the Christian era it took on a new form, doubtless because of the presence there of a considerable Judeo-Christian community. The Gnostics were never an organized or united church or cult. Some remained pagan, while others professed to be Christian, though they were immediately denounced as heretics. Their most celebrated figure was probably the thaumaturge Simon Magus, of whom what is doubtless a slanderous account appears in the Acts of the Apostles. Their most important teachers were Marcion and Valentinus.

Deriving their doctrines partly from Iranian, partly from Egyptian and partly from Orphic-Pythagorean sources, and mingling them with their own readings of the Christian writings whose canon was then just being established, the Gnostics recognized the startling differences of tone and spirit between the New and the Old Testaments, and, while they did not deny the historicity of the Old Testament narrative, they decided that its cruel, vengeful and tyrannical deity, Jehovah, or Yahweh, could not be the true God. On the basis of their Old Testament readings they concluded that the physical world was evil, and the creation of an evil being, the Demiurge.

The Demiurge, as described by Hans Jonas in *The Encyclopedia of Philosophy*, bears a remarkable resemblance to Yahweh, the Lord Creator of *Not Wanted on the Voyage*. Far from being the true God, the Demiurge is the product of a Fall due to a crisis in the divine realm.

> Early in the descending series—and marked by all the deforming defects of the Fall whose fruit he is—appears the Demiurge, the monstrous and benighted archon (lord) of the nether powers. This widespread Gnostic figure, telling symbol of the Gnostic hostility toward the world, is clearly a polemical caricature of the Old Testament God, and the identity is made explicit by frequent transference to him of well-known utterances and actions of God from the Biblical text. Pride, ignorance and malevolence of the Creator are recurring themes in Gnostic tales. . . . He is always a problemical and never a venerable figure. . . .
>
> He believes himself to be the only God and engages in creations chiefly designed to satisfy his ambition, vanity, and lust for dominion.

Yahweh, though he is in fact the creator of the imperfect world that rebels against his tyranny, is thus presented in both Gnostic doctrine and in Findley's book as a pseudodivine imposter, a representative or embodiment of the forces of darkness, and hence a diabolical figure, which of course would fit in with Mottyl's view of his minister Noah as demoniacal. But if Yahweh is to be taken as a manifestation of the Gnostic Demiurge who has made the earth the place of death and cruelty that it is, what are we to make of the "rogue" angel who—having "joined the human race"— appears in drag as Lucy and so finds her way onto the ark as the bride of Ham?

Lucy, of course, is Lucifer, the name given in Patristic writings to Satan before his rebellion against Jehovah. His origins lie back in Greek mythology when, as Phosphoros, he was the minor god who represented the morning star—the planet Venus as she appears at dawn. Taken over by the Romans, Phosphoros became Lucifer, the light-bearer, and was represented by a male figure carrying a torch. With him, as the old saying goes, pride went before a fall; hence the other saying, proud as Lucifer. Why the church fathers should have picked upon such a minor classical deity to be transformed into the great antagonist of God is something of a mystery, one of whose most interesting features is the fact that in Christian tradition Christ, and Satan as Lucifer, share some of the same epithets. Both are referred to as "the morning star" and "the son of the morning," and certainly Milton was more than a little dazzled by the light Lucifer could generate even in hell.

Here, with the appearance of Lucifer in *Not Wanted on the Voyage*, we come to another Gnostic idea, that of the eternal messenger, the emissary from the world of light who, as Jonas remarks, "outwits the archons, awakens the spirit from its earthly slumbers, and imparts to it the saving knowledge from without." Linked with the idea of the eternal messenger is the other widespread Gnostic legend in which, on the morrow of creation, the Demiurge exults like Yahweh with the Old Testament proclamation, "I am God and there is none other than I," and a voice echoes from on high, "Thou art mistaken! Above thee is First Man."

Buddha, Zoroaster, Jesus and Mani, all of them men, were variously identified by the Gnostics as messengers from the world of light. It does not stretch the pattern very far to see among them the Creator's traditional antagonist, Lucifer, since those presented as the enemies of Yahweh, now identified as the evil Demiurge, must necessarily be regarded as good. If the identification of Lucifer as the great adversary had not taken place after the Augustinians had won their victory over the Gnostics, we can fairly assume that he, bearing the very name and emblem of Light, would have been included among the messengers of the gnosis.

In *Not Wanted on the Voyage*, it is true, Lucifer is identified as the son of Yahweh, but he is the son who commits the unpardonable sin of questioning, and so he is cast out. And now, just as Christ joined the human race by incarnation and became the Son of Man, so Lucifer joins it by choice and marriage, and in a supreme act of defiance does so at the very time when Yahweh, the evil Demiurge, has decided to destroy humanity and the rest of his creation. In acting thus, it is clear, he finally severs his link with the Demiurge and with all the evil he has done.

And when we observe Lucy's nature through the innocent yet experienced mental eye of Mottyl, she appears before us as one of the compassionate beings whom the Gnostics chose as their messengers of Light.

Bip had wanted to know if Mottyl had ever known a rogue angel and Mottyl had said; "*no*". She might still have said no. Nothing she knew of Lucy made her think of violence or contentiousness. And Lucy's only fear was of wolves and dogs and foxes—and they were just as afraid of her—a stand-off. Surely, above all, it was wonderful that Lucy was one of them, in the bowels of the ark—that she was opposed to Doctor Noyes—opposed to his experiments—opposed to his Edict—opposed to his methods and his tactics and his . . .

Mottyl had almost thought; *evil ways*.

Why had she stopped herself, when she was so obviously right?

They were *evil* ways.

Even the fading of the powers of giving and destroying life that Lucifer had enjoyed in his original "home," the heaven of Yahweh, can be taken as a sign of his separation from the realm of the Demiurge and of his identification with the other messengers, who wielded no supernatural powers when their time of testing came—for Jesus in his crucifixion, for Mani in his martyrdom, for the Buddha when he died of eating putrid meat out of politeness. They shared the human fate, and so Lucifer, for all his angelic aspects, means to do. The role he has accepted is to pose the alternative vision (hence his appearance as a woman in opposition to the paternalistic regime of Yahweh and Noah), to foster and sustain the spirit that questions and rebels, the spirit that, like Ivan Karamazov, rejects the injustice of a world where a single child suffers, and "returns God his ticket." It is the spirit of Lucifer, as a Gnostic might see him, veritable bearer of light, that hovers over the last sentences of the book when Mrs. Noyes sits one night on the deck of the ark with Mottyl in her lap.

> She laid her hand on Mottyl's head. Here was this cat, whose sight had been taken by Doctor Noyes, and down below them all was the world that had been destroyed by Doctor Noyes (with some help from his illustrious Friend) and all that remained of the world was what, to all intents and purposes, had been seen by this old blind cat and by herself—sitting long ago and rocking on their porch above the valley. And now, Noah wanted another world and more cats to blind. Well—damn him, no, she thought.
>
> "No!" she said.
>
> Mottyl heard her—and stirred.
>
> Mrs. Noyes said; "I didn't mean to wake you. I'm sorry. Sorry—but not sorry. Watch with me, Motty—you blind and me with eyes, beneath the moon. We're here, dear. No matter what—we're here. And—damn it all—I guess we're here to stay."
>
> Mrs. Noyes scanned the sky.
>
> Not one cloud.
>
> She prayed. But not to the absent God. Never, never again to the absent God, but to the absent clouds, she prayed. And to the empty sky.
>
> She prayed for rain.

Here is one answer to the query that rests in Lucy's mind about the "rumour" of "another world." If that new world is to be like the last or the present (for here Findley is clearly equating the antediluvian and post-diluvian worlds and directing our attention to the condition of living beings now), if it is to perpetuate the cruelties and injustices that exist between men and men, and men and animals, then we must reject it and pray for rain, which is a conclusion any good Gnostic would have freely accepted.

And so in the great ambivalences of the conflict between our desire to live and our fear of living, the complex fabulist and parodic structures of *Not Wanted on the Voyage,* which is so much more than a novel, are finally knit and knotted. And not merely knit and knotted within itself, but also knit and knotted to Findley's earlier books, for all in their various ways end with the defiance of actual history, whether recorded or revealed, since it is the chronicle of multiple deaths and for that reason alone must be reconstructed. Robert's "not yet" and Mauberley's "*I am*" and Mrs. Noyes's "I guess we're here to stay" form a holy triad, a threefold insistence on the power of the human spirit over negation and death.

# PART TWO

# 10

## CANADIAN POETRY

### The Emergent Tradition

**A**nthologists and literary historians usually set order in a literary tradition, and generally the anthologists appear, as they have done in Canada, before the historians. This has been especially the case in poetry, more easily selectable than prose, and ever since Edward Hartley Dewart published his pioneer *Selections from Canadian Poets* in 1864, three years before Confederation, they have been, explicitly or implicitly, presenting our poetry as an expression of the national spirit. A. J. M. Smith's anthologies, *The Book of Canadian Poetry* and the *Oxford Book of Canadian Verse*, were landmarks in the study of Canadian poetry, for they not merely established a canon of the tradition but they also presented a critical view of Canadian poetry seen as a whole, as well as offering critical insights into the work of individual poets.

The emergence of a strong critical tradition over the past quarter of a century has removed the need for anthologists to offer overt assessments of the work they present, but selection is still a critical act. When Margaret Atwood's *New Oxford Book of Canadian Verse* appeared in 1982, twenty-two years after Smith's second anthology, it offered a new view of Canadian poetry that took into account the changes in the scene over the past quarter of a century.

Considering such anthologies as Smith's and Atwood's is one way of understanding the tradition of Canadian poetry; the piece that follows, which began as a long review essay, offers my own view of the progression of English-speaking poetry since Robert Hayman started writing it in Newfoundland in the sixteenth century and serves as an introduction to the subsequent essays on significant individual poets.

**A**nthologies have a special role in young and emergent literatures. They are not, like the various Oxford Books of English Verse, meant to commemorate with suitable examples the high points of an established tradition, the masterpieces that have endured the fires of criticism and survived. An *Oxford Book of Canadian Verse*, as exemplified in Smith's original in 1960 and Margaret Atwood's *New Oxford Book of Canadian Verse* appearing in 1982, discovers rather than commemorates; it takes its place beside the emergent criticism of a young literature to examine the nature of individual creation in such a situation and to define the collective trends that are still developing.

Thus, when the poet A. J. M. Smith compiled the first important (one could equally call them "great") anthologies of the poets of Canada, *The Book of Canadian Poetry* (1943) and *The Oxford Book of Canadian Verse* (1960), he was doing much more than picking collections of good or even significant poems. He was discovering and charting the lines of a new tradition, establishing a canon, and in the process developing insights into the kind of poetry the Canadian environment and Canadian history have encouraged. Smith not only made the act of selection a critical process; to *The Book of Canadian Poetry* he also wrote a long and brilliant introduction which was a pioneer document in Canadian historical criticism, and he introduced each poet with a concise and insightful prefatory note. Our view of Canadian poetry and our sense of the possibilities of Canadian criticism were both greatly enlarged by this pioneer book.

Appearing in 1943, *The Book of Canadian Poetry* was thus not only a definitive anthology of its country's poetry up to that time but it also stood at the beginning of Canadian criticism. By the time Smith published the first *Oxford Book of Canadian Verse,* the two functions had grown apart; the appearance in 1959 of the quarterly *Canadian Literature,* with Smith writing in its first number, had confirmed the development of a critical tradition in Canada, and it was appropriate that Smith's new anthology, while still exploratory, should give the appearance of presenting a literature whose criteria were more or less established.

Nevertheless, Smith's *Oxford Book* remained tentative in the sense that he was bringing forward new poets in rather striking numbers, and this was even more the case with his *Modern Canadian Verse,* published seven years later in 1967. Even today, with Atwood's *New Oxford Book of Canadian Poetry,* the difference from the standard anthologies of literatures with long traditions is striking. When Helen Gardner brought out her *New Oxford Book of English Verse* in 1972, only ten out of the two hundred poets were still alive; out of Atwood's 121 poets, eighty-eight are still living, and sixty-five of these were not in Smith's *Oxford Book.* Not only are Canadians still in a position, like all peoples with newly defined literatures, of living with their classics, for half-legendary pioneers of modernism like Dorothy Livesay and Earle Birney are still among us; they have also been living since the 1950s in a period of what one might call continuing renaissance, which has thrown up a succession of remarkable new poets and is still doing so.

Margaret Atwood herself is one of that succession of poets (her rapid rise to recognition as a kind of junior classic began in the mid-1960s), but she is also an acute critic and a scholar respectful of the past as well as sensitive to contemporary trends, so that she seemed from the beginning an excellent choice for the task of compiling an anthology suited for the 1980s, to replace Smith's *Oxford Book,* which had long been out of print. And, grudging though one may be here and there about choices that conflict with one's own preferences, she has put together a collection that stands well beside its predecessors, both because of its good organization and because of the richer resources from which she has been able to select. For among the striking characteristics of recent Canadian poetry has been not only its proliferation but also its variegation. Looking at the very youngest of the new poets she introduces, on whom she is taking the greatest chances, Margaret Atwood justly remarks on their retreat from the self-conscious nationalism of recent decades into the kind of concern for the actual craft of writing that is one of the signs of a maturing literature:

> There is a renewed interest among many of them in the intricacies of rhetoric, and an emphasis on the poem as consciously crafted. None of them is like any of the others, which is an indication of the variety and energy still being generated by the writing of poetry in Canada.

Of course, any anthology embracing a succession that, however tenuously, stretches nearly four centuries from Robert Hayman in Newfoundland down to the present is bound to build itself around a nucleus of poems that have stood the wearing of time ("old chestnuts," as Margaret Atwood calls them), and there are plenty of these in the early pages of the *New Oxford Book.* Still, Atwood has notably trimmed the earlier poets, in comparison with Smith's selections, and a fifth of the way through her anthology we are already up to F. R. Scott and A. J. M. Smith, the poets with whom one customarily associates the emergence of Canadian modernism during the 1930s.

Yet, brisk though Margaret Atwood's selection of the early Canadian poets may be, it is a shrewd one. It begins with that engagingly smug Jacobean, Robert Hayman, the first poet to write in English about what eventually became Canada. Hayman was given an orange by Drake (and wrote about it) and became the friend of Ben Jonson and also in 1621 the governor of Harbour Grace. He looked on Newfoundland from a viewpoint that combines the roles of early publicity agent and utopian fantasist, and one has to remember that he wrote shortly after the completion of *The Tempest* when one reads such an evocation of idyllic insularity as this:

> The Aire in Newfound-land is wholesome, good;
> The Fire, as sweet as any made of wood;
> The Waters, very rich, both salt and fresh;

The Earth more rich, we know it is no lesse.
Where all are good, *Fire, Water, Earth and Aire,*
What man made of these foure would not live there?

Hayman provides English Canadians with a useful counter to the French poet Marc Lescarbot, who was writing in Acadia only a decade or so before, but his efforts were isolated and the real English Canadian poetic tradition began nearly two centuries later with the Loyalists and the early immigrants from Britain to Upper Canada at the end of the eighteenth century. Most of them were, as Margaret Atwood remarks, "displaced persons who brought their language and their preoccupations with them." Sometimes, as in the younger Oliver Goldsmith's *The Rising Village,* they tried to perceive the New World as materially kinder if culturally cruder than that they had left, but more often they resembled Standish O'Grady with his bitter invocations of the land:

Thou barren waste; unprofitable strand,
Where hemlocks brood on unproductive land,
Whose frozen air in one bleak winter's night
Can metamorphose *dark brown hares to white!*

As Margaret Atwood remarks of them, "these poets, very early on, sound two notes that have sunk deeply into the Canadian poetic tradition; the elegiac, a mourning of homes left and things lost; and the satiric, a bitter account of dismal surroundings, both social and geographical." But as the nineteenth century went on, and native-born poets began to replace immigrants, other strands did appear: notably the idea of a Canadian poetic tradition, which had been inconceivable for the first immigrant writers, still attached to their memories of lost fatherlands. The earliest idea of establishing a tradition was to turn back to previous and perhaps stronger periods of English poetry, which explains the powerfully anachronistic neo-Jacobean dramas that Charles Heavysege wrote in his spare time as a woodcarver in Montreal, and Sangster's detached landscapist poems that remind one of some late Augustan tinged with Romanticism (Samuel Rogers, perhaps) passing through a new country.

There is a real sense of something new entering Canadian poetry with Isabella Valancy Crawford towards the end of the 1870s. The diction, the imagery and the metrical shape of her poems are not greatly different from English later Romantics, and if Keats and Shelley had not written, and Landseer had not painted, Crawford would not have been quite the poet she became. What is new in her is the fact that she gives herself to poetry as none of her Canadian predecessors had done. As Margaret Atwood says, "in Crawford's world everything is alive, everything is sentient, everything has a shape that can be imaginatively comprehended.'' Her poems grip our imaginations because they are moved by frustrated passion and by the power of an inner vision that had little to do with the objective world in which the poet lived. The bizarre hidden personality of this woman of obscure life emerges most strikingly when she uses her generally conventional imagery to serve her fantasy:

> They hung the slaughter'd fish like swords
> On saplings slender—like scimitars
> Bright, and ruddied from new-dead wars,
> Blaz'd in the light—the scaly hordes.

Crawford inhabits a private land of the poetic persona. It is with the so-called Confederation poets (Wilfred Campbell and Charles G. D. Roberts, Bliss Carman and Archibald Lampman and Duncan Campbell Scott) that writers begin to inhabit a recognizable Canada and the first intimations of a truly Canadian poetic voice are heard. By this time, at least in eastern and central Canada, the pioneer age had ended. The links with the mother countries were thinning out, and for the new generations love for the land of childhood experience was more real than nostalgia for a land one had never seen. In giving voice to this transference of emotional allegiances, the Confederation poets at their best not only celebrated Canadian scenes, which Sangster after all had already done, but also observed with considerable accuracy the human life they fostered and found the language and imagery to describe them. A realism inevitably entered into the process, as it always does when writers have to recognize the actual nature of the world they inhabit before they can apply to it the transfiguring processes of the imagination.

And so, in Roberts and Lampman, in Scott and at times in Carman, we see not only a strange luminous factualism in evoking the landscape but also a new use of imagery, of language, of poetic form. It emerges in lines and verses more memorable, because more original, than any used before in Canada. There is that magically unprecedented line from Roberts's sonnet, "The Mowing": "The crying knives glide on; the green swath lies." And there is that final verse of "Low Tide at Grand Pré," which has given Bliss Carman a lasting niche among Canadian poets:

> The night has fallen, and the tide . . .
>   Now and again comes drifting home
> Across these aching barrens wide,
>   A sigh like driven wind or foam:
>   In grief the flood is bursting home.

Margaret Atwood rightly gives fair representation to these poets, though she confesses to "a sneaking preference" (which I share) for Duncan Campbell Scott: "Although I recognize that the other poets are lusher and more graceful, Scott's condensed tragedies have a starkness and a moral jaggedness that evoke darkness rather than the lights and half-lights of Lampman." And Atwood, as her own poems show, recognizes the uses of darkness. But I find Scott interesting also because, like Roberts to a certain extent but unlike the metrically conservative Lampman, he felt uneasily that a new approach to the Canadian land needed a new formal expression, and in the end went very near to free verse. Already in 1905 "The Forsaken" has a broken-line pattern which shows how eager Scott was to seek in unconventional metrical forms a way of giving expression to the strange things he had seen in the Canadian North.

> But in the frost of the dawn,
> Up from the life below,
> Rose a column of breath
> Through a tiny cleft in the snow,
> Fragile, delicately drawn,
> Wavering with its own weakness,
> In the wilderness a sign of the spirit
> Persisting still in the sight of the sun
> Till day is done.

Scott lived until 1944 to overlap the poets we regard as the first Canadian modernists, and one of his late poems, "En Route," written in 1935 and included in the *New Oxford Book,* carries to its farthest degree the desire of the Confederation poets to find authentic expression for their intense involvement with the natural setting. "En Route," which tells of a train stopping "for no apparent reason / In the wilds," does not merely show the innovatory influence on Scott of the imagist movement he lived to witness; it even ends with a quiet statement of the validity of that encounter between the concrete and the transitory which is the essence of imagist thinking.

> Traces there are of wild things in the snow—
> Partridge at play, tracks of the foxes' paws,
> That broke a path to sun them in the trees.
> They're going fast where all impressions go
> On a frail substance—images like these,
> Vagaries the unconscious mind receives
> From nowhere, and lets go to nothingness
> With the lost flush of last year's autumn leaves.

This gradual liberation of the verse of Roberts and Scott is perhaps the principal thread of continuity in Canadian poetry during the early twentieth century, for after the almost simultaneous appearance of Roberts, Carman, Lampman and Scott in the 1880s and the early 1890s, no poet of major significance made an appearance until E. J. Pratt published *Newfoundland Verse* a third of a century later in 1923. And Pratt has always seemed a somewhat anomalous figure, leading towards modernity by turning to the past. He chose epic and mock epic forms, he went back to the seventeenth century for Hudibrastic metres in which to write his often heavy-handed satires, but he did explore the use of the Canadian vernacular in poetry and he early on recognized the importance of Canadian history and geography as a basic subject matter.

A very different figure was W. W. E. Ross, whose importance as a Canadian modernist poet was only belatedly recognized. Ross published his first volume, *Laconics,* in 1930, and the very title is revealing; he brought to Canadian poetry a new simplicity of expression and a stress on imagistic clarity that had not been seen before. Although he has remained little known, his influence on the poets of the 1930s and 1940s was considerable, and his "Rocky Bay" (unfortunately not included in Margaret Atwood's *New Oxford Book*) is almost a model for a certain type of Canadian landscape poem:

> The iron rocks
> slope sharply down
> into the gleaming
> of northern water,
> and there is a shining
> to northern water
> reflecting the sky
> on a keen cold morning.

Certainly one of the ingredients of Canadian modernism as it appeared in the 1930s was an imagist way of looking which, by stressing the visual, enabled the Canadian poets to see their environment and translate it into words with an appropriateness their predecessors never attained. Poems of this period like F. R. Scott's "Lakeshore" and A. J. M. Smith's "The Lonely Land" (both included in the *New Oxford Book*) are good examples of this process at work and have a clear relationship to Ross's sharper imagism.

> This is a beauty
> of dissonance,
> this resonance

of stony strand,
this smoky cry
curled over a black pine
like a broken
and wind-battered branch
when the wind
bends the tops of the pines
and curdles the sky
from the north.

But the poets who worked together in Montreal during the late 1920s and the 1930s, and in the process created a modernist movement in Canada (notably Scott and Smith and A. M. Klein), were much too polymorphous in attitude to confine themselves to imagism in their search for alternative ways of expression to the worn-out nineteenth-century examples most Canadian poets were still following. They found affinities with the English poets of the 1930s and with earlier masters like Pound and Eliot. A. J. M. Smith applied the arts of the pasticheur in the best sense as he parodically echoed seventeenth-century poets while at the same time he was writing naturalistic poems about the Canadian landscape, and A. M. Klein turned to the rich imagery of Jewish tradition and the resounding English of the Jacobeans to create his extraordinary elegiacs of modern life seen *sub specie aeternitatis*.

Indeed, what strikes one now, in the 1980s, about these poets is that they were much less of a movement in the sense of sharing their visions or their voices than the literary historians with their neat patterning of the past have led us to believe. Yet the idea of something going on in a collective way cannot be entirely dismissed. The modernist poets did form interlocking groups like that which centred on the *McGill Fortnightly Review* (Smith, Scott and others) and the later Montreal groups associated in the 1940s with *Preview* (P. K. Page, Patrick Anderson, Scott, Klein) and *First Statement* (Irving Layton, Louis Dudek and the Toronto poet Raymond Souster). These groups were partly associations of convenience among poets who found it difficult to get their work published in ordinary periodicals or by ordinary publishers, but the fact that they were in this common predicament and sought a shared solution arose from the circumstance that each in his or her way was rebelling against conventional poetics and seeking a way of expression that suited a personal vision. A vague cultural nationalism was at large among these poets as it has been among some of their successors, but we are going at it the wrong way if we see the self-conscious desire to create a Canadian national poetry as the main factor in what happened either collectively or individually. It was the desire to find their own voices that was primary, and the movement to create a distinctive

Canadian poetry that was secondary and less consciously motivated, emerging only through the poets realizing that they could be fully themselves only by living in their own place and time and giving expression to the experience they knew. But the means of giving that expression they often had to find elsewhere, and for rough convenience Canadian poets of this period can be divided into the Anglophiles and the Americanophiles.

Not only Smith and Scott were influenced by English poetry of the time. Patrick Anderson, the leading spirit of *Preview,* was actually a temporarily transported English poet. Dorothy Livesay rightly in retrospect dates her poetic awakening from her discovery of Auden and Spender, who showed that lyricism and a social conscience were compatible; though now, late in a long career, it is not her Marxism of the 1930s but her intense feminism that emerges most strongly, a feminism less political than concerned with the personal intensities and ambiguities of the passional life.

> I walk beside you
> trace
> a shadow's shade
> skating on silver
> hear
> another voice
> singing under ice.

Earle Birney, who like Livesay has become one of the enduringly important voices in Canadian poetry, first found a new way of talking about Canada through his study of Old English poetry, whose density and power, and even whose diction, were strongly present in his early poems. Since then, in decades of restless experimentation, he has developed a conversational loping rhythm that serves to convey sharp visual images and to hint at their philosophic implications, as in "Bear on the Delhi Road," one of his many vivid travel poems.

> They are peaceful both    these spare
> men of Kashmir    and the bear
> alive is their living    too
> If    far on the Delhi way
> around him galvanic they dance
> it is merely to wear    wear
> from his shaggy body the tranced
> wish forever to stay
> only an ambling bear
> four-footed in berries.

P. K. Page, whose intermittent career also dates from the 1940s, clearly began writing under the influence of the socially aware British poets of the 1930s and 1940s, but has moved into an extraordinarily individual combination of verbal economy and visionary intensity; as Margaret Atwood says, she is "both a dazzling technician and a tranced observer who verges on mysticism," seeing, indeed, the technique as part of the trance.

> And choir me too to keep my heart a size
> larger than seeing, unseduced by each
> bright glimpse of beauty striking like a bell,
> so that the whole may toll,
> its meaning shine
> clear of the myriad images that still—
> do what I will—encumber its pure line.

If the poets of the *McGill Fortnightly Review* and *Preview,* as well as contemporary mavericks like Earle Birney and Dorothy Livesay, tended to look towards British models for their modernist inspiration, the rival *First Statement* group set going another recent Canadian trend by finding its lead among New World poets; for them any Old World, even an Old World in revolt, was anathema. This was the beginning of Ezra Pound's powerful if intermittent role as a model for Canadian poets; it would be revived in the 1960s, filtered through Black Mountain glass, among the group around the magazine *Tish* in Vancouver, with which were associated such poets as George Bowering and Frank Davey. Neither Dudek nor Souster (and even less Irving Layton) appears as a mere imitator of Pound; indeed, the difference between their styles shows how each took one aspect of Pound and transformed it to his own poetic purposes.

Louis Dudek is more the philosophic poet, concerned with historic issues on a global scale, and so it is the Pound of the *Cantos* whose echoes we sometimes catch, though what is actually said is an evident projection of Dudek's highly individual sensibility, seen at its best, I think, in those long sequences like *Atlantis* of which Margaret Atwood unfortunately gives us no examples.

> I seem to peer through time, as through a tottering mansion,
> to glimpse the shapes beyond, the spectral bone-men
> who lived, and died, and believed.
>
> And see the new religion fearfully replacing the old,
> burning temples,
> knowing, past cure, how sure their reasons were

    against the old idols,
who now are burned themselves, with the sure fire of reason.

Nothing stands, we say, we moderns.
All's flux, an art of mathematics—of fiery matter,
while the old gods gutter and die in the flames.

An earlier Pound, the imagist, stands behind Raymond Souster's poetry. Souster has refined and adapted imagism, turning it into a remarkable instrument for bringing the visible world clearly alive in our minds while giving it a transparency through which we see the poet's mind ironically reflecting, with the thought always a consequence of the experience, but often vast implications spreading out from the thought. Souster has written so eloquently of Toronto and its life that he has become that rare phenomenon, an urban regional poet; yet one of his most memorable poems, which shows all his virtues of economy and vividness, is "The Hunter":

I carry the ground-hog along by the tail
all the way back to the farm, with the blood
dripping from his mouth a couple of drops at a time,
leaving a perfect trail for anyone to follow.

The half-wit hired man is blasting imaginary rabbits
somewhere on our left. We walk through fields steaming after rain,
jumping the mud: and watching the swing of your girl's hips
ahead of me, the proud way your hand holds the gun,
and remembering how you held it
up to the hog caught in the trap and blew his head in

wonder what fate you have in store for me.

At most, Irving Layton's attachment to Pound, and later to William Carlos Williams, was tenuous. Although he has developed a powerful poetic persona, his choice of modes and influences has been eclectic and his performance has been erratic. The Dionysian attitude (one can hardly call it a philosophy) behind his poetry derives from Nietzsche and partly from Lawrence, whose *Pansies* was an extremely bad poetic influence on him. Essentially he is a kind of hyper-Romantic, reaching a poetic extravagance of diction and a density of imagery that are far removed from anything Pound or Williams would have accepted, and at times, with luck, he can be very good. His "Tall Man Executes a Jig," the longest of the pieces in Margaret Atwood's selection of his work, is certainly one of the best poems written in Canada.

191

Clearly, the groupings of Canadian poets in the 1930s and 1940s had their purpose, giving mutual support in material and moral ways in a milieu that was at best indifferent but often hostile to anything that appeared experimental in literature or art. As the situation gradually changed, as the public attitude to poetry improved and the poets themselves became more self-assured, building up through the 1950s to the explosive decade of the 1960s, such needs diminished, and it becomes misleading, I believe, to pay too much attention to talk of schools and movements. Some poets, like the austerely religious Margaret Avison, have always seemed too uncompromisingly themselves to be linked in any way with other writers. Others, like Al Purdy, show in their work so broad a grasp of what it means to write poetically of Canada that one immediately recognizes the justice of Margaret Atwood's estimate of his role as an epitomizing one, and of her talking of him as a "giant figure" in terms of the poetry of "indigenous myth" and "the rediscovery of history." Yet Purdy stands, in his own very idiosyncratic way, quite outside categorization.

Nevertheless, he shows in his career the way in which Canadian poets seemed to flower in the atmosphere of renaissance, the mood of excitement and innovation, that came into Canadian writing during the 1960s. Purdy's early verse was conventional and constrained, but during the late 1950s, when he was already forty, his style began to develop rapidly. He was eclectic in accepting influences, and perhaps the greatest influence of all was that of the audiences with whom, on reading circuits, he tried out his verse. Purdy writes very directly from experience, so that his poems often read like fragments of autobiography or travelogue. As Atwood says, "he blends the cadences of real speech and a gangly eloquence in, typically, elegiac poems that place the human figure like a tiny dot at the intersection of geological time and astronomical space and yet manage to assert its importance." There is a haunting, unillusioned love of the land in Purdy's poems that is more telling than any stridently nationalist verse can be:

> This is the country of our defeat
> > and yet
> during the fall plowing a man
> might stop and stand in a brown valley of the furrows
> > and shade his eyes to watch for the same
> > red patch mixed with gold
> > that appears in the same
> > spot in the hills
> > year after year
> > and grow old
> plowing and plowing a ten-acre field until
> the convolutions run parallel to his own brain.

Purdy's melding the sense of history in a new country suddenly grown old in its feelings with the awareness of place as a visual reality has perhaps enlightened rather than inspired many younger poets, so that a genuine poetry of place and time now exists in Canada, represented by such writers as John Newlove, Sid Marty, Andrew Suknaski and Dale Zieroth, all represented in Atwood's volume, and also by Patrick Lane, perhaps the largest figure among them, and by Alden Nowlan, whose Maritime background detached him from the western preoccupation with nature-in-the-large that one finds in the other poets I have just named. In Lane the wish not to "sing other than our lives," as he once put it, produced a stoic pessimism that did not rule out an intense compassion for the dispossessed, whether men or women rejected by society, or animals living under the harsh laws of nature or the threat of man's predation.

> The poor, the broken people, the endless suffering
>
> we are heir to, given to desire and gaining little.
> To fold the arms across the breast and fly
> into ourselves. That painless darkness or stand
>
> in the field with nothing everywhere and watch
> the first flakes falling and pray for the deliverance
> of the grass, a dog's death in the snow? Look
>
> there. Stark as charred bone
> a magpie stuns his tongue against the wind
> and the wind steals the rattle of his cry.

It is not, however, very far in feeling (if not in territory) from Lane's frequent poems about animals wantonly destroyed by man or nature to Alden Nowlan's splendid poem "The Bull Moose"; they speak alike the empathy for the wilderness that has permeated so much of recent Canadian poetry, in contrast to the earlier pioneer hatred of the wilds. Nowlan makes a potent symbol out of his old bull moose, who, recognizing the onset of his own death, comes out of the wild into the village, where the people pet and persecute him until

> just as the sun dropped in the river
> the bull moose gathered his strength
> like a scaffolded king, straightened and lifted his horns
> so that even the wardens backed away as they raised their rifles.
> When he roared, people ran to their cars. All the young men
> leaned on their automobile horns as he toppled.

There is another strain running through Canadian poetry in the 1960s which is more concerned with the artifice, in the best sense, of verse making, and more directed to the inner landscape of memory and myth, of dream and feeling. Its intellectual dependences can be exaggerated, and have been, for at one time there was much talk of a group of poets, a mythopoeic school, emerging under the influence of Northrop Frye's critical theories. The poets most often named in this connection were James Reaney, Jay Macpherson and Eli Mandel. Frye himself rejected the role of guru and pointed out rightly that the opinions of critics never lead to poetry. And in fact, as they have developed, it has become clear that these poets do not have much in common except perhaps a tendency to revolt against historical actuality. Reaney cultivates in his elaborate parodies of the bucolic mode a kind of mock innocence that can be annoying, as it is in the sillier poems of Blake, but can also lead to nostalgic poems of great and sad intensity, like "The School Globe," and poems of Yeatsian fantasy, like "Granny Crack":

> I was a leather skinned harridan
> I wandered the country's roads
> Trading and begging and fighting
> With the sun for hat and the road for shoes.

Jay Macpherson has listened to Blake too, but to his more powerful visions, which she has absorbed without any surrender of intellectual acuity, so that her poems, rich in wit and conceit, make one see her as a belated metaphysical.

> You were my soul; in arrogance I banned you.
> Now I recant—return, possess me, take my
> Hands, bind my eyes, infallibly restore my
> Share in perdition.

Among the other poets who displayed the extraordinary variegation in Canadian poetry that took place during the 1960s and 1970s are Leonard Cohen and Gwendolyn MacEwen, George Bowering and Michael Ondaatje, and, perhaps most deserving of mention because her clear, spare purity of poetry has so long gone unrecognized, Phyllis Webb. At the end of her volume Margaret Atwood moves beyond the poets who are by now accepted, taking a calculated risk on a dozen or so very young poets in order to maintain the open termination that Smith also gave in his *Oxford Book*. Her choices, I think, are good; many of them will remain as recognizable presences in the tradition.

Finally, there is the editor herself. This part of the volume has been selected by William Toye, at Margaret Atwood's request, and it has been well done. Margaret Atwood's role as a poet has tended to be confused by her broader fame as a novelist, an innovatory critic and a public personality observed and read by a larger and different audience from that which has read her poetry with growing appreciation since the middle 1960s. At the end of her introduction, Margaret Atwood applied a series of descriptive adjectives to Canadian poetry which I think could even more appropriately be applied to her own: "spiky, tough, flexible, various, and vital." How various one can see when, after the sharp astringencies of so many of her poems about the relations of the sexes, one comes to the tenderness of a poem like "Variation on the Word *Sleep*."

> I would like to watch you sleeping,
> which may not happen.
> I would like to watch you
> sleeping. I would like to sleep
> with you, to enter
> your sleep as its smooth dark wave
> slides over my head
>
> and walk with you through that lucent
> wavering forest of bluegreen leaves
> with its watery sun & three moons
> towards the cave you must descend
> towards your worst fear.

Such verses represent a poetry in Canada that, as Margaret Atwood argues, is "finally . . . its own," and of age.

# II

# THE JOURNEY OF DISCOVERY

## Nineteenth-Century Canadian Narrative Poets

Early Canadian poets tended to be at their best—which often was not very good—in the larger poetic forms, such as the long narrative and the verse drama. These were really public forms, concerned mainly with social experience as distinct from the essentially private experience that is reflected in lyric and elegiac verse. Even if the dramas tended to be closet plays, ill adapted for the stage, they were still inclined to project—or sometimes to challenge—collective values as distinct from individual ones.

By the latter third of the nineteenth century, when Isabella Valancy Crawford was writing, the social mood was rapidly changing, since modern transport and industry were transforming the pioneer society and making the distances of the new land less threatening and more penetrable. A safe and relatively stable society emerged, and the poets began to write less in the defensive forms that project collective experience and more in the briefer, more personal forms that stress individual perception and experience—the forms mostly used by the Confederation poets.

Only when a collective purpose re-emerged, as Canada was moving from the stage of contented colonialism to that of refined nationhood, did the more public forms appear again, most notably in the epic and mock epic poems which E. J. Pratt wrote to strengthen a sense of our history as Canadians.

Whatever the weaknesses of the earlier narrative poets, who preceded Pratt by half a century and more, they laid the foundations of our poetic tradition.

It is possible that if Canada has any epics, they are, with the exception of certain poems by E. J. Pratt, in prose. Indeed, outside the dramatic genre—which includes the poetic closet plays of Charles Mair, John Hunter-Duvar and Charles Heavysege in the nineteenth century and an interesting variety of verse plays for radio and stage about a century later— long poems of any kind and quality have been rare except in a limited period of the early Victorian era and the years immediately preceding it. And even if the decades from the end of the Napoleonic wars to Confederation do offer a weighty-looking list of narrative or at least long discursive poems, only a few are of lasting interest.

Until recently it was not easy to study any of the representative works of Canada's most prolific period in long poems. Verse was written then for even smaller audiences than today and was usually published in small editions which were not reprinted. Charles Sangster's "The St. Lawrence and the Saguenay" did not appear again for 116 years after its first printing in 1856. Howe's *Acadia* has never been published in full; even the incomplete version appearing in 1874 had to wait 98 years for second printing. Heavysege's *Jezebel* had to wait 104 years after its original appearance in the January 1868 issue of the *New Dominion Monthly* before it finally appeared within covers in a slender pamphlet presented by the Golden Dog Press of Montreal.

Recently, however, a fair number of Canada's Victorian and pre-Victorian long poems have become available to readers. David Sinclair's collection, *Nineteenth Century Narrative Poems*, which appeared in the New Canadian Library, included *The Rising Village* by Oliver Goldsmith the younger, Joseph Howe's *Acadia*, Sangster's "The St. Lawrence and the Saguenay," Alexander McLachlan's *The Emigrant* and Isabella Valancy Crawford's "Malcolm's Katie," all as they were originally published, together with lengthy extracts from William Kirby's rambling 178-page poem, *The U.E.: A Tale of Upper Canada. Nineteenth Century Narrative Poems* appeared in 1972, which was something of an *annus mirabilis* in revivals, since not only did Sangster's "The St. Lawrence and the Saguenay" have its second reprinting then in a collection of his poems which appeared in the University of Toronto Press's Literature of Canada series, but in the same series and the same year "Malcolm's Katie" also appeared in a facsimile reproduction of the 1905 edition of Isabella Valancy Crawford's *Collected Poems*.

The reasons why we are interested enough in such poems as I have mentioned to read them again after a century of neglect go beyond a mere academic concern. We read them because of our desire to find the roots of a culture that has at last grown apart from its parent cultures, and because we want to understand our ancestors and predecessors in the land. We read them, as we become conscious of our perilous relationship with the natural environment, because they depict in often vivid terms the life of a pristine Canada when the mechanical age was hardly beginning, and because most of their authors are closely preoccupied, though in a different way from us, with a concern for the environment that for them is expressed in a desire to tame and transform it. We also sense the irony implicit in the fact that the humanizing conquest of the wilderness they celebrate led inevitably to the destructive unbalancing of natural relations which we begin to fear may incur our own destruction.

As Roy Daniells has pointed out, in reading these mainly pre-Confederation poets, "We sense . . . one profound change of sensibility, now that pioneer days are past and gone. It is the loss of confidence, of cheerfulness, of joy, of eagerness" (*Canadian Literature* 56). And we do so, uneasily aware of an ironic division in our own attitude towards such qualities. For if we envy the cheerfulness and joy of these poets, if we admire their confidence and eagerness, it is with the sense that such admirable traits, because they were united with a less admirable lack of prophetic insight, produced those very consequences in terms of the thoughtless exploitation of the natural world that have made our age one of anxiety rather than confidence, of apprehension rather than joy. The fullness of living they celebrated passed into the excess of living we lament, and so, when we read such poems as "The Rising Village" and even, despite its dark undertones, "Malcolm's Katie," we find ourselves torn between two emotions: a quasi-romantic nostalgia for a time that could produce what Roy Daniells has also called "this élan, this ineradicable optimism and abounding hopefulness, this chorus of testimony to the ultimate goodness of life," and at the same time a certain knowing pity for a generation that did not recognize the threat of the "little cloud . . . like a man's hand" that came up out of the sea towards them.

When we turn from the phenomenon of our own interest in the narrative poems of early Canadian literature to the poems themselves, three questions immediately confront us. Why was the long discursive poem with its narrative line so popular in the colonial period? Why is there a gap of almost fifty years between "Malcolm's Katie," the last long narrative poem of the earlier period, and the next significant poems of that kind published by E. J. Pratt in the 1920s? And why were the narrative poems that appeared during that interlude the kind of spare and compact verse tales of which one finds good examples among the works of Charles G. D. Roberts and D. C. Scott or, on another level, of Robert W. Service?

The answer to these questions is that the long narrative poem was an essential transitional form which reflected not only the efforts of Canadian poets to find a way of writing that expressed their experience in a raw, half-dependent society but also the gradual and reluctant realization by men of taste and intelligence that their hopes of building in the New World a purified version of the society they had left behind in the Old World were doomed to frustration.

Essentially, in the discursive and quasi-philosophic form that it most often assumed in nineteenth-century Canada, the long narrative poem was the close descendant of the kind of long reflective poem, with its essentially social orientation and its desire to project an ordered world in an ordered form, that flourished in Britain through most of the eighteenth century and, somewhat modified by the influences of Scott and Byron, survived in the works of writers like Hood and Praed and Samuel Rogers well into the nineteenth century. This was poetry characterized by bland sentiment rather than by the ordered rage of the Restoration poets or the ordered passion of the Romantics. Because of its stylized vocabulary and phrasing, its metrical regularity and a selection of images and sentiments almost as formalized as Homer's, it was comparatively easy poetry to write, dependent on intent rather than inspiration; any man of letters with a sense of the sound of words could practise it reasonably well.

It was admirably suited to the colonial situation. Since pioneer cultures are inevitably conservative, the continuity of values and forms must be preserved precisely because experience is changing, and in the case of writers working within such a culture, their very isolation makes them seek the security of accepted forms rather than the adventure of new ones; the adventures find their place in the content of the narrative.

*The Rising Village,* first published in 1825, more than half a century after the elder Oliver Goldsmith's *The Deserted Village,* and the first Canadian narrative poem of any distinction, displays these characteristics in an extreme degree. Oliver Goldsmith was not merely the great-nephew of the celebrated writer who was Dr. Johnson's friend. He was also the son of a man who had left the United States rather than accept republican government, and he himself was born in the Loyalist town of St. Andrews not long after it was established. While it is true that his own life, spent largely in the city of Halifax and abroad, was remote from the pioneer past, he had heard from participants of the hardships involved in setting up a new community in the wilderness, and in writing of such a community he was taking a subject near the hearts and memories of his fellow colonists.

Yet the colonial desire to proceed within a safe framework of conventions determined the form of his poem. He decided not only to write in the same form as *The Deserted Village,* down to the vocabulary and the rhyming iambic couplet, but also to make his poem specifically a counterpart to his great-uncle's work, contrasting the growth of Maritime rural society from the emigrant village of his infancy with the decline of Irish and English rural society from the pre-enclosure villages of the elder Oliver's infancy. He makes the relationship specific when, in the early lines of *The Rising Village,* he remarks:

> If then adown your cheek a tear should flow
> For Auburn's village, and its speechless woe;
> If, while you weep, you think the "lowly train"
> Their early joys can never more regain,
> Come, turn with me where happier prospects rise,
> Beneath the sternness of Acadian skies.

And in his portrayal of the mainly happy outcome of settlement in the New World, there seems no doubt that he has in mind passages in *The Deserted Village* where emigration is portrayed as a tragic end for those who have been displaced from the sufficient existence of the English cottager. It is a "dreary scene" indeed to which the elder Goldsmith takes his dispossessed peasants as he portrays them attempting to make their settlement beside the Altama River in Georgia.

> Far different there from all that charmed before,
> The various terrors of that horrid shore;
> Those blazing suns that dart a downward ray,
> And fiercely shed intolerable day;
> Those matted woods where birds forget to sing,
> But silent bats in drowsy clusters cling;
> Those poisonous fields with rank luxuriance crowned,
> Where the dark scorpion gathers death around;
> Where at each step the stranger fears to wake
> The rattling terrors of the vengeful snake;
> Where crouching tigers wait their hapless prey,
> And savage men more murderous still than they;
> While oft in whirls the mad tornado flies,
> Mingling the savaged landscape with the skies.

The wilderness of *The Rising Village* is by no means lacking in its terrors of wild beasts howling around the backwoods cottage, or of "savage tribes in wildest strain" who "oft in sternest mood maintain / Their right to rule the mountain and the plain" and who "doom the *white man's* instant death." North American experience was still too near the horrors of wars conducted by British and French with Indian auxiliaries for the vision of settling the wilderness to be wholly without shadows. But they are shadows to be dispelled by "patient firmness and industrious toil," and in the end there emerges a new Auburn, though different from its English original, for while the Deserted Village represented the end of a tradition of long-matured skills and customs, the Rising Village has all the makeshift quality of pioneer life. Indeed, it is when the younger Oliver sets out to describe that life with ironic zest that his poem attains its greatest vigour, using the couplet to satiric effect in a manner that recalls Pope rather than the earlier Goldsmith.

For example, the pedlar who used to wander through the emergent settlements is shown assuming a "merchant's higher title," and there follows a sharply concrete description of the contents of a backwoods store:

Here, nails and blankets, side by side, are seen,
There, horses' collars and a large tureen;
Buttons and tumblers, fish-hooks, spoons and knives,
Shawls for young damsels, flannel for old wives;
Woolcards and stockings, hats for men and boys,
Mill-saws and fenders, silks, and children's toys;
All useful things, and joined with many more,
Compose the well-assorted country store.

The "half-bred" Doctor arrives:

No rival here disputes his doubtful skill,
He cures, by chance, or ends each human ill;
By turns he physics, or his patient bleeds,
Uncertain in what case each best succeeds.

From this point, the poem loses its temporary grip on actuality. A tenuously pathetic love motif is introduced in the sad tale of poor Flora driven mad by wicked Albert's betrayal, and the poem ends with patriotic and pro-British invocations:

Thy grateful thanks to Britain's care are due,
Her power protects, her smiles past hopes renew,
Her valour guards thee, and her councils guide,
Then, may thy parent ever be thy pride!—

and with a vision of the apotheosis of Acadia as "the wonder of the Western skies . . . / Till empires rise and sink, on earth, no more."

In other early Canadian narrative poems, with the theme of emigration and settlement in the wilderness remaining so popular as to be almost constant, one finds the same divergence as in *The Rising Village* between vast stretches of mere verse distinguished by no more than the trite thought and clichéd images made familiar by eighteenth-century sentimental poetasters, and the occasional passages whose actuality keeps them immediate even for us who read them a century or more afterward. Often it is the writers less polished in a conventional sense who achieve this effect most frequently, so that while Standish O'Grady's *The Emigrant,* projected in four cantos of which only the first was completed, seems as a whole a rambling and amateurish piece, yet on almost every page there are lines where a flash of sharp, original imagery opens a glimpse of the author's vigorous and independent mind. Pursuing his sardonic course, O'Grady seems to have realized, as the later nineteenth-century Canadian poets did, that the sharp condensed tale in verse is more effective among the necessities of a new society than the longueurs of the traditional discursive verse. As a consequence, one of the best fragments of early Canadian poetry is his Barhamesque passage, embedded in *The Emigrant,* on the discomfiture of the devil in frozen Quebec.

> Old Nick took a fancy, as many men tell,
> To come for a winter to live in Sorel,
> Yet the snow fell so deep as he came in his sleigh,
> That his fingers and toes were frost-nipt on the way.
>
> In truth, said the demon, who'd ever suppose,
> I must go back again with the loss of all those;
> In either extreme, sure it matters me not,
> If I freeze upon earth or at home I'm too hot;
>
> So he put back his sleigh, for he thought it amiss,
> His clime to compare to a climate like this;
> And now 'tis resolved that this frightful new-comer
> Will winter in hell and be here in the summer.

In Joseph Howe's *Acadia,* another incomplete and roughly constructed work (though composed by the most versatile of early Canadian men of letters), the natural vigour of the poet, his zestful interest in scenes of action, his sharp feeling for the physical beauties of his native Nova Scotia, emerge to redeem the poem's formal lameness and sameness.

> There the smooth lake its glassy bosom shows,
> Calm as the wearied spirit's last repose;
> Here frowns the beetling rock high o'er the tide,
> Fanned by the branches of the forest's pride;
> Here gently sloping banks of emerald dye
> Kiss the pure waves that on them softly lie,
> While buoyant flowers, the lake's unsullied daughters,
> Lift their bright leaves above the sparkling waters.
> There foams the torrent down the rocky steep,
> Rushing away to mingle with the deep,
> Shaded by leaves and flowers of various hues;
> Here the small rill its noiseless path pursues,
> While in its waves wild buds as gently dip
> As kisses fall on sleeping Beauty's lip.

The turns of phrase are often hackneyed, the conceits worn, as a language much used may be hackneyed and worn but carry genuine feeling, which this poem abundantly does as it continues with its identification of trees and flowers by specific tint and form, eventually creating in the mind's eye a landscape glowing from within like the magically perceived landscapes of adolescence. And indeed, reading Howe, and later reading Sangster and Crawford, one realizes what a splendid and pristine world the poets saw as their habitation; it was a perception proper to the youth of a people in a land yet incompletely possessed by either mind or hand.

An especially striking aspect of Howe's *Acadia* lies in its dichotomy of attitude towards the Indian. Considered in ideal terms, the Indian still appears in the poem as the "noble savage" invented and admired by eighteenth-century writers who had never left Europe, and Howe spends many lines, after he has described the wild landscape of Nova Scotia, telling of the life, simple in its appropriateness to such an environment, which the Indians led in their undisturbed past.

> But, when the white man landed on the shore,
> His dream of gods and spirits soon was o'er;
> He saw them rear their dwellings on the sod
> Where his free fathers had for ages trod;
> He saw them thoughtlessly remove the stones
> His hands had gathered o'er his parents' bones;
> He saw them fell the trees which they had spared,
> And war, eternal war, his soul declared.

At this point the noble savage of European invention is transformed by circumstance into the revengeful scourge of so much North American experience, and the most vigorous and best passage of *Acadia* is one that tends to contradict the generally bucolic nature of the rest of the poem: a vivid imaginative reconstruction in verse of the massacre of a settler and his family by Indians who attack by night. Howe pities the victims, yet there is obviously a part of the mind of this fierce fighter for rights and liberties that feels with the savage victors, and their inevitable and doomed resentments, as Goldsmith never did.

\* \* \*

The emigrant theme is treated in a variety of ways by the early nineteenth-century Canadian poets, though the treatment is always to a large degree derivative from British masters. Alexander McLachlan, in another of many poems entitled *The Emigrant,* presented what was less a narrative poem than a suite of songs and poetic episodes loosely woven around the record of a mythical emigrant settlement. McLachlan's models are numerous, though Burns was probably his closest master, and he stands outside the tradition of eighteenth-century gentility to which Goldsmith and Howe belong. Coming of poor origins, he remembered old injustices more sharply than did his contemporaries. His "Lean lank Tom, the politician" sings of England like a latter-day John Ball:

> "The squire's preserving his game.
>     He says that God gave it to him,
>   And he'll banish the poor without shame
>     For touching a feather or limb.
>
> "The Justice he feels very big,
>     And boasts what the law can secure,
>   But has two different laws in his wig,
>     Which he keeps for the rich and the poor.
>
> "The Bishop he preaches and prays,
>     And talks of a heavenly birth,
>   But somehow for all that he says,
>     He grabs a good share of the earth. . . ."

And there is the old Scots piper, Donald Ban, remembering the destruction of the habitations of the clansmen when they were dispossessed and forced to emigrate. For Donald emigration has brought no real betterment; old, blind and poor, he wanders in the settlements, playing the laments for people of other cultures who do not understand, and dying in loneliness. The fundamental difference between McLachlan's view of what had been achieved in Canada, and that of earlier poets like Goldsmith and Howe and even of contemporaries like Sangster, emerges when one contrasts with their essential optimism the suggestion McLachlan projects that at the time he wrote, with Canada changing from a collection of settlements into a nation, the simple goodness of the pioneering life, with its values of mutual aid and mutual trust, was fading fast.

> Much remains still to be told
> Of those men and times of old,
> Of the changes in our days
> From their simple, honest ways,
> Of the quacks on spoils intent,
> That flocked to our settlement,
> Of the swarms of public robbers,
> Speculators and land jobbers,
> Of the sorry set of teachers,
> Of the bogus tribe of preachers,

Of the host of herb physicians,
And of cunning politicians.
But the sun has hid his face
And the night draws on apace.

For the emigrant narrative, Charles Sangster substitutes a tenuous and unnecessary love story as he takes his reader on a full-scale guided tour of the two rivers of his longest poem's title, "The St. Lawrence and the Saguenay." The inclination towards the journey as an element of narrative structure which Sangster showed in its most extreme form was linked with the rapid increase in the facility of travel in Canada round about the mid-nineteenth century. The railway, curiously, did not strike the imagination of these poets, perhaps because so much of early North American experience had oriented them towards the waterways as natural channels of communication; it was the steamboats, which made water transport quicker and even safer, that appealed to their imagination, and one senses genuine delight and wonder as Kirby says: "But passing on, the rapid steamer glides / Smooth as a swan upon the glassy tides," or as Sangster evokes "The strong steamer, through the watery glade / Ploughing, like a huge serpent from its ambuscade."

Sangster was perhaps the most facile versifier among early Canadian poets, and with the exception of Hunter-Duvar and Isabella Crawford, the most versatile poet in a merely technical sense. Yet, except for brief exceptional passages, "The St. Lawrence and the Saguenay" remains the least tangible and the least memorable of the poems I mention. This is partly because it lacks the strong thematic spinal structure that is needed to sustain a long discursive poem. But it is equally due to the level and enamelled quality of Sangster's verse, always smoothly running and usually consisting of a chain of familiar metaphors linked by banal thoughts. This level tone, combined with a scarcity of fresh and striking images, makes it hard for us actually to visualize what Sangster is trying to tell us, and there remains in the mind a luminous and rather misty image like those created by the Canadian academic painters of the same period, who found themselves defeated by the attempt to capture a vastness which they could never quite encompass, a harshness they could never quite admit.

Occasionally, Sangster jolts out of his even pace with some authentic perception, some original image, and one gets a fleeting sense of a different poet behind the conventional façade. As he describes the Thousand Islands, for instance, there is one moment when one seems fleetingly to be witnessing the emergence from this bland poet's unconscious of some harsh germ of myth.

> Here nature holds her Carnival of Isles.
> Steeped in warm sunlight all the merry day,
> Each nodding tree and floating greenwood smiles.

So, in the usual Sangsterian manner a verse begins, and then the mood abruptly shifts:

> And moss-crowned monsters move in grim array;
> All night the Fisher spears his finny prey;
> The piney flambeaux reddening the deep,
> Past the dim shores, or up some mimic bay;
> Like grotesque banditti they boldly sweep
> Upon the startled prey, and stab them when they sleep.

Yet we return to conventionalized Indians and "their birchen fleet," to duck hunters and picnickers, and the dread Fisher never repeats his startling emergence.

Charles Heavysege was a poet of quite a different tone and quite a different character. He had strength rather than accomplishment, passion rather than polish, inner urge rather than outer amenity. His efforts to express himself in the mid-Victorian age as if he were writing in the reign of James I had at times ludicrous consequences, particularly when he failed to remember how the connotations of words and phrases changed. Sangster, cautious and meticulous, would never have been trapped into a solecism like that which Heavysege unconsciously commits when he makes Ahab cry out to Jezebel: "Take back thy bloody vineyard!" But Sangster, on the other hand, could never have made a story of the ancient world so passionately immediate as Heavysege made *Jezebel*, transforming the stern prose of the Bible into a poetic form that in no way diminishes it.

*Jezebel*, of course, provided an occasion to which Heavysege's approach was perfectly adapted. Such a story could never have been satisfactorily rendered in any kind of verse that was being written by other Canadian poets at that time. It needed the power and darkness of an archaic language spoken by a living man, and this is what Heavysege provided. Moreover, given the strongly religious cast of English-Canadian society in the Confederation age, when the Bible was by far the most familiar of all books, it could be argued that if the colonial situation demanded the use of borrowed styles, Heavysege's Jacobeanisms were less out of place than the Augustan gentility of Goldsmith or the neoclassicist fancies of Sangster.

But is there an element beyond the mere re-creation of long-dead passions that accounts for the peculiar tension one senses running through the poem? Is there an element that makes *Jezebel*, set in another place and time, nearer to the other narrative poems—with their settings in recent Canada—than at first sight appears? It seems to me there may have been.

Implicit in almost all the poems I have discussed is the sense of Acadia or Canada as a land with its own selfness, its own way of existence that must be preserved. The difference of this land from the republic to the south is sometimes only implied, as in "The St. Lawrence and the Saguenay," or is expressed indirectly through an emphasis on loyalist values, as in *The Rising Village* and *Acadia*.

*Jezebel*, of course, is not overtly about Canada and the United States, but it is about a land threatened with alien domination, represented by the foreign queen and the infidel and materialistic faith of Baal she seeks to impose. *Jezebel* was probably written in 1867 and appeared in 1868, the year after Confederation, in a Montreal magazine—the *New Dominion Monthly* —whose very title stresses its nationalist inclinations.

When one further considers the central role Heavysege gives to the episode of Naboth's vineyard, which takes up the whole of the middle canto of the poem, the underlying parallels become even more interesting. Heavysege expands the biblical version to represent Ahab wandering in his palace garden, enjoying sunlight after storm, forgetting the slaughter on Mount Horeb, and immediately coveting Naboth's vineyard; as soon as the strife in his kingdom ends, in other words, he becomes rapacious for the land of others, as American politicians did for Canadian land after the Civil War was over. And he significantly expands Naboth's biblical answer ("The Lord forbid it me, that I should give the inheritance of my fathers unto thee") to read:

> I cannot yield thee that which is not mine,
> But was my father's, and must be my son's.
> Ask me not for it, then; yet beg aught else,
> And I will give it thee; but God forbid
> That I should yield thee mine inheritance.

There follows the sequence in which Naboth is falsely accused and then killed so that his land may pass into Ahab's hands.

Heavysege, it seems evident, was not expanding and elaborating the biblical story without a topical purpose, for during the years leading to Confederation the story of Naboth's fate was much in Canadian minds as a parable reflecting fears of invasion and annexation. In 1867 no less a figure than Sir John A. Macdonald declared: "A brilliant future would await us were it not for those wretched Yankees, who hunger and thirst for Naboth's field." One does not have to speculate outrageously to imagine the reading many Canadians must have given *Jezebel* when it appeared in 1868, particularly as they related Naboth's death by false accusation to the suggestion of certain American leaders that Canada be handed over to settle the *Alabama* claim, which was no concern of Canadians.

Roy Daniells has pointed out that "Isabella Crawford is in a somewhat different class, both in sensibility and in craftsmanship," from the other nineteenth-century narrative poets. "Malcolm's Katie," as he pointed out, has qualities that are both mythic and melodramatic. But though there are passages in "Malcolm's Katie" of a lyrical intensity and excellence unattained by previous Canadian poets, they are combined with a powerful tale of love, jealousy and conflict welded on to a thematic structure not unlike that of the earlier narrative poems, embracing the settlement and conquest of the wilderness, and ending in a patriotic invocation.

> I would not change these wild and rocking woods,
> Dotted by little homes of unbark'd trees,
> Where dwell the fleers from the waves of want,
> For the smooth sward of selfish Eden bowers.

Yet even on the social level—and Crawford is openly conscious of this, describing her hero Max as "social-soul'd"—there is evident a sense that the Canadian world has moved irrevocably beyond the simplicities of the pioneer beginnings.

> Then came smooth-coated men with eager eyes
> And talk'd of steamers on the cliff-bound lakes,
> And iron tracks across the prairie lands,
> And mills to crush the quartz of wealthy hills,
> And mills to saw the great wide-arm'd trees,
> And mills to grind the singing stream of grain;
> And with such busy clamour mingled still
> The throbbing music of the bold, bright Axe—
> The steel tongue of the Present, and the wail
> Of falling forests—voices of the Past.

It is curious but significant that while Max rather simply boasts, "My axe and I, we do immortal tasks; / We build up nations—this my axe and I!" the long speech by the villain Alfred, exposing the mortality of nations as of men, is far more telling.

Here we may have a clue to the reason for the interlude, the half-century from Crawford to Pratt, in which no significant long narrative poems were written by Canadians. Crawford retained within a precarious balance her warring inclinations towards socially oriented narrative and inwardly oriented lyrical verse. Within herself she represented the conflict point that arises in any culture when the poetry which uses accepted means to chart the emergence of a new society becomes outmoded, because as society grows individual expression it once again seeks a voice, and an original voice at that. The poets who followed her were concerned with the latter need, and even the narratives they wrote were no longer of social import; instead they narrowed individual experience, individual achievement and defeat, into their small compass. It was only when, after creating Canada, Canadians had to some degree identified themselves, that the social themes emerged again with E. J. Pratt in longer poems, raised often into myth and, at Pratt's best, distanced into the epic dimension which the earlier narrative poets never attained.

# 12

# THE TYRANNY OF GOD

*Charles Heavysege and the Canadian Tradition*

**A**lready, in Timothy Findley's fable, *Not Wanted on the Voyage,* we have seen a Canadian writer questioning Divine Providence and reviving an ancient gnostic argument that the God of the Old Testament was evil and not good.

But Findley was not the first writer in our tradition to do this. Well over a century before, in the 1850s, the working-class poet, Charles Heavysege, had raised it in his powerful, imperfect drama, *Saul.* Later, in his long poem *Jephtha's Daughter,* Heavysege was to take as his subject another biblical story and declare a doubt of the justice of God's will. What gives these works their special agony is that Heavysege writes them as a practising Christian and not as a free thinker, for *Saul* was published two years before that skeptic's Bible, *The Origin of Species,* and it seems likely that Heavysege was influenced by earlier Christian tendencies to reject the arbitrariness of Jehovah's judgements and commands.

With all the grandeurs and absurdities of his verse, Heavysege was an example of a kind of writer who has appeared recurrently in Canadian literature: large in vision, powerful at times in expression, yet flawed by a chronic awkwardness in handling the language. Frederick Philip Grove was a similar case in prose; so to a lesser degree is Hugh MacLennan and in our generation Rudy Wiebe—clumsy giants whose importance cannot be denied since in some half-conscious way they image forth the great preoccupations of their times.

**T**oday, in the late twentieth century, writers in Canada are aware of each other and in constant contact, because there are enough of them to make a viable literary society; such an environment fosters and fertilizes their originality and strength of vision. By contrast, one of the most discouraging aspects of a writer's life in mid-Victorian Canada was usually its isolation. Writers were few, most of them lived by other means than writing, and, since the infrastructure of a Canadian literary world in terms of publishers, periodicals and a public hardly existed, they relied largely for whatever literary income they might earn on publication abroad. Often they seemed to stand, like Charles Heavysege, as solitary figures in an unresponsive setting, developing highly personal visions that seem to have little immediate relation to the world around them, and, since there is so scanty a local tradition as yet, looking into the general past of English-speaking literature for their myths and their models. Yet because they persisted, because they left ambitious works that stand like Regency follies in an unfriendly landscape and evoke a certain—albeit often grudging—admiration, they have their place and represent a distinct and necessary phase in the succession by which Canadian writing developed into a tradition of its own.

The information that can be scraped together regarding Charles Heavysege's life is scanty, as it is with other early Canadian writers who were his contemporaries, like Charles Sangster and Isabella Valancy Crawford. All the accounts agree that he was born on 2 May 1816. But there is a sharp difference of opinion as to the place where he was born.

J. C. Stockdale, in the *Dictionary of Canadian Biography,* states that it was Huddersfield in Yorkshire; Solly Bridgetower, in Robertson Davies's highly satirical *Leaven of Malice,* declares that, on the day we all agree on, Charles Heavysege first saw the light of day in Liverpool. The American poet and novelist Bayard Taylor, who sought Heavysege out in Montreal and wrote a sympathetic account of him in the *Atlantic Monthly* in 1865, also gave his birthplace as Liverpool. Later, in correspondence with another American writer, Charles Lanman, Heavysege agreed that Taylor's article was "generally correct," though he also said that "his ancestors on the paternal side" came from Yorkshire. We can assume that Heavysege was born in Liverpool of a Yorkshire family.

Otherwise, the known facts reveal a boy born into a poor family and forced to leave school at the age of nine, which was not unusual in the 1820s. He was apprenticed to a woodcarver and worked from thirteen to fifteen hours a day all through his childhood. "I was," he remembered, "what is usually styled religiously brought up, and taught to consider not only the theatre itself, but dramatic literature, even its best examples, as forbidden things." However, his mother was more indulgent than his father, and he managed to persuade her to give him "covertly . . . a few pence daily for a cheap edition of Shakespeare that was then being issued in parts." Yet Bayard Taylor gained the impression that Milton was "the first author that made a profound impression on his mind." If one adds the Bible, which must have been constantly present in such a home as his, one probably has the sum of Heavysege's childhood literary influences. It was the kind of self-education that sustained a whole lineage of English working-class dissenting writers from John Bunyan onward.

At the end of his apprenticeship, Heavysege set up his own woodcarving workshop in Liverpool and at one point employed several hands, but he had neither business ability nor the ambition to make a fortune, and by his thirties he had certainly begun to divert his energies to writing poetry, for his first work was published in 1852 in both Liverpool and London. It was *The Revolt of Tartarus,* an epic in the Miltonic tradition, and it aroused little attention.

The next year he emigrated to Canada and began to work for a Montreal firm of cabinetmakers. He had not given up his literary ambitions and combined his two occupations, for the poet John Reade, who met him in 1858, recorded:

> Heavysege told me that he was accustomed to compose while he was engaged at work, the occupation of his hands not interfering with the efforts of his mind. Speaking especialiy of *Saul,* he said that in this way he had elaborated some of the livelist scenes.

In 1855 Heavysege's first Canadian-published book appeared, in Montreal—a volume of sonnets. Not a single copy appears to have survived. But the work to which Heavysege devoted most of his energies at this time was his verse drama, *Saul.* The first edition appeared in 1857, and much of his later life was to be spent on working over this massive work for subsequent editions, of which the second appeared, in London as well as in Montreal, in 1859, while a third appeared in Boston in 1869 and was reprinted in New York in 1876, the year of his death.

As this publishing history suggests, *Saul* attracted much more attention abroad than in Canada. Emerson and Longfellow admired the play and a copy reached Nathaniel Hawthorne, who was United States consul in the poet's home town of Liverpool; Hawthorne showed it to the English poet Coventry Patmore, who anonymously wrote a laudatory notice in the *North British Review* which described *Saul* as "indubitably one of the most remarkable poems ever written out of Great Britain."

A second play, *Count Filippo: or, The Unequal Marriage,* was published in 1860; astonishingly, to modern readers, it was too sexually explicit for Victorian tastes, and gathered poor notices and few readers. In the same year, Heavysege left his carver's bench, and, at the urging of some of his friends, who thought it a more congenial occupation for a poet, became a reporter on the Montreal *Transcript.* Later he joined the staff of the Montreal *Witness,* of which he became city editor; he remained at the *Witness* until 1874, two years before his death.

It was an unhappy choice, which the more perceptive of his friends regretted. John Reade remarked: "I never saw him spending his intellectual strength in this way without feeling how lamentable his choice had been." Heavysege himself told Charles Lanman: "You will know that to be the reporter and local editor of a daily newspaper does not permit of the seizing of those inspired moods, which come we know not how, and leave us we know not wherefore." Apparently Heavysege's day at the Montreal *Witness* did not end until eight or nine o'clock in the evening, so that to do his own writing he had to work far into the night; when his wife remonstrated that he would harm his health, he answered that he would prefer to shorten his life rather than cease to write. When he did give up this drudgery and retired to devote himself to writing, it was too late; he died two years later of what was described as "nervous exhaustion."

Given the frustrations of this latter period of his life, it is not surprising that Heavysege's production of new works should have slowly diminished after the completion of *Saul* and *Count Filippo*. In 1864 he published two poems, *The Dark Huntsman,* a narrative of 160 lines, and *The Owl,* a poem of twenty-five stanzas of which no copy seems to have survived. At the Shakespeare Tercentenary in Montreal that year he delivered an ode whose complete version has also vanished. In 1865 he published both his worst work, a novel called *The Advocate,* and one of his best, the long narrative poem *Jephtha's Daughter,* which was accompanied by a group of sonnets, some of them revisions of the lost *Sonnets* of 1855. The last of Heavysege's works to be published was another narrative poem, *Jezebel,* which appeared in the *New Dominion Monthly* in January 1868.

\*     \*     \*

In dealing with poets like Heavysege, one is almost inevitably forced into the relativist position that is implied in all of Northrop Frye's references to early Canadian poets. We can regard them as "major" poets only in relation to their time: biggish frogs in a very small pool. Their importance in providing the first literature of any interest in a land that as yet had none of its own cannot be denied. Nor can the fact that perhaps their very isolation, in a community which remained unconvinced that anything good could be written in a colonial setting, may have been responsible for the kind of forlorn power which, at best, the work of poets like Heavysege and Isabella Valancy Crawford reveals. Judged by later Canadian standards, and even British standards in their own time, their writing often seems uncouth, derivative, perversely archaic for poetry written in what aspired to be a "new land." These poets lacked restraint; they lacked freshness of diction and imagery; they lacked a distinctive "poetic voice"; they lacked taste. And, as Norman Newton once remarked in *Canadian Literature,* these lacks are intimately related to the very nature of their work. "Apparently Heavysege's genius and his lack of taste were inseparably related; he could write 'correctly,' but only by writing dully." Heavysege was a poet of natural power and an obsessive preoccupation with the conflict between human and divine justice, whose dramatic architecture was ramshackle at

213

best and whose lack of a true ear led him to write both some of the most inept verse ever published in Canada and—occasionally—some surprisingly good poetry.

*Saul* is, at first sight, a daunting book, for, like so many of the other closet dramatists (for example Thomas Hardy in *The Dynasts*), Heavysege welcomed the removal of the limitations of length that stage performances imposed; the second and best edition of the play runs to 328 pages—well over ten thousand lines. This choice of a lengthy reading structure in preference to a compact acting one notably affected the work, making it more repetitious and at the same time more psychologically searching than it might otherwise have been, since the lack of a need for constant dramatic interaction between the characters meant that Saul himself became larger than the rest not only in physique but also in moral complexity, and his lengthy soliloquies tended to carry the burden of the play's intent to a much greater extent than did the actual dialogue.

In this sense *Saul* comes near in spirit to the introspective psychological novel, with its action turned inward. Yet there is no lack of at least reported physical activity, for the alarms and excursions are endless. Time and again the Philistines invade, or Saul attacks them, until one's mind is numbed by the repetitious descriptions of battles. A dramatist writing for the stage would have had to pick and choose, as Peter Haworth eventually did when he trimmed the great bulk of *Saul* in 1973 into a successful two-hour acting script for CBC radio.

Heavysege follows the biblical account in the Book of Samuel, but shifts the weight of priestly and antimonarchical prejudice in that narrative by presenting Saul as a heroic figure—as he explicitly acknowledges in his introduction—pitted against a vindictive priesthood interpreting the commands of an arbitrary and capricious Jehovah, of whom the demon chorus chants derisively at the beginning of the play:

> Mocketh all things the Creator,
> Mocketh his own realm of nature;
> Think no sons of earth he'll spare
> Who smote the nobler things of air.

The action begins with Saul's anointing as king by Samuel and ends with his death in a final battle with the Philistines, after he has finally severed his loyalties to Jehovah by communing with a necromancer, the Witch of Endor. The divine cards are stacked against Saul from the beginning, since Samuel at the time of his anointing declares that the decision of the Israelites to be ruled by kings is displeasing to the Lord, and Saul is constantly placed in situations where his impatience or even his compassion lead him into acts of disobedience to Jehovah's orders for which he is implacably punished, first by the madness caused by an "evil spirit from the Lord," then by the rise of David, whom the alienated Samuel raises up as his rival for the kingship, and finally by his death at the hands of the Philistines, whose victory seems on this occasion to have been divinely engineered to get rid of Saul and have David crowned in his place.

Saul is presented as the typical tragic hero, his flaws being pride and an inclination towards human compassion that jars with divine implacability. Except for various intruders from the spirit world, the remaining characters come mainly from the biblical narrative, but by the end of the play they seem curiously diminished in comparison with the central figure; David is reduced to a bloodthirsty prig and Samuel to a mean-spirited old man untroubled by the arbitrariness of Jehovah's commands and hypocritically insisting on his love for Saul while laying traps for him. In fact the only character as interesting as Saul is the demon Malzah, the "evil spirit from the Lord," a kind of inverted Ariel who speaks some of Heavysege's most amusing and some of his most absurd lines and who enters subtly into the moral structure of the play, for he in the end shows compassion for Saul while Jehovah does not:

> Why did I ever, thoughtlessly, engage
> To make his soul more wretched than my own? . . .
> 'Twas in an evil hour I came to tempt him:
> For this most vile transaction ends not here;
> But I shall ever self-upbraidings know
> Oft as I meet him in the realms below.

Strong as the influence of Milton is in *Saul* — which is a more curious battleground than *Paradise Lost,* since here the demonic forces are conscripted to serve Jehovah against human beings — it is not the devils but Saul himself who resembles the Miltonic Satan; both Satanic stature and the essential conflict with God are transferred to the human hero, and there are times when mere humanity collapses under the burden even before the end, for grand and sombre though the king may be, he is mortal, and we know that he is doomed in a way the angels — even the fallen ones — are not. Thus our sympathy is drawn towards his predicament with, as Heavysege said, "its picturesque grandeur, its sadness and tragic issue," and towards his stance when, sick and guilty for massacres committed at Jehovah's command, and moved to pity for the victims, he declares:

> But that I dare not let my thoughts have birth,
> Much less array these embryo thoughts in words,
> I should deliver me of such conception
> As would appall the reverent ear of men,

And make me seem, even what I fear I am,
The Omnipotent's accuser.

Perhaps, when our feelings are so aroused in Saul's favour, it may seem pointless to ask where Heavysege's feelings lay. Sandra Djwa in her introduction to her collection *Saul and Selected Poems* (1973), argues that "ultimately . . . Heavysege views Saul's offense as Shakespeare did that of Macbeth, as an offense against degree," and she disagrees with T. R. Dale's argument in a 1959 *Canadian Forum* article that *Saul* is "a potentially dangerous and explosive work" in its suggestion that, in its hero's words, "the Almighty greater is than good." Dale, I suggest, is certainly right about the effect of *Saul,* though Djwa may be right about the poet's intent. Yet even when I consider the intent of *Saul,* it seems to be written in such a way that, given human and demonic and angelic testimony, we can make our own judgements between a human and a somewhat more repellent divine morality. Certainly the often excessive elaboration of the arguments Saul offers in his many soliloquies suggests that Heavysege was anxious to give him ample space to state a case against the Almighty.

One cannot after all ignore the rebellious antinomian element within the dissenting tradition which dispensed Christians from the laws of the Old Testament Jehovah and which even in the nineteenth century gave its touch of radicalism to the nonconformist sects—to one of which Heavysege belonged—and which led to a constant restless pushing out to the frontiers of theology. In a period when both Coleridge and Godwin started off as dissenting ministers on strange odysseys, and when so many of the Romantic poets—like Byron in *Cain* and Shelley in *Prometheus Unbound*—dismissed Jehovah and his cognate, Zeus, as tyrants, it is not unlikely that Heavysege may deliberately have been giving us the option to regard Saul as a Prometheus, posing human compassion against divine implacability.

As a play *Saul* suffers all the defects inherent in the closet drama, defects that careful editing might have modified. Its sprawling structure, its abundance of pointlessly repetitious episodes, its often staggering wordiness, would have made it at any time unsuitable for a stage performance, an unsuitability compounded by the fact that Heavysege had neither an eye for stage action nor an ear for stage dialogue; even trimmed to size, it is so much a literary rather than a theatrical work that only in the disembodied and intensely verbal medium of radio drama could *Saul* re-establish its credibility. Yet the feeling of passion is always there, sometimes submerged and sometimes overt, the sense that Heavysege was stirred to the heart by Saul's predicament and that all his verbal excesses were part of the passion.

In *Saul* Heavysege is indeed often at his best in descriptive passages incidental to the main theme in which an uncharacteristic visuality appears. These range from sudden sharp and immediate images like Saul's "I feel the demon move / Amidst the gloomy branches of my breast," or the demon Zaph's Tennysonian figure, "Or where the brook runs o'er the stones, and smooths / Their green locks with his current's crystal comb," to bleak but haunting evocations, like that of a soldier approaching David's hiding place at En-Gedi, which suggest that Heavysege might have been remembering some actual north country landscape of his pre-Canadian days:

> Wilder and barrener this region grows:
> Till naught but sheep, and they of smallest size,
> Draw from it sustenance. No fields of corn
> Are here, nor rye or barley, neither roots
> To fare the frugal shepherds who appear
> Dwelling within the doors of bleak starvation;
> A rising melancholy moorland, that
> Ascending keeps, until the sterile hills
> Seem to be hanging in the sombre clouds.
> What that hath life can harbour there?

Here and there, also, one encounters philosophizing passages where the rhetoric is muted and a feeling emerges so deeply personal that one senses a more than coincidental identification between Heavysege, beset by the problems of creation in an unresponsive land, and Saul, beset by the problems of moral living in an unresponsive universe ruled by an arbitrary deity. For example:

> To hunt or to be hunted make existence;
> For we are all but chasers or the chased;
> And some weak, luckless wretches ever seem
> Flying before the hounds of circumstance
> A-down the windy gullies of this life,
> Till, toppling over death's uncertain verge
> We see of them no more.

If any character in the play is Heavysege's persona, it is certainly not Samuel or David; it is clearly Saul, and this is perhaps our best answer to his intent. Whatever his didactic purpose, his artistic intent puts him clearly, if not on the devil's side, at least on Saul's, and knowing it.

Any problems that exist with the intent of Heavysege's other play, *Count Filippo*, are more easily stated if not solved, since it is a much simpler work and one in which artifice counts for much more, and feeling for much less, than in *Saul*. The play begins with a brief and perhaps defensive introduction by Heavysege:

> Next in enormity to a breach of the marriage relation, stands its mutual contraction by youth and years. To give a truthful, though fictitious, instance of the sad issue of such an ill-omened union as the latter, is the aim of this drama.

Actually, *Count Filippo* deals with both adultery and marriage between an older man and a younger woman, the second providing the temptation for the first, and it does so in a way suggesting that originally, before he wrote his moralistic little apologia, Heavysege was mainly concerned with trying out various dramatic models and ended with an unhappy mongrel of a play. Yet there may be more to it than a mere failed experiment.

The plot, which proceeds somewhat more directly than that of *Saul,* concerns the elderly minister of an old Tuscan duke who sets out to arrange a marriage in a neighbouring court for the ruler's unwilling son and heir, Hylas. While the count is away at Arno (which Heavysege presents as a city rather than a river), Hylas is egged on by the libertine Gallantio to seduce Filippo's young wife; the corruption of Paphiana, wife of the neighbouring landlord Gonardo, by Gallantio himself is the subplot of *Count Filippo*. Volina immediately after her seduction falls into bitter remorse. In the end, after Filippo returns and Gonardo reveals the results of his assiduous spying in the guise of a gypsy minstrel, the old duke dies of distress on hearing of all this wrongdoing, Gallantio is sentenced to be tortured to death, Filippo, Hylas and Volina all decide to retire into various cloisters, the first to expiate his fault in marrying a young woman, the other two to expiate their adultery. Only Gonardo and Paphiana of the principal characters remain in the world, he the epitome of the eternal jealous husband, she of the eternal defiant wife.

Although the plot, other than the dénouement, seems to be borrowed from Alfieri, the play has a great deal in common with earlier English Italianate comedy. The plot of the old husband deceived by the young gallant is a common one among Cavalier playwrights, from Beaumont and Fletcher, whose verse Heavysege's at times resembles, down to such Restoration writers as Etherage, Wycherley and Aphra Behn, and the comic old cuckold Gonardo, the cynical libertine Gallantio and the defiant adulterous wife Paphiana would not have been out of place on the London stage in the reign of Charles II. But the other side of the play, the remorse and moral self-condemnation, and the inordinately mawkish manner of their expression, belong rather in the next century, the age of sentiment and Samuel Richardson.

It seems to me that here we have something more than a clumsily amateur attempt to bring together two incompatible approaches to the drama, one defiantly amoral and the other stubbornly moralistic. There is a divided moral being at work in *Count Filippo,* and one not entirely in tune with his world.

Much in *Count Filippo* would have appealed to Victorian readers, and to Victorian audiences if it had been produced, notably the scenes of regret for sins committed and the Gothic devices by which nature with its storms and its sinister moonlight effects provides a kind of supernatural backdrop to the heavy play of emotions.

But there are aspects that Victorian Canadian readers found disturbing. The duke, ruler and arbiter of justice and morals, is revealed as having been a libertine in his youth and not particularly repentant for it; he presides over a court whose morals are so easy that Hylas was already an apprentice rake with some practice before he began his assault on Volina. Ordinary loose behaviour seems to be condoned when Volina cries out: "More heinous sin than Magdalen's is mine; / Adultery, worse than a virgin's lapse." Two adulteries take place in the play, and one couple caught *in flagrante delicto,* Gallantio and Paphiana, are unrepentant to the end, and are even presented as if they were meant to earn our grudging admiration. Count Filippo, by his admission of wrongdoing in taking a young wife, which almost condones Volina's lapse, must have seemed to good Victorians a destroyer of the two pillars of their paternalistic world, the subordination of the young to the old and the infantilization of women by their subordination to husbands who domineered them *in loco parentis.*

And, though Freud was far ahead, it is hard to think that Heavysege's fellow Montrealers would be entirely blind to the sexual imagery that gives a kind of febrile vitality to the conventional patterns of *Count Filippo.* Gallantio, expectedly, is profuse in such suggestive metaphors: "She is a landscape, wrapped indeed in snow, / But underneath, the heated, golden mine"; "Again, take your artillery to the breach"; "While he, afraid to row into her haven / (Or heaven rather)" and the delightfully anachronistic "the touch is love's electric line." But Hylas speaks them too: "Why do you fear the snake that you have charmed?" And so, more obliquely, does even Volina, reflecting an obsession with the moon as a necromantic symbol that occurs repeatedly in *Saul:*

> I am the moon, 'twould seem, to rule his tides.
> Then flow, tides, toward the moon, and bathe this shore;
> Yet flow nor here too oft, lest some should say,
> The moon is mad, or tide has lost its way.

Among such passages are the best, most vital fragments of poetry in *Count Filippo,* and they bespeak a hidden revolt against current morality that parallels the hidden revolt against an implacable deity in *Saul.* Here indeed was more of the "potentially dangerous and explosive" quality that T. R. Dale found in *Saul,* and it is hardly surprising that the Victorians tended to ignore rather than condemn *Count Filippo* (since condemnation would have exposed a guilty knowingness on their part) and that Heavysege, in his persona as the respectable Christian workingman sedulously bettering himself, should have spent a good deal of his time in later years pathetically cleaning up *Count Filippo* for republication.

Of Heavysege's four narrative poems, the first predates either of the plays, having been published originally the year before Heavysege set sail for Canada. *The Revolt of Tartarus* is a Miltonic pastiche, a blank verse poem of six books which is really interesting only because its theme already projects Heavysege's central obsession with revolt against an arbitrary deity. As in *Saul,* the rebel—who this time is Satan himself and not a surrogate—is defeated, but there are ironies to the situation as there are to *Paradise Lost,* which suggest that Heavysege's mind is no more single in this work than it is in *Saul.* Essentially, *The Revolt of Tartarus* is a pendant to *Paradise Lost,* for it begins when Satan, having been punished by God for the corruption of Adam and Eve, sets out on a revengeful journey to the outer galaxies of the universe in search of further Edens to be destroyed. Satan's quest is frustrated, but a final ambiguity—foreshadowing the appointment in *Saul* of the demon Malzah to be the unwilling "evil spirit from the Lord"—is provided in the suggestion of ultimate complicity between God and devil in the fact that when the lesser fallen angels stage a revolt in Hell during Satan's absence, the latter is reinstated as the ruler of the underworld, and thus, in showing a government of Tartarus parallel to the government of Heaven and sustained by it against rebellion, Heavysege is, knowingly or not, suggesting their mutual indispensability and hence a kind of Manichean equality between them.

The next two narrative poems, like *Saul,* deal with episodes in the Bible that, once again, show Old Testament situations where obedience is placed above mercy, the doctrine of the children paying for the sins of the fathers is mordantly evoked, and the insistence on compassion and forgiveness that characterizes Christianity has no place except in the minds of doubters or rebels. Reading these poems, it seems hard to agree with Sandra Djwa's suggestion that in them Heavysege was "affirming his own faith in Christian obedience," since in fact they concern a pre-Christian world which the Gospels superseded, and we cannot ignore the fact that before he wrote *Jephtha's Daughter* Heavysege had been reading Euripides' *Iphigenia,* which has the same theme of a child sacrificed to an implacable deity who demands the literal keeping of promises and appears impermeable to argument or compassion. In fact, of course, Iphigenia was saved by the pity of Artemis to become her priestess, and so Heavysege is right in suggesting that the fate of Jephtha's daughter is "more fraught with . . . grim fate";

there is indeed an especial grimness in the fact that Jephtha, remembering
the divine substitution of a ram for Isaac, hopes as much will be granted to
him as to Abraham, and waits for a sign. The silence that follows is described—powerfully, if somewhat Tennysonianly, as Djwa remarks—in
the best-known passage of the poem:

> He said, and stood awaiting for the sign,
> And hears above the hoarse, bough-bending wind,
> The hill-wolf howling on the neighbouring height,
> And bittern booming in the pool below.
> Some drops of rain fell from the passing cloud,
> That sudden hides the wanly shining moon,
> And from the scabbard instant dropped his sword,
> And, with long, living leaps and rock-struck clang,
> From side to side, and slope to sounding slope,
> In gleaming whirls swept down the dim ravine
> (Ill omen!): and, mute trembling, as he stood
> Helmless (to his astonished view) his daughter,
> All in sad disarray, appeared.

In *The Bush Garden* Northrop Frye, who evidently shares the view that
Heavysege is seeing the tragedy of Jephtha and his daughter through a
Christian as distinct from an Old Testament eye, offers a provocative
comment:

> To Heavysege, a man who, like Jephtha, worships a God who demands fulfil-
> ment of a rash vow of sacrifice even if it involves his own daughter, is really a
> man in the state of nature: he has identified his God, if not with nature, at any
> rate with a mindless force of inscrutable mystery like nature, and all Jephtha's
> questionings and searchings of spirit are the looks of intelligence directed at
> blankness, the attempts of a religious pioneer to find a spiritual portage through
> the heart of darkness.
>
> In this poem Heavysege has put together certain essential ideas: the contrast
> of human and civilized values with nature's disregard of them in a primitive
> country, the tendency in the religion of such a country for God to disappear be-
> hind the mask of nature, and the symbolic significance, when that happens, of
> human sacrifice and the mutilation of the body. . . . Once one has carefully
> read this narrative, the essential meaning of many fine Canadian poems leaps
> out of its derivative and conventional context.

Frye places this passage in a discussion of nineteenth-century Canadian
narrative poems that treat of God and nature in similar ways, and clearly
the implicit suggestion is that Heavysege is reflecting in his own way the

general horror and fear of the wilderness that was part of what Frye has described as the garrison mentality of early Canadian immigrants. In other words, despite all the appearance of his Jacobean language and forms, Heavysege was a true Canadian writer at heart.

There is no evidence that Heavysege experienced the actual Canadian wilderness, though we do know, as his imagery suggests, that he was excited by the violence of the country's storms, and one of his daughters remembered that he "loved Canada's . . . silent country, and the snow." Certainly he was likely to have heard enough about the wilderness to share the general attitude towards it of Canadian townsmen, and it is possible that he was aware enough of popular Darwinism to absorb some of its sense of an indifferent and brutal nature. So we can accept Frye's interpretation as perhaps correctly describing a half-conscious identification on Heavysege's part between man in the primitive world of ancient Palestine and man in the primitive world beyond the towns in Canada.

Another long poem, *Jezebel,* is to all appearance a biblical story like *Jephtha's Daughter,* and an equally ambivalent one. Overtly it takes the orthodox line of showing Ahab as a weak man, which is contrary to what the historical record suggests, and Jezebel is portrayed with zest as the ruthless woman who destroys her husband and herself by the extremity of her wilfulness. But covertly one is led to see Elijah, like Samuel, as another fanatic and cruel servant of Jehovah, and the massacre of the priests of Baal as atrocious and arbitrary like the massacres that touched Saul's conscience and set him against God. However, as I have shown in the preceding essay, *Jezebel* is most interesting as a disguised political poem, related to Canadian fears of a militant post–Civil War United States at the time of Confederation, and to get a final insight into the nature of Heavysege's Christian faith we must turn to the other surviving long poem, *The Dark Huntsman.*

Writers on Heavysege up to now have tended to minimize the differences between the two versions of *The Dark Huntsman.* Both deal with the theme, often rendered in verse by European poets, of Death as a dark huntsman seeking with his hounds for souls, but the first version, published as a booklet in 1868, is not only almost three times as long as the second but also much more elaborate in its imagery and sometimes more naively absurd, as in the description of Death's hounds—"each fierce as a dragon; / Like embers their eyes, their jaws foaming like flagon." It is also much more galloping in its rhythms, which suggest that Heavysege had recently been reading Edgar Allan Poe, whose "The Raven" is said to have influenced his lost poem, *The Owl,* published in the same year as *The Dark Huntsman:*

The blasts of his bugle grew wilder, more eerie
While gaily he galloped, as one never weary
Adown the dim valley, so doleful and dreary,
And woke the tired twilight with echoes forlorn.

Death calls the dreamer, who feels bound to obey, until he awakens:

An agony shook me,
All manhood forsook me,
I woke—'twas a dream at the dying of day.

The second version, besides being shorter, is starker in both rhythm and imagery, and though the hunter and his hounds disappear into Hades, the poem ends not with the thought that this has been merely a dream, but with a much more sombre reflection:

For who that is mortal can meet without fear
The figure endowed with the Fate-winged spear?
Or temper his breath
At thy presence, O Death,
Who hunteth for souls as one hunteth the deer!

It was written shortly before Heavysege's death, and it may indicate that in his last days his thoughts turned towards his end and *The Dark Huntsman* came anew into his mind. It is significant, in view of the attempts of some critics to present Heavysege as a pious Christian poet, that the thought of death is accompanied by no thought of redemption. Indeed, the poem reads as fatalistically as anything written in classical antiquity, and the dead are represented as they are in the *Odyssey,* living in a "Land of Shadows" where "the Ghosts of thy Fathers glide grey."

The sonnets that were printed with *Jephthah's Daughter* contain some of the best of Heavysege, perhaps because he was forced to work within circumscribed forms, even if, like his contemporary Sangster, he often used them irregularly. Occasionally he breaks into Heavysegian absurdities, such as "Open, my heart, thy ruddy valves," but the poem which follows that awkward opening is a neatly wrought and even humorous conceit. In the other sonnets, if the central thoughts are usually rather conventional, the poems are wrought with a kind of solemn and substantial eloquence and are better-crafted than most of Heavysege's work. Sonnet XIV, which shows how difficult Heavysege found it to escape from his cosmologies even when describing natural phenomena, is a good example.

The stars are glittering in the frosty sky,
Frequent as pebbles on a broad sea-coast;
And o'er the vault the cloud-like galaxy
Has marshalled its innumerable host.
Alive all heaven seems! with wondrous glow
Tenfold refulgent every star appears,
As if some wide, celestial gale did blow,
And thrice illume the ever-kindled spheres.
Orbs, with glad orbs rejoicing, beam,
Ray-crowned, with lambent lustre in their zones,
Till o'er the blue, bespangled spaces seem
Angels and great archangels on their thrones:
A host divine, whose eyes are sparkling gems,
And forms more bright than diamond diadems.

There is a power here that shows Heavysege at his best a not unworthy disciple of Milton, and a better poet than either of his principal rivals in the mid-nineteenth century, Charles Sangster and Charles Mair.

Such Victorian poets, wrestling with the angels and demons of the past, haunted by the doubts and hopes of their age, relating uncertainly to their half-tamed environment, and as yet unequipped with the tools of myth and language needed to give it expression in a mature and responsible literature, represent a necessary phase in the development of Canadian writing. Their strange obstinacy, which made them continue despite all discouragement, was a necessary quality if literature were to persist in the Canadian New World and prepare the way for the emergence of a distinctive Canadian tradition which would have its first flowering among the young poets of the 1880s like Roberts, Lampman and Duncan Campbell Scott, and come to maturity among the young modernists of the late 1920s like A. J. M. Smith, W. W. E. Ross and F. R. Scott.

# 13

## F. R.  SCOTT

### Canada's Man for All Seasons

The link between poetry and the polis is an ancient one, and in every age the isolated, antisocial kind of writer, the *poète maudit,* has been opposed by the writer conscious of his role as citizen. Perhaps the ancestor of them all was the great Greek dramatist Aeschylus who, when he composed his own epitaph, ignored his triumphs in the theatre and emphasized only the fact that with his fellow Athenians he had fought in the ranks of spearmen at Marathon for the defence of their city, which in fact meant the defence of Hellenic civilization and in the long run of Western civilization in general.

There have been such citizen writers through the ages, like Milton and Marvell in the years of the Commonwealth, like Lamartine, Hugo and Zola in nineteenth-century France, like Tolstoy who stepped forward as the conscience of Tsarist Russia and Thoreau who first clearly enunciated the principles of civil disobedience as a corrective to an unhealthy society.

Such writers, who dare to risk the purity of their art in the service of humanity, appear rarely, and there have not been many in Canada, where the occupation of politician has always been regarded with mistrust. Even F. R. Scott, who is probably our best example of the poet as aware and active citizen, avoided taking political office and subjecting himself to the temptations of holding power.

Nevertheless, as well as acting during the late 1920s and the 1930s as the impresario of poetic modernism in Canada, Scott played a key role in the development of a viable socialist movement in Canada, and as a lawyer he won court victories that enlarged our civil liberties. He was also a fine poet, and that is not incidental to his contribution to the polis, for Frank Scott was in many ways a divided personality and even a divided poet.

Two volumes that appeared towards the end of F. R. Scott's long life summarize, while we await the inevitable biography, the multiple and varied achievements of one of Canada's most versatile intellectuals. One was the *Collected Poems,* which appeared in 1981, and the other, published in

1983, was a symposium entitled *On F. R. Scott: Essays on His Contributions to Law, Literature and Politics.*

*On F. R. Scott* was the eventual product of a festival held in February 1981 in downtown Vancouver, far from Scott's own Laurentian country. There was much sad irony to the occasion. The many tribes to which Scott belonged—literary and political and juridical—gathered in parley as he himself sat like a wise old chieftain, receiving praise and blame with equal impassivity.

On first sight, indeed, it seemed as though everyone who mattered in his various worlds was present, from Thérèse Casgrain to Tom Berger, from Audrey Thomas to Iona Campagnola, from David Lewis to Pierre Trudeau. But then one began to count up the absences, especially among the poets one regarded as Scott's peers: Earle Birney and Dorothy Livesay, P. K. Page and Irving Layton, all were absent, while many people of little importance in Scott's life or in the Canadian literary world were there. Towards the end of the celebration, in rooms crowded with often inconsequential company, I began to hear an irreverent echo ringing in my mind—an echo from, of all people, Frank Scott:

> Shall we go round the mulberry bush, or shall
> We gather at the river, or shall we
> Appoint a Poet Laureate this fall,
> Or shall we have another cup of tea?

Of course, the beverage sampled was rarely tea, and I am sure Scott was the last person—despite the flattering attention—to see himself as poet laureate. But when the proceedings of the conference finally appeared as *On F. R. Scott,* and all confronted one in cold print, it was evident that the mulberry bush had indeed been there and much circled. Many of the items from participants chosen for their celebrity rather than their insight were so insubstantial and irrelevant that one wondered anyone had thought them worth preserving.

There were indeed some interesting recollections from people who knew Scott in his various manifestations—Louis Dudek as poet, David Lewis as political activist, Gerald Le Dain as lawyer. Dudek was full of insights into Scott's poetry, and David Lewis warmly personal in a way that is touching when one remembers how soon afterward Scott would be speaking his funeral oration. But apart from the fact that few of Scott's closest poetic contemporaries were invited to recollect or assess, there were no commentators sufficiently critical to point out the glaring inconsistencies in the legal-political stances of this man of high social conscience but not always of comparable good judgement.

Nevertheless, the symposium did indicate the multiple ways in which

Scott laid his mark on the life of Canada. For, as well as a poet, Scott was a notably nonprofessional politician. Although in poetic ways he was influenced by the English writers of the 1930s, he never followed the example set by so many of them by flirting with communism. He was too much of a natural democrat for that, and he also saw that extreme minority movements were unlikely to channel and satisfy the discontent and sheer despair so prevalent in the 1930s among workers, farmers and everyone else at the lower end of the bottom-heavy totem pole of Canadian society in the age. But he believed that such people could be drawn to democratic socialism.

Farmer and labour organizations already existed in Canada, and at the beginning of 1932 Scott with Frank Underhill and a number of other Toronto and Montreal academics came together to form an intellectual wing of the movement, the League for Social Reconstruction. Later in the same year the league took part with other groups in founding a social-democratic party, the CCF, the lineal ancestor of the NDP. Scott was among the CCF's first members, and in 1935 he helped to frame the party's basic document, the famous Regina Manifesto, which called for a "social order . . . in which economic planning will supersede unregulated private enterprise and competition."

For a quarter of a century Scott remained a moving influence in Canadian social democracy. He was president of the League for Social Reconstruction from 1935 to 1936, from 1942 to 1950 national chairman of the CCF, and from 1958 to 1961 a member of the National Committee for the New Party which resulted in the foundation of the NDP.

Politics, like poetry, however passionately he followed it, was one of Scott's avocations, filling the leisure of a busy life. His profession was the law. He was called to the bar in 1927, and in 1928 he joined the faculty of law at McGill and remained there until his retirement in 1964.

Under the right-wing government of Premier Duplessis in Québec, Scott devoted himself to the defence of civil liberties, which were imperilled by such measures as the notorious 1937 Act To Protect the Province against Communist Propaganda, otherwise known as the Padlock Law because it provided for any building to be closed and padlocked for a year if the police suspected it was being used in the cause of communism. Scott fought the law through the courts, and finally in 1957 it was declared *ultra vires* by the Supreme Court. In the famous Roncarelli case he vindicated a restaurant owner who has stood as bondsman for Jehovah's Witnesses being persecuted by the Québec government. Roncarelli's licence had been taken away and his business ruined, but Scott succeeded in getting damages awarded against Premier Duplessis for "gross abuse of legal power."

Scott's speciality was constitutional law, and the precarious unity of the Canadian federation was always one of his concerns. Living in Montreal, with its two cultures striving side by side, he was conscious before most other English Canadians of the need to give French-speaking Canadians a more genuinely equal status within the confederation. He welcomed the "quiet revolution" of the 1960s which showed Québecois beginning to take their lives into their own hands, and from 1963 to 1967 he served on the Royal Commission on Bilingualism and Biculturalism, whose report led to the Official Languages Act of 1969. Throughout Scott's career as a constitutional expert, the protection of the rights of minorities, whether of race, religion or culture, was one of his leading concerns.

Yet, with seeming inconsistency, Scott was also a convinced political centralist, and the conflict this caused with his civil libertarian principles was shown by the stance he assumed during the October Crisis of 1970. Faced with a situation on which strong central government and the liberties of a considerable number of individuals had to be weighed against each other, Scott opted for the first. The authoritarian seemed to triumph over the libertarian within him.

I am voicing here a point of personal disagreement which existed between Scott and me ever since we first met in the early 1960s. In literary terms our attitudes were not far apart, and Scott contributed some interesting items to *Canadian Literature* while I was editing it. But I never accepted the centralism of his interpretation of the Canadian constitution, and I always believed that to rely on the state—as he did—to safeguard the liberty of individuals was like confiding a herd of antelope to the care of a pride of lions. Scott never took full account of the corrupting nature of power, perhaps because he was never tempted to share it. Yet his devotion to the preservation of civil liberties was genuine, and his legal victories helped immeasurably in the general liberalizing of court interpretations of the law and even of legislation. We might be much less free as persons now if it had not been for his work in the 1950s.

In the essay he contributed to *On F. R. Scott,* Louis Dudek suggests we can best understand Scott's poetry if we see it in terms of polar opposites, and this pattern might well be extended to his life. The authoritarian existed beside the libertarian. The public ideal existed beside the private sensibility. The social planner existed beside the individual rebel. And in his poetry the harshly didactic voice existed beside the purely lyrical. Such contradictions, rare in our staid society, mark Scott as an exceptional being in his time and place, a Canadian of historic importance as well as a historically important Canadian poet.

It is to the poetry we now turn, for Scott first attracted attention as a poet, and it is undoubtedly as a poet that he will be longest remembered. It was while a law student at McGill that he began to publish poetry. Some of the earliest appeared in the *McGill Fortnightly Review* which Scott helped to found in 1925 and which for its short life (it came to an end in 1927) served as the first mouthpiece for the modern movement of poetry in Canada. One of his associates was the poet and anthologizer A. J. M. Smith, and another was Leon Edel, later the biographer of Henry James.

In one of his early poems Scott said of Canada: "It will choose its language . . . / A tongue to shape the vowels of its productivity." He and other poets of his time consciously attempted to find a form of writing more appropriate to the Canadian experience than the colonial way of imitating British styles and British sentiments. And while he continued writing his own poetry, his enthusiasm for the new ways of writing made him an eager poetic entrepreneur. After the *McGill Fortnightly Review* expired, he was involved in another short-lived magazine, the *Canadian Mercury*. In 1936 he and A. J. M. Smith edited the epoch-making anthology, *New Provinces,* which included not only their own verse but also that of E. J. Pratt and A. M. Klein and acted as a kind of manifesto for the new Canadian poetry.

The Montreal renaissance in English poetry carried on well into the 1940s, and Scott remained in the thick of it, helping in 1942 to found *Preview,* the magazine on which he worked with A. M. Klein, P. K. Page and Patrick Anderson. When the *Preview* group joined the rival *First Statement* group of John Sutherland, Louis Dudek, Irving Layton and Raymond Souster, Scott remained on the editorial board of *Northern Review,* the journal that resulted from the union, until 1947.

Because of the difficulties of publishing during the depression years, Scott's own first book, *Overture,* did not appear until 1945, two decades after he first began to publish his poems in periodicals. It was followed by *Events and Signals* (1954), *The Eye of the Needle* (1957) and *Signature* (1964); in 1966 the best poems of these volumes were put together in *Selected Poems.* Later, Scott showed his versatility in a series of excellent translations of French Canadian poets, and some of these were included in his 1973 volume, *The Dance Is One.*

Like the poets of the 1930s in England, Scott in his youth wrote many poems of social protest. He was deeply convinced of the injustice of a system that could produce the misery of the depression years, and he also believed that a more rational and humane system could be attained. Poems like "Dedication" expressed his commitment:

> From those condemned to labour
> For profit of another
> We take our new endeavour.
>
> For sect and class and pattern
> Through whom the strata harden
> We sharpen now the weapon.

Till power is brought to pooling
And outcasts share in ruling
There will not be an ending
Nor any peace for spending.

Many people nowadays—and I among them—find a poem like that rather obvious in statement and rather naive in the assumption that a mere shift in the balance of political power will solve the world's problems. But Scott was only giving a Canadian expression to what world-famous writers like Stephen Spender and George Orwell and André Malraux believed at the time, and, as we have seen, he was not content merely to write poems about social injustice and social change.

Even in his youth, Scott wrote other kinds of poems, and the fact that his *Collected Poems* appeared only in 1981, when he was already eighty-two, long tended to mask the variety of his approaches and the versatility of his poetic talent. The individual collections had appeared at long intervals of nine or ten years between volumes, and only the few aficionados who followed his periodical publication closely and repeatedly read his earlier books had any real idea of the scope of his work or even of its volume. It was, indeed, somewhat astonishing to see at the end of his career that the *Collected Poems* ran to almost four hundred pages, for Scott's annual production of poems had always seemed scanty in comparison with that of prolific verse writers like Irving Layton and Al Purdy.

The *Collected Poems* was assembled mainly by Scott himself, and it was characteristic of the man's essential honesty that in putting the pieces together he made no attempt to conceal literary weakness or intellectual folly. There are plenty of misfiring shafts of wit, like "Eclipse":

I looked the sun straight in the eye.
He put on dark glasses.

There are plenty of ephemeral squibs, like his riposte to Pratt's *The Last Spike:* "Where are the coolies in your poem, Ned?" And there are moments of hollow rhetoric when the poet's usually sharp ear seems to have waxed up, such as the last verse of his uncharacteristically pompous poem on the death of Gandhi:

India, India, the load of your history
Presses down upon the springs of your progress,
For man is heir of his past, yet his spirit
Leaps, in an instant, over the Himalayas.

What Scott obviously understood very well is that a poet's collection is much more than a garland of the best poems, more even than a monument to a memorable career, which is what it probably seems to the publisher and to most of the readers. It is an autobiographical document as well, since in what he keeps and leaves out, and in the way he arranges what is left, his own sense of the shape of his creative life and its final meaning will be made clear.

In his *Collected Poems* Scott has rearranged the contents of his earlier volumes in order to emphasize the autobiographical pattern as he sees it. The form is thematic rather than chronological, reflecting the various currents into which his mental life and its poetic expression have run: social anger, political speculation and utopian vision, for example, but also the ironies of life, the pities of death, and that sense of communion with what Albert Camus called the "benign indifference of the universe," which emerges in Scott's often noble poems of the bare northern landscape, where the preoccupations of old and dying cultures can be left behind, like "New Paths."

> Child of the North,
> Yearn no more after old playthings,
> Temples and towers and gates
> Memory-haunted thoroughfares and rich palaces
> And all the burdensome inheritance, the binding legacies,
> Of the Old World and the East.
>
> Here is a new soil and a sharp sun.
>
> Turn from the past,
> Walk with me among these indigent firs,
> Climb these rough crags
> And let winds that have swept lone cityless plains,
> Gathering no sad tales of past endeavour,
> Tell you of fresh beauty and full growth.

There have been a few omissions from past volumes, but nothing that subtracts from any aspect of Scott's total achievement as a poet. It is, in the best sense, a warts-and-all collection, offering his less inspired divagations as well as his real triumphs.

One of the earliest items is a fragile love lyric from 1924—when Scott himself was twenty-five—called "Below Quebec." Its final verses convey the poet's special sensibility:

No stream-swirl nor ebb
Of sea round these cold coasts
Speaks of the pulse and throb
In our close breasts,

Nor tells you what pain
The night would work
If I were alone
Under this old cloak.

There is nothing experimental about such a poem, which hardly seems the kind to be written by someone destined to play a role in the Canadian poetic renaissance. Yet among the dichotomies in Scott that made Louis Dudek think of his achievement as a kind of marriage of polar opposites was the contrast between such a traditional lyrical impulse, dealing with close and personal feelings, and the often harsh didacticism we have seen in "Dedication" and see also in the bald, naive declarativeness of a poem like "Creed":

The world is my country
The human race is my race
The spirit of man is my God
The future of man is my heaven

There are times indeed when it is hard to reconcile the jarring tones and obvious messages of such simplistic verses with Scott's role as one of the precursors of modern poetry in Canada, not only as an impresario and editor but also as a practitioner. And then we read the poems that represent the other side of Scott, not so single-minded as Smith in his literary aims, but just as conscious that Canadian poetry needed a new voice and a clear vision. In one of his northern poems, "Laurentian Shield," he evokes the sense of an inarticulate, expectant land, "Not written on by history, empty as paper," and continues: "This waiting is wanting. / It will choose its language."

Given the time at which he was writing, it was natural that Scott, when he was seeking a new vision as well as a new language, should have turned towards imagism, to which T. E. Hulme had originally been inspired by the Canadian landscape. W. W. E. Ross was already in his own way adapting imagism to the Canadian setting which, whatever its deficiencies in traditional culture, was full of stimuli to the visual imagination. Scott also took to imagism, but went beyond it. There are poems of his that are as spare and as clear-sighted as anything H. D. wrote or as any Japanese haiku, like "Winter Sparrows":

Feathered leaves
   on a leafless bush.
Dropping to feed
   they fly back to the stems.

But at his best, like other major poets of his time, he uses the simple insights of imagism to support the complexities of his poetic vision. A fine example—and deservedly one of his best-known poems—is "Lakeshore," written in 1950 at a time when he had absorbed the major influences of modernism and had moved into his own maturity as a poet. The poem begins with a stanza that in its sharp observation and clear statement, in which metaphor is slightly and discreetly used, is imagist in effect.

The lake is sharp along the shore
Trimming the bevelled edge of land
To level curves; the fretted sands
Go slanting down through liquid air
Till stones below shift here and there
Floating upon their broken sky
All netted by the prism wave
And rippled where the currents are.

But the next two verses, departing from purist imagism, make a free and complex use of metaphor to introduce the poem's theme, which is really the essential unity of all life:

I stare through windows at this cave
Where fish, like planes, slow-motioned, fly.
Poised in a still of gravity
The narrow minnow, flicking fin,
Hangs in a paler, ochre sun,
His doorways open everywhere.

And I am a tall frond that waves
Its head below its rooted feet
Seeking the light that draws it down
To forest floors beyond its reach
Vivid with gloom and eerie dreams.

The poem continues into a long meditation on man's separation from his past in nature, the process of evolution that is also a process of isolation, and swings round in the last two stanzas, with their bold and sudden introduction of the great biblical image of the flood, to a contemplation of the isolation of the poetic mind, envisioning all and yet by that token isolated from all.

> This is our talent, to have grown
> Upright in posture, false-erect,
> A landed gentry, circumspect,
> Tied to a horizontal soil
> The floor and ceiling of the soul;
> Striving, with cold and fishy care
> To make an ocean of the air.
>
> Sometimes, upon a crowded street,
> I feel the sudden rain come down
> And in the old, magnetic sound
> I hear the opening of a gate
> That loosens all the seven seas.
> Watching the whole creation drown
> I muse, alone, on Ararat.

The solitary man of this poem is indeed the polar opposite, as Dudek argued, of the social man who figures in the more didactic and propagandist poems. And so all the aspects of Scott that we need to remember are contained in *Collected Poems*. They are the clues to the other, more public but perhaps also more ephemeral manifestations of his varied achievements.

# 14

# TRANSMUTING THE MYTH

## *Dorothy Livesay and the 1930s*

The 1930s, the period when Canadian writing moved into its modernist phase, was also a period when most writers were highly disturbed by the condition of their world and when many of them moved into political activism.

How active the writer should become was often a matter of agonized discussion. George Orwell believed that in our time a writer could not fail to be politically oriented, but he also argued that it was fatal to subject oneself to the disciplines of a party; a writer could be at most a guerilla skirmishing on the edges of the main army. Writers who did join political movements very often found that they were being led into the kind of writing that offended their sense of artistic honesty, and all the famous English writers who supported the Communists with varying degrees of closeness— Auden, Spender, Day Lewis—finally ceased from fellow travelling to follow their individual courses.

Canadian writers, too, experienced this kind of conflict. Some, like F. R. Scott, made known their political views and even did some political organization, but avoided the total commitment that the extremer parties demanded, so that they never faced the acuter problems of choice. Other writers did commit themselves in active ways to the organizations of the far left, and either became submerged or escaped into the freedom of their personal visions. There is no point in mentioning those who submitted; they were simply lost to literature. Perhaps the best example of the writer who escaped to a later career of highly distinctive work is Dorothy Livesay. Livesay wrote a good deal of mere propaganda in the 1930s but later found in the difficulty and pain of human relations and in the changing viewpoints of aging people the material for some of the strongest and most original of Canadian poetry. For her it was the crucial period of her acceptance of political imperatives and her self-liberation from them.

The writers whom we now tend to regard as typical of the 1930s made their own myth, which is by no means a creation of hindsight. Indeed, it is critics and historians in later decades who have begun to reduce to proper proportions the pretensions of a literary trend whose representatives in the very titles of their journals and anthologies—*New Verse* and *New Writing, Twentieth Century Verse* and *Contemporary Poetry and Prose, New Signatures* and *New Country*—sought to identify all that was significant of the times and all that pointed towards the future with their own socially conscious poetry and their own largely documentary and repertorial prose. In Canada, on a much slighter scale, the same phenomenon emerged among a relatively small group of writers, leftward inclined and impatient with currently accepted literary attitudes, who attempted to pre-empt the future in publications which, largely in imitation of their British contemporaries, they called *New Provinces* and *New Frontiers*.

Even then it was evident that not everything being written at the time was in the same spectrum as the poetry of Auden or Day Lewis or the prose of George Orwell or Edward Upward. Yet such was the power of the myth of the Thirties, from about 1931 when it first began to surface, until the end of the Spanish Civil War in 1939, that to a young person living and writing at that time, as I did, other writers really did seem to have receded into irrelevance.

In ways which it is not easy to explain, the times left their lasting mark on those who lived through them. I have often thought that the reason was the strength of the mutually contradictory emotions that swayed us—the sense of an ineluctable doom created by the rise of fascism and by the virtual certainty of a catastrophic war this year or the next, and the sense of almost messianic hope that was offered to some of us by what they believed to be the socialist paradise of the U.S.S.R. and to others (including myself) by the anarchist-inspired upsurge of free communitarianism among Spanish peasants and factory workers in Barcelona between 1936 and 1939.

Neither the dread nor the hope was fulfilled as we had expected. The war, bad as it was, did not turn out to be the total disaster, the apocalyptic Armageddon, we had expected; the Moscow trials revealed the hollowness of Soviet promises, and the Spanish experiment had been ruined by conflicts within the Republican ranks long before Franco's armies marched into an unresisting Barcelona. Yet the apprehensions and the hopes dissolved so quickly that the state of mind they had created lingered in our consciousness despite all the disillusionment, and I do not think there is a writer alive, touched by the myth of the Thirties when it was still a living myth, who does not look back with regret on his life at that time, when writing was so inextricably mingled with political action, and on the self he then was before he lost his dread and his faith and became, in Stephen Spender's telling phrase, "rotted by a modicum of success." And because there is this kind of mental continuity, preserved rather than destroyed by the unpredictability of events, it seems to me that such writers always remain affected, in their work as well as in their way of life, by the consciousness of that past, just as Stendhal was permanently affected by the more glorious early phase of the Napoleonic adventure. I see this in myself, I see it in English poets like Spender and Roy Fuller whose roots go back to that time, and I see it in Canadian poets like Earle Birney and Dorothy Livesay whose activities for a time spilled over from literature into politics.

It is Dorothy Livesay I am specifically concerned with in the present essay, but I have dwelt on the extraordinary durability of the myth of the Thirties and its retentive hold over certain minds and talents because it seems to me that here we have one of the most important clues to why Dorothy Livesay became the kind of poet she is, a poet intensely sensitive to issues and relationships which, even when she presents them in highly personal ways, are at base social—for instance, the concern over the relationships between men and women that tends to dominate a 1960s volume like *The Unquiet Bed,* and the concern over the difficulties of growing old in a world so oriented to the young that is evident in a 1970s volume like *Ice Age.*

To understand the full role of the 1930s in Dorothy Livesay's development as a poet, one cannot rely merely on the magnificent *Collected Poems,* subtitled *The Two Seasons,* which she published in 1972. In that book she was making a selection of her best work, the work by which she would wish to stand in the eye and ear of posterity, rather than a collection of everything she had written. She recognized that her work of the 1930s was so uneven in quality, and so often subjected to the imperatives of partisan propaganda, that a great deal had to be left out. Thus *Collected Poems,* though relatively full in respect to other periods, presents an incomplete record of what Dorothy Livesay was writing at this early and important stage in her poetic career.

Fortunately there exists an invaluable companion volume, published in 1977. Entitled *Right Hand Left Hand,* it bears the subtitle, *A True Life of the Thirties.* It is not a memoir so much as a scrapbook of the decade, edited by David Arnason and Kim Todd, but put together out of material saved from the past by Livesay herself; presumably she also had a considerable hand in arranging this volume which charts out the formative years of her life as a poet.

Apart from the relatively short passages of recently written narrative continuity whose spidery italics tie the volume together like webs of strong gossamer, everything comes from the Thirties, and this gives the compilation a flavour very reminiscent of that period, for the 1930s was the decade when the documentary came into prominence in many fields—writing, radio, film, even the stage. In England the younger poets went around gathering *faits divers* for Mass Observation, and some of them even made

237

collective poems out of the nuggets they had gathered, while George Orwell went off to the north of England and came back with the factual diaries and the masses of figures he stuffed into *The Road to Wigan Pier*. Original facts, and if possible original documents to support them, were one of the passions of the era.

In this sense *Right Hand Left Hand* is very much of a Thirties book, even if it was put together four decades later; it is a sound guide—with a real flavour of the times—to Dorothy Livesay's own attitudes and activities and to the intellectual ambiance in which she then lived. It includes letters between Dorothy and her family, newspaper items, playbills of left-wing dramatic ventures, photographs, an interview about Dorothy with her best friend of the period, and drawings by artists with whom she associated.

Interesting as all this biographical and background material may be, the important features of the book are Dorothy Livesay's own writings during the Thirties; most of them have never been collected. They include articles and radio scripts defending the socially conscious poetry of the period; reportages of Orwellian journeys to depression-stricken villages in the Crow's Nest Pass; a group of short stories about repressed and exploited people; a radio play and a brief and bald agitprop sketch, and some twenty-one poems, a third of which did not appear in *Collected Poems*.

What *Right Hand Left Hand* really illuminates is the interplay in Livesay's life at this period between her political urges and her personal desires. The left hand of politics did not always want to know what the right hand of love or mere loneliness demanded. This struggle between the collective and the personal runs through Livesay's poems and her actions during this period; the personal was perhaps more ascendant than it seemed, for Livesay never went where she did not want to go.

On the verge of the Thirties, when she was nineteen, Livesay published in 1928 her first book of verse, *Green Pitcher*. These poems were charming juvenilia, somewhat romantic, somewhat derivative. Even in her second volume, *Signposts*, which appeared in 1932, the nostalgia for the passing hour so evident among the Canadian colonial poets was still strongly present, while the reader was aware of the influence of American women poets far removed from the political struggle, like Elinor Wylie, Edna St. Vincent Millay and, increasingly, Emily Dickinson, who gave Livesay a shape to which she could begin to mould her own sharply individual images, as in "Wilderness Stone."

> I dreamed that I dwelt in a house
> On the edge of a field
> With fire for warmth
> And a roof for a shield.

But when I awoke I saw
There was nothing at all
But rain for my roof
And wind for my wall.

Good as it is, there is little in such a poem, or in most of the other pieces in *Signposts,* to suggest that by the time the book was actually published Dorothy Livesay would have taken, in her life and in her writing, a sharply leftward direction, though one long poem, "City Wife," about the difficulties of an urban woman accepting the necessities of a farming existence, foreshadowed her later poems of the difficulties of human relationships.

At the University of Toronto, and in Paris between 1931 and 1932, Livesay encountered the young radicals whose arguments stirred her generosity and her anger and propelled her towards involvement with the Communist party and the various cultural groups that were associated with it. After returning to Canada in 1932, she became a founding member of the Progressive Arts Club. She contributed to the Communist literary magazine, *Masses,* which appeared between 1932 and 1934, and when it ceased publication she was one of the founders and editors of the more broadly based *New Frontier* that took its place. She was influenced by the ideas about a people's theatre that were current among left-leaning intellectuals at the time. She wrote agitprop plays to be performed at the Toronto Progressive Arts Club and was closely involved in the Workers' Experimental Theatre and the Toronto Theatre of Action. She was also active in such front organizations, set up by the Communists to attract liberal sympathizers, as the League against War and Fascism and the Youth Movement for Peace.

Like many intellectuals attracted towards communism at that period, she developed an almost masochistic yearning to shed her past, and in identifying herself with the workers, to cast off the very attributes of the culture in which she had developed as a poet. Writing to one of her closest friends in July 1932, she said:

As for communism, it's a working-class movement and I realize now that it's no use trying to spread it anywhere except within the proletariat. It is alien to the other classes, they do not *feel* that way and so they cannot think that way. I want to think and belong to, work for the proletariat.

A few years later, in 1936, Livesay gave a talk on the CBC entitled "Decadence in Modern Bourgeois Poetry"; she attacked and dismissed to oblivion those favourite targets of left-wing poets and critics at the time,

T. S. Eliot and the Sitwells, but at the end she made an exception for Edith Sitwell's *Gold Coast Customs,* which she classed as a "different and extremely important piece of work," even though its general theme, like that of *The Waste Land,* was "sterility, death, and finally, mysticism."

> The more specific theme is ironic: namely, the comparison between the so-called brutal customs of the Gold Coast natives, and the customs of an English society lady holding parties oblivious of London's poor. To my mind this poem is socially valuable, in spite of its mysticism. The knowledge in it that death is coming to destroy the present system is exceedingly marked. This theme has meaning for a dying bourgeoisie; this theme is a confession of defeat. It adds one more important conviction to the certainty that bourgeois art is dead, that a new art, the art of the proletariat, is being born.

There is little doubt that when Dorothy Livesay went to report on life in the mining communities of the Rockies for *New Frontier,* her motives were not entirely those of the objectively observing journalist or even of the ardent propagandist. She stayed with the people and wished to have a sense of sharing their lives as a kind of human communion. But one suspects that she may indeed have found working-class existence almost as impenetrable for someone reared in another class as Orwell had done on the road to Wigan Pier. Certainly she maintained her contact with bourgeois relatives and even visited them when she was on her reporting expeditions, and when she reached the West Coast in 1936 and settled in Vancouver, she married a theosophist accountant named Duncan McNair and organized a circle of middle-class amateur writers to provide material for *New Frontier.* The desire to become assimilated seems to have vanished with the realization that it could not be fulfilled, though throughout her life Dorothy Livesay has remained quick to empathize with unjustly treated people. Years after the Thirties ended, in 1947, she wrote *Call My People Home,* her documentary poem for radio on the wartime expulsion of the Japanese from the coast of British Columbia.

By the time Dorothy Livesay reached Vancouver, the peak of her involvement in left-wing activities was already past. The Spanish Civil War and its special griefs and enthusiasms merely prolonged loyalties that were already dwindling. Although that conflict inspired her to a few good lyrics and one interesting mini-epic called "Catalonia," it is evident that as the decade went on Livesay ceased to be militantly active in left-wing causes and turned increasingly to the personal and poetic life.

Yet there was never the kind of wounding break with this area of her past that afflicted so many former Communists and fellow travellers. Indeed, what is especially striking about the recollections written in the 1970s for *Right Hand Left Hand* is the way in which Dorothy Livesay regards her past, with total honesty and at the same time without self-condemnation. There is neither guilt nor bitterness when she writes about her life between 1932 and 1936; these were the actions that came naturally to her at the time, and she asks no pardon for them, nor indeed does she spend much time explaining what seemed and seems to her so natural; she presents and describes but in no sense offers an apology. Let me quote two passages to illustrate the honesty with which she treats memories. The first arises from her agitational-cultural activities in Montreal between 1933 and 1934.

> I learned a great deal about Communist tactics of penetration and camouflage; but I was too committed to be shocked. It was only years later that the false actions and fractional tactics were revealed to me in their true light. This did not cause me to hate the communists or to red-bait; rather I was disgusted with myself for having been so duped. But I believe I let myself be duped because no one except the communists seemed to be concerned about the plight of our people, nor to be aware of the threat of Hitler and war.

The second is the last passage of *Right Hand Left Hand,* telling of her feelings early in World War II:

> All our perspectives had changed since that Sunday morning when Churchill's voice came over the radio saying that he was giving his support to Stalin. They were joining together to defeat Hitler! This was a moment of intense emotion for us. Soon all the comrades who had been in jail were released. The unemployed men and women joined the army and the communists, though never permitted to go to the front, marched down the streets of Canada in battle dress. We were all in high hopes again that this time it truly would be a war that would change the world. Instead, we received Hiroshima.

And in that last sentence the future years of reassessment, of realizing life on a deeper level than politics, and of Dorothy Livesay's major poetry, are opened before us. For the poetry she wrote in the Thirties, apart from its ephemeral political content, is interesting to us as a bridge of maturing powers which united the juvenilia of *Green Pitcher* with the work of the 1960s and 1970s that made her the equal of any other poet writing in Canada today or in the past.

One way of approaching Livesay's poetry of the Thirties is to consider the pieces that were left out of *Collected Poems* and included in *Right Hand Left Hand.* One assumes they were regarded as poetically inadequate but autobiographically interesting, and most of them are indeed the kind of proletcult poems that were being published at the time by mainly forgotten party-lining poets in magazines like the Canadian *Masses* and the English *Left Review.* But a good poet leaves almost nothing she writes untouched by the personal, and these poems remind us at least with how much direct sincerity Livesay involved herself in left-wing activities. "Growing Up" may be strident in its statement that coming to maturity is an arrival at political consciousness, yet through the red veil of party images and party diction, genuine impulses that stir the writer's own feelings are perceptible:

> Now I am alive, having created
> My breath one with yours, fighter and toiler,
> My hands ready with yours, young worker
> To crush the boss, the stifler,
> To rise over his body with a surge of beauty—
> A wave of us, storming the world.

"Rain in April," with its attempt to identify with the plight of the unemployed during the depression, retains in some of its lines the sharp perception of the physical world which characterized Dorothy Livesay at her best:

> Give us rain in April: for rain is harsh
> Reveals the sidewalks where we tread
> Cracked, and caked with mud. It blows and beats
> Against the worn-out shutters and the walls,
> It sweeps away the lethargy of spring.

But the poem advances towards a painfully obvious identification of the real spring with the figurative spring of the revolution:

> We must be ready, as the fields prepare
> For May, and the flowering of our may-day hour—
> For the sweep from uncertain April into red growth,
> For the bursting of our shackles, into power!

And in a long rhetorical poem entitled "Canada to the Soviet Union" there are loud and empty lines which it is hard to distinguish from translations of contemporary poems being written in Russia by party poetasters like Demyan Byedny at the behest of Stalin and his cultural commissars:

> Because of you we have learned that soon "this kind of thing"
> Will flower above the ruthlessness
> Of the bosses' Iron Heel.
> We shall see beauty rising from the roofs of factories
> We shall see armies marching through new fields of wheat:
> We shall be unashamed to face you, comrades!

For our children will have songs, at last
To spur their eager feet!

Livesay tells us how, after three years when she had "abandoned writing any poetry that was personal," she found herself "seeking some relief from the orthodox Marxian literature I had been consuming for so long—*Masses, The Daily Worker,* and countless pamphlets and political tracts. . . . What was my astonishment and unbelief to find some slim volumes of English poetry—revolutionary poetry but full of lyricism and passion!" She had discovered in Greenwich Village bookshops the poets so often and so wrongly described as typical of the English Thirties, "C. Day Lewis first, then Spender, then Auden and MacNeice." None of her friends and comrades took any interest in this discovery, and the sense that she was alone in the new line she began to follow under the influence of the English poets must have been a strong factor in her withdrawal from the ranks of left-wing orthodoxy. It was at this period that she wrote poems like "The Outrider" and "Day and Night," which E. J. Pratt, then editing the *Canadian Poetry Magazine,* described as "a splendid bit of work."

Because of the circumstances of the Great Depression, which discouraged any kind of adventurous publishing for most of the Thirties, these poems which Dorothy Livesay wrote when she was extricating herself from the bonds of proletcult remained scattered in periodicals until they were finally collected in *Day and Night* and published as late as 1944. In a sense the late publication was not inappropriate, for the volume splendidly presents the transition to the mature Livesay of later years which was achieved under the influence of socially conscious poets who never abandoned their personal visions for the sake of a cause outside themselves: Shelley seems to be present as much as Spender and Day Lewis, and one is aware of them less as shaping influences than as attendants in a rite of passage. "The Outrider" shows a deliberate effort to escape the urban preoccupations of orthodox Marxism and to see the harshness of prairie life as historic reality and personal endurance at the same time.

The year we came, it was all stone picking:
Sun on your fiery back, and the earth
Grimly hanging on to her own. At the farm's end
A cedar bog to clear. But in the dry season
Not enough drink for the cattle.
The children gathered blueberries, and ate corn meal.
We danced no festivals.

Children stretched lean to manhood. One day
Wind prying round, wrenched free the barn

And lightning had the whole hay crop
Flaming to heaven. Trying to save the horse
Arthur was stifled. His black bones
We buried under the elm.

And "Day and Night" is a largely successful attempt to convey the rhythms of mechanical toil in the very structure as well as the sentiment of the poem:

One step forward
Two steps back
Will soon be over:
Hear it crack!

The wheel may whirl
A roundabout
And neighbour's shuffle
Drown your shout.

The wheel must limp
Till it stands still
And crumpled men
Pour down the hill.

Day and night,
Night and day,
Till life is turned
The other way!

In the poems of this period, the latter years of the Thirties and the beginning of the Forties, Dorothy Livesay is turning more and more towards what, in the introduction to *Collected Poems,* she terms "another source of poetry, quite outside one's conscious experience." And more and more one is aware of the kind of vision that comes to a poet when she has assimilated political doctrines to such an extent that, in so far as the mind does not reject them, they are absorbed into the personal unconscious and emerge transformed. This happened in a poem for voices about Louis Riel which I regard as an important transitional work. Entitled "Prophet of the New World," it was started in 1945, the year after the publication of *Day and Night* had marked a period by giving definitive form to Livesay's late poems of the 1930s; the final chorus of "Prophet of the New World" looks back indeed to the world of collective action that so dominated the poems of the preceding decade, but forward also to the flowering of the personal vision, the exploration of the natural and the particular, that dominate Livesay's late and best poems.

> Now the dark plunge of the year is done:
> we make new prophecies
> and stand, unhelmeted
> facing remote certainties.
> In the mind's eye bare branch
> Leaps with encircling green—
> the pushing, probing blades.
> These will be here, come bomb
> or barbs of love lost, lost; come fire
> to hospital, museum, home

Yet never, entirely, has the influence of the Thirties as she knew them leached out of Livesay's poetry. Always, in the sense that our agonies are typical as well as personal, one hears the echo of a time expressed poignantly in one of the poems she did not reject, a sonnet entitled "Comrade." In the octet the poem addresses the lover who first awakened her; in the last lines she voices a sentiment that reflects what, for a brief and crucial three or four years of that momentous decade, her view of the right way must have been:

> My dear, it's years between; we've grown up fast
> Each differently, each striving by itself.
> I see you now a grey man without dreams,
> Without a living, or an overcoat:
> But sealed in struggle now, we are more close
> Than if our bodies still were sealed in love.

# 15

# IN THE BEGINNING
# WAS THE QUESTION

## The Poems of Phyllis Webb

In recent years Canadian writers—whether in fiction or in verse—have been less inclined to see themselves as the voices of causes or collective visions. A few exceptional individuals—Milton Acorn is an example—remain attached to some kind of political messianism, but even the overt concern over nationalism that not long ago preoccupied poets like Dennis Lee and to an extent Margaret Atwood has dwindled as it has become evident that indeed we have a mature literature from which the colonial outlook has vanished even if it has not vanished from our political life.

The variegation of our literature that has come with its maturity, and which in some ways accords with the postmodernist preoccupation with deconstruction, means that there is indeed place for writers who still gain their creative impulses from political enthusiasms and nationalist ideals, just as there is a place for any other kind of writer. But it means also that literature has become, perhaps more than it ever was in Canada, a matter of private visions and explorations, of the subjective examination of life and death and of the refinement of style, the distillation of language, to give the truest expression to what the poet finds at the end of his or her quest.

Few poets have carried this questing and questioning farther than Phyllis Webb, a poet of reclusive life and the reverse of a prolific writer. Webb has produced, in a lifetime of work, a relatively small group of poems, but they show at once such concern for the craft and such intensity of vision that her career seems almost exemplary, the way in our age of the true poet.

Frank Davey once argued that in Phyllis Webb's poetry "Canadian literature reaches its greatest depths of both worldly and metaphysical desolation," yet he gave her work a special and even crucial significance in the development of postmodernism that he envisioned in his somewhat polemical survey of modern Canadian writing, *From Here to There*.

Phyllis Webb's poetry stands at the juncture between the modernist and postmodernist sensibilities. In it the modernist's rejection of the secular and material and his campaign to purify the language have reached their ultimate end.

246

Beyond lie only suicide and silence. From the fragments and silences of this end, however, the post-modern recognition of a vast, disjointed, but sufficient cosmos can begin. In Canadian poetry, Webb's clears the way for the creative junk-gatherers—bp Nichol, Gerry Gilbert, Victor Coleman—who will ask much less of the world than she, but find much more.

Davey was writing in 1974, during Phyllis Webb's longest period of apparent poetic silence, when it might easily have been concluded that the sparse structure of *Naked Poems* (1965) represented her final abdication of creative intent. Since then, with the publication of *Wilson's Bowl* in 1980, it has become clear that *Naked Poems* in fact represented a period of searching and resolution that enabled Webb to go forward with sureness into even better work than she had done in the past, so that now—with the more recent publication of that splendid selection from her work, *The Vision Tree* (1982)—she stands as one of the best of living Canadian poets, and Davey's suggestion that minor, inconsequential figures like bp Nichol, Victor Coleman and Gerry Gilbert might be going beyond her in developing a postmodernist canon seems merely a manifestation of his critical partisanship.

Yet, though he saw Webb's *Naked Poems* as terminal works because of their starkness, Davey did recognize her exemplary honesty. "Not believing in the competence of the human intellect, and disillusioned by the examples of 'order' which the everyday world provides, she trusts only the naked fragments of experience—and trusts even these not enough to forge for them an extensive speech." It is my contention, which I shall develop in this essay, that all of Webb's career has been directed towards the development of speech, first intensively and later extensively, and that she has come closer than any of her contemporaries not merely to forging the proper speech of poetry but also to determining its proper purpose. At the same time I accept the accuracy of Davey's insight in placing Webb at the point where modernism, as it was manifest in Canadian poetry, expands into a field whose variegation of talents and approaches made it more complex and sophisticated by far than the literary garbage collection which he seemed to envisage as postmodernism.

Phyllis Webb has compelled the attention of readers with a remarkably small production of poems. The *Selected Poems* of 1971, though it contained the pieces she wished to retain from twenty years of work, amounts, if one leaves out John Hulcoop's long introduction, to only 116 sparsely printed pages. *The Vision Tree,* appearing eleven years later as a second selected poems, contains 134 pages of verse; *Wilson's Bowl,* the result of fifteen years of work after the appearance of *Naked Poems* in 1965, contains 73 pages of poems.

Even if one could envisage Phyllis Webb sanctioning a collection of her poems, including the pieces that have been dropped successively in compiling *Selected Poems* and *The Vision Tree,* it would still be a relatively slight volume, for although she began publishing in Alan Crawley's *Contemporary Verse* in the early 1950s, her publication—if not her production—has always been sparse. There seems to have been a reluctance involved in all her decisions to release a poem into print or oral reading. In fact, the extent of her publication has become steadily less copious over the years.

Phyllis Webb collaborated with Eli Mandel and Gael Turnbull in a joint volume, *Trio,* in 1954. Two years later, in 1956, she was able to publish a new volume of her own, *Even Your Right Eye.* It was six years before her next volume, *The Sea Is Also a Garden,* appeared in 1962; this was followed three years later by *Naked Poems,* a collection of poems ground to a hard gemlike transparency and abstraction. Then followed a long period of apparent silence. The *Selected Poems* of 1971 contained nothing written after 1965, and during this period Webb contributed few poems to periodicals. Yet she continued to write in reclusion, to polish and, very often, to discard. The "Kropotkin Poems," on which she worked for years until they became—as she herself wryly admitted—a "legend," never reached completion as the self-contained suite she had planned. Yet finally, in 1980, a new book, *Wilson's Bowl,* appeared, which showed she had moved into more expansive views and more complex forms than those so sparsely delineated in *Naked Poems.* In 1982 a tiny volume of short poems, *Sunday Water: Thirteen Anti-Ghazals,* appeared, and when *The Vision Tree,* the second selected poems of her career, was published in 1982 it contained a scanty half-handful—three poems of moderate length—written after the publication of *Wilson's Bowl.*

The careers of many Canadian poets—perhaps responding to an expansive movement within the culture—have been marked by a growing exuberance in production and in manner; Al Purdy is a notable example. In others, like Margaret Atwood, the self-conscious disciplining of the manner has not lessened the volume of production. For Phyllis Webb, growing maturity as a poet has meant growing withdrawal—a narrowing of contacts with the world paralleling a narrowing of the circle of the creative self that is in keeping with the somewhat solipsistic character of much of her verse.

Webb has said—though she said it in *Trio* more than thirty years ago—that "The public and the person are inevitably / one and the same self." This may have been true of the Phyllis Webb who in the year of her graduation from the University of British Columbia stood as a CCF parliamentary candidate. It has not been true for many years of the poet who in 1970 wrote to John Hulcoop, "I *will* keep removing myself farther and farther from my friends," and who, in an article she wrote for *Maclean's* in 1971, remarked:

I've settled temporarily for island waters and quiet parenthetical ways. Salt Spring Island on the west coast is a good place for star-gazing and navel-gazing, a nice shy corner of the universe which doesn't clamour for recognition or glory. A good place, maybe, for getting a perspective on life and times.

In 1986, fifteen years afterward, Phyllis Webb still lives on Salt Spring Island and seldom goes away. And she is still, as she became very early in her career, the poet concerned with personal emotions, the loneliness of life, the knife-edge paths on which we painfully dance our way to death. Art she has seen as a "remedy"—no more; as a "patched, matched protection for Because." Yet, having committed herself to poetry, she has also committed herself to the perfection of the craft and to that ultimate preoccupation of poets, the rightness of the line. In "Poetics Against the Angel of Death," the last poem of her second complete volume, *The Sea Is Also a Garden*, written just before she started on the experiment of rigour of *Naked Poems*, she demonstrated how in the poet's mind the way of saying becomes virtually identical with what is said.

> I am sorry to speak of death again
> (some say I'll have a long life)
> but last night Wordsworth's "Prelude"
> suddenly made sense—I mean the measure,
> the elevated tone, the attitude
> of private Man speaking to public men.
> Last night I thought I would not wake again
> but now with this June morning I run ragged to elude
> The Great Iambic Pentameter
> who is the Hound of Heaven in our stress
> because I want to die
> writing Haiku
> or, better,
> long lines, clean and syllabic as knotted bamboo. Yes!

Phyllis Webb wrote her equivalent of Haiku in the lean small *Naked Poems*. The spirit in which these laconic statements were written had already been anticipated years before in the early poem, "Is Our Distress," which was included in *Trio*.

> This our inheritance
> is our distress
> born of the weight of eons
> it skeletons our flesh,
> bearing us on

we wear it
though it bares us.

The philosophic pessimism—in unguarded moments breaking down into self-pity—which these lines suggest tends to control the development of thought and also of form in Phyllis Webb's poems. There is a devolution away from the elaborate and the assured, a devolution that led her towards the simplified view of the anarchists (hence the "Kropotkin Poems"), the view that the less one demands of existence, the less one has to defend. One of "Some Final Questions," the last section of *Naked Poems,* reads:

*Now you are sitting doubled up in pain.*
*What's that for?*

doubled up I feel
small like these poems
the area of attack
is diminished

Such lines say much about the poetic as well as the philosophic rule by which Phyllis Webb brought herself to live. Like organisms that shrink in hostile seasons, like bulbs or knotty corms, her poems for a while became small, simple, as packed with meaning as stone artifacts. During this time, by one of the paradoxes that haunt literary reputations, public awareness of her seemed to grow the farther she personally retreated, even when, for a long time after *Naked Poems,* it seemed that she had stepped into silence. What she had in fact stepped into was a further wrestling with poetic form out of which she emerged as a writer who had deliberately discovered the limitations and hence, by implication, the powers of her talent, and so she could write, in the poems of *Wilson's Bowl,* those "long lines, clean and syllabic as knotted bamboo," of which she had dreamed years before.

Having sketched out what I think one must describe as the history of a poet—the record of writing and publication—rather than the biography of the person called Phyllis Webb, whatever mysterious links may exist between person and poet, I propose to take a closer look at the poems, proceeding by way of an examination of Webb's views of her own creative development. I am encouraged in this procedure by a confidence in the self-examining honesty with which she has always approached both the inner world from which her poems seem to emerge and the manner in which, as poems, they are developed.

"In the beginning was the word, but was it followed by a question mark?" Webb asks in one of the handful of radio lectures included in her single prose work, *Talking*. The particular talk, "The Question as an Instrument of Torture," was produced during 1971 in the CBC "Ideas" program that Phyllis Webb herself created. It dealt with "the question" in all the sinister levels of ambiguity the phrase has acquired over the centuries and developed its metaphysical as well as its physical implications. Always, at the back of the talker's mind, one feels there was a constant referring back to the poetry that was her principal vocation. How far, one wonders, did the torment of questioning, as well as the question of torment, produce the state of mind out of which creation emerged? At the end of her talk she dismissed as "suggestive, but finally not very satisfactory," Heidegger's rejection of the question as self-defeating and his advocacy of the surrender to pure Being. Having said this, she continued:

> I have suggested that curiosity is of the mind and body both and may be unappeasable except at the level of Heidegger's mysticism. At any level its condition should be regarded as critical. Kierkegaard, hardly one of the sunniest philosophers to have meditated on the tasks of the self, was, like most of us, still caught on the hook of questions. And of the question as an instrument of torture he seemed to know something. What he knew was despair.

With questioning—and here lies much of its agony—comes detachment; the binding links to dogmas, to institutions, even to settings, shred away, as the Buddha and others have taught. Expressing that not-attachment as she had achieved it in political terms after her partisan youth, Webb once remarked: "I am a voter who has never voted for a winning candidate, and a law-abiding anarchist. No party would have me if they knew what I really think. I won't have any of them because I know what they really think." Even the loyalty to location that one might assume from Phyllis Webb's resolute and lasting reclusion on Salt Spring Island seems a matter of attachment less to place than to privacy. "I'm a regional poet," she has said, "in the sense that the West Coast is my psychic homeland, but that's about as far as it goes." Far enough, one might say, remembering how often and how memorably Webb has evoked in her poems the true feelings of that psychic home. But this does not take away from the fact that, as her whole work showed, she had never felt the rootedness of a true regional poet, the consolation in setting, like Thomas Hardy for instance, or Al Purdy in his Roblin Mills mood. "I did not have to reach Dante's 'midway this way of life,' " she remarked in a marvellously illuminating "Ideas" talk on Proust in 1970, "to experience the dark wood, the lost way."

The factor of questioning shows itself in a number of ways in Webb's attitude to her poetry. There is, for example, her willingness to examine the work of other poets whose approach is unlike her own and whose attitude she finds in many ways unsympathetic, and to conclude, if that is where her reading leads her, that they are genuine and meaningful voices. It

251

would be hard to think of two poets less alike than Webb and Al Purdy, and her first reaction to his work was clearly unenthusiastic. Yet after reading his *Poems for All the Annettes,* she wrote a review of the book for *Canadian Literature* in 1963 in which, though she criticized the clutter and excess of some of the poems, she nevertheless recognized, at that comparatively early date, Purdy's potential standing among Canadian poets.

> After reading Alfred Purdy's *Poems for All the Annettes* I have come to the conclusion that he is one of the few important voices in Canadian poetry today. It has taken me some time to arrive at this verdict because the method in this book is open to criticism and because the tone of much of Purdy's work is, at first reading, offensive. And deliberately so.

It is reasonable to expect that a critic who could be enquiring enough to come to an understanding of a writer so unlike herself should, as a poet, have the questioning curiosity that would open her mind to learning from writers temperamentally nearer to her. This curiosity was demonstrably active at the time of the famous poetry seminar held in 1963 at the University of British Columbia, when a clutch of literary missionaries came at Warren Tallman's invitation to instruct the Canadians in the ways of postmodernist wisdom. They were Allen Ginsberg, Robert Creeley, Robert Duncan, Charles Olson and Denise Levertov.

It was salutary and inspiring to see Phyllis Webb, already a poet of standing who had recently established herself in the Canadian literary world with her second book, *The Sea Is Also a Garden,* sitting there among the student versifiers and gaining a great deal more from the occasion than most of the participants. There was no question of what is commonly understood as derivation; she was not seeking to absorb ideas or attitudes or imagery or even language; those aspects of her poetic presence were already established. But she had come to the point where the form of the poem was all important, and from some at least of these poets she could learn.

In 1964, in an interview with Dorothy Livesay that was eventually published in *CVII,* Phyllis Webb talked about this occasion. She had obviously, and understandably, learnt nothing from Allen Ginsberg, whose poetry is all noise and no craft, and perhaps little from Creeley, of whom she talked with cautious praise. But from Charles Olson and Denise Levertov she did attain what she felt was a greater understanding of ''a problem that had been puzzling me for a long time,'' the reasons why a poet breaks a line in a certain way. This may seem a somewhat technical problem, but in poetry, far more than in prose, the precision of the technique is the key to formal success. Webb had by now recognized that the line—not the phrase which is a grammatical rather than a rhythmic unit—is the basic component of the poem. But she was interested in the broader aspects of form, and it was here that she found her meeting with Robert Duncan the most important during the 1963 seminar. She told Dorothy Livesay:

> Robert Duncan has the most to offer me because he is a great explorer in the realm of form. Since I am attempting to move into larger forms and since he handles these with great skill I have been studying him quite carefully. And because he is very interested in *sound*, especially the vowel sounds, the melodic tone that he can acquire through a skilful manipulation of these vowels in his poetry.

These contacts did not lead Webb into imitation. They did lead her to a questioning of her poetic methods, and it was this that set her working on the *Naked Poems,* in which, as she told Dorothy Livesay, she was trying "first of all to clarify my statements so that I could see what my basic rhythms were; how I *really* speak, how my feelings come out on the page"; she was also trying "to get away from a dramatic rhythm, from a kind of dramatic structure in the poem itself, and away from metaphor very often."

Almost two decades later, Webb wrote two groups of notes on her views of poetry, entitled respectively "On the Line" and "Up the Ladder: Notes on the Creative Process." Here she talked less of the formal and technical aspects of *Naked Poems* and more of the psychological implications of such an experiment, such a "question." "The short line is 'for candor,' says Duncan. Or Terror, say I. Notes towards a Poetics of Terror. Pull down thy vanity." And she remarked—without adding her own comment —that "Kroetsch sees anxiety as central to the short-lined *Naked Poems*—and the post-modern long poem generally." In "Up the Ladder" she asks—questioning again—"Is resistance, in the psychoanalytic sense now, the actual subject coming about? Or is rebellion against the inner censor the more exact source of the poem?"

A year before this, in June 1980, she had written the brief preface to *Wilson's Bowl;* the first sentences of this, as naked in their way as *Naked Poems,* are worth quotation as a recent insight into Webb's view of her own creative process.

> "I am both too big and too weak for writing. I am *alongside* it, for writing is always dense, violent, indifferent to the infantile ego which solicits it." I was so grateful to Roland Barthes when I discovered that passage in *A Lover's Discourse* because it so perfectly describes my relationship to writing, and I don't think I could ever myself have explained the blood-line with such precision. My poems are born out of great struggles of silence. This book has been

253

long in coming. Wayward, natural and unnatural silences, my desire for privacy, my critical hesitations, my critical wounds, my dissatisfactions with myself and the work have all contributed to a strange gestation.

So we see in Webb's view of her own poetic progression, as we shall find in the poetry itself, what John Hulcoop in his introduction to the 1971 *Selected Poems* called "a movement away from a self-pitiful obsession with the despairing self and towards a much more self-critical preoccupation with language as a means of proclaiming or presenting the nature of present things."

What one immediately notices in the early poems of *Trio* is the somewhat explicit statement of the personal pessimism and the sense of dissatisfaction with the world that made Webb's early critics inclined to dismiss her as excessively negative, and that tended for long to restrict the breadth of her readership. The assurance of her craft, even then, engendered admiration; the mood of her poems created disturbance. The technique still verged on the traditional; the lines were irregular, but there were still rhymes and assonances, and even puns.

> The eye's lid covers
> the I aware,
> the hand hovers
> over, then plunders
> emerging despair.

The drama of appearance and reality, of the private and the public life in confrontation, is also there, projected in dream images:

> On the apparent corner of two streets
> a strange man shook
> a blue cape above my head,
> I saw it as the shaking sky
> and was forthwith ravished.

Time passing and pain continuing are the constants of Phyllis Webb's world at this period, and patience—"love withdrawn / into the well"—is the sustaining element.

> Patience is the answer
> poised in grief—the knowing—
> it is the prose of tears
> withheld and the aging,
> the history in the heart

254

and futures where pain
is a lucid cargo.

Yet there is an equilibrium of force and fate expressed in a particularly
good early poem, "Chung Yung," that curiously was not included in the
*Selected Poems* of 1971, but was reinstated in *The Vision Tree* of 1982.

Purchases have been made
Wisely or imprudently
Neither all being lost
Nor all gained;

Balance, delicate
Yet fibred,
Proves a pivot
Around which are described
Immaculate arcs.

There is a strange Pythagorean serenity to this poem that is absent from
most of Webb's early work, and which appears only intermittently in her
later writings.

More typical, at least until after the formal and emotional purgation involved in the writing of *Naked Poems,* is the mood of the fine but bleakly
elegiac poem "Lament" in Webb's first volume, *Even Your Right Eye,*
which frames a rigorously unhopeful view of existence.

Knowing that everything is wrong,
how can we go on giving birth
either to poems or the troublesome lie,
to children, most of all, who sense
the stress in our distracted wonder
the instant of their entry with their cry?

For every building in this world
receives our benediction of disease.
Knowing that everything is wrong
means only that we all know where we're going.

Yet we survive through the thought of "a virtuous land," the insubstantial
vision of a "place of perfect animals and men," and this is "why we frame
our lonely poems in / the shape of a frugal sadness."

In the last phrase, of course, is the anticipation of her forthcoming development, for, as Hulcoop remarked, "meaning to exercise economy and

avoid waste, *frugal* is the perfect word with which to describe the poetry in *Naked Poems*." And, indeed, the idea of nakedness as a quality of poetry is already there, to parallel the idea of frugality, in another poem of *Even Your Right Eye*.

> Poetry
> is cloaked in sheer
> profundities of otherness,
> its ambiguous nakedness its serene capacity
> for wisdom; nothing denied
> until entirely known.

These lines occur in the first section, "Poetry," of a double-headed poem entitled "Two Versions"; the second part, entitled "In Situ," is perhaps the more important in Webb's mind, for it contains the phrase "vision tree" which she later used as the title for her second selected poems. It is a series of almost Blakeanly gnomic statements about the poet and his role which sets up a creator's ethic different from that of ordinary men, and as a statement of aspects of the poetic mind that remain fairly constant in Webb's viewpoint it deserves lengthy quotation.

> The poet in his tree of hell
> will see life steadily and see it well.
>
> The world is round.   It moves in circles.
>
> The poet in his vision tree
> imparts immaculate necessity
> to murder, ignorance and lust.
>
> The world is round.   It moves in circles.
>
> Poetry, the poet's curse,
> will look, for better or for worse
> like a simple monk in meditation
>
> cloaked in apparent deprivation:
> in its ambiguous nakedness
> glows the raiment of its otherness.
>
> The world is round.   It moves in circles.

> With laughter in his haunted face,
> a madman captive in a leaf's embrace,
> the poet wildly shakes his tree . . .

> The world is round.   It moves in circles.

Such a poem, with its phrases that will be repeated at later crucial points in Webb's career—"vision tree" and, again, "ambiguous nakedness"— sees the poet at the centre of a world that moves in its necessary cycles. Nothing he can do will affect such destined patterns, and so, in his "vision" he can record without judgement "murder, ignorance and lust." Unlike Arnold's poet, he does not see life "whole"; he sees it "well," which means that he sees it in all its pain and negation. Yet poetry, though it accepts deprivation, asks nothing of existence, is willingly naked, still "glows in the raiment of its otherness," a statement that takes us to the other poem of major importance in *Even Your Right Eye*, "Marvell's Garden," since here the suggestion is clearly made that the "otherness" of the poet's vision lies in its emphasis on form, as a philosophic as well as a prosodic entity.

> And yet Marvell's garden was not Plato's
> garden—and yet—he *did* care more for the form
> of things than for the thing itself—
> ideas and visions,
> resemblances and echoes,
> things seeming and being
> not quite what they were.

I become aware as I discuss these poems that the "otherness" of poetry is meant not merely to be a different kind of vision but also a different kind of morality. Always in her poetry, but increasingly as time goes on, Phyllis Webb shows herself hostile to conventional systems of morality, to political organization of any kind, and to consolatory religions that offer fragile hope or anything less rigorous than the question she poses in a slightly later poem than "Marvell's Garden," called "Breaking": "What are we whole or beautiful or good for but to be absolutely broken?"

But there is the other morality of the craft that too demands its denials and its deprivations, its willing self-disciplines. The link between the sentiments and the forms of moralist—as distinct from moralistic—writing has always been close; the compact, undecorated and largely unmetaphorical forms of the récits of André Gide and Albert Camus, and of the 1930s parable-novels of Morley Callaghan, are directly related to the fact that these writers are using their fiction to project moral problems, and that in the process of creating an austerity of word as well as of thought they bring together a morality of art and a morality of action that are parallel, that resonate together, but are neither identical with each other nor necessarily interdependent.

Thus it is no accident that Phyllis Webb, as she has proceeded according to the morality of art towards the impoverishment of form for the sake of greater ultimate richness, has also practised austerities and simplifications in her life and has sought the reclusion that all good artists, like all saints, find necessary at some time in their careers.

The second volume of her poems, *The Sea Is Also a Garden,* is a rich book in its variety as well as in its strength of accomplishment. There are complex verse legends like "Love Story" and "A Tall Tale," fine exercises in visualization like "Two Pears: A Still Life," and a number of brittle and glittering poems like "Images in Crystal" and "The Glass Castle," in which the sharpness and transparency, the fragility and the reflected luminosity of glass come together in an image of the human mind at its most clear and perhaps most vulnerable to breakage.

> The glass castle is my image for the mind
> that if outmoded has its public beauty.
> It can contain both talisman and leaf,
> and private action, homely disbelief.
>
> .    .    .
>
> I do not mean I shall not crack the pane.
> I merely make a statement, judicious and polite,
> that in this poise of crystal space
> I balance and I claim the five gods of reality
> to bless and keep me sane.

But perhaps the most important poem of the book, projecting the quintessential Webb, is the long address "To Friends Who Have Also Considered Suicide." It is a poem in intent at once serious and satirical, in tone at once grave and strangely gay. It is, for Webb's poems of this time, exceptionally expository, arguing a point with a kind of logic and coming to a conventionally shocking conclusion, yet carrying more force than, say, Swift's *Modest Proposal,* since we know that Swift never really thought except satirically of breeding babies for the table, while Webb is quite evidently one of those who have considered suicide, and hence she can look on the question with a complicitous and even an amused eye. In doing so, she finds a morality in the thought of suicide, an honesty that contrasts with the self-deception of those who might condemn it as violence towards oneself and yet condone the violence that destroys others.

> Some people swim lakes, others climb flagpoles,
> some join monasteries, but we, my friends,
> who have considered suicide take our daily walk
> with death and are not lonely.
> In the end it brings more honesty and care
> than all the democratic parliaments of tricks.
> It is the "sickness unto death"; it is death;
> it is not death; it is the sand from the beaches
> of a hundred civilizations, the sand in the teeth
> of death and barnacles our singing tongue:
> and this is "life" and we owe at least this much
> contemplation to our western fact; to Rise,
> Decline, Fall, to futility and larks,
> to the bright crustaceans of the oversky.

"To Friends Who Have Also Considered Suicide," apart from its theme, is a good poem in which to study Webb's development at this point in the early 1960s. Important traditional devices like rhyme and unimportant ones like the capitalization of line beginnings have been abandoned. There is minimal—though effective—use of metaphor. The tone has become conversational but not colloquial, for Webb has never abandoned the feeling that poetry has its own tone and its own voice, which are not those of prose; this is why she confesses to a difficulty in writing prose. In considering the metrical structure of the poem, it is interesting to refer back for a moment to the last poem of *The Sea Is Also a Garden,* "Poetics Against the Angel of Death," which has already been quoted, with its expressed intent to elude "the Great Iambic Pentameter," and to explore Haiku, "or, better, / long lines, clean and syllabic as knotted bamboo." For in "To Friends," whose hortatory tone and argumentative expansiveness are very far from Haiku, we do find the lines—mostly between ten and twelve syllables long and stressed irregularly—offering at least an approach to her "long lines, clean and syllabic . . ."

In fact, it was towards the alternative form, the Haiku, that Webb actually turned after she had published *The Sea Is Also a Garden,* having once again and rather curiously prefigured her *Naked Poems* in a piece entitled "Bomb Shelter," which begins with the statement, "Nakedness is our shelter," and ends with the exhortation:

we must . . .
. . . in our nakedness
and in our peace abide.

The link between writing "To Friends Who Have Also Considered Suicide" and the embarcation on the enterprise of *Naked Poems* seems a clear transition. Suicide, after all, is a form of ultimate austerity, and as such it has been seen in Asian cults—like Jainism—where some kind of self-immolation is regarded as the logical end of the ascetic path towards enlightenment. But the voluntary impoverishment of poetry implied in such reductive verse making as *Naked Poems* is itself an ultimate austerity and for the poet an immolation of all her pretensions, which amounts to a kind of suicide, different mainly because it allows the possibility of revival. It is perhaps significant that the poem in *The Sea Is Also a Garden* nearest in spirit to *Naked Poems* is also a celebration of almost Taoist quietism. It is called "Sitting."

The degree of nothingness
is important:
to sit emptily
in the sun
receiving fire
that is the way
to mend
an extraordinary world,
sitting perfectly
still
and only
remotely human.

Perhaps the most striking feature of *Naked Poems*—and the most certain evidence of Phyllis Webb's virtuosity as well as of her inspiration—is the great variety of mood and meaning which she induces in these small poems. They are demonstrations as exemplary as anything the Japanese achieved of what the poet can do with minimal resources. The volume is divided into five sections. "Suite I" and "Suite II" deal respectively with love fulfilled and love receding, both conditions presented inexplicitly and through sensation and feeling.

MOVING
to establish distance
between our houses.

260

It seems
I welcome you in.

Your mouth blesses me
all over.

There is room.

There are interludes of withdrawal:

TONIGHT
quietness.   In me
and the room.

I am enclosed
by a thought

and some walls.

Yet at the culmination of the relationship there is the sense of climax and
fulfilment.

YOU
took

with so much
gentleness

my dark

But Suite II involves the lover's withdrawals and the poet's admission of
her failure to dispel attachment.

*Then you must go.*
*I sat cross-legged*
*on the bed.*
*There is no room*
*for self-pity*
*I said*

*I lied*

Yet by the end of Suite II the lover has become the muse, and the acceptance of detachment brings the benison of inspiration.

*You brought me clarity.*

*Gift after gift*
*I wear.*

*Poems    naked*

*in the sunlight*

*on the floor.*

It is these poems that follow in the remaining sections of *Naked Poems*. The first, in the section entitled "Non Linear," are largely visual in their impact, often pure clusters of images.

An instant of white roses.
     Inbreathing.
A black butterfly's
     twitch and determined
collapse on a yellow round.

But they are interspersed with nonvisual notations of states of mind attained during the discipline of poetic rigour.

I have given up
complaining

but nobody
notices

And it becomes evident that *Naked Poems* is in one of its aspects a temporary departure from Webb's preoccupation with the line. Here the emphasis is on the nucleus of meaning, the tiny cluster of words taken as a whole, dense and self-contained as a pebble. This is what gives such gnomic strength to the last section, "Some Final Questions," which we must read not merely because it brings us back to one of Webb's abiding preoccupations, the question, but also because of the laconic ambiguity of the answers, that finally defeat the questioner, as in the last three pages of the book, which sparsely lay out some seven compact lines.

*But why don't you do something?*

I am trying to write a poem

*Why?*

Listen. If I have known beauty
let's say I came to it
asking

*Oh?*

And so the problem of the question reaches a standoff solution as the questioned poet reveals herself an asker, and what she asks we can only assume are questions.

A questioning so rigorous as the *Naked Poems* must reveal not only the need for answers but also their difficulty. It was to finding them, not only in poetic forms but also in positive visions, that Webb devoted the decade and a half between the appearance of *Naked Poems* and that of her most recent completely new collection, *Wilson's Bowl*. The most important of those visions, with which Webb wrestled for years and failed to bring to a final solution, was that associated with the anarchist activist and writer Peter Kropotkin and his life, recorded partly in his own *Memoirs of a Revolutionist* and partly in the biography of him, *The Anarchist Prince*, which Ivan Avakumovic and I wrote together and published in 1950.

*Wilson's Bowl* is in fact a miscellaneous collection of poems written under the various impulses of fifteen years, and formally they are dominated by Webb's return to working on the line, the syllabic line certainly, but not necessarily the long line, for though there are some poems with flowing long lines like "Fyodor," and even one suite of prose poems ("Letters to Margaret Atwood"), there are also some highly effective narrow column poems of short lines like "Socrates" (back to the old game of questions and answers) and some telling experiments in fractured lines like "Treblinka Gas Chamber."

              fallingstars
                     "a field of
                            buttercups"
                     yellow stars
                            of David
                                   falling

And having gained confidence in the liberation of her line, Webb can return, albeit with some irony, to traditional forms; there is an "Imperfect Sestina" and a dream poem in Audenesque metre entitled "Composed Like Them."

Despite Webb's confession of failure, the fragments of the "Kropotkin Poems" still dominate *Wilson's Bowl*. She remarked that the plan was "too grand and too designed" in concept, with "the 'body politic' and 'love's body' as interchangable polymorphous analogues in an ideal world," and indeed the idea of this large and complex work on the nature of power does seem alien to Webb's main preoccupations as a poet up to this time concerned with the world's suffering and with personal loss and its quietist alleviation. Yet not only is the whole first part of the collection—"Poems of Failure"—derived from the failed Kropotkin project, but a Kropotkin elegy appears in the section called "Portraits" and another in the section called "Crimes," so that the "mind so vast and intimate" of Kropotkin broods over the whole volume, and here the sense of loss that is strongly present is really the sense of the lack of the power to become the kind of intellectual poet, the poet of grand and sweeping concepts who could have done justice to them. And, poignant as her gestures to Kropotkin may be, there is an even greater poignancy to the penultimate section of the book which, like the volume as a whole, is called "Wilson's Bowl."

It centres around a petroglyphic carving by prehistoric Indians, a perfectly round bowl on the cliffs of Salt Spring Island that reflected the moon at certain phases and was given its name in honour of Wilson Duff, an anthropologist with a mind too original for his profession who committed suicide in 1976. Some of the poems echo Indian legends, but the core of the suite is the story of Lilo Berliner, the woman who named Wilson's Bowl; she had conducted a correspondence with Duff, close to intimacy, though they never met, and she almost certainly understood his mythopoeic ideas of Indian artifacts better than his professional colleagues. A year after Wilson Duff's death, Lilo herself walked into the sea from a Salt Spring Island beach, having left his letters to her on Phyllis Webb's doorstep. Here were two people, haunted by unaccepted ideas, who had not merely considered suicide, and Webb, in friendship for Lilo (for she hardly knew Duff), in compassion, in admiration, perhaps partly in envy, wrote those elegiac poems, more modest than the great suite she had planned on Kropotkin, yet more intimate and more certain in their union of form and feeling.

> What was the path she took?
> As winding as her gut
> with the pain in it?
> Along the beach?

To the caves in the hill?
Path of her mind turning
on symbols. Civility and
the Wild Woman's scream.
And horror. Horror.
Path to the beach
at full moon at last
joy of that mean water,
the manic ride out in the bay.

Since *Wilson's Bowl* appeared, Phyllis Webb has been writing, as is her wont, slowly and with much discarding, and has published few poems. But whatever comes now, her deliberate small *oeuvre* has already entitled her, for the clarity of her vision and the dedicated impeccability of her craft, to a first place not merely among recent Canadian poets but in the whole poetic tradition of our land.

# 16

# METAMORPHOSIS AND SURVIVAL

## Notes on the Recent Poetry of Margaret Atwood

If one of the signs of the maturity of a literary culture is variegation, the tendency for writers to follow highly individual rather than collective goals, another is versatility, the willingness of a writer to try new forms and her or his ability to master them. Pioneer societies may be adventurous physically, but almost of necessity they are unadventurous culturally. Their art forms are conservative, and such artists as they produce, almost invariably amateurs, are cautious and unexperimental. The writer of many parts, the all-round man-of-letters, does not flourish in such settings. If very occasionally a poet ventures into fiction, as Charles Heavysege does with *The Advocate,* the result is likely to be lamentable, as was conversely the case when William Kirby, who wrote one good novel, *The Golden Dog,* tried his hand at poetry in *The U.E.: A Tale of Upper Canada.* The importance of Charles G. D. Roberts, apart from a few fine poems and animal stories, lies in the fact that, in the last decades of the nineteenth century, he offers the first Canadian example of the kind of literary virtuosity that makes a true man-of-letters, willing to try his hand at any genre and succeeding reasonably well in most.

Not many writers, even in a mature literature, show such versatility, and it would probably be unfortunate if all poets and novelists wandered much from their chosen genre. But, as Oscar Wilde said of himself, those who do stand in a symbolic relation to their age; they seem to concentrate its light as in a prism and to dispense it in various directions; even if there are only a few of them at any one time, they attest to the vitality of the literary culture.

In our own time Margaret Atwood has shown herself an extraordinarily versatile woman-of-letters. She is a fine and always disturbing novelist. She is an excellent critic and, as *Survival* showed, a provokingly polemical literary historian. And she is one of the best poets of her time. Her more recent poetry reflects the dominant themes of all her writing—tenacious survival and constant metamorphosis.

"My purpose," says Ovid in the opening lines of *The Metamorphoses*, "is to tell of bodies which have been transformed into shapes of a different kind. You heavenly powers, since you were responsible for these changes, look favourably on my efforts."

In Margaret Atwood's more recent books of verse, *You Are Happy* (1974), *Two-Headed Poems* (1978), *True Stories* (1981) and *Interlunar* (1984), the theme of metamorphosis flows with remarkable strength, and even though she is not so consistent as Ovid in exemplifying it in all her late poems, it becomes a powerful uniting current. At one point, indeed, the paths of Ovid and Atwood cross, for Circe, perhaps inevitably, finds a place in the mythologies of both poets. Yet it is no more than a crossing, for Ovid is, like Virgil, directing his sequence of changes towards the foundation of Rome, and Circe enters as an incidental figure in the story of Aeneas. But Atwood is concerned with the story of Odysseus, whose encounter with Circe takes up a great deal of *You Are Happy*, and Odysseus was of course the universal survivor, the great resister of magic transformation, though in another way one might call the *Odyssey* a Western *Book of Changes*, for no poem tells more powerfully how the very struggle to sustain his true self against the assaults of experience changes a mortal hero steadily and irrevocably. As Atwood has it in the "Circe/Mud" cycle in *You Are Happy*:

> Your flawed body, sickle
> scars on the chest, moonmarks, the botched knee
> that nevertheless bends when you will it to
>
> Your body, broken and put together
> not perfectly, marred
> by war but moving
> despite that with such ease and leisure
>
> Your body that includes everything
> you have done, you have had done
> to you and goes beyond it.

In a past essay I found the essence of Atwood's earlier writings implied in one of the most concise and powerful poems of *Power Politics*:

> Beyond truth,
> tenacity: of those
> dwarf trees & mosses,
> hooked into straight rock

believing the sun's lies & thus
refuting / gravity

& of this cactus, gathering
itself together
against the sand, yes tough
rind & spikes but doing
the best it can

And I commented, in what I still feel is a valid summary of the most striking feature of Atwood's first decade of writing, whether in verse or prose:

> Here is not merely an attitude to life that is evident in all Atwood's
> writings—an attitude appropriate to an age when survival has become the great
> achievement. Here is also the metaphor that expresses a personal poetic, even a
> personal ethic. To be (tenacity) is more certain than to know (truth); one does
> the best one can, shapes one's verse like one's life to the improbable realities of
> existence ("the sun's lies"), and in this age and place the realities impose a
> defensive economy, poems close to the rock, poems spiny as cactuses or
> calthrops.

But tenacity does not obviate change; it merely makes it slower and yet
at the same time more irreversible, and even in Atwood's earlier writings
the theme of change and the myth of metamorphosis are there, conveyed in
powerful metaphors like the cake-woman in *The Edible Woman* which
Marian MacAlpin eats in order to cure and transform herself, and in the
submersion-surfacing imagery which accompanies the narrator's metamorphosis in *Surfacing* through a regression (magic transformation) into
animality that heralds her move into a new level of understanding in a
world of benign cosmic indifference, where "The Lake is quiet, the trees
surround me, asking and giving nothing." The poems are full of subtler
images of change. Eskimo sculptures become the memories of shapes felt
in the hand; the decay of totem poles makes them seem more living than
the wooden people who look at them; strawberries in a dream garden turn
into the blood that pioneers sweat.

Often change is used in these earlier poems to emphasize the continuity
that is inescapable, the haunting survival of the past in the present it has become, as in the strange poem of the revenant Mrs. Moodie that ends *The
Journals of Susanna Moodie*, "A Bus along St. Clair: December":

> It would take more than that to banish
> me: this is my kingdom still.

Turn, look up
through the gritty window: an unexplored
wilderness of wires

Though they buried me in monuments
of concrete slabs, of cables
though they mounded a pyramid
of cold light over my head
though they said, We will build
silver paradise with a bulldozer

it shows how little they know
about vanishing: I have
my ways of getting through.

  •    •    •

Turn, look down:
there is no city;
this is the centre of a forest

your place is empty.

But though the past permeates the present, the present hastens with ever greater speed into the future. This is another aspect of change that occurs in Atwood's earlier writing, nowhere more powerfully than in the extraordinary metamorphic poem that in *Power Politics* suddenly expands the private war between lovers into the universal war that is history. The perceiving persona who speaks throughout the book sees, almost cinematographically (as in a movie run at ever-increasing speed), the progression of feminine experience with herself as a kind of everlasting Penelope at the centre of it:

At first I was given centuries
to wait in caves, in leather
tents, knowing you would never come back

Then it speeded up: only
several years between
the day you jangled off
into the mountains, and the day (it was
spring again) I rose from the embroidery
frame at the messenger's entrance.

  •    •    •

269

But recently, the bad evenings
there are only seconds
between the warning on the radio and the
explosion; my hands
don't reach you

and on quieter nights
you jump up from
your chair without even touching your dinner
and I can scarcely kiss you goodbye
before you run out into the street and they shoot

This is a Penelope whose Odysseus never returns. "At first I was given centuries" in fact points forward to the poems preoccupied with the increasing atrocity of political relations in our time that play so important a part in Atwood's *True Stories,* published a decade after *Power Politics.* But this is only one of the many ways in which metamorphosis, as metaphor and myth, has become perhaps the most important thematic element in Atwood's most recent poetry. This increasing emphasis on change and changes does not mean an abdication of Atwood's earlier preoccupation with survival, with the tenacity that lies beyond truth. But it does mean the development of a more fluid sense of the possibilities of the poet's own vision, accompanying and interacting with certain changes in her personal ambience that enter into the content of her poetry.

There is a haunting imagist sufficiency about the title poem of *You Are Happy;* imagism passes through practice into theory as Atwood tells of a winter walk, beginning with a verse that is an irregular haiku: eighteen syllables arranged four, nine, five instead of seventeen arranged five, seven, five, but otherwise traditional in its natural image and seasonal setting:

The water turns
a long way down over the raw stone,
ice crusts around it

The poem proceeds with the walk which the poet and her companion take, wandering to the open beach, seeing the unused picnic tables, the brown gravelly waves. The headless carcass of a deer lies in a ditch; a bird runs across the road in the pink glare of the low sun. All is stated in images, until the last five lines, which expound the very core of imagist doctrine, the subordination of idea to image:

When you are this
cold you can think about
nothing but the cold, the images

hitting into your eyes
like needles, crystals, you are happy.

Only in the very last phrase, "you are happy," is the emotion that the images have carried through the poem explicitly stated.

This poem exemplifies the startling actuality that is one of the striking features of so many of the items in *You Are Happy*. Such poems are related to the life which Atwood took up when in the early 1970s she retreated to live in old Loyalist country at Alliston, Ontario, in a way re-enacting Susanna Moodie's experiences, since she too was involved in a kind of pioneering, getting an old farm back into shape and some degree of production. They are often poems about place, but unlike Al Purdy's poems about the Loyalist country, they are not really about time in the historic sense; Atwood is less concerned than Purdy about ancestors and prefers to find them in myth and literature rather than in the kind of genealogical speculation through which he pushes backward to the roots of our past, or at least of his.

It is living or reliving at most, rather than remembering, that is important in poems like "You Are Happy," or like "November," "Digging" and "Late August," in which the poet projects anew the images of country living that belong to the pioneer tradition rather than evoking the tradition itself.

The dead sheep found in "November" hangs in the barn as "a long fruit covered with wool and rotting" and becomes in the poet's mind "a legacy," out of which emerge the bitter maxims of the poem's final lines:

Kill what you can't save
what you can't eat throw out
what you can't throw out bury

What you can't bury give away
what you can't give away you must carry with you,
it is always heavier than you thought.

The past that is "always heavier than you thought" hangs like a miasma over "Digging," where the poet digs dung in the barnyard as if it were a way of exorcising anger, grudges, "old remorse." And when the exorcism has worked, there is the pure flame of experience, as in "You Are

271

Happy,'' and the rich contentment of "Late August" that takes up the Keatsian theme—"Season of mists and mellow fruitfulness"—and makes out of it an exceptional Atwoodian poem in which the characteristic astringency is dissolved and a dreaming sensuality bridges the Romantic generations far more effectively than Keats's Canadian imitators did in the 1890s, with their precise metrical and metaphoric derivations. "Late August" is

> the plum season, the nights
> blue and distended, the moon
> hazed, this is the season of peaches
> with their lush lobed bulbs
> that glow in the dusk, apples
> that drop and rot
> sweetly, their brown skins veined as glands
>
> .   .   .
>
> The air is still
> warm, flesh moves over
> flesh, there is no
>
> hurry

There is a kind of verbal *trompe l'oeil* in such poems. Time and change seem to have been stilled: "there is no / hurry." And the illusion of timelessness is of course a quality of both imagist poetry and of the kind of Romantic verse that was most strikingly exemplified in Keats's odes. What is so clearly present is so in time, as well as space, and we have the sense of suspension in an eternal moment. But the very phrase, "eternal moment," gives the illusion away. Time starts up when we close the page, and we know that change has produced what the poet—and we vicariously —experience as changeless, and that change will afterward break the spell. It is Atwood's acknowledgement of the coexistence of the sense of timelessness and changelessness that special times and moods confer on us, with the reality of change, that gives *You Are Happy* a range and a poignancy which make it more complex in its perplexities and its rewards than any of Atwood's earlier volumes.

The double core of the book is formed by the two groups of poems linked with the Circe myth in its Odyssean variant. Metamorphosis in the true Ovidian sense is the theme of the "Songs of the Transformed," sung by beasts who were men before they were changed by Circe. They stand before us in their bestial natures, speak in their animal voices, yet through the masks of their transformation they project the aspects of our humanity we normally conceal but which are now released because the deceptions by which we safeguard them are no longer needed. Thus, often in their final lines, the speakers in these poems make reflections that are totally and appallingly human in their implications, as when the pig declares:

> I am yours. If you feed me garbage,
> I will sing a song of garbage.
> This is a hymn.

For the rat says:

> You'd do the same if you could,
>
> if you could afford to share
> my crystal hatreds.

There is a difference between natural metamorphosis and magic transformation, and the more we read the "Songs of the Transformed," the more we realize that the change of appearance which has taken these creatures out of humanity has left unchanged the core of instinct which the relationships necessary to human society have modified and moralized. Turned into animals, men exhibit without inhibition the worst characteristics of the human beast, just as, when political or religious hysterias are deprived of their protective mutuality, men, who have not even grown fur or horns, will exhibit the negative traits which we call bestial but which in fact are more deeply human than we dare admit.

"Songs of the Transformed" have to be read beside the "Circe / Mud Poems." Ostensibly this cycle of monologues that Circe addresses to Odysseus concerns, like *Power Politics,* the combination of need and conflict that dominates female-male relationships, but the implications run deeper.

The mud woman, crucial though she is, occupies only one poem of the cycle; a traveller told Circe that he and his friend constructed her in boyhood: "She began at the neck and ended at the knees and elbows; they stuck to the essentials." Making love to her soft moist body was ecstasy:

> His love for her was perfect, he could say anything to her, into her
> he spilled his entire life. She was swept away in a sudden flood.
> He said no woman since then has equalled her.

Circe, in a way, is the equivalent of the mud woman, which is why they are linked in the title of the cycle. She owns the island and in a sense she *is* the island:

> This is mine, this island, you can have
> the rocks, the plants
> that spread themselves flat over
> the thin soil, I renounce them.
>
> You can have this water,
> this flesh, I abdicate.

And this is what gives her the powers. She is a manifestation of the earth mother. She names the island and what is on it, and to name is magically to control and to transform. "The fresh monsters are already breeding in my head." And she transforms men not into what they are not but into what, essentially, they are:

> I did not add the shaggy
> rugs, the tusked masks,
> they happened.

Her victims are transformed because they do not have the will to become more than they are, to change instead of being changed, whereas it is the will to say always "Onward," of which Circe accuses Odysseus, that saves him from her magic:

> You are impervious
> with hope, it hardens you,
> this joy, this expectation, gleams
> in your hand like axes

And because he has resisted transformation and remained his ever-changing self, the threat of departure is always there. As Circe says to him: "Don't evade, don't pretend you won't leave after all: you leave in the story and the story is ruthless."

The myth—the story which "is ruthless"—tells of Odysseus's departure. There are other islands to which he comes, and it is a poem about two islands, Circe's and another, that ends the "Circe / Mud Poems." On the first island *"the events run themselves through / almost without us."* Magic transformations are predictable because they are always alike; they are the transformations that strip the human forms from men and women, and in other ways they will continue to haunt Margaret Atwood's later books. But there is the other island:

> The second I know nothing about
> because it has never happened;

this land is not finished,
this body is not reversible.

And this land which "is not finished" one can think of metaphorically as
modern life that has not yet made its own myths, or in a broad sense as
Canada, or in a narrow sense as the farm where the couple of the unmythi-
cal poems lives and where the time is neither past nor future but always,
imagistically, now:

We walk through a field, it is November,
the grass is yellow, tinged
with grey, the apples

are still on the trees,
they are orange, astonishing.

It is also a land where, as a later poem of *You Are Happy* says:

we keep going,
fighting our ways, our way
not out but through.

*Two-Headed Poems* seems like a strange oasis of relative calm between
the appalling mythical transformations that occupy so much of *You Are
Happy* and the horror of human atrocities grown habitual that casts such a
shadow over *True Stories*. I do not think there is any book by Atwood in
which one captures quite the same sense that it is good to be alive and human, and that in some way, not heroic or spectacular, the manner in which
men live can make the world a little more than endurable. In *Two-Headed
Poems* the irony that in some of Atwood's earlier poems appears merely
corrosive becomes transformed into a kind of solvent of anger.

It may be irrelevantly biographical to remark that the four years dividing
*Two-Headed Poems* from *You Are Happy* was a time of literary success for
Margaret Atwood and to all appearances of greater personal happiness. Yet
the fact is that a sense of unexpected contentment is projected by the poems
in the volume most closely linked to the actualities of an existence, largely
dominated by the presence of Atwood's young daughter. There are myths
here, indeed, but they are the myths of daily living, incorporated in such
undramatic transformations as dolls or Hallowe'en heads made of paper
bags, symbols whose very humbleness and indefiniteness give them more
protean possibilities than the ritual magic of Circe with its permutations
limited by tradition:

Paper head, I prefer you
because of your emptiness;
from within you any
word could still be said.

With you I could have
more than one skin,
a blank interior, a repertoire
of untold stories,
a fresh beginning.

Other, more sombre transformations do indeed appear in *Two-Headed Poems;* after all, it is a title that reminds us of Janus, the god of beginnings and endings, and the very first poem of the book—"Burned Space"—talks of the fundamental transformation that occurs when the timelessness of the natural cycle is dislocated by human intervention:

Before the burn, this was a forest.
Now it is something else:

a burn twists the green
eternal into singed grey

history: these discarded
stag-heads and small charred bones.

The statement is environmental propaganda; the poem is art. Perhaps the elegiac is the only mood that can be didactic and at the same time poetic.

There are two cycles within *Two-Headed Poems* entitled "Daybooks." My first reaction when I read them was to think of Robert Frost; like so many of Frost's poems, they seemed to me concrete and suggestive nota-tions on country living. But in fact, without ceasing to resemble Frost, they are nearer to Hesiod's *Works and Days,* with the strange combination one finds in those archaic Greek poems of a realistic sense of the difficulties of country life with an awareness of the emotional sustenance that is also a part of rural living. One of the most appealing poems in the "Daybooks" cycles is "Apple Jelly," which describes and decorates, and at the same time celebrates, opening out to a generous mood of awareness and accep-tance that is far different from the tight simplicities of *Power Politics* and other poems of earlier periods:

No sense in all this picking,
peeling & simmering

if sheer food is all
you want; you can buy it cheaper.

Why then do we burn our hours
& muscles in this stove,
cut our thumbs, to get these tiny
glass pots of clear jelly?

Hoarded in winter: the sun
on that noon, your awkward leap
down from the tree,
licked fingers, sweet pink juice,
what we keep
the taste of the act, taste
of this day.

Sometimes the remembered taste of country life has, as in Hesiod, a bitterness quite different from the winter sweetness of apple jelly; yet in the end, as another poem, ''Nothing New Here,'' declares, there is a frugal compensation that Hesiod would appreciate:

(. . . this broken
garden, measure
of our neglect and failure, still
gives what we eat.)

There is here, once again, tenacity, that recurrent alternative *leitmotiv* of Atwood's writing.

It is appropriate that *Two-Headed Poems* should be, as well as everything else, a lesson in existence. In ''You Begin,'' the poet is talking to her daughter, starting with images, things, colours, words, the stuff of poetry, and coming to man's primordial and distinguishing gift, the hand:

The word *hand* anchors
your hand to this table,
your hand is a warm stone
I hold between two words.

This is your hand, these are my hands, this is the world,
which is round but not flat and has more colours
than we see.

It begins, it has an end,
this is what you will
come back to, this is your hand.

*True Stories,* appearing in 1981, seven years after *You Are Happy,* represents the end of a cycle, and on the personal and the physical level it is all summed up in the poem "High Summer":

Goodbye, we credit

the apple trees, dead
and alive, with saying.

They say no such thing.

Reading this poem, one is aware that there are no claims made; the past is not insistent, as it is in Purdy's poems about the same countryside. The myth, the story we invent for our own solace and protection, is meaningless except to its inventors, we are told. But so also is the "true" story that pretends to be the opposite of myth, as the title poem tells us:

The true story is vicious
and multiple and untrue

after all. Why do you
need it? Don't ever

ask for the true story.

Yet much of *True Stories* in fact consists of a kind of poetic actuality, a continuing oblique comment on the world that is our here and now. Poetically, it contains some of the best verse Atwood has yet written, honed down to a stark directness, an accuracy of sound, yet always lit with that visual luminosity and sharpness which make poetry more than a mere verbal exercise, a Swinburnian patterning of sound. And it tells us, once again, after the relatively benign interlude of *Two-Headed Poems,* not only of the abdication of reason suggested in the title poem, but also of the tyranny of the senses and the cruel proximity of violence and love.

One of the striking aspects of *True Stories,* which it shares with much of *Two-Headed Poems,* is the metaphoric process by which thoughts merge into sensations, so that the mind seems imprisoned in its flesh, yet things in

a curious and compensating way become liberated into thought, so that a
landcrab is not only its hard evasive self but also a concept:

> a piece of what
> we are, not all,
> my stunted child, my momentary
> face in the mirror,
> my tiny nightmare.

And even though in a sequel, "Landcrab II," the poet remarks, "You're
no-one's metaphor," it is the previous concept that stays in the mind, just
as a longish poem later in the book called "Mushrooms" builds up inevitably to the final unknotting of a metaphor:

> Here is the handful
> of shadow I have brought back to you:
> this decay, this hope, this mouth-
> ful of dirt, this poetry.

This constant interplay between the sensual and the intellectual, between
things and thoughts, provides the formal remoteness from which Atwood,
like Auden's "Just," can exchange her messages. For these are poems
that, even while they warn us not to rely too much on reason—even our
own reason—are nevertheless saying factual things about the world in
which love exists—but also survives—on sufferance, threatened by the
kinds of violence and injustice that none of our civilized theories or codes
of conduct can comprehend.

The poems assembled in the middle section of *True Stories*—"Notes
Towards A Poem That Can Never Be Written"—read often like a verse abstract of the more harrowing sections of Amnesty International reports.
They too are poems of metamorphosis, of the frightful transformations,
without magic, that the malign human intelligence can alone invent.

> I think of the woman
> they did not kill.
> Instead they sewed her face
> shut, closed her mouth
> to a hole the size of a straw,
> and put her back on the streets,
> a mute symbol.

These poems depict a condition of unreasoning barbarity, where cruelty
and death are no longer tragic but merely gratuitous, absurd in their horror.

> you're unable
> to shake the concept of tragedy,
> that what one gets
> is what's deserved, more
> or less; that there's a plot
> and innocence is merely
> not to act.

It is no longer a world for taking sides, since "such things are done as soon as there are sides."

These poems may not—cannot—portray the rational, since they are concerned with areas of human existence from which reason has abdicated. Yet in themselves they are rational. They are also, taken together, one of the most intensely moral pieces of writing I have read in recent years, and no less so because they savage romantic notions of love, motherhood, and so on, and show how much myths can imprison and, indeed, destroy.

Yet *True Stories* is not all negation; its very moral intensity makes that impossible. It is about human cruelty and about human love, yet the two are far less fatally intertwined than they were in earlier Atwood poetry, like *Power Politics*. Cruelty is immediate and, at its worst, impersonal; love is a necessary contradiction to a world of violence. In "Small Poems for the Winter Solstice," the speaker asks her lover:

> How can I justify
> this gentle poem then in the face of sheer
> horror?

And she answers her own question: "I know you by your / opposites." It is through the presence of the opposites that we endure. The last lines of "Last Day"—the last lines of the book—are an image of renewal.

> This egg
> in my hand is our last meal,
> you break it open and the sky
> turns orange again and the sun rises
> again and this is the last day again.

*      *      *

*Interlunar,* which is Atwood's most recent book of verse at the time of writing this essay, and her tenth in all, is perhaps on balance the most serene of her volumes. It is not without its notations on human cruelty, though the inclination now is to reflect on the indifference of nature and the universe to all the evil that men do.

I would say the stones
cry out, except they don't.
Nothing cries out. The light falls on all of this
equally. Fear and memory
work their way down into the earth
and lie fallow.

There are also times when the poet seems to look forward, as in earlier
volumes, to the end of the kind of life we now cherish, to a time

when language
will shrink to the word *hunger*
and the word *none*.

But much more interesting about *Interlunar* is the sense one has throughout these poems, which are written in the familiar laconic Atwood voice
with a pitch as true as ever, of an almost animist pushing to the edges of
human consciousness, a return, in more complex and varied ways, to the
mental world of *Surfacing*.

Sometimes—in a more subtle way than in the "Songs of the Transformed" in *You Are Happy*—Atwood evokes the animal world in a curious
mingling of empathy and myth. The book is divided into two sections, the
larger bearing the title of the collection as a whole, "Interlunar," and a
smaller group of "Snake Poems," with which the volume begins and
which was originally published separately in a limited edition.

"Snake Poems" is a closely knit sequence in which, essentially,
Atwood is reflecting on the difference between the snake as a creature in
nature and the snake as an inhabitant of myth, and so, along with the ordinary snakes that are beautiful beyond human sympathy and are killed
with shovels and sometimes eaten, she poses the mythical "white snake"
and "blue snake" that, like the serpent in Genesis, promise knowledge,
liberating and destructive.

On one side you have the creature that lives outside the human world and
the world of warm-blooded animals:

Alone among animals
the snake does not sing.
The reason for them is the same
as the reason for stars, and not human.

And considered in this way the snake—that quintessentially lonely
creature—represents the cruelty of mere appetite at its most extreme:

281

There are no leaf-eating snakes.
All are fanged and gorge on blood.
Each one is a hunter's hunter,
nothing more than an endless gullet
pulling itself on over the still-alive prey
like a sock gone ravenous, like an evil glove
like sheer greed, lithe and devious.

Yet by his very alienness, the snake stirs in one thoughts of a realm beyond normal human experience. The snake, in the poet's mind, becomes ''an argument for poetry,'' a ''long word, cold-blooded and perfect.'' Also,

Unfurling itself from its cast skin,
the snake proclaims resurrection
to all believers.

And, in the lost paradise,

Love is choosing, the snake said.
The kingdom of god is within you
because you ate it.

Here we are involved in transformations of meanings and beings, in states of mind in which the poet can say, of the world of normal perception, ''It's only one version. / So is the sun.'' Even that normal world, if we observe it for itself, is a place of gratuitous miracle:

the real
flowers, goldenrod and purple asters,
the light spilling out of them
unasked for and unused.

But poems like ''The Saints'' convey a pure sense of the irrational mystery of existence and the power of the mysterious:

Now they seem to have no use,
like the colours on blind fish.
Nevertheless they are sacred.

They drift through the atmosphere,
their blue eyes sucked dry
by the ordeal of seeing,

exuding gaps in the landscape as water
exudes mist. They blink
and reality shivers.

In a series of poems about Orpheus and Eurydice, the half-worlds of
death-life, flesh-spirit, are suggested with sometimes a marvellous kind of
negative imagery, as when the shade of Eurydice is evoked:

> moving and still
> both, like a white curtain blowing
> in the draft from a half-open window
> beside a chair on which nobody sits.

The last Orpheus poem ends with an astonishingly Shelleyan declaration of
the poet's will to have his poetry survive:

> They have cut off both his hands
> and soon they will tear
> his head from his body in one burst
> of furious refusal.
> He foresees this. Yet he will go on
> singing, and in praise.
> To sing is either praise
> or defiance. Praise is defiance.

Two of the poems of *Interlunar* stand apart as remarkable by any standards, and show how, at this midpoint in her career, Atwood has mastered
all the craft of poetry and has used it to draw out the numinous from the
normal. One of them is "Heart Test with an Echo Chamber," an autobiographical poem, at once descriptive and transfigurative in its recording of a
routine medical test.

> Dressing, I am diaphanous,
> a mist wrapping a flare.
> I carry my precarious
> heart, radiant and already
> fading, out with me
> along the tiled corridors
> into the rest of the world
> which thinks it is opaque and hard.
> I am being very careful.
> O heart, now that I know your nature,
> who can I tell?

The other is the title poem, ''Interlunar,'' which ends the book, a poem about light and darkness, about protecting love, enclosed within a kind of nature poem that stirs with the sensations of smell and hearing which come into their own in darkness, and ends with an invocation of the lake's silence.

> We have come to the edge:
> the lake gives off its hush;
> in the outer night there is a barred owl
> calling, like a moth
> against the ear, from the far shore
> which is invisible.
> The lake, vast and dimensionless,
> doubles everything, the stars,
> the boulders, itself, even the darkness
> that you can walk so long in
> it becomes light.

The poet is, for once, at peace.

There are, in my view, a number of criteria of poetic excellence that apply in our time, in addition to a compulsive devotion to expression in verse: intense visual awareness; sharp verbal accuracy that makes, to adapt Orwell's metaphor, verse like a windowpane; deep moral sensitivity; the intuitive wisdom that in the last resort will accept the irrational as truer than the rational. Atwood, as her most recent volumes have shown, has all these qualities in abundance. She has also the over-reaching vision without which such qualities would in isolation be ineffective. Seen from this point in her life, her work—in prose and verse alike—presents a unity that reflects her dominant themes, tenacious survival and constant metamorphosis.

# 17

# PATRICK LANE

## *The Poetry of Place*

One of the striking features of recent Canadian poetry is the number of practitioners who have been autodidacts, without university training but with a varied experience of life. P. K. Page and Al Purdy, Raymond Souster and Gwendolyn MacEwen, John Newlove and Milton Acorn, Alden Nowlan and Patrick Lane, the subject of this essay; they form a notable group among living Canadian poets, and their presence shows that formal scholarship and poetic inspiration are unrelated factors. It also demonstrates how absurd are the pretensions of those who run so-called creative writing schools within the universities and presumptuously claim they can fashion writers.

Unlike some university-educated writers who claim to be worker poets, Patrick Lane is a genuine proletarian who from necessity worked many years as a labourer and at other dead-end jobs before he ever set his pen to writing verse. Work, a roving life and an observant eye gave him the basic material for his poetry, and he became one of those recent western poets who developed a strong consciousness of place, bringing the western landscape and its way of life, hitherto the province of realistic fiction, into Canadian poetry.

Lane has not remained a mere landscape poet. He is also highly conscious of the way a physical setting will conserve, and like a stone giving off at night the accumulated heat of the day, will project the spirit of the past, as he showed in his poems about the Andes and their Inca ruins. His poetry has revealed not only a serious attitude to life (a melancholy nihilism) but also an equally serious sense of craft, so that his technique has steadily progressed from his loose early free verse notations to patterns of growing intellectual and verbal complexity, and from being to all appearance one of the simplest of our poets, he has developed into one of the most sophisticated, without benefit of the academy.

The experiences of the working life and its peripheral incidents—spending nights in jail, living the life of the city streets and slums and the lonely road—have entered deeply into Patrick Lane's poetry and helped to create its characteristically plebeian tone. They have also led him to evolve the concept of the poet as outlaw that has influenced his life, the way he looks at the world, and the kind of poetry he writes. In an essay entitled "To the Outlaw," printed in *New: American and Canadian Poetry* in the spring of 1971, he elaborated that concept of the Nietzschean role of the poet:

> Outside the law is a place that is beyond even freedom, for to be free you must be free of something or someone and no-one is free that *must* live. Beyond freedom, beyond all temporal boundaries of ethics and morality is a place called beauty where the outlaw resides in bondage and in that beauty is a burning beyond all knowledge and understanding. It is from there that the poem comes. It is there the outlaw lives.

Patrick Lane began to publish his work in the little magazines of Vancouver during the 1960s, when the city became one of the most important Canadian centres of poetic activity. Earle Birney, Dorothy Livesay and Milton Acorn were there, Margaret Atwood and Al Purdy lived in the city for periods during the decade, and among the younger poets who began to emerge in Vancouver at this time were John Newlove, George Bowering, and Patrick's brother Red Lane, whose career was cut short by his death before the 1960s had half ended.

Lane published books, pamphlets, and broadsheets of his poems at fairly regular intervals, amassing more than twenty titles by the mid-1980s. Most of these were little-press publications in small editions that quickly went out of print; the most important volumes were brought out by established publishers and tended to be selections of poems already issued in more ephemeral form. They are *Beware the Months of Fire,* published by the House of Anansi in 1974, *Poems New and Selected,* which was published by the Oxford University Press in 1978 and won the Governor General's Award for poetry in that year, and *Old Mother* (1982), also published by Oxford. For another reason, a fourth collection has special significance. This is *Unborn Things: South American Poems,* issued by Harbour Publishing in 1975 and inspired by the travels Lane made shortly beforehand in Peru, Ecuador and Colombia—his first major journey outside North America.

What becomes evident as one follows Lane's publications over the years is the steady and conscious development of an individual voice, of a philosophic attitude for dealing with a view of life that is not optimistic, and of a distinctive poetic persona; just as impressive are the growing masteries of form and language that are shown when one compares the early poems of his first book, *Letters from the Savage Mind,* with the recent meditative poems of volumes like *The Measure*.

*Letters from the Savage Mind* consists of fifty-five poems composed in the first three or four years of Lane's activity as a poet. The volume is dedicated to his brother, Red Lane, and the longest poem, "The Carnival Man," is a kind of bizarre elegy on the dead poet, with dreamlike recollections of childhood fairs disguising what is essentially a poem of loss and remembrance, with its frenetic imagery of lights and sounds and childhood wonders quietening down to the last moving threnodic lines:

> I shall search
> in the empty field
> for a puff of dry corn
>
> I shall crawl on the ground
> searching for stones
> among dry hulls of dead lilacs
>
> I shall weave a coat
> from the strands of his red hair—
> it will ride on my shoulders like the night

There is in these early poems by Patrick Lane a great deal of the rather flat and painful simplicity that characterized so much of his brother's work. Often the imagery is too soft-edged to be apprehended clearly, and the result is a kind of wavering vagueness out of which no clear intent emerges: for example, the last stanza of the opening poem of *Letters,* "If I Travel Alone":

> If I travel alone
> I'll turn to stone
> and it shall be silently
> without benefit of
> a sun's burning
> or a thousand years
> without a moon
> as a tree walks
> into stone and silence
> with my hair rustling

Only five of the fifty-five poems in *Letters from the Savage Mind* were eventually picked for Lane's later collections, and this suggests that he would have us regard most of these early poems as the apprentice work of a writer who developed largely through his inclination towards self-rejection. The pieces that have survived are worth special consideration not only because they show that even in his early years Lane was capable of writing the occasional striking poem but also because they indicate the directions his work was later to follow.

All five are poems that present a situation. We are invited to consider a scene in which the poet is involved; he is there physically and he is moved emotionally, and his feeling is conveyed by an appropriateness of language and a sharpness of imagery that make us sensible that we are at the same time experiencing actuality and living within the poet's imagination, which extends the dimensions of the actuality we see. In this way, a brief poem becomes dense with meaning. Take, for example, "Three Days after Crisis in Cuba":

> Looking at cougar tracks
> by my back door with Bill;
> pads in the mud.
> He showed me where grass was bent in soft ground.
>
> Rain on my hard hat,
> squatting there among waterpuffed stems.
>
> He shot a crow
> from where we sat;
> it hangs above his record player—
> glass eyes,
> black feathers,
> it flies on a thread
> when you open the door.

Nothing is said about Cuba except in the title: there is nothing that is obviously a metaphor for the crisis. But this is not in the strict sense a metaphoric poem, in which the images can be taken as figures intended to reinforce our perception of what is being told by creating supporting analogies. Rather, it is a symbolist poem, in which we are expected to perceive correspondences rather than figurative likenesses. The cougar and the crow and the arbitrary killing of the crow are images that have nothing to do with the crisis itself, but, because they are images of fear—and particularly fear of the unpredictable—they suggest the state of mind of those who have lived through the crisis, just as the hard hat suggests the futility of human efforts to cope mentally with such situations, and the dead crow that flies, but on a thread, suggests how illusory the hope of escape from the cruel and gratuitous catastrophes of existence.

"Treaty-Trip from Shulus Reservation" is the kind of poem we shall see Lane writing frequently in later years, in which human degradation is evoked with objective honesty yet with a compassion that mingles with pessimism—a pity that what is must be. There are two drunken Indians. The man leans against a dusty wall, struggling with the "drunken buttons / on his fly."

His raven woman
knelt in the dirt
like some aged black
supplicant bird.

She vomits on the man's feet, and he raises his knee to strike her in the face while, apparently unaware of what is going on, an Indian child is wildly bouncing her ball against the same wall. The poet, in his role of agonized witness, contemplates the scene:

I hung there
in the sightless night
like a hooded
jesse-bound hawk
my quiet hammered breath
held in rhythmic beat
with the bouncing ball
that neatly caught
flew out
from the child's small hand
to thump on the flat red wall.

In "Legacies," the poet sits smoking a cigar that is part of the meagre inheritance coming to him from a grandfather he saw only once, yet whom, as he sits and consumes the legacies, he recognizes as

forebear,
passing my father to me
in one sudden moment
on a prairie night . . .
begat
begat

There is a sense here of the continuity of human relationships, in the mind at least, that will run right through the line of Lane's poetry as he tells of marriages broken, children lost, friends departed or dead, but all remembered. The continuity is fraught with sadness, for no human relationships are seen as secure, no lives immune from catastrophe. Even in "Act of the Apostles," when Lane writes of three children who have not yet departed (they eventually will), it is the poet seeing his own flaws reflected in his progeny:

> I catch an image
> of myself
> inside their eyes
> and all alone
> I live in fear
> of the sepulchral
> shadow of a tree.

Another characteristic Lane theme emerges in the fifth of these early poems that he chose to keep, "Loving She Stood Apart." The lover lies watching the woman as she undresses, turned away from him:

> afraid she was
> of the wanting to need
> me watching her.

She begs him to turn out the light, and at last he does so, and

> so quietly my mind
> shut out the sight
> and I was blind to
> her but O the night

Here is a tenderness that seems the opposite of the consciousness of the cruelty in human relationships that pervades so many Lane poems, yet it is a tenderness that recurs not only in the poet-persona's attitude to women but also in his gentleness towards those who are wrecked by life. The cruelty appals this agonized witness, but the victims do not, and the moments that are somehow exempt from cruelty are treasured. No critics have been more mistaken than those who have assumed, from the content of his poems, an essential brutality in Lane's vision, a rejoicing in the violence and horror he sees in the world. Rather, like the classic Buddhist, he finds in the recognition of life's horrors, or the terrible things men do to men and even more to other beings, the reason for an ultimate compassion, for a desire to nurture love where it survives.

*Separations* appeared in 1969, and it shows the growing power and assurance of Lane's poetry. Almost three-quarters of these forty poems eventually emerged in one or other of his definitive collections, and they include some of the poems by which he is now best known, such as "Prospector," "Calgary City Jail," "Elephants," "Wild Horses," "Ten Miles In from Horsefly," "The Water-Truck" and "For Rita—in Asylum."

In *Letters from the Savage Mind* it was the characteristic Lane themes, the characteristically pessimistic view of life, that began to emerge. In *Separations* we encounter, much more often and more pronouncedly, the epiphanic episodes that Lane handles so well. The personal myth of the poet is developed, undoubtedly largely based on an actual life, though that is not what concerns us as readers so much as the mental arrangements of that life which form the armature of the poems. The very titles of the poems I have mentioned tend to define the perimeters of that myth. It embraces the wanderer, in "Ten Miles In from Horsefly," shovelling manure from a barn to get lodging and food; the worker who is neither efficient nor zealous, in "Elephants" and "The Water-Truck"; the man torn by the suffering of animals yet taking part in their destruction in "Wild Horses"; the enemy of conventional society in "Calgary City Jail"; the sexual predator who yet laments women as the supreme victims of social ills in "For Rita —in Asylum," and the wondering child (precursor of the suffering man) in "Prospector."

What is so compelling about these poems is that they are visual and reflective at the same time. We are shown a scene, an episode, in such a way that we cannot do other than consider its implications, how the particular reflection that emerges from it may affect our view of the life we share with the poet. Lane never offers us an abstract thought; he presents a concrete and particular instance, and from that, if we wish to go such a way, we can abstract our own conclusions, but the act of abstraction is not part of the role the poet accepts.

Yet, as the debris which chokes our memories of the imagist movement shows, no amount of concrete presentation will have this effect of stirring the mind outside of reason if it does not move on multiple levels of perception and if it is not associated with a technical mastery of the poetic medium. It is for their advances in both these directions that the poems in *Separations* are notable.

To begin there is the development of the multiple perceptions and the ironic juxtapositions which such multiplication inevitably involves. "Elephants" is a work poem in the sense that it presents the poet-narrator in a work situation. But it is not a work poem in the conventional sense of displaying merely the hard life of the toilers. The point it drives at does not, in fact, have much to do with the work situation in which it begins. As it opens, the poet is sitting with two other workers on a road project: "all of us waiting out the last hour / until we go back on the grade." Trying to forget the clatter of machinery

> pounding stones and earth to powder
> for hours in mosquito-darkness
> of the endless cold mountain night

he occupies himself with a slow creative process, a shaping like that of making poetic images, as he sits with his knife and carves out of a chunk of brown soap an elephant, which he intends to give an Indian boy "who lives / in the village a mile back / in the bush."

As he cuts away and talks to the boy, his mind moves from the work situation, and he tells the child, who does not know what an elephant is,

> the story
> of the elephant graveyard
> which no one has ever found
> and how the silent
> animals of the rain forest
> go away to die somewhere
> in the limberlost of distances
> and he smiles at me

The Indian boy's smile is the ironic turning point of the poem, for it brings the fantasies home to roost. What he now tells the poet is of the graveyard where his people have been buried "so far back / no one remembers when it started." When the poet asks where the graveyard is,

> he tells me it is gone
> now where no one will ever find it
> buried under the grade of the new
> highway.

And so the wheels have turned full circle. We are all endangered species, our lives likely to be buried by history, and we are all involved in the universal complicity that finds the poet working on the highway that has buried the Indian cemetery at the same time as he is giving the Indian boy a totemic image of the greatest of all land animals, doomed for its very greatness.

Perhaps "Elephants" is more complex in its ironies than some of the other poems I have mentioned, and more oblique, for the extinction of the elephants is not linked directly with the actions of men as the destruction of other animals is in "Wild Horses." But even here we are involved in matters which bring us face to face with a crucial question: to what degree is Patrick Lane a moralist poet? Already we have noticed his Nietzschean statement that "beyond all temporal boundaries of ethics and morality is a

place called beauty where the outlaw resides,'' and it is from the place outside good and evil that he sees the poem emerging. In fact, evil exists,
quite clearly defined, in Lane's poems, and the witness's agony, repeated
time and again, represents his judgement and at the same time his acceptance of guilt.

The whole point of "Wild Horses" lies in the poet's involvement as
both actor and witness. He sees the gun fired—and he holds it. "Wild
Horses" begins obliquely with the expression of a longing for an innocent
contact with the free beings of the wilderness—something like the primitive man's encounter with the spirit animals:

> Just to come once alone
> to these wild horses
> driving out of high Cascades,
> raw legs heaving the hip-high snow.
> Just once alone. Never to see
> the men and their trucks.

But in the poem, as in the poet's experience, the men and the trucks are
there. The "stallion with five free mares / rush into the guns." They are
all killed. "Ice bleeds in their nostrils / as the cable hauls them in." And
then the poem itself bleeds away to human callousness:

> Later, after the swearing
> and the stamping of feet,
> we ride down into Golden:
>
> *Quit bitchin.*
> *It's a hard bloody life*
> *and a long week*
> *for three hundred bucks of meat.*
>
> That and the dull dead eyes
> and the empty meadows.

A similar pattern, of the poet as witness, also taking part in the action,
though not initiating it, and then displaying the signs of remorse, occurs in
later poems, notably in "Wild Dogs." Here the poet begins by talking of
the dogs that have run wild in the mountains and formed themselves into
packs, which kill the cattle. The mill is shut down in winter, and the poet's
mates invite him to join them in killing the wild dogs; though his wife does
not like it, he goes, without trying to explain.

How do you explain
what men do

there's a special
hatred for wild dogs
we go to hunt
because we were
their masters
it's not for food
we kill them
or even pleasure
but the fear
we thought we'd lost
so long ago

The dogs are trapped on the road, and the poet thinks of Spartacus and his slaves "free in the hills / of Rome" while he watches the dogs milling round and round "as I wept / and they blew them / to pieces."

There are balancing sentiments at work here. The poet invents a reason in human nature and in men's relation to other creatures to explain the massacre in which he is taking part. But then he suddenly sees the animals as, in their own way, equivalent to human beings who seek their freedom, and in the end *he* weeps as *they* blow them to pieces. In other words, at the very end some impulse within him makes him refrain from taking part in the killing as he had done in "Wild Horses."

Yet the sense of the complicity of the witness remains, and emerges perhaps in its most extreme form in "If." As he is making love to a woman, the poet remembers a grotesque and terrible scene in Tiajuana, a woman weeping with pain as a burro fucked her on a sideshow stage. Remembering, he no longer wants the woman he is with:

I am obscene.
I am one of those who laughed
when the burro dropped her on the floor.

To see, and to fail in rejection, is to be guilty of whatever you witness; the implication is clear.

It is impossible to consider these as merely poems about the human condition; they are poems making a judgement on mankind's role in the natural world. When Lane quotes Céline in the epigraph to *Beware the Months of Fire,* saying that we must realize "how devilish men can be," and saying also "we must tell the whole thing, without ever altering one word,—everything that we have seen of man's viciousness," he is implying a moral reason for what he writes in his poems. He is not merely saying this is how the human condition is; he is saying also how terrible that it should be so. And so he stands among the pessimistic moralists, like Céline and Swift and Orwell, writers fascinated and horrified by the way in which men have shown themselves more destructive, more gratuitously cruel, than all the animals. If one wants to catch in Lane the opposite vision that also haunts those dark nightmarists, the elusive vision of a world in grace, it exists in the late poem "I Am Tired of Your Politics," in which Lane seems to be cautioning himself as well as his readers when he says:

> We must not hide
> our innocence, the distant
> singing we call love.

After arguing that poets should sing of such rare and positive things as "Peace, wisdom, / excellence in the small / affairs of the heart," he goes on to ask, not pity, but respect for living beings, and in the last two excellent verses of the poem—a reflective narrative as so often in Lane—he is really saying that misfortune is inevitable, but the worst crime is to despise those who are unfortunate:

> Listen, once when I was
> young, I knew a woman
> natural as beauty, brave
> with all the mysteries
> she was born to.
> Let us not pity her.
> The sad compassions
> are of little use.
> She left her love
> in a thousand beds
> until she lost her mind
> and fell into the
> dream called death.
>
> Let us respect her now,
> give her at least the desire
> that she could be in the sun
> with her hurt head resting
> on her pale white hands.
> The will is not holy.
> One moves in stillness.
> Look, even the birds

are decently silent
while she sleeps.

Reading through this series of poems that are clearly related by theme, one is aware of the growing mastery of the craft of poetry that Lane has established. Plainness and the search for the true word were always his virtues as a poet, but in the early works they were accompanied often by an unsought roughness of tone, an unfocussed vagueness of imagery, a clumsiness of rhythm. In some ways, what he has achieved is a progression from naive poetry to a very sophisticated poetry. In the late pieces, one is aware of a constant balancing of the sound and the intent, of the visual element and the thought, and also of a steady moving into the tradition, as a result of which the verbal texture of the poems becomes close-knit yet elastic. There is a careful balancing of syllables in the lines, and a pattern in which the polysyllabic words stand out in emphasis within a basic weave of simple monosyllabic words. Alliteration is modestly present ("left her love," "beauty, brave," "her hurt head," "dream called death"), and in other later poems one finds the occasional rhyme, but just as traditional is the conversational-reflective tone—as old at least as Wordsworth in its ancestry—that Lane achieves in so many of the later poems. In a poem like "I Am Tired of Your Politics" one is in fact reminded, from the title to the end, of the later Yeats, and a poet who can proclaim such affinities without mere imitation has gone a long way towards maturity.

*Mountain Oysters* is the volume that perhaps more than any other raises the question of whether Lane is a regional poet, since so many of its pieces spring out of his experiences in the mountain country of British Columbia, where he was born and reared and where he spent a great deal of his working life. Indeed, eighteen of the twenty-one poems would have been impossible without these experiences, and a number of them, like "Wild Dogs," "The Black Colt" (later "The Black Filly") and "Mountain Oysters," vividly portray episodes in which the poet-persona is directly involved. They are largely poems about violence done in one way or another to animals. The black colt is tethered in an open field during a frightful mountain storm in order to terrify it into submission. In "Mountain Oysters" a sheepherder bites off the balls of his rams, and the poet

enjoyed them with him
cutting delicately
into the deep-fried testicles.

Mountain oysters make you strong
he said
while out in the field

the rams stood holding their pain
legs fluttering like blue hands
of old tired men.

Dying and living, the bird is an image that recurs throughout Lane's poems, taking various forms—the dead crow in *Letters from the Savage Mind,* the redwing blackbirds in "Fireweed Seeds" and a number of manifestations in *Mountain Oysters,* including "The God Who Is Goshawk," symbolic of the survival urge with its paradoxical need to destroy, and the blue jay who reaches "unreasonable death," smashing its "fingernail skull" as it hits a boxcar in panic flight:

Blue wings harden in my hand.
Bones crack, hollow as the wind
where it creeps on high snow
levelling mountains with the land.

In later volumes, the bird dashing itself to death against a wall or a window or dying from cold will become a recurrent image, reaching its climax in "Ice Storm," in which weather, unaided by men, contrives a massacre, and the poet rages, not against his own kind, but against the indifferent cruelty of the universe:

As if the snow was more than just a prison.
Ice like an eyelid closing on the birds
beneath the snow. As I am more than just

the owner of this field, knowing every bird
I free, I'll find another dozen dead.
My foot jerks back from cold,

angry now, shaking my fists at the rare
explosions below me, feet breaking through
the icy cloud cover of their tombs.

In "The Bird" the implications of this recurrent image are made evident. The poet speaks to a child who has caught a bird and held it in his hands, thinking that in this way he will learn to fly, but the bird dies, and the poet says:

Only words
can fly for you like birds
on the wall of the sun.

A bird is a poem
that talks of the end of cages.

And so the bird becomes a symbol of poetic activity, but also of freedom, as indeed the wild dogs were in other poems, and here the relationship between the poet and the natural world reaches its greatest ambiguity,
for it is with the wild things of this world that he senses the greatest affinity—they, like him, are beyond ordinary human commerce or morality
—yet he joins with other men in the destruction of what are, in effect, his
totemic counterparts. And here we come to the element of ritual magic in
Lane's poems, for he resembles the primitive hunter who will kill a sacred
animal, like a bear, for food, but will placate its spirit by apologetic ritual
chants.

Into all these poems there enters a vivid sense of the mountain region
where the poems take place, and from whose way of life they are derived in
theme and imagery alike, and the same happens in the volumes that follow
closely after, *Hiway 401 Rhapsody, The Sun Has Begun to Eat the Mountain* and *Passing into Storm,* except that in these the focus shifts from the
hard death of animals to the hard life of men, as in poems like "Thirty
Below":

Men on the pond
push logs through constant ice.
Faces stubble with frost.
No one moves beyond the ritual
of work. Torment of metal
and the scream of saws.

In "Thirty Miles In from the Coast" a man waits with the frozen corpse of
his wife stored in a shed until spring; in "Gerald" a boy is persecuted into
insanity by the cruel discipline of his religious fanatic of a father, and in
"Sleep Is the Silence Darkness Takes" Lane narrates, as a kind of exemplum of Western Canadian history, the story of a man bred on a pioneer
farm, growing up to manhood in the hardrock mines and surviving the war
to return "and pour my soul / into the pocketbooks of others who stole /
my brains and used them for their gains / because of privilege, birth or
prior right—." This poem is dedicated to Lane's father, but it is wise when
considering any of Lane's narratives to expect a measure of invention. For
in another poem, "The Witnesses," also purportedly about his father (this
time in the role of a rodeo rider, the McLeod Kid), he says:

What if I try to capture an ecstasy that is not
mine, what if these are only words saying

this was or this was not, a story told to me
until I now no longer believe it was told to me

The witnesses dead, what if I create a past
that never was, make out of nothing
a history of my people whether in pain
or ecstasy, my father riding in the McLeod Rodeo

But whether the witness evokes an actual incident or an episode conjured
by the mind, the faithfulness to place and to historical moment remains in
all these poems, and in this way, when he is writing about the interior of
British Columbia, Lane does evoke in a convincing way the spirit of a
region where he has lived and suffered. The difficulty about classifying
him as a regional poet arises when one encounters Lane writing with equal
intensity and authenticity about other regions than his native British
Columbia. In *Unborn Things: South American Poems* (1975) (some of
whose pieces had already appeared in *Beware the Months of Fire* a year
before) Lane comes up from an immersion in life along the Andes with a
series of splendid and convincing poems, and in his most recent volume,
*Old Mother* (1982), the notably dominant region in terms of settings,
themes and recorded experiences is the prairies, where Lane has been
living for the past few years, though this volume also contains a group of
poems written on a journey to China.

*Unborn Things* is a group of threnodies on the lost past of the Incas, al-
ternating with appalled presentations of the here and now in which the descendants of those who created the Andean civilizations survive. In a
sense, they are a continuation in another place of Lane's earlier poems recording with mingled delight and anger the splendour of the world and the
shame of what man has done to it and to his fellow inhabitants. The difference is that in *Unborn Things* Lane is writing within a context of history
and myth that gives his poems a special colour and richness of imagery
which his Canadian work, with its faith to place, necessarily lacks.

The heart of the book is a suite entitled ''Machu Picchu,'' which evokes
the past of that lost final fortress of the Inca realm, perched on its splendid
crags above the jungle and the rivers. It tells of the departure of Manco
Capac, the last Inca, who is to die in a Spanish ambush, of the dying out of
the Virgins of the Sun in their mountaintop refuge, and of the fate as an ar-
chaeological site and a tourist centre that Machu Picchu now shares with
other tragic loci of history and myth, with Mycenae and Elsinore, with
Taxila and Persepolis:

Today we lay in the Temple of the Virgins
As centuries filled our mouths with moss.

They have stripped away the jungle.
They have torn the winding cloths.
They have scattered bones to the wind.

Strangers walk through the ruins.
They talk of where they come from,
Where they are going.
As we lay in this roofless room
They stoned a snake.

It crawled out of the earth
To lie in the brilliant sun.
Coils of its body like plaited hair,
Eyes of cracked stone. They left it
Broken, draped on a fallen wall.

The kind of quasi-Lawrencian transference that equates modern brutality
to a snake people fear with the Spaniards' destruction of a civilization they
could not understand is extended to other poems in *Unborn Things,* poems
concerning the present-day life of the Andes. "At the Edge of the Jungle"
is a poem about disillusionment in a romantically anticipated place. The
narrative of horror begins with a dog burying its head in the Amazonian
mud to evade the flies that swarm on his sore eyes; it ends with a tethered
rooster whose beak children have cut away so that he cannot eat. It is a
fine, appalling poem; I recognize its authenticity from having made the
same journey over the Andean Sierra and down to the Amazonian head-
waters. It ends:

Diseased clouds bloom in the sky.
They throw down roots of fire.
The bird drags sound from its skin.
I am grown older than I imagined:
the garden I dreamed does not exist
and compassion is only the beginning
of suffering. Everything deceives.

A man could walk into this jungle
and lying down be lost
among the green sucking of trees.
What reality there is resides
in the child who holds the string
and does not see

the bird as it beats its blunt head
again and again into the earth.

There is a curious footnote to be made to this poem and to the title poem
of the volume, "Unborn Things." They appeared, as "July" and "June"
respectively, in *Beware the Months of Fire,* but they were, as Lane admits
in his prefatory note to *Unborn Things,* "printed in versions where,
through changing a few key geographical words, they reflected a British
Columbia locale." Lane gives no explanation as to why he made the
changes, though he admits it was an "error," as becomes evident when
one reads on and encounters a cluster of images that has no imaginable
place in a British Columbian locale, but is authentically Latin American:

a broken melon bleeds a pestilence
of bees; a woman squats and pees
balancing perfectly her basket
of meat; a gelding falls to its knees
under the goad of its driver.

Lane's ability to grasp the essential imagery of a series of regions and his
power to create a self-consistent myth out of the lost history of the Incas
mark him as a great deal more than a regional poet in the way we apply that
term to writers whose inspiration comes from a single small area and its
traditions, like William Barnes or John Clare. He is on a much wider scale
a poet of place and time, committed to considering human communities in
relation to their geographical environments and their places in history.

Each of the larger collections of Lane's poems consists mainly of works
collected from the smaller earlier volumes, with a few added new pieces—
more in the case of *Poems New and Selected* than in the case of *Beware the
Months of Fire.* What is most interesting in these books is the method of
selection and arrangement. In the case of *Beware the Months of Fire,* both
these tasks were apparently done by Margaret Atwood, then the active editor of House of Anansi, which published the book, though it seems unlikely that Lane had nothing at all to do with the process of choice and ordering. In the case of *Poems New and Selected,* Lane seems to have made
his own choices, possibly with some advice from William Toye, the editorial director of the Oxford University Press in Toronto.

The arrangement of *Beware the Months of Fire* tends to be in thematic
groups, which would fit in with Margaret Atwood's critical inclinations at
that period. For example, six poems about men's relations with animals are
grouped together at one point; these are followed by four poems about experiences connected with work in the interior of British Columbia; next

301

come four poems and a long prose dialogue about the vagabond levels of city life; and then seven love poems of various kinds, followed by five of the poems from South America later included in *Unborn Things*. The arrangement of *Poems New and Selected* is chronological rather than thematic, with groups of poems from the various books following each other in succession, and a group of thirteen previously uncollected pieces bringing the book to an end.

One notices clearly in *Poems New and Selected* the formal change in Lane's poems, the tendency to create fairly regular syllabic structures within traditional stanzaic forms, which becomes evident in the poems of *Unborn Things* and of the year or so immediately preceding that volume, and which accompanies a remarkable advance in poetic skill since the rather loose and unsure poems Lane was writing in the early 1960s. There is also a shift towards a more reflective type of poem, philosophically concerned with human destiny and moving into those verges of the numinous that prose can hardly penetrate. This results in poems quite different in their gravity of tone, in their deliberate balancing of correspondences and connotations, and even in their visionary symbolism, from the earlier poems. "Still Hunting" is a fine example, with its contemplative probing of the reality of death:

> A single banner of sky between two mountains:
> neither the beginning nor the end of clouds.
> Somewhere all the animals have happened
> and I wait and pray I will know
> the difference between the animal and man,
> pray for the gift of a death
> to break this glacial waste of time—
> that when I shoulder the empty body
> I will have something to walk with
> be it ice, air, stone or man; pray
> I will find the road where I left it
> in the tree-line far below.

And in one of the later, previously ungathered pieces in *Poems New and Selected,* significantly entitled "Wild Birds," the poet sees a flight of crows fighting the wind:

> Baffled, returning, knowing the landfall,
> they beat their wings against a strength
> greater than their own.

He goes on to develop his philosophic theme: the way humankind's chaotic nature in a chaotic world frustrates all dreams of order. It is, made clear and articulate, the philosophy that unites Lane's poetry from beginning to end:

> We are all of us
>
> as those birds I saw at sea blown outward
> against their will. I read the books
> and dreamed the dream that words could change
> the vision, make of man a perfect animal
> and so transformed become immortal.
>
> What else was there to dream? Not this,
> not this beating against the wind. Chaos
> is our creation and the god we wished was man:
> to turn again into the thing we are, yet be
> black cinders lost at sea, the wild birds failing.

Since the appearance of *Poems New and Selected,* Lane has published three collections of verse, each with its own special character. In *No Longer Two People,* poems written by Lane and Lorna Uher appear in alternation, and the resultant dialogue marks a departure for a poet who up to now has been a monologist, talking to, rather than with, his readers. Lorna Uher is speaker as well as reader; she is the fellow poet, sharer of experience and idea. The result of the collaboration is that in this collection one poet writes at her best and the other seems to move out of his stance as the agonized witness into that of the engaged and involved man, the half of a unity of feeling. It is unnecessary to ask biographical questions. The relationship, so far as the reader is concerned, is one between personae and achieves its validity on that level. As a dialogue of disembodied voices on radio, it found its appropriate medium and was impressive because of the elegiac undertone to its lyrical intensities. *No Longer Two People* builds up to a strange gravity as the speakers see their lives advancing through the debris of the past towards the paradoxical regeneration of winter. Both their final poems evoke the rot of a late garden where the tomatoes hang shrivelled with frost on the black vines. The woman concludes:

> And we await
> the forgiveness of winter: drifts
> to bury all the dead we left behind.

Then we will come to one another
with the simplicity of trees
stripped branches holding all
that will survive.

And the man, more ambiguously, sees himself breaking

a trail through the snow.
There is no looking behind.
Everywhere the wind covers my passing.

Is he really leaving the old past of ruined relationships, as his earlier remark "Now is the time / for patience" suggests? Or is he just acting once
again to the habitual pattern? One suspects the latter when he contradicts
the woman by saying:

There is no forgiveness,
only a blind woman calling out her dead,
the snow, the broken earth.

This stubborn ambiguity takes one back to the relationship between person
and persona, and also between animus and anima, and to the ways in which
poetic structures become detached from the life they purport to represent,
as the Picasso epigraph suggests:

Though these two people once existed for me, they exist no longer. . . . They
are no longer two people, you see, but forms and colours; forms and colours
that have taken on, meanwhile, the idea of two people and preserve the vibra-
tion of their life.

The transition to *The Measure*, which is dedicated to the other poet of
*No Longer Two People*, is a clear one. For here, as well, Lane is working
among the haunting correspondences between art and the actuality that provides its content. His own statement introducing the poems emphasizes this
fact. For, beginning with the platitudinous remark that "the old stories
aren't dead and neither is the art of telling them," he goes on to say:

The poems here are mostly narratives, their form a direct result of their content,
their content a direct result of a life lived. Even as one allows the poems to be,
one selects among the many images in order to find those whose shape will
define a way of being alive. There are a number of voices speaking here. Each
one struggled into being on its own. If there is a violence reflected among them
it is only because I care deeply for the many lives I have seen wasted uselessly.

The intellectual confusion of such a statement is obvious, yet it is a necessary confusion in a poet who has based so much of his writing on actual experiences, and in the end realizes, if the poem is good, it has very little to do with the power of the experience. It is, as he says, a matter of selecting among the images, which means creating an abstract order, an area of detachment among the concrete and particular facts of existence. And this is one of the principal problems and tasks of the narrative as distinct from the epic poet.

For the unepic writer of narrative poems is dealing, not with the affairs of gods and heroes, but with the affairs of ordinary human beings and perhaps of animals. And the essence of narrative poetry is really trapping those moments in life that are either typical or epiphanous, either that which explains or that which astonishes, and presenting them in a shape that, as Lane remarks, "will define a way of being alive."

A narrative poem need not tell a story at length, as Wordsworth's often do. It can present a single image that portrays or even implies action which reveals through its symbolic power something profound about existence. "Chinook" is the shortest poem of *The Measure*, but the truth it tells is as complex as an ice-flower:

> Beneath the tree, glutted on winter
> apples, seven sparrows lie
> drunk, beating small wings on snow
> as if they could fly into it
> and make of ice an element as free as air.

And a life doomed to loneliness, which many poets would take pages to evoke, is embraced in the hardly longer form of "Coming Home":

> Coming home drunk
> I want you to be
> not there. I want
> the empty bottle
> the broken glass
> and the backs of my friends
> as they leave me. But
> most of all I want you
> not to be there.

But by no means all the poems in *The Measure* are as brief or as gnomic in their intent as these. "I Am Tired of Your Politics" is one of them; here a general statement is made about the goals of poetry, and the personal history of the "woman / natural as beauty" is introduced to illustrate it. In

"Blue Valley Night" the poet draws out of the past a recollection of his days as first-aid man at a lumber mill and tells the story of his relationship with alcoholic old Charlie, who gets drunk regularly at the end of the month on lemon extract. The poem is elaborate, building through the savage comedy of human degeneration to the inevitable tragedy when Charlie, putting on what is left of his best clothes, goes out to march into the front of a train. His death creates the merest ripple in the universe:

> In the cedars, crows
> lift in their feathers,
> lift and settle
> in their sleep.

And in "Something Other than Our Own" the savage comedy plays out in a different way as the poet and his companions from the bunkhouse watch an enraged husband with a gun stalking his wife's naked lover (armed only with a guitar) through the piles of lumber in the frozen yard. As the naked man stumbles down the railway track into the snowy distance and the husband gives up his hunt, the watchers laugh, and the poet goes back to his bunk to dream of a woman.

Perhaps it is the inevitability of the human comedy, and the strange dignity of those for whom it has turned into tragedy, that is the clearest theme of *The Measure*. If one can talk of the book having a lesson, it is that of respect for life, no matter how ludicrous, how debased, how alien it may seem to us who are observers. It comes round again to the conviction that observation is not enough; there must be the passion and the complicity of witness.

Lane's most recent book, *Old Mother,* is also his most overtly experimental, but this statement immediately involves one in considering what we really mean by terms like *experimental* and *avant garde* in a country like Canada whose distinctive literature is still young and has only recently emerged from the cautious conservatism of early pioneer writers. I suggest that in such a situation the experimental artist is far less concerned with formal considerations than his counterpart in a country with an established literature. In the arts of a young country, the first task—once the defensiveness of the pioneer has been dissolved—is to define and embrace the land, to understand the interplay of history and geography that has shaped the society for which the poet or the novelist or the painter, each in his special language, speaks. In an old country, it is the shifts of sensibility and perception within an established order that are the concerns of those who move on the forward edge of art. The difference, essentially, is between the process of exploration and the process of invention—between the discovery of what is existing and the creation of what does not yet exist. What the two situations have in common is that they both represent that thrust into the unknown which is the ultimate aim of all true artists.

In terms of these definitions, it seems to me that Lane has always been experimental and always avant garde since he has been constantly seeking the forms that would most appropriately express a kind of living which has not yet found its place in literature. In such a task, the content often assumes an importance in relation to the form which it may not have in the more abstract and disembodied poetry of older cultures, and this means that very often a stark narrative structure, with a language stripped down to largely monosyllabic simplicity, such as one often encounters in Lane's earlier poetry, is the appropriate and therefore the experimentally correct vehicle.

Nevertheless, Lane's recent work, ever since his visit to the Andes and his encounter with the old cultures of the Incas and the Spanish Americans, has shown a growing complexity, manifested, as we have seen, in the greater sophistication of language and the resort to technically more elaborate forms that are characteristic of poets working in more long-established literary traditions. This echoes a general tendency in Canadian writing—and painting as well—to make the further step, from the stage of exploration to the stage of invention. We see it in the fiction writers who have moved from the naturalism of the early prairie novelists to the artifice of writers like Timothy Findley and Margaret Atwood, and it appears now among the poets, and in Lane's case within the work of a single poet, so that in *Old Mother* one sees him involved in the exploration of poetic ingenuities in a way that reminds one how much his affinities were always divided between the Canadian poets who explored the immediate environment and the European decadents who were much more concerned with the horror of human existence in any environment.

Already in the naming of a previous volume, *The Measure*, there is a hint of Lane's closer attention to the prosodic aspects of his work, and though the "measure" of the title poem seems to be an existential one—

> What is the measure then, the magpie in the field
> watching over death, the dog's eyes hard as marbles
> breath still frozen to his lips?

—one soon becomes aware, reading through the book, of the extent to which poetic measures, as well as existential relativities, have become increasingly important to him.

In the first version of Lane's most recent volume, the key word was repeated in the provisional title, "Weights and Measures"; later the book was retitled *Old Mother*. The formal concerns of the poet are made very clear in the central sequence of the volume, "The Weight" (meaning the weight of the past, of ancestry), where the second staggered stanza ends:

which is duty
not to deny
      the neck burned
             calling the dead to come
eyes buried
      alive again
          once more
             the sprung
measure

The "sprung measure" is evident throughout this central (in place as well as significance) section of *Old Mother*. It is partly a variant of Hopkins's practice of "sprung rhythm," gaining emphasis through splitting the lines according to the natural pauses and emphases of speech, but it is also a visual element in the layout of the text, which relates it to contemporary concrete poetry, and it accompanies an associational grouping of concepts and thoughts that reminds one—and not too distantly—of classic modernist works like *Ulysses,* and the *Cantos* of Ezra Pound.

All this may seem to project the image of a Lane coming late to awareness of the variants of poetic postmodernism, and that would be unjust since the erudition that makes him acutely aware of poetic events has long been evident. It is really the content of "The Weight" that has dictated this poly-experimental approach since here, in the grotesque ancestral figure of "old *Jack Lane,*" his putative descendant Patrick is enacting—for an audience of poets gathered in by name: Marty, Purdy, Newlove, Suknaski, Kroetsch, etc.—the cruel seeding and subjection of the land. This is poetry that defies exposition, yet—especially in the section of the sequence called "The Dance"—it moves the reader to a strange alternation of bitterness and nostalgia. The past—we are told and believe—was frightful to live through; is beautiful in recollection. And here one lips that paradox which haunts every significant Canadian writer of our generation, the gap between what happened, which was actuality, and what we choose to remember, which is history.

History, in fact, haunts the earlier poems of *Old Mother,* such as "Buffalo Stones" and "Indian Tent Rings," which move Lane out of other pasts linked to a departed present into the prairie of an immediate present. In "Indian Tent Rings" the poet compares his own reactions as a man of the West to the evidences of a past culture with those of the American visitors who relate everything they come across to the archaic remains they have seen in the lands of classical civilizations. Yet in the end he concludes:

> It is enough they are here, the woman
> caught in the circle and the man
> circling below her, his eyes
> trying to find a thing more than an idea,
> a bit of pebble carved into himself.

In these poems, the relativity of pasts is perhaps the most important theme: the suggestion that the unrecorded histories of peoples without writing may be as important as those of elaborately literate cultures.

At the end of the original "Weights and Measures," the contrast between the primitive and the civilized was emphasized in a cruel sequence, "The Chicken Poems." In *Old Mother* these poems do not stand apart; they are included, and somewhat scattered, in the section called "Prairie Poems." But even in this rearrangement, they stand out for their bleak horror. The intent of these poems is on one level obvious. Chickens bred by modern methods—trapped in their functions of egg-layers and meat-providers—are the ultimate exploitees, the final slaves of human beings. Yet even they have their own orders of domination and subjection, their own mindless cruelties, and here there is a curious series of juxtapositions, with the victor inevitably becoming victim. In "Monarch II," the cock kills an intruding rooster:

> His crowing stuns the air.
> The hens flutter, wings
> cowled and tails held high.
> Monarch stabs at the barred bird
> then stalks toward the garden
> where young worms have risen after rain.

In "Monarch IV" the same cock is crippled because he twisted his tendons during the fight. Detecting his sickness, his own hens attack him. It is left for the lowest in the pecking order, a bird almost deprived of plumage, to deliver the *coup de grâce:*

> She circles carefully
> as if her scabs might crack,
> and keeping safe from her white sisters
> stands above her king. The rooster

twitches and his one eye opens
to a sky whose sun has gone.
With a stab she returns him to the dark.

In Lane's early poems the bird was always the image of flying free, of liberation. But in "Archaeopteryx," another poem of *Old Mother* that appeared in the original "Chicken Poems" sequence, the prehistoric creature is "the bird of aeons. / The thing you kill." The chickens are all victims as distinct from free flyers. Yet a human being is shown as no better or more fortunate than the bird victims, for at the end of another poem, "Wings,"

> The hawks have flown the sky,
> following a darker wing.
> I stand alone, a thing of bones,
> a wingless thing who cannot find the wind.

*Old Mother* ends with the sequence "China Poems," written as a result of Lane's visit, with a group of other Canadian writers, to China in 1981. In them he shows the same power of empathizing with a strange landscape and of catching the resonances of another people's history as he did in Peru. "Silk Factory" is a good example; it demonstrates admirably the way the patterns of the past—dragon and phoenix in the white brocade woven in the factory—survive in modern China, and not only in artifacts but also in the human condition exemplified in the lives of the silk weavers:

> A weaver-girl
> laughs at a young man and he trips on nothing.
> When she moves he cannot see where he is going.
> Grey with silk dusk, windows rattle
> and the glass is frosted with snow.
> The bitterness of Ch'en T'ao is long ago
> and the shuttles are no longer lumps of ice.
> Still, the brocade the weaver-girl makes
> is not for her, and the young man, though
> he labours for many years, will never buy
> the white silk she works so hard to weave.

The human condition, Lane is suggesting in these poems, modifies and largely frustrates all political hopes. The "China Poems" accept no ideology; they do accept friendship, human warmth, and there is a tenderness to their tone that is in striking contrast to the ferocity with which, in the chicken poems, Lane handles the fates and the natures of both beasts and men trapped in unnatural ways of existence, whether as exploiters or exploited. In the "China Poems" birds return to their role of flying free, like the swallows in "Over the Slow Rivers":

> Sing to me of the tireless, the endless,
> the coming and the going that are leaves:
> sing the female and the male of things
> among the empires of the air, bright warriors,
> none as swift as you in the blue worlds.

# INDEX

317